Nietzsche's Earthbound Wisdom

Nietzsche's Earthbound Wisdom

THE PHILOSOPHER, THE POET, AND THE SAGE

Keith Ansell-Pearson

THE UNIVERSITY OF CHICAGO PRESS
CHICAGO AND LONDON

The University of Chicago Press, Chicago 60637
The University of Chicago Press, Ltd., London

Published 2025
Printed in the United States of America

34 33 32 31 30 29 28 27 26 25 1 2 3 4 5

ISBN-13: 978-0-226-83925-7 (cloth)
ISBN-13: 978-0-226-83926-4 (e-book)
DOI: https://doi.org/10.7208/chicago/9780226839264.001.0001

Library of Congress Cataloging-in-Publication Data

Names: Ansell-Pearson, Keith, 1960– author.
Title: Nietzsche's earthbound wisdom : the philosopher, the poet, and the sage / Keith Ansell-Pearson.
Description: Chicago : The University of Chicago Press, 2025. | Includes bibliographical references and index.
Identifiers: LCCN 2024042410 | ISBN 9780226839257 (cloth) | ISBN 9780226839264 (ebook)
Subjects: LCSH: Nietzsche, Friedrich Wilhelm, 1844–1900.
Classification: LCC B3317 .A58 2025 | DDC 193—dc23/eng/20241003
LC record available at https://lccn.loc.gov/2024042410

♾ This paper meets the requirements of ANSI/NISO Z39.48-1992 (Permanence of Paper).

For friends known and unknown

The fact that I get along well with wisdom and often too well is because she reminds me so much of life!

Nietzsche, “The Dance Song,” *Thus Spoke Zarathustra*

Contents

Abbreviations of Nietzsche's Works

For the original German, for both published and unpublished material, I have utilized mainly *Friedrich Nietzsche: Sämtliche Werke: Kritische Studienausgabe* (*KSA*). I have occasionally modified translations, without stating so in every instance. Where an English translation is not available, I have translated the material myself. I have used the available translations of the posthumous fragments collected in the Stanford University Press edition of *The Complete Works of Friedrich Nietzsche* (*SUP*). These texts are cited by volume number and page number. Volumes 1–13 of the *Kritische Studienausgabe* are cited by volume number and fragment number, with the note number given in square brackets; I provide page numbers only where a given note extends across more than one page. Volume 14 of the *Kritische Studienausgabe* is cited by volume number and page number. The *Kritische Gesamtausgabe* (*KGW*) is cited by volume number, part number, and page number. *Ecce Homo* is cited by chapter title and section number. *Nietzsche contra Wagner* is cited by chapter title and, where available, section number. *Dithyrambs of Dionysus*, *Philosophy and Truth*, *Philosophy in the Tragic Age of the Greeks*, *The Pre-Platonic Philosophers*, and *Writings from the Late Notebooks* are cited by page number. *Twilight of the Idols* is cited by chapter title and aphorism number. *On the Genealogy of Morality* is cited by essay number and aphorism number. *Thus Spoke Zarathustra* is cited by part number, chapter title, and, where relevant, section number. *The Anti-Christ*, *Beyond Good and Evil*, *The Birth of Tragedy*, *The Case of Wagner*, *Dawn*, *David Friedrich Strauss*, *The Gay Science*, *Human, All Too Human*, *Human, All Too Human II*, *On the Utility and Liability of History for Life*, *Mixed Opinions and Maxims*, *Schopenhauer as Educator*, *Richard Wagner in Bayreuth*, *The Will to Power*, and *The Wanderer and His Shadow* are cited by aphorism or section number.

AC	*The Anti-Christ*
BGE	*Beyond Good and Evil*
BT	*The Birth of Tragedy*

CW	*The Case of Wagner*
D	*Dawn: Thoughts on the Presumptions of Morality*
DD	*Dithyrambs of Dionysus*
DS	*David Friedrich Strauss: Confessor and Writer*
EH	*Ecce Homo*
GM	*On the Genealogy of Morality*
GS	*The Gay Science*
HH	*Human, All Too Human*
HH2	*Human, All Too Human II*
HL	*On the Utility and Liability of History for Life*
KGW	*Werke: Kritische Gesamtausgabe*
KSA	*Friedrich Nietzsche: Sämtliche Werke: Kritische Studienausgabe*
KSB	*Sämtliche Briefe: Kritische Studienausgabe*
MOM	*Mixed Opinions and Maxims*
NCW	*Nietzsche contra Wagner*
PT	*Philosophy and Truth: Selections from Nietzsche's Notebooks of the Early 1870s*
PTAG	*Philosophy in the Tragic Age of the Greeks*
PPP	*The Pre-Platonic Philosophers*
SE	*Schopenhauer as Educator*
SUP	Stanford University Press edition of *The Complete Works of Friedrich Nietzsche*
TI	*Twilight of the Idols*
WB	*Richard Wagner in Bayreuth*
WLN	*Writings from the Late Notebooks*
WP	*The Will to Power*
WS	*The Wanderer and His Shadow*
Z	*Thus Spoke Zarathustra* (in four parts)

Volumes of Nietzsche's Unpublished Fragments, Stanford University Press

For details of translators, see the bibliography.

Unpublished Fragments from the Period of "Human, All Too Human II" (Spring 1878–Fall 1879). Vol. 4.

Unpublished Fragments from the Period of "Unfashionable Observations". Vol. 11.

Unpublished Fragments from the Period of "Human, All Too Human I" (Winter 1874/75–Winter 1877/78). Vol. 12.

Unpublished Fragments from the Period of "Dawn" (Winter 1879/80–Spring 1881). Vol. 13.
Unpublished Fragments from the Period of "Thus Spoke Zarathustra" (Summer 1882–Winter 1883/84). Vol. 14.
Unpublished Fragments from the Period of "Thus Spoke Zarathustra" (Spring 1884–Winter 1884/85). Vol. 15.
Unpublished Fragments (Spring 1885–Spring 1886). Vol. 16.

Introduction

> Whoever looks into himself as if into vast space and carries galaxies in himself, also knows how irregular all galaxies are; they lead into the chaos and labyrinth of existence.
>
> Nietzsche, *The Gay Science*, aphorism 322

> Does anyone wish to walk these paths with me? I *advise* no one to do so.—But you want to? Then let's go.
>
> Nietzsche, note of 1885

I aim with this book to provide readers with fresh and instructive insights into Nietzsche's philosophical character and identity, including his character as a "poet-philosopher" and his identity as a thinker who conceives the project of philosophy as a philosophy of the future. To do this I focus attention on the conceptions and figurations of the philosopher, the poet, and the sage we encounter in the texts of his middle and late periods (1878–88). In considering attempts to define philosophy and poetry as parts of the repertory of the mind and also as classic exercises to be renewed and refreshed, Wallace Stevens (1997, 864) invites us to reflect on this difference between them: the philosopher hopes to give us a world that will always remain to be discovered, and the poet hopes to give us a world that will always remain to be celebrated. In Nietzsche, we are offered, extraordinarily, perceptions into both kinds of worlds and as worlds of earthbound knowledge and wisdom.

I place the emphasis in this study on the middle and late periods of Nietzsche's writings on account of taking cognizance of his disclosure in a note of 1877 that he has abandoned the metaphysical-artistic views of his early writings (*KSA*, vol. 8, fragment 23 [159]). In addition, I personally find the middle and late writings to be his most philosophically mature and highly pertinent to our continuing efforts to understand the human, indeed inexhaustibly so.[1] Nietzsche's middle writings of 1878–82 include the two volumes of *Human, All Too Human* and are made up of three texts—*Human, All Too Human*, *Mixed Opinions and Maxims*, and *The Wanderer and His*

Shadow; *Dawn*; and *The Gay Science*—with the latter work being by far the best known. *Thus Spoke Zarathustra* was composed in the years 1883–85, and Nietzsche himself regarded it as his most important book but also an "*unintelligible* book" since it is based on experiences peculiar to himself and born of a feeling of profound solitude.[2] In confiding this to his friend Franz Overbeck, however, he highlights another point about the book and one we should connect with as readers of it and perhaps even apply to our encounter with all his books: "[I]f the book is insufferable to you, perhaps a hundred *details* in it will not be!" (*KSB* 7, p. 223; see also Middleton 1996, 254). *Late Nietzsche* refers to the texts published between 1886 and 1888. The period commences with the publication in 1886 of *Beyond Good and Evil* and includes texts such as *On the Genealogy of Morality*, *Twilight of the Idols*, *The Case of Wagner*, *The Anti-Christ*, and *Ecce Homo*. It also includes book 5 of *The Gay Science* with its remarkable suite of aphorisms that was added to the second edition of the text published in 1887.

In *Ecce Homo*, Nietzsche writes that if he had credited *Thus Spoke Zarathustra* with another's name it might have taken two millennia's worth of acumen to guess that the author of *Human, All Too Human* (1878) is also the visionary (*Visionär*) of *Zarathustra* (1883–85) (*EH* "Why I Am So Clever" 4). Although the way he conducts his philosophizing in the two texts is indeed strikingly different, it is possible to discern that the future-oriented character of his thinking is already in play in his middle writings of 1878–82. One of my main claims, then, is that the constructive project that characterizes the books of his middle period deeply informs *Thus Spoke Zarathustra* and the books of his post-Zarathustra period and thus that the typical periodization of his corpus stands in need of revision. The typical approach to periodization alleges, first, that *Zarathustra* marks a clear break from the books of the so-called middle period and, second, that the books of the post-Zarathustran period (1886–88) are meant to attract an audience worthy of the teachings of Zarathustra. Both assumptions simplify Nietzsche's philosophical project in the years 1878–88 and end up distorting it. By showing the persistence of the new wisdom developed in the writings of the middle period in *Zarathustra* and the books of the post-Zarathustran period I shed new light on the project that these books are intended to advance. The books of the post-Zarathustran period need to be seen not simply as destructive in their aims but rather as critical and destructive in the service of implementing the philosophical project that is being carried out in the books of the middle period.

Nietzsche considered his books to be distinguished by virtue of their wealth of psychological insight, their fearlessness in the face of great dangers, and their sublime candor.[3] He regarded his middle writings—such as *Dawn* and *The Gay Science*—as his most congenial and personal books, the ones he himself preferred, and the texts of his late period as the more far-reaching and important on account of their unfashionable critique of the present (*KSB* 8, p. 341; Middleton 1996, 299). In a note, he reveals that the choice that people make with respect to his books gives him food for thought (*KSA*, vol. 11, fragment 38 [15], p. 616; *SUP*, 16:173). Although most widely read for his late texts, such as *On the Genealogy of Morality* and *Twilight of the Idols*, today his middle writings, such as *Dawn*, are being rediscovered and studied afresh as whole books, and this provides us with a much richer picture of his philosophizing than is typically the case as well as a keener sense of his intellectual development on which he prides himself as having (*D* 481).[4] The focus I adopt in this book, along with the close readings I offer of the middle writings, enables me to cast fresh light on *Thus Spoke Zarathustra*, which, I show, grows out of these writings and is intimately related to them. Commentators persistently misinterpret Nietzsche's philosophical project. For example, it has been argued by one illustrious commentator that the doctrine of the superhuman repeats the same pattern that we find in the case of the ascetic ideal—the ideal that Nietzsche scrutinizes in essay 3 of *On the Genealogy of Morality*—in which human life is accorded value only to the extent that it is a means to something that brings about its negation (see Clark 1990, 273). Nietzsche's focus, however, is not with creating anything otherworldly or transcendent, as is the case with ascetic ideals that have served to foster a hatred of the conditions of human existence, expressing a "fear of happiness and beauty" and "a longing to get away from appearance, transience, growth, death" (*GM* 3.28). Moreover, Nietzsche has been foregrounding a discourse on sacrifice well before *Zarathustra* and his positing of the superhuman. If human beings are to become serious about the passion of knowledge, they will need to be courageous and show a degree of magnanimity that heretofore has been found wanting in humanity (see *D* 551). The project we find at work in Nietzsche's middle writings is an anticipation of and a preparation for the teaching presented in *Zarathustra*.

Philosophically Heterodox

In this study, I do not seek to make Nietzsche conform to a readily recognizable conception of philosophy as practiced in academic philosophy departments today since this serves only to distort and domesticate his philosophizing. Nietzsche's thinking is rooted in the history of thought and literature. Throughout this study I place him into dialogue with a range of philosophical and literary figures, notably ones who either were important to him or, in my view, serve to enrich our understanding of his intellectual character and his ideas. Indeed, it is from Stendhal that Nietzsche derives his conception of what constitutes a good philosopher.[5] I provide references to further reading on various figures in many of the notes, and readers who wish to pursue their own readings and research may find the links I establish in this study of value. Works of poets and storytellers were just as important to Nietzsche as works of philosophy and not just on the level of style, as we shall see in chapter 5 on the poets. He discloses that Dostoevsky is the only psychologist from whom he felt he had anything to learn (*TI* "Reconnaissance Raids of an Untimely Man" 45; see also *AC* 31).[6] Aldous Huxley (1929, 231) held the view that works of fiction are sometimes worth a whole library of treatises on the theory of knowledge and the nature of reality.[7] This is a view we should take seriously. Huxley (2001, 28) expands on it in "Vulgarity in Literature" by suggesting that modern psychologists "systematize and de-beautify the vast treasures of knowledge about the human soul" we find in novels, plays, poems, and essays, and he mentions the likes of Shakespeare, Blake, Stendhal, and Dostoevsky. Santayana's appreciation of the way William James pursues psychology, or the life of the mind, as a literary subject as well as a scientific one helps us see the attraction a figure like Dostoevsky held for Nietzsche. The candid psychologist employs the imagination to break through false conventions, to throw off prejudices and scientific shams, and to examine human nature in terms of a bold voyage of discovery: "[I]n this sense Shakespeare is a better psychologist than Locke or Kant" (Santayana 1968, 300).

Nietzsche confesses to being philosophically heterodox.[8] He is not the typical philosopher who, as Robert Nozick puts it, is "beset by the temptation to say everything explicitly" (1989, 273). He invites his readers to participate in the act and task of thinking and to have the full range of experiences that it is possible to have from learning and self-education—including harsh self-examination—and this is why he speaks of the possibility of his readers having the chance to experience ecstasies of learning from reading him. He seeks to elicit in us a feeling of high-spirited freedom (*HH* 206).[9] He writes tellingly about his way of doing philosophy in this aphorism from *Human, All Too Human*: "[T]he relief like, incomplete representation of a thought or of a whole philosophy has more effect than working it out thoroughly does: we leave more for the reader to do, he is roused to continue shaping and to think through to the end what has set itself before him in such strong light and shadow" (*HH* 178).

A draft Nietzsche wrote but discarded for the section "Why I Write Such Good Books" in *Ecce Homo* is an invaluable document for understanding his manner of doing philosophy.[10] Let me draw attention to three key points he makes. First, he admits that his writings are difficult, and he hopes this will not be an objection. The difficulty stems, he knows, from the fact that we encounter in his writings "the most *abbreviated* language ever spoken by a philosopher." In addition, he says, it is poor in formulas but alive and artistic. This means, he goes on to suggest, that as commentators and readers we must follow a procedure opposite to that required by most philosophical literature, so long-winded it must be condensed if it is to be understood. "I," Nietzsche writes, "have to be diluted, liquified, mixed with water, else one upsets one's digestion." Second, he discloses that with him silence is his key instinct in contrast to the garrulity of other philosophers: "I am *brief*; my readers themselves must become long and comprehensive in order to bring up and together all that I have thought and thought deep down." To comprehend him properly we must be able, he insists, to see a problem in its proper place, by which he means the context of the other problems that belong with it and are attached to it. It helps if we have an appreciation of "the topography of various nooks and the difficult areas of whole sciences and above all of philosophy." Third, and finally, he tells us that he speaks only of what he has lived through and that there is no opposition in his case between thinking and life: "My 'theory' grows from my 'practice'—oh, from a practice that is not by any means harmless or unproblematic."

Anyone who reads Nietzsche will immediately recognize the truthful character of what he says in points 1 and 2. His language *is* an abbreviated one, and, moreover, he *is* brief, and taken together these two features of his writing mean that the reader does indeed have to "become long and comprehensive" to understand him. The task is to attempt to do this in a felicitous and wise manner. We need to keep these points firmly in our minds when we read Nietzsche and engage with his texts, and it will help if we take seriously his plea for slow reading and the need for us to be friends of *lento* in an age of work, hurriedness, and overhastiness (*D* preface 5).

Robert Pippin has rightly drawn attention to the fact that Nietzsche constantly raises in his writings the issue of how to read the philosophical terminology and framing of his work as well as pointing to the danger of reading him as a conventional essayist or writer, let alone an orthodox philosopher.[11] Pippin insists that the important and relevant point is not to simply take note of Nietzsche's resistance to incorporation into traditional theory since this point is obvious; rather, we need to reflect on what this resistance means and amounts to and in terms of reflecting on the issue of just "what Nietzsche is trying to *do* with his books" (2010, xv). Such a question poses itself to anyone who encounters the "strange, witty, and graceful texts" from the middle period, as Michel Foucault (1988, 33) described them, such as *The Wanderer and His Shadow*, *Dawn*, and *The Gay Science*.

Need we go so far as Pippin, however, in his contention that with these writings Nietzsche has given up on philosophical theory? Here, Pippin admits to taking his bearing from an argument of Bernard Williams, chiefly, that Nietzsche, like Wittgenstein, was "trying to say something about what it might mean for philosophy itself to come to an end, for a culture to be 'cured' of philosophy" (2010, xiv). If, however, we pay close attention to what Nietzsche himself discloses in his middle writings, especially concerning how he conceives his relation to a free-minded intellectual culture, we discover that one of the aims he has is to move philosophical education in a new direction through the book form. Today, he thinks, we are living in an age of self-education and peer education, with the result that the teacher is becoming superfluous in the usual form it assumes, and the way forward now consists in fostering philosophical friendship through the appreciation of new kinds of books and of writing (*WS* 180).

When we reflect on the character of his books, cognizance needs to be taken of the warning Nietzsche gives to shortsighted readers: "Do you think that this work must be patchwork [*Stückwerk*] because it is (and has to be) given to you in pieces [*Stücken*]?" (*MOM* 128). We may be tempted when encountering Nietzsche to express sympathy with Cioran when he maintains: "Nietzsche is a sum of attitudes, and it only diminishes him to comb his work for a will to order, a thirst for unity. . . . His philosophy, a meditation on his whims, is mistakenly searched by the scholars for the constants it rejects" (1956/1987, 151). This, however, fails to understand the nature of Nietzsche's fusion of the analytic and the lyrical and how, as one of the freest writers who meditates on matters that concern much more than his whims, he engages in philosophy as a *search*. It is a search that, following the event of the death of God and the collapse of moral and other absolutes, assumes the form of, on the one hand, an experimental inquiry and, on the other, a creative positing.[12]

When we read Nietzsche, we are struck by the voice that is addressing us, often in an intimate manner and inviting us to probe our beliefs and opinions, our virtues and values, and our moral presumptions and prejudices. Nietzsche advises us to proceed experimentally with the things that we encounter and that provoke us into thinking, in which we are "sometimes angry, sometimes affectionate toward them and allow justice, passion, and coldness toward them to follow one upon the other." Thus: "One person converses with things like a policeman, another as father confessor, a third as a wanderer and curiosity seeker. Sometimes one wrings something from them through sympathy, sometimes through violent force; reverence for their mysteries leads one person forward and eventually to insight, whereas another employs indiscretion and roguery in the explanation of secrets"

(*D* 432). It is prudent, therefore, for a philosophy in search of new wisdom to involve a multiplicity of faculties, methods, and procedures: "The thinker needs imagination [*Phantasie*], the leap upward, abstraction, desensualization, invention, presentiment, induction, dialectics, deduction, critique, compilation of material, the impersonal way of thinking, contemplativeness, and comprehensiveness, and not least justice and love towards everything present" (*D* 43). Nietzsche tells us explicitly himself that his writings seek to appeal to those in whom a task wishes to be incarnate and come into the world and who are willing to continue the task (*HH* preface 7). He warns the thinker, however, against canonizing himself and turning himself into a binding institution for the future of humankind, and he advises us not to become fools of piety with respect to the teachings of the sage and not be damagers of knowledge (*D* 542).

System and Aphorism

Karl Löwith described Nietzsche's philosophy as a system in aphorisms. This is a curious claim to make since we know that Nietzsche takes himself to be not narrow-minded enough for a system and he explicitly states that the will to system displays a lack of integrity (*TI* "Maxims and Barbs" 26). Löwith (1997, 11–21) is aware of this and has in mind an open system of reflection as opposed to a closed one, in which an open system is one that encourages experimentation and is open to new horizons of questioning as well as to its own testing. Baudelaire spells out well the reasons why we should have distrust in a system. He is especially incisive on the ultimate frustration one experiences in trapping oneself inside a system that seems to give one the freedom to pontificate as one likes until one realizes that "a system is a kind of damnation that condemns us to perpetual backsliding" and prevents one from attaining what is truly desired: an "abundant impartiality" (2006, 117–18).[13] Baudelaire expresses a preference for intellectual modesty, which is a virtue Nietzsche also champions in his writings from 1878 to 1888 (*HH* 2; *AC* 13, 14).

The word *aphorism* stems from the Greek *horos* (horizon or boundary). Lawrence Buell suggests that the characteristic structure of the aphorism implies two kinds of boundary crossing: "a thrusting past banality to further reaches of insight, and an ongoing energy flow that reforms insight continuously in a transmissible form that invites perpetual continuation of the game" (2003, 156). We can apply this insight into the nature of the aphorism to Nietzsche's stylistic practice. In the middle writings we find him engaged in a passionate search for knowledge and keen to provoke readers to take up further and complete for themselves the thoughts and ideas that are being advanced. As we ourselves become adept in the art of thinking, the ideas we read and hear will start to appear in the form of a chain (*MOM* 376). Indeed, this is precisely how Nietzsche conceived his practice of the aphorism and how he wished his books to be read. In a note from 1885, for example, he writes that the "profoundest and most inexhaustible" books will continue to "have something of the aphoristic and abrupt character of Pascal's *Pensées*" (*KSA*, vol. 11, fragment 35 [31]; *SUP*, 16:91), while, in another note from the same year, the year he was drafting notes and sketches for the book that becomes *Beyond Good and Evil*, he reflects on his books made up of aphorisms that contain thought chains standing between and behind them (*KSA*, vol. 11, fragment 37 [5]; *SUP*, 16: 142). He presents his philosophy as a developing one and encourages the reader to be active in the process of learning. As Gary Saul Morson (2012, 200) notes, our imagination and intellect can be stimulated by an incomplete effort as much as by a finished product, and his insight that aphoristic writers provide readers with "ideas in development" is a good one. Philosophy becomes in Nietzsche not only an art of thinking but equally an adventure in it.

Évelyne Grossman (2023) points out that originally the aphorism was a sentence-like phrase designed to define a concept or sum up a received truth or piece of wisdom. Subsequently, however, it came to suggest placing received truths in a fresh light with the attempt to dismay common sense by breaking with entrenched habits of thinking and generating surprise. For Nietzsche human stupidity can be defeated not only by developing well-argued criticism but also by depriving it of its good conscience (*GS* 328). One way to do this is through confronting it with novel styles of thinking and writing. Even more daringly and boldly, Nietzsche, Grossman (2023, 89–90) points out, pursues truth not simply as something to be simply found but rather as something that is to be produced and presented as provisional interpretation. In a recent study of the aphorism, Andrew Hui seeks to show that Nietzsche refuses to spoon-feed his readers: "[H]e intends for them to engage in a hermeneutic agon, an existential struggle as perilous as a tragic hero's encounter with the Theban monster" (2019, 154–55).[14] This insight captures, however, only one aspect of Nietzsche's aphoristic writing, albeit an important one. Equally important is his commitment to a style that attempts to provide his readers with pathways to the sublime. We typically construe Nietzsche as a philosopher of the tragic, and, indeed, in *Ecce Homo* he declares that he is the *first* tragic philosopher (*EH* "The Birth of Tragedy" 3). However, he also reveals in that text: "The art of *grand* rhythm, the *grand style* of phrasing, as the expression of a tremendous rise and fall of sublime [*sublimer*], of superhuman passion, was first discovered by me" (*EH* "Why I Write Such Good Books" 4). We should also take note of what is said about aphorisms in the discourse "Reading and Writing" in part 1 of *Zarathustra*: "[They] should be peaks, and those to whom they are spoken should be big and tall of stature." As a writer of aphorisms Nietzsche aims not to leave his readers drifting and stranded in heavy, black clouds but to enlighten and elevate them. Consider, for example, his conception of the figure of the father confessor and the scene depicted in an aphorism of *Dawn* where we may encounter paths rising to the sublime:

> To be able to be humble so as to be accessible to many and humiliating to none! To have experienced much injustice and crawled through the worm tunnels of every kind of error in order to be able to reach many hidden souls along with their secret paths! Always in a type of love and a type of self-interest and self-enjoyment! To be in possession of a dominion and at the same time inconspicuous and renouncing! To lie constantly in the sun and the kindness of grace and yet to know that the paths rising to the sublime [*Erhabenen*] are right at hand!—That would be a life! That would be reason to live, to live a long time. (*D* 449)[15]

One further point is worth noting, and it concerns how we might enjoy and profit from the experience of reading Nietzsche's books. In an aphorism in *Dawn*, Nietzsche notes that, although the thinker aspires to be rigorous and unrelentingly bold, he complicates the search for knowledge by accepting that along the way he will encounter "streams with many bends and turns and secluded hermitages." Thus, the thinker may make for himself "a brief idyll with islands, trees, grottos, and waterfalls," but such an idyll will be only temporary since one needs to move on again, "past cliffs" and forcing oneself "through the hardest stone" (*D* 530). Nietzsche titles this aphorism "The Thinker's Digressions." Digressions provide the thinker with places to rest and to pause for thought and even hostels for housing and inhabiting them to become better acquainted with them. This does not mean, however, that there is not a project unfolding and with a definite search under way.[16]

Naturalisms

In recent years there has been a renaissance of interest in Nietzsche as a philosophical naturalist, which is how he was received in some quarters at the beginning of his reception in the early part of the twentieth century.[17] Questions now at the forefront of research on Nietzsche include, What kind of naturalist is Nietzsche? And what role does naturalism play in his philosophizing as a whole? It merits noting that, unlike a naturalist such as Santayana, Nietzsche is not a thinker who develops his intellectual project by working through the problematic of naturalism in a concerted manner.

Naturalism has a rich but marginal history in philosophy, including notable ancient thinkers such as Epicurus and Lucretius, and encompassing Spinoza and Hume as early modern and modern thinkers and the work of Santayana in the twentieth century. Naturalism allows for no cosmic exceptionalism and construes the human being as fully part of nature, in which it has no special metaphysical value and enjoys no privileged place in the natural order (there is no kingdom within a kingdom, as Spinoza puts it). In its materialist form, naturalism does not recognize or allow for any immaterial agencies or supernatural powers. Nietzsche is a strong naturalist in this sense, calling for the shadows of God to cease eclipsing our understanding of the universe, and keen to expose the errors involved in applying anthropomorphic notions to it, so that we may now relate to a "de-deified nature" and in this way both "discover" nature and "redeem" it (*GS* 109).[18] He writes of the need to translate humankind back into nature as a way of mastering the many "vain and gushing [*schwärmerischen*] interpretations that have been painted over the eternal basic text of *homo natura*" (*BGE* 230). Seeking to free himself of human vanity, he chooses to speak of genuine knowers as "hermits and marmots."[19] Disciplined by science, such free spirits seek to resist metaphysical bird catchers who endeavor to teach the human that it is higher than nature and of a different descent to the rest of it.[20]

As a way of understanding the world, naturalism, then, goes against the ingrained habits and the vanity of the human mind. Highlighting the dangers of wanting to inhabit the "fairyland" of idealism, Santayana notes how "a deified nature has generally inspired a religion of melancholy," and he poses the question: "Why has man's conscience in the end invariably rebelled against naturalism and reverted in some form or other to a cultus of the unseen?" He adds to this cultus the attachment human beings display to "senseless oracular prejudices," their "persistent search for invisible regions and powers," and their penchant for metaphysical explanations that, in fact, explain nothing. We can regard the situation as ironic given that it is the voice of nature that cries out to us to look, to act, and to enjoy. The answer to why the human mind tends to rebel against naturalism is no doubt obvious: it reminds us of our "essential impotence and mortality, while the logical fancy . . . is saddened of its own insignificance." In calling us back from the irresponsible flights of human imagination, naturalist and empiricist philosophies seem only to dispossess us of our nature and leave us cramped into our life. Why, therefore, should one wish to be a naturalist in the face of naturalism's corrosive disillusionment of the world? The answer that Santayana gives—and that is also at work in Nietzsche if not stated so explicitly by him—is in my view the best one, namely, that true wisdom can come only by way of disillusionment. We should welcome empiricism and naturalist philosophy because, as Santayana points out, they work against both "logical patriotism" and the "attachment to homespun ideas" (2011, 116–18). However, there is not only disillusionment but also the hope of new wisdom. As we shall see as this study unfolds, for Nietzsche new dawns are on the horizon, and new stars can be generated, but they are not to be found where we typically see and locate them—above us. In Nietzsche, naturalism gives rise to a futurism centered on the discovery of possibilities of life.[21]

Christopher Janaway (forthcoming) has drawn attention to the fact that Nietzsche calls the task of translating the human back into nature a strange and crazy one, and he asks why he should hold this to be the case (see *BGE* 230). He argues that Nietzsche is, in fact, acknowledging the aporetic character of his investigative task and suggests that caution is therefore required in interpreting him as an ardent naturalist. Nietzsche, he maintains, provides no satisfactory answer to the question concerning the value to be attached to a naturalist self-investigation, and he thus consciously leads his readers into an aporia that he does not resolve. Indeed, Nietzsche wants us to acknowledge the extent to which we are practicing a kind of intellectual self-cruelty when we engage in the task in which we question our transcendent aspirations, undermine our self-certainties, and expose our self-deceptions. Moreover, a picturesque effect should be neither demanded nor expected from truth and the inquiries of knowledge, and we should resist the temptation to give free rein to human pomp by eulogizing free spirits whose will to knowledge is guided by excessive honesty. Although gleaming, festive words such as *the love of truth*, *the heroism of truth*, and even *the love of wisdom* make philosophers swell with pride, they are incompatible with the task of translating the human back into nature.

Janaway's interpretation overlooks the ways in which value can be accorded to a project of naturalism. Although this value may not be readily transparent to human beings, the task has an important role to play in developing a mature humankind, even if this entails undergoing a process of disillusionment. Nietzsche holds that we are entitled to an attitude of hopefulness involving feelings of expectation and anticipation, but he also knows there can be no guarantees and that hazards lie ahead, and this means that recognition of the task as a strange and crazy one cannot be avoided. If we see naturalism as simply a component in his philosophizing—an important and necessary one—and take full cognizance of his character as a poet-philosopher who has a dedication to futurity, then it becomes possible to see that his project does not remain caught in an aporia (although it is clearly caught in complexity and difficulty). As I noted above, naturalism in Nietzsche is to pave the way for novel and quite possibly urgent ways of thinking about the future. Although I am in sympathy with aspects of Janaway's interpretation, I hold that Nietzsche's commitment to naturalism is stronger than he supposes and that its true value comes into view when it is seen in conjunction with his commitment to the future.[22]

Although the renewed interest in Nietzsche as a naturalist is to be welcomed, the concerns he has over the limited ambitions of empiricism and naturalism should not, then, be overlooked. And, as we shall see as this study unfolds, his interest in the human being concerns itself with much more than qualia, such as an interest in "complete human beings" and "the whole human being" (see esp. chaps. 4 and 5).[23] The philosophy Nietzsche develops in his writings is linked to several intellectual commitments, including self-cultivation, and centered on the mastery of the passions, the discovery and fashioning of possibilities of life, and the passion of knowledge. Unless we attend to the topics I am highlighting as important in this study, we do not know who Nietzsche is as thinker and writer. Like Santayana after him, he is aware of the inadequacy of an apathetic naturalism that is unable to attend to issues of value and significance in a philosophically mature manner.[24] There is a need to challenge the positivistic school of criticism that overlooks the highest functions of the human being. Santayana states this well when he claims: "The environing world can justify itself to the mind only by the free life which it fosters there." Furthermore, all observation is observation of brute facts until such facts are digested and disciplined by us, "embodied in humane impulses," and "become the starting point for a creative movement of the imagination, the firm basis for ideal constructions in society, religion, and art." Santayana provokes us further when he argues that, in contrast to an apathetic naturalism unconcerned with the future of human life and its development, "all the errors and follies of religion are worthy of indulgent sympathy." However questionable and objectionable free-spirited thinking must find these errors and stupidities, they at least represent the effort, however misguided, to interpret and utilize the material of experience for ennobling ends and "to measure the value of reality by its relation to the ideal" (Santayana 1900/1989, 5). We shall see how similar thoughts steer Nietzsche's thinking on the "ideal" of the superhuman (chap. 6 below) and his conception of philosophy as intellectual vision (chap. 7 below).

In the volumes of *Human, All Too Human*, Nietzsche aims to promote a new kind of wisdom to be based on an enthusiastic love of philosophy (and art), one in which the focus is on examining and exploring the human being in all its defective character, including undertaking the diligent study of its passions and delusions, and the hope is that something new will emanate from human beings that will in time change the character of humankind. In *Thus Spoke Zarathustra* (1883–85), and as an avowed poet-philosopher, Nietzsche is the visionary teacher of the death of God and the superhuman as the new meaning of the earth. In *Beyond Good and Evil* (1886), philosophical thinking is described as a mode of intellectual vision (*Blick*) (*BGE* 252). As we shall see, the visionary aspect of Nietzsche's thinking has nothing to do with the visions of the mystic, of which he is severely critical. Indeed, he advises us to be on our guard against so-called geniuses who claim to be capable of visions and to have seen things others do not see. We are to be cautious, not credulous, when confronted with the claims of mystics and find them fantastic (*D* 66). When Nietzsche writes against visionaries, he has in mind fantasists. He writes pointedly: "The visionary [*Der Phantast*] denies the truth to himself, the liar only to others" (*MOM* 6).

Although Nietzsche is concerned with the fate of the human animal and offers an ultimate teaching of the superhuman, his fundamental philosophical character is of a highly sober and composed kind, involving a commitment to the importance of nuance in the exercise of thinking and of measure in the cultivation of the emotions. He seeks to enliven thinking through an admixture of aphoristic and poetic—broadly speaking, "literary"—forms, utilizing in his writings of this period modes of storytelling, such as parables, imaginary conversations, and imaginatively depicted scenarios, presenting readers with arresting thoughts and novel insights, keen to entertain them and engage their deepest attention. In the preface to *On the Genealogy of Morality*, for example, he makes it clear that with the text he is offering a "Dionysian drama on the fate of the soul."[25] He punctuates his texts with question marks and asks unsettling questions, wishing to provoke serious reflection on matters individual and social.

Wisdom as a Hiding Place

Although it has long been customary to interpret Nietzsche as *the* antisage, the figurations of the sage we encounter in his writings are highly varied, and pursuing a nuanced approach is advisable in seeking to comprehend and get the proper measure of him on questions of wisdom (see, e.g., Maurois 1940, 217). What is clear is that he does not aspire to assume, whether in his middle writings or his late texts, the lofty character of the archetypal sage that we find depicted in Spinoza's *Ethics*, where wise humans are said to so suffer "scarcely any disturbance of spirit" since being conscious by eternal necessity of themselves and of God and of things they are in possession of "true peace of mind" (Spinoza 1985, pt. 5, proposition 42 scholium). Examining Nietzsche on the sage can, once again, reveal important insights into his complex and unorthodox philosophical character.

In book 5 of *The Gay Science* (1887), Nietzsche reflects on cultivating knowledge as a passion and spells out some of the distinctive features of the genuine seeker of knowledge, who cannot simply be a disinterested observer, "outside, indifferent, secure, and objective." He contests the identification of the sage with the true philosopher since it is a mistake to conceive the philosopher as one who is simply clever, "bovine," and "pious," seeking only peace of mind and the "meekness of country pastors that lies in the meadow and *observes* life seriously while ruminating" (*GS* 351). He is keen to mark a distinction between the true philosopher and the wise person who professes to live as a sage, insisting that the true philosopher is driven by a "great *passion*." It is insufficient to have the presumption that one simply *is* a human being of knowledge and in possession of complete wisdom. Rather, the philosopher must be possessed by the passion of the search for knowledge and prepared to welcome the hazards involved in the pursuit that may necessitate living *unwisely*. The figure of the philosopher is mistaken by most human beings for an ideal scholar or a religiously elevated and enthusiast of God or the divine. But Nietzsche asks whether such wisdom might be a detachment from life and a form of escape? He responds by declaring the genuine philosopher to be someone who lives unwisely and imprudently, constantly putting himself at risk by playing "the wicked game" (*BGE* 205). If he is to be an experimenter, the philosopher cannot allow himself to live a life of timid virtuousness (*KSA*, vol. 11, fragment 35 [24]; *SUP*, 16:89).

Nietzsche mounts a biting attack on the immodesty of sages when they profess their devotion to wisdom. In his criticism, he has in mind people who are ashamed of their existence and for whom education, books, possessions, solitude, and mind or spirit have become so many poisons.[26] Those people who for whatever reason have turned out badly end up in a state of perpetual revenge and display a will to revenge against existence itself. Such people even claim to have transcended mortal human existence and reached the heights of a sublime morality, a morality of command and "thou shalt," giving themselves an appearance of superiority, so attaining "the pleasure of an *accomplished revenge*," at least in their imaginations. Nietzsche writes bitingly: "Always big moral words. Always the rub-a-dub of justice, wisdom, holiness, virtue. Always the Stoicism of gesture." For such people a sage-like way of life is a way of concealing what they lack; indeed, they wear, Nietzsche says, idealistic cloaks, strutting about as "incurable self-despisers," and are, in fact, "incurably vain" (*GS* 359). He acknowledges that among these born enemies of the spirit there does on occasion come into being a rare piece of humanity that others revere, such as the saint and the sage (*der Weise*). In such a figure, the vices that characterize a vengeful spirit can lead to the creation of new virtues, and Nietzsche gives the example of St. Augustine to illustrate the kind of person he has in mind.[27] He is, however, deeply critical of the way of life the saint and the sage seek to inspire in others. In the case of a figure like Augustine, for example, we are confronted with one of "those monsters of morality who make noise, make history." Augustine encapsulates the vengeful figures who, in their cultivation of so-called wisdom, seek revenge on those who are in possession of liberality of mind and seek to honor the free-spirited life. If we look at examples from Greece and India, Nietzsche argues that the philosophers' putative wisdom may well show itself to be a screen by which they hide from the mind or the intellect and seek to save themselves because they have become "weary, old, cold, hard." Such philosophers perhaps gain a premonition that the end is near, and, like the prudence animals have before they die, they go off by themselves, "become still, choose solitude, hide in caves, and become *wise*" (*GS* 359; see also *BGE* 288).

Nietzsche is encouraging his readers, then, to develop a suspicion about the figure of the philosopher-sage who is taken to be a figure of exemplary true or genuine wisdom but who may, in fact, be hiding or retreating from life.[28] The saintly sage he is depicting proclaims to be a serious human being in possession of certainty but one who is only a few steps away from being a moral fanatic.[29] Nietzsche suggests that the "magnificent overweening presumption" in calling oneself wise is best left to the actors of mind or spirit (*GS* 351). He has a distrust of big moral words and gestures, as we find articulated in the pretensions of the archetypal sage. Indeed, we find there is a lot to be said in praise of folly and finding wisdom in unwisdom. Once we become suspicious of the piety and self-righteousness of the sage, we might cease wanting to be philosophers and become philasophers instead: "[f]riends of folly, good company for itinerant musicians and foolish folk" (*KSA*, vol. 12, fragment 4 [1]; *SUP*, 16:408). Nietzsche calls this philosophy *one* of his philosophies, and he wishes it to be called not the *love of wisdom* but instead "the *art of mistrust*" (*KSA*, vol. 11, fragment 34 [196]; *SUP*, 16:58). His distrust of big words and gestures also informs his critical reception of various writers and literary figures, including the political and moral designs of Victor Hugo. He finds Hugo "shallow and demagogical, on his belly before all big words and gestures, a flatterer of the people who speaks with the voice of an evangelist to all lowly, oppressed, deformed, crippled people and does not have a whiff of what discipline and honesty [*Redlichkeit*] of the intellect are, what intellectual conscience is—on the whole an unconscious actor, like nearly all actors of the democratic movement" (*KSA*, vol. 11, fragment 38 [6], p. 602; *SUP*, 16:161). In just as firm and witty terms, he writes: "His spirit afflicts the French like an alcoholic drink that is both intoxicating and *befuddling*. When his stupefying babble commences, it makes our ears ring: and we feel pain, as when a railroad train carries us through a dark tunnel" (*KSA*, vol. 11, fragment 26 [454]; *SUP*, 15:251).[30]

Itinerary

The first two chapters of the book are devoted to illuminating some important aspects of Nietzsche as a thinker and writer. Chapter 1 examines Nietzsche as a cheerful thinker and writer who has a predilection for certain kinds of books, namely, honest books and cold books. There is nothing facile about being motivated by cheerfulness in one's work and holding it to be important in one's attachment to life itself. Illuminating his preference for cold books affords insight into how Nietzsche conceives philosophy as an exercise in disillusionment but one that does not need to result in cynicism or nihilism. He seeks to show that good thinkers express the happiness that lies in thinking well, and this is an experience they wish to share with the reader. In chapter 2, I examine the role the intellectual virtue of honesty plays in his writings and his conception of the passion of knowledge. If we are to commit ourselves to knowledge, then it must be pursued as a passion and not simply as an ethos: the *amour-plaisir* or *amour-vanité* of knowledge is not sufficient; rather, something nobler and more heroic is required of us, including a willingness to develop and embrace knowledge that challenges human vanity and our presumptions about the world. For the thinker who has this dedication to knowledge, existence is lived magnanimously. Free-spirited thinkers console themselves in entertaining the thought that the personal sacrifices to knowledge they make may contribute to the greater health of a future humanity.

In chapter 3, I endeavor to illuminate key aspects of Nietzsche's conception of a free-spirited philosophy. I aim to showcase the remarkable range and psychological subtlety of Nietzsche's aphoristic mode of philosophizing in his middle writings as well as illuminating his conception of the philosopher as a wanderer and the way of life that is attached to it. Chapter 4 focuses on the topic of Nietzsche on the passions, including examining his relation to Stoic teaching on the emotions. I show the extent to which Nietzsche adheres to philosophy's commitment to teaching the mastery of the passions. In addition, I illuminate his criticism of Stoicism and show why it is erroneous to characterize him, as Martha Nussbaum has done, as a Stoic. It is important that we do not simplify his position on the passions but also cognize the subtle character of his appraisal of them. The topic of the passions is central to having an adequate understanding of Nietzsche on the poets, and this is the focus of chapter 5. Nietzsche makes special demands of the poets, including the need for them to master the passions. Poets are significant figures for him because, when they assume the guise of seers, they provide signposts to the future by offering images of new kinds of human beings.

In chapter 6, I provide essential insight into *Thus Spoke Zarathustra* in relation to the main themes of my book and offer a close reading of several salient aspects of this strange text in which Nietzsche becomes the poet as seer he calls for in his middle writings. I pay special attention to seeking to illuminate Zarathustra's philosophical character as a poet who is a fool and a liar. This development in his writing should not be taken to mean that Nietzsche has abandoned a concern with the passion of knowledge and truthfulness and now assumes the guise of a straightforward liar. As I seek to show, the issue of the fool is a complicated one in Nietzsche's writings and is best construed in the context of his attempt to posit a philosophy of the future where the future is unknown and uncertain. Zarathustra is a passionate seeker of knowledge committed to truthfulness and a fool and a poet at one and the same time. The fool may well be, as the wisdom of ages gone by has it, in possession of the third eye and so able to provide humankind with new ways of seeing and feeling. "What is original in a human being," Nietzsche writes, "is that he *sees* a thing that all do not *see*" (*KSA*, vol. 9, fragment 12 [80]; *SUP*, 6:435). This "seeing" is not that of the entranced mystic but rather the perception of the sober and serene philosopher. It is essential that Nietzsche's character as a poet-philosopher is not treated in a cavalier or glib manner and that his philosophy of the future, which is such an integral part of this character and necessarily speculative, is comprehended in the context of the fundamental problems he wrestles with. In chapter 7, the final chapter of the book, I turn my attention to the late Nietzsche (1886–88), especially *Beyond Good and Evil.* I endeavor to illuminate several key features of his philosophizing in his late period and centered on questions concerning vision and perception. I focus on the nature of his critique of our attachment to "objectivity," be it of the kind we find in the modus operandi of the scholar or Flaubert's conception of the art of the novel. I also examine Nietzsche's identity as a philosophical legislator and his advocacy of spiritual (*geistig*) Caesarism, where *Caesar* stands for the eternal symbol of authority and the earthly kingdom (see Berdyaev 1952, 69). This chapter also illuminates two important aspects of his critique of naturalism: first, the "literary" naturalism that is developed in the modern French novel and, second, the philosophical naturalism that eliminates "the choosing, judging, interpreting subject as a principle" (*KSA*, vol. 12, fragment 9 [178], p. 442; *WP* 95). Nietzsche opposes any mode of thinking that denies human agency and involves our fatalistically submitting to alleged matters of fact.

The books Nietzsche published in the ten-year period 1878–88 constitute a veritable laboratory of thinking, and his notebooks of this period demonstrate the deeply reflective and boldly speculative character of his thinking. Today we can continue to benefit in our bid for intellectual maturity from both the middle and the late Nietzsche, especially once we see him, as Paul Valéry (1968, 337) urged us to do, as a living force. When Freud said of Nietzsche that he had a more penetrating knowledge of himself than anyone who had ever lived and was likely to live, he had in mind not some personal self-knowledge but a universal discovery, one in which the ancient invitation to know oneself refers not simply to individual personality but to the human animal as such.[31] We are still in need of this discovery and of Nietzsche too as one of its bravest and boldest voyagers.

[CHAPTER ONE]

Books and Cheerfulness

Nature and books belong to the eyes that see them.

Emerson, "Experience"

Writing should always show a victory, specifically an overcoming of *oneself*, which can be communicated to others for their benefit; but there are dyspeptic authors who write only when they cannot digest something and it remains stuck in their teeth: they then attempt to vex the reader with their annoyance and exert power over him; they, too, want to gain victory, but over others.

Nietzsche, *Mixed Opinions and Maxims*, aphorism 152

"You are a philosopher, Dr Johnson. I have tried too in my time to be a philosopher; but I don't know how, cheerfulness was always breaking in." The truth is, that philosophy, like religion, is too generally supposed to be hard and severe, at least so grave as to exclude all gaiety.

James Boswell, *Life of Johnson* (1791)

Honest Books

Nietzsche favors "honest books" (*MOM* 145), "cold books" (*MOM* 142), and "European books" (*WS* 214). In his middle writings, he presents himself as a good European and is keen to de-Germanize himself (*WS* 87; *MOM* 323). He encourages his readers to "bear the flag of the Enlightenment farther" and aligns himself with figures such as Petrarch, Erasmus, and Voltaire (*HH* 26). He also seeks to entice his readers to return to the world of classical antiquity and its geniuses of meditation, such as Seneca and Plutarch (*HH* 282), and he finds a restoration of meditative modes of thinking in modern French writers such as Montaigne, La Rochefoucauld, Fontenelle, and Chamfort. The appeal of these writers is that they avoid using obscurantist and bombastic language, a feature of German philosophy that ruins most of it for Nietzsche. The books of these writers elevate themselves above changes in national taste and philosophical hues and contain, he contends, "more *real ideas* than all the books of German philosophers put together." He even locates a questionable style in mentors such as Goethe and Schopenhauer, with the former said to want to "embrace clouds more than is proper," and the latter wandering "continually among the likenesses of things, rather than among the things themselves" (*WS* 214).

Despite his criticism of him, Nietzsche did learn valuable lessons about style from Schopenhauer, who holds that style "is merely the silhouette of a thought," that "to write obscurely or badly amounts to thinking in a dull or confused manner." Simplicity, he maintains, is a sign of both truth and genius, with style obtaining its beauty from one's thoughts: thoughts do not become beautiful simply through style. The most important thing is to have something to say and to have the desire to communicate one's truths and insights to the reader in a clear way. Schopenhauer contrasts this practice of philosophy's love of wisdom with the style taught by the "pseudo-philosophy of the universities," which is the style of the prolix and the ponderous: "stilted, vague, equivocal" (1851/2015, 465–66). Even though Nietzsche is a severe critic of Schopenhauer's philosophy—of his metaphysics and his ethics—he admires him for displaying in his work the "good will for clarity and reason, which so often makes him appear so English and un-German" (*GS* 99).

In *The Wanderer and His Shadow*, Nietzsche argues that improving one's style can indeed aid our efforts to improve our ideas since it forces us to strive for clarity (*WS* 131). He also appeals in this text to "the grand style," where the beautiful gains victory over the colossal or, more literally, the monster (*das Ungeheure*) (*WS* 96). When we encounter things that seem too large to comprehend, we need to feel confident that we have the intellectual resources needed to confront them, able to transform powerful experiences into something beautiful, and no longer fearful and stuck in an attitude of puzzled awe or dread. Indeed, the best style is said to be one that is bound up with the expression of moods, especially the mood that is the most desirable to communicate and convey, that of the human being who is "spiritually joyful, bright, and sincere and who has overcome his passions." In this style, the features of feeling can be clarified, and in great art we can identify the attempt "to check feeling in its tracks" (*WS* 88, 136). The desire to display more feeling than one possesses corrupts style. The commitment to being a master of one's passions—be it in one's own life or in language and art—is one that Nietzsche never relinquishes. In a note from 1885, for example, he writes in favor of human beings of passion who are at the same time masters of their passions and of their passion for knowledge (*KSA*, vol. 11, fragment 38 [20]; *SUP*, 16:174). And, in the preface to *The Anti-Christ*, he writes of the "economy of the great style" that can hold together its strength and its enthusiasm.

The coldness Nietzsche espouses is in large part bound up with encouraging mistrust, which he sees as a healthy attitude to have. In aphorism 207 of *Dawn*, for example, he encourages his readers to take an interest in the morality of antiquity, and he does so in the context of a powerful criticism of German moral culture that he finds lacking in personal distinction and self-command: "To subordinate oneself, to follow publicly or in secret—that is virtue for the Germans. Long before Kant and his categorical imperative, Luther had spoken out of the same sensibility." By contrast, the Greeks and the Romans display an entirely different sensibility. Nietzsche calls it a "Mediterranean form of feeling" that seeks to guard against unconditional trust. With this feeling, one has in the last recess of one's heart "a little bit of skepticism for each and every thing, be it god, human, or concept" (*D* 207). Here skepticism is being advocated not as a way of life but as a healthy component within life, serving as a useful aid that does not stop us from living our lives with passion and dedication but encourages us to live with a healthy dose of self-reliance (*D* 163; *GS* 21).[1]

Nietzsche praises books that bring out honesty in readers (*MOM* 145). They do this, he thinks, by coaxing out our hatred and antipathy, "which canny shrewdness otherwise knows how best to conceal." In the experience of reading a book, we experience a rare freedom, namely, of experiencing an honest confrontation with ourselves. For once, we might say, the social mask comes down: "[W]e let ourselves go in reading a book, however much we restrain ourselves with regard to human beings" (*MOM* 145).[2] Ordinarily, we conceal ourselves in the noise of sociability and in affability. Reading, however, is an experience of solitude. In the experience of reading, we are open to inspiration and provocation, and implicit in this aphorism from *Mixed Opinions and Maxims* is the idea that reading is a form of friendship. Proust too has the insight that reading is a form of sincere friendship and that that is why it is of such value. It is, a friendship with the absent and often with the dead, "unencumbered with everything that makes other friendships ugly" (2011, 33).

Cold Books and Cheerfulness

Nietzsche links the communication of philosophical cheerfulness with a cold and sober mode of thinking, as in this aphorism: "*Cold books.* The good thinker counts upon readers who are receptive to the happiness that lies in good thinking: so that a book appearing to be cold and sober can, when seen with the right eyes, seem to be played upon by the sunshine of intellectual cheerfulness [*geistigen Heiterkeit*] and a true source of comfort for the soul" (*MOM* 142).[3] In German, the term *Heiterkeit* also means "serenity," "clarity," and "limpidity," as in the senses of an unclouded sky and of an unclouded mind or expression in speaking or writing. Cheerfulness is construed by Nietzsche not only as a state of the mind achieved by the genuine thinker but also as a quality of books in relation to the reader. Good thinkers, he stresses, express the happiness that lies in thinking well, and it is an experience they wish to share with the reader. Cold and sober books are able not only to cool down readers but also to cheer and refresh them, so allowing them to participate in the happiness of good thinking; good thinkers and readers take pleasure in and are reinvigorated by bathing "lasciviously in ice-cold streams" (*KSA*, vol. 9, fragment 11 [339]; *SUP*, 6:419). It is in this sense that the sunshine of intellectual cheerfulness can serve as a genuine source of comfort for the soul. In contrast to the false comfort offered by the dogmas of religion and metaphysics and their salutary, soothing errors, the cheering comfort Nietzsche prefers is based on good thinking and serves as a stimulant to action and the need to change one's life (*HH* 109).

All sensations of happiness for Nietzsche have two things in common: "*abundance* of feeling and *high-spiritedness* within it, such that one feels like a fish in water and leaps about in it" (*D* 439). He develops the point by suggesting that the thinker "leaps into *his* water, thus he attains *his* serenity [*Heiterkeit*]" (*D* 440). The water thinkers swim in and navigate may in fact be not only cold but also boundless and so difficult to chart that it requires brave seafarers. Indeed, it might be a completely open sea, of the kind Nietzsche depicts in *The Gay Science* 343, where he writes about the emotions that free spirits experience in the face of the event of the death of God. In contrast to unendangered and comfortable forms of the feeling of being at home in the world, Nietzsche considers cheerfulness to be an essential aspect of thinking and living dangerously (*GS* 283). The thinker as creator and not just as contemplator, then, lives in the great stream of thought and feeling, and even his dreams at night follow this stream; he requires repose and quietude from life to become clear about the nature of his task, not as a way of retreating or withdrawing from life. To be cheerful means to face the danger of the happiness we encounter in Homer: "to enjoy a strong bold, audacious soul, to go through life with a calm eye and firm step, always prepared to risk all—festively, impelled by the longing for undiscovered worlds and seas, people, and gods" (*GS* 302). This risk-taking—to be practiced with an attitude of calmness and steadfastness—is a crucial component in Nietzsche's conception of the practice of philosophical cheerfulness.[4]

While there is a need to be critical of simple, naive cheerfulness as well as superficially cheerful thinkers and writers, it is not necessary to go along with the attacks made by slanderers of cheerfulness, namely, those who regard cheerfulness as a naivete or even as a self-delusion: "People who have been deeply wounded by life are suspicious of all cheerfulness, as if it were childlike and childish." Cheerfulness, according to these slanderers, is entirely misplaced, being the result of either a childlike and childish lack of awareness of the suffering inherent in life or the self-deception of a sufferer or a sick person who "wants to gulp down one last minute of life's intoxication." Nietzsche sees this as a gross slander on cheerfulness that reveals something about the slanderers themselves: "But this judgment on the cheerfulness of life is nothing other than its refraction through the somber terrain of fatigue and disease." Such a judgment is to be pitied in the same way the slanderers pity cheerfulness as childlike and childish since their slander is itself "something child-like and childish, but from that *second childhood* that succeeds old age and precedes death" (*D* 329). Denying the possibility of different kinds of cheerfulness is not a substantiated judgment about the cheerful life but rather the expression of weakness, fatigue, and sickness of the spirit.

Nietzsche partly echoes the slanderers in suggesting that "the eternal cheerfulness of the common people and of children" is due to "the poor power of the eye," which cannot see far enough to bring threats and evils into focus. Not only is the superficial cheerfulness of the common people and of children shortsighted, but it also proves to be especially vulnerable since it is sustained by a "feeling of security, of comfort, of benevolence," which is in turn merely engendered by the temporary absence of danger, of uneasiness, and of evil. When danger is lurking, the feeling of security and, with it, superficial cheerfulness are vulnerable to attack and easily breakable. Superficial cheerfulness is to be considered directly proportional to the dullness of the eye—"[h]ence the gloominess and grief—akin to a bad conscience—of the great thinkers," who have better vision and awareness of the evils of life (*GS* 53). Nietzsche endorses neither superficial cheerfulness, which is shortsighted and vulnerable, nor the melancholy of the deep thinker, which might lead one to despair and resignation and to become a slanderer of cheerfulness.

Cheerfulness is not to be understood simply as the immediate reflection of an author's state of mind. As Timothy Hampton (2022, 14 [see also 17]) has helpfully suggested, it "can be a technique, a way of managing oneself and influencing others," and, as such, it has an aesthetic dimension along with moral and psychological aspects. Not only is cheerfulness a factor in writing; it is also a stylistic tone and effect to be composed. Indeed, reading and writing themselves may be construed as uplifting practices (Hampton 2022, 21). Nietzsche, for example, thinks that the modern age has forgotten the art of reflection or observation, in which it is possible to gather maxims "from the thorniest and least gratifying stretches of our lives" to make ourselves feel better, to give ourselves a lift and a tonic. We can return to life from an encounter with thorny problems revivified rather than depressed and with "presence of mind in difficult situations and amusement in tedious surroundings" (*HH* 38). There is a need, therefore, for modern spirits to learn how to derive pleasure from the art of the maxim, from its construction to its tasting. Nietzsche recommends a return to the great masters of the psychological maxim, and he refers specifically to La Rochefoucauld and his spiritual and artistic relatives. Today, he finds, although there is an appreciation of these writers of maxims, it is one without real discipline or exercise: "[T]hey praise them because they cannot love them, and are quick to admire, but even quicker to run away" (*HH* 35). Just as the modern acceleration of life is leading to a superficial engagement with life, so Nietzsche finds that modern readers taste the maxims of the great psychologists in all too hasty fashion when the task is to savor the maxim and to go slowly.

Nietzsche and Montaigne

Nietzsche is critical of the desire to feel comfortable in the world and takes to task the way modern intellectual culture reduces Montaigne's conception of philosophy as a way of life to little more than achieving personal serenity and peace of mind (*BGE* 208; see also *WB* 3).[5] In a fragment from the period of volume 2 of *Human, All Too Human*, he writes: "We become travelers, 'wanderers,' when we are nowhere at home" (*KSA*, vol. 8, fragment 40 [20]). In the preface to *Human, All Too Human* of 1886, he explains that the process of the great liberation of the spirit is set in motion when "a will and a wish awaken to depart at any cost for somewhere else": "'Better to die than to live here,' . . . and this 'here,' this 'feeling of being at home' is all that up until now the soul had loved!" (*HH* preface 3). And, in book 5 of *The Gay Science* from 1887, he commends his secret wisdom and *gaya scienza* to free spirits and good Europeans who are homeless and feel compelled to embark on the sea like emigrants: "We children of the future, how could we be at home in this today? We feel disfavor for all ideas that might lead one to feel at home even in this fragile, broken time of transition" (*GS* 377). In these instances, Nietzsche disapproves of the feeling of being at home as an uncritical sense of satisfaction and passive acceptance of present opinions and ways of life. In contrast, and as we have seen, he deems his mode of cheerfulness to be a way of thinking and living dangerously. As he puts it in a note from his late period: "Concerning the misunderstanding of 'cheerfulness' (*Heiterkeit*). Temporary redemption from protracted tension, the exuberance, the saturnalia of a spirit who consecrates and prepares himself for protracted and terrible resolutions. The '*fool*' in the form of '*science*'" (*KSA*, vol. 12, fragment 2 [166]). For Montaigne, there is no more certain sign of wisdom than gaiety and "constant cheerfulness [*rejouissance*]": "[H]er state is like that of things above the moon, ever serene." Moreover, in philosophy, we should find "nothing more gay, more lusty, sprightly, and I might almost say frolicsome": "She preaches nothing but merry-making and a good time" (2003, 144 [I. 26]). Although Nietzsche on occasion enjoys a little philosophical merrymaking, his cheerfulness, linked as it is with much fateful questioning, is clearly of a more profound character. Still, he expresses admiration for Montaigne for being a rich and thoughtful naturalist, in contrast to today's thoughtless naturalists (*PT*, 118), and for his "brave and blithe skepticism" (*KSA*, vol. 11, fragment 36 [7]; *WP* 367).

Robert Pippin has identified a "Montaigne problem" (2010, 23) in Nietzsche's philosophy. How is it possible that Montaigne combines intellectual honesty, centered on drawing attention to the weaknesses of human beings, with an affirmative orientation toward life? In other words: "[*H*]*ow*, [Nietzsche] wants to know above all, did Montaigne manage to exhibit such a thoroughgoing skepticism and clarity about human frailty and failings without Pascal's despair and eventual surrender?" What Nietzsche finds interesting in Montaigne, Pippin goes on to claim, is that "Montaigne ended up a thoughtful, ferociously honest, cheerful free spirit, someone who had succeeded at the task of 'making himself at home in the world.'" Pippin holds that Nietzsche never succeeded in reaching the "Montaigne-inspired *ideal*" of being at home in the world: "The fact that his prose sometimes lapsed into a shrieking intensity, the occasional hysteria, the drift into the maudlin and the sentimental, the hatred venting through some passages, do [*sic*] not at all evince a Montaigne-like peace of mind." The conclusion to be reached is unavoidable: "For all his aspiration and admiration Nietzsche never succeeded in writing with the kind of 'cheerfulness,' '*Heiterkeit*,' and balance of Montaigne" (Pippin 2010, 10–11, 121).

Issue can be taken with this reading on several fronts. Pippin tends to assume that Nietzsche wants to take his example from Montaigne; he also tends to equate philosophical cheerfulness with the task of making oneself feel at home in the world and achieving peace of mind. In suggesting that Nietzsche might not after all be a cheerful thinker and writer, he fails to entertain the possibility that in his work skepticism might well work very differently to the ends of tranquility it serves in Montaigne. To bring out the difference between Montaigne and Nietzsche as cheerful thinkers and writers it is not necessary to impute to Nietzsche as Pippin does the sentiments and emotions of a maudlin writer—shrieking tones, hysteria, hatred—that are simply not a feature of his writings and that serve only to conceal exemplary aspects of his philosophical character. Although Nietzsche is a philosopher of hope and intellectual boldness, his fundamental philosophical character is of a highly sober and composed kind.

Melancholy Authors and Cheerful Wisdom

In a study of cheerfulness, Christopher Hampton argues that Nietzsche retains the salutary, generative dimension that previous thinkers associated with cheerfulness but dispenses with its psychological depth. He claims that Nietzsche associates cheerfulness with aesthetic experience (Hampton 2022, 174) and, furthermore, that, along with writers such as Emerson and W. B. Yeats, he locates it not in individual psychology but in the medium of art itself and as "the violence of form" (2022, 194). Helpfully noting that *Heiterkeit* "takes us back to etymological roots suggesting 'bright,' 'clear,' 'shining'" (2022, 189), he concludes by equating Nietzsche's cheerfulness solely with the "divinely artificial art" of surfaces that he speaks of in the second edition of *The Gay Science* (*GS* preface 4) and that seems to be an adoption of Emerson's advice to learn how to skate well on them.[6] While this is undoubtedly an aspect of Nietzsche's use of cheerfulness, it is important not to overlook how it is also linked in his work to the task of undertaking bold intellectual inquiry and mining the depths of the human psyche.

Both Emerson and Nietzsche connect high spirits with cheerfulness. Emerson writes: "[P]ower dwells with cheerfulness; hope puts us in a working mood, whilst despair is no muse, and untunes the active powers" (2003, 141). And Nietzsche asks: "[W]hat could be more necessary than cheerfulness? Nothing gets done without a dose of high spirits" (*TI* foreword). In *Ecce Homo*, Nietzsche also describes the tone of *Twilight of the Idols*—whose working title was *Idleness of a Psychologist*—as both "cheerful and fateful" (*EH* "Twilight of the Idols" 1). This cheerful fatefulness has to do with the attempt to overthrow old idols or truths. Indeed, the foreword to *Twilight* is largely devoted to the theme of cheerfulness, which is understood as a proof of an excess of strength that involves the capacity to recover and to return stronger from the serious and, at times, depressing business of sounding out and overthrowing idols. Here Nietzsche admits that the greatness and difficulty of the task of the revaluation of all values "forces him to keep running out into the sunlight to shake off a seriousness that has become heavy, all too heavy" (*TI* foreword).

In the preface to *On the Genealogy of Morality*, Nietzsche refers to cheerfulness as a reward for "brave, diligent, subterranean seriousness"

(*GM* preface 7).[7] The reward in question refers to the liberation one secures for oneself when treating burdensome subjects seriously—problems of morality in this instance—but no longer feeling intimidated by them.[8] Once you have seen *through* certain problems and *beyond* them too, you can now encounter them cheerfully. While noting Nietzsche's utilization of the metaphor and imagery of dawn in his writings, Hampton overlooks its connection with the daybreak that emerges for Nietzsche precisely from tunneling in these depths and being rewarded for one's patience and diligence (see *D* preface 1). Nietzsche offers this helpful advice to good soldiers of knowledge: "'We must take things more cheerfully [*lustiger*] than they deserve, especially because for a long time we have taken them more seriously than they deserve'" (*D* 567).

In *The Wanderer and His Shadow*, Nietzsche draws a distinction between melancholy authors and serious ones: "Anyone who puts on paper what he *is suffering* will be a melancholy author: but a *serious* one, if he tells us what he *has suffered* and why he is now at rest amid joy" (*WS* 128). According to this distinction, melancholy authors are amid their suffering and have not yet overcome it. As a result, their thinking and writing is trapped in a state of agitation that takes the form of a melancholic or cheerless form of seriousness.[9] Nietzsche holds that pessimistic thinkers and melancholy authors contribute to misanthropy by giving all things the blackest and gloomiest colors, increasing the horror, and getting us to sense that things are more terrifying than they in fact are (*D* 561). Indeed, much of the fear that grips us and holds us back in our lives is of the kind Nietzsche calls *fantasized* fear, which we can comprehend in terms of "that malevolent, apish goblin who leaps onto a person's back at the very moment he is already most burdened" (*HH* 535). In response to the pessimist, he writes: "[W]e have no way of preventing people from *darkening* us. . . . But we shall do what we have always done: whatever one casts into us, we take down into our depth—for we are deep, we do not forget—*and become bright again*" (*GS* 378). Truly serious authors have conquered their suffering, and, from a position of a hard-won joy, they seek to speak about serious matters with a genuinely cheering cheerfulness that invigorates and emboldens the reader.

While his opinion of Montaigne as a cheerful thinker and writer remains constant in his writings, Nietzsche changes his mind about Schopenhauer. In his unfashionable observation on him as educator, Schopenhauer is said to be cheerful because his thought has conquered the most difficult things (*SE* 2).[10] In the middle writings, however, he holds that Schopenhauer's philosophy "remains the mirror image of an ardent and melancholy youth" (*MOM* 271).[11] Nietzsche finds a lack of development in

Schopenhauer's thinking and holds that he chose to barricade himself in: "[H]e neither enjoyed himself much nor suffered much. . . . His passion for knowledge was *not great* enough for him to suffer on its behalf: he barricaded himself in. His pride, too, was greater than his thirst for knowledge, in revoking, he feared for his reputation" (*KSA*, vol. 9, fragment 6 [381]; see also *D* 481).

In *The Wanderer and His Shadow*, Nietzsche surprisingly attributes to Xenophon's Socrates in *Memorabilia* a "cheerful [*fröhliche*] form of seriousness and a *playful wisdom*." He considers this to be the best spiritual condition for human beings to advance themselves ethically and rationally (*WS* 86).[12] While in the early and late writings he tends to associate Socrates with decadence, in *The Wanderer and His Shadow* he privileges him over the figure of Christ and the Bible. His observation echoes what Emerson says in his journal: "I do not see in him [Jesus] cheerfulness: I do not see in him the love of Natural Science: I see in him no kindness for Art; I see in him nothing of Socrates, of Laplace, of Shakspeare. The perfect man should remind us of all great men. Do you ask me if I would rather resemble Jesus than any other man? If I should say Yes, I would suspect myself of superstition" (2010b, 424). Nietzsche seems to agree with Emerson that the life and words of Christ—at least as conveyed in the *New Testament*—are characterized by a cheerless form of seriousness and an excessively solemn wisdom.[13]

In his middle writings, Nietzsche imitates Socrates to some extent with his own attempt to produce a cheerful form of seriousness as the principal tone of philosophy.[14] In *The Gay Science*, for example, he attacks the "clumsy, gloomy," and stiff intellect of scholars who equate thinking well with "taking the matter *seriously*" (*GS* 327; see also *GS* 177), launching a campaign against the prejudice held by these all-too-serious scholars, according to which: "[W]here laughter and gaiety are found, thinking does not amount to anything" (*GS* 327). In *Beyond Good and Evil*, he tells his readers that his gay science serves as an antidote to the overly nationalistic, scholastic, obscure, and grave way of expression characteristic of the latest German style (*BGE* 293). He goes so far as to say that he would "rank philosophers according to the level of their laughter" (*BGE* 294).[15] Similarly, in *Ecce Homo*, he construes playfulness "as a sign of greatness" and its "essential presupposition," admitting that he does not know "any other way of handling great tasks than as *play*" (*EH* "Why I Am So Clever" 10).[16] The key insight, then, is that, in the forms of gaiety, laughter, and playfulness, cheerfulness is not incompatible with negotiating serious matters. Rather, a cheerful style of thinking and writing is a requirement for dealing adequately with grave philosophical matters and executing important tasks of thinking.

"Cricket-Cheerfulness"

It takes some time for Nietzsche to arrive at a fully cheerful mode of thinking and writing. Although cheerfulness is one of the central themes in his first book, *The Birth of Tragedy*, he does not consider it to be a cheerful one. In "An Attempt at Self-Criticism," the preface written for the second edition (1886), he introduces the book as "a youthful work full of youthful courage and youthful melancholy" (*BT* preface 2). Similarly, and in the same period, *Human, All Too Human* is characterized as a "melancholic-courageous book" (*HH* preface 2). It is important to note, however, that both books are described not only as melancholic but also as courageous. Although Nietzsche acknowledges that in these texts he is not at rest amid joy, he does not see himself as a merely melancholy author (*WS* 128). Indeed, courage is one of the intellectual virtues that is continually associated by him with cheerfulness. In *Ecce Homo*, Nietzsche says that in *Human, All Too Human* "almost every sentence is the manifestation of a victory" (*EH* "Human, All Too Human" 1). As we shall see, he believes he fully succeeds in securing this victory in the form of true cheerfulness only in *Dawn*.

In his preface to the second volume of *Human, All Too Human* (1886), Nietzsche tells a story about his search for a practice of cheerfulness between the years 1878 and 1880. While his early writings, such as *Richard Wagner at Bayreuth*, reveal a "melancholy turn of phrase," Nietzsche discloses, in *Human, All Too Human*, that there "lies something of the almost cheerful and inquisitive coldness of the psychologist" dealing with "a multitude of painful things" (*HH2* preface 1). Importantly, the cheerfulness of *Human, All Too Human* is associated with cold philosophical and psychological investigation as well as with a mode of handling suffering. In line with the preface to the first volume, Nietzsche deems the overall project of the work to be "almost cheerful," implying that true cheerfulness has not been fully achieved at this point in his intellectual development. He further complicates the picture: "It was at that time that I learned the art of *presenting* myself as if cheerful, objective, inquisitive, above all, healthy and malicious. . . . What perhaps constituted the attractiveness of these writings will nonetheless not escape a subtler eye and sympathy—that a sufferer and a renouncer speaks here as if he were *not* a sufferer and a renouncer. Here balance, composure, even gratitude toward life *shall* be upheld" (*HH2* preface 5). The three books contained in *Human, All Too Human* are said to be attractive because in them a sufferer and a renouncer speak as if he were neither, presenting himself *as if* cheerful—when in fact he is not. The "as if" dimension is key here. Nietzsche affirms that what he learned at that time is not so much the art of being cheerful but rather the art of disguising himself as a cheerful thinker and writer. But why does he describe his feigned cheerfulness as attractive? Moreover, why should *we* find it attractive?

The passage mentioned above might seem to be merely suggesting that sufferers and renouncers can be cheerful only when feigning cheerfulness: all that is left to them is to pretend to be cheerful when in fact they continue to suffer and renounce life in private. This would be cold comfort to readers of Nietzsche and offer an uninteresting example of a philosophical life. As becomes evident in the remainder of the preface, much more, however, is being suggested. In 1886, Nietzsche links his feigned cheerfulness to a desire to return to health: "Just as a doctor puts his sick patient into totally alien surroundings . . . I forced myself, as doctor and patient in a single person, into a reversed, untested *climate of the soul*, and especially into a diverting wandering abroad, into the unknown, toward a curiosity about every sort of strangeness." Presenting himself as if cheerful is a critical stage in the evolution of this developmental process. As the sick patient in the period of convalescence, he goes on to say, he learned how to stretch his hands toward "new nourishment, a new sun, a new future," both personally and philosophically: "[A] lot of cricket-happiness, cricket-cheerfulness [*Grillen-Munterkeit*], a lot of quiet, light, subtler foolishness, hidden enthusiasm—all of this ultimately resulted in a great spiritual strengthening, an increasing pleasure and abundance of health. Life itself *rewards* us for our stubborn will to life, for a long war such as I waged at that time against the pessimism of weariness with life" (*HH2* preface 5).[17]

"Cricket-cheerfulness" or made-up cheerfulness is, though feigned, significant in that it signals a wish to return to health and might ultimately result in such spiritual strengthening, and so aid our overall feeling of well-being. In *Dawn*, Nietzsche observes that it is proper to noble spirits to affect constant cheerfulness: "Just as [a noble individual] knows how to preserve the appearance of ever-present, dignified physical strength, he also wishes, through constant serenity and civility even in distressing situations, to maintain the impression that his soul and his spirit are equal to all dangers and vagaries" (*D* 201). This is further explained in a preparatory note for this aphorism: it is proper to noble spirit "not to seem tired even when standing for hours, i.e., one affects constantly dignified physical strength and a psychic feeling of power through constant serenity and civility" (*D* "Notes," p. 327). Nietzsche, then, is explaining how he practiced a form of cheerfulness by simulating and seeking to enact a cheerful mode of thinking and writing.[18] The two volumes of *Human, All Too Human* are found attractive by him because they teach "a *lesson of health*" and a "*disciplina voluntatis*"

(*HH2* preface 2). In practicing and learning the art of presenting oneself as cheerful, one exercises and strengthens one's spirit and will to life. To put it simply, the lesson we can draw from Nietzsche's experience is that by willfully enacting cheerfulness one might become cheerful.[19] We find this encapsulated in the motto, "Fake it until you make it."

The search for cheerfulness is construed by Nietzsche as an essential part of a struggle against "*Romantic pessimism*" that puffs up and interprets personal experiences into "general judgements" and "world-condemnation" and that he finds dreamily dissolute (*HH2* preface 2, 5). This is the kind of pessimism that "destroys the spirit's severity and mirth and makes every sort of vague desire and fungal covetousness proliferate" (*HH2* preface 3). However, Nietzsche seeks to overcome any simplistic opposition between a cheerful mode of thinking and writing and a specific kind of pessimism: "[T]here is a will to the tragic and to pessimism that is as much the sign of severity as of strength of intellect (of taste, feeling, conscience). With this will in our breast, we do not fear the frightening and questionable aspect characteristic of all existence; we even seek it out" (*HH2* preface 7; see also *GS* preface 4). In searching for a cheerful mode of thinking and writing, Nietzsche seeks to triumph over his youthful tendency toward Romantic pessimism. The practice of a made-up cheerfulness helps him bolster his intellectual courage and reclaim the right to a cheerful pessimism that is characterized not only by fearlessness but also by risk-taking in investigating terrifying problems.

Nietzsche thinks he first achieves a perfect cheerfulness in *Dawn* (1881): "The perfect lightness and cheerfulness, even the exuberance of spirit that is reflected in this work, was accompanied not only by the deepest physiological weakness, but by an excess of painful feelings as well" (*EH* "Why I Am So Wise" 1). The text is conceived as emerging from and reflecting a cheerful spirt that speaks of a cheerfulness that goes with suffering and the acknowledgment of psychological weakness. In achieving cheerfulness amid several days of unremitting headache and the vomiting of phlegm, he writes that he had a dialectician's clarity par excellence and could think with cold-blooded lucidity about things that in healthier conditions he was not enough of a mountain climber and not cold enough for (*EH* 'Why I am so Wise' 1).

In the preface to the second edition of *The Gay Science*, Nietzsche writes that the last book of his middle writings "is nothing but a bit of merry making after long privation and powerlessness, the rejoicing of strength that is returning, of a reawakened faith in a tomorrow and the day after tomorrow, of a sudden sense and anticipation of a future, of impending adventures, of seas that are open again, of goals that are permitted again, believed again" (*GS* preface 1). *The Gay Science* is presented as the expression of a full cheerfulness, even more perfect than the one reflected in *Dawn*. While Nietzsche sees his newfound cheerfulness in the latter as inseparable from psychological weakness, the cheerfulness of the former is linked with high spirits, with an exuberance of joy, with a greater sense of possibility, and with an overall increase in spiritual strength. Although the kind of *Wissenschaft* that Nietzsche seeks to promote in *The Gay Science* is technically *fröhliche* (gay or joyful) rather than *heitere* (cheerful), gaiety and joy are deeply and intimately connected to cheerfulness (Lanier Anderson and Cristy 2017, 1541 n. 11). This connection is more explicitly drawn in the preface to *On the Genealogy of Morality*: "[C]heerfulness, in fact, or to put it into my parlance, that gay science—is a reward: a reward for a long, brave, diligent, subterranean seriousness for which, admittedly, not everyone is suited" (*GM* preface 7). In a preparatory note for the preface to the second edition of *The Gay Science*, Nietzsche laments a misunderstanding of his cheerfulness in the book, especially by all-too-serious scholars: the gaiety of his scientific investigation and his cheerful mode of thinking and writing are mistaken for a lack of rigor and profundity, whereas the book emerged from a triumphant condition, a victory over and gratitude toward the serious problems he had been grappling with in his previous writings (*KSA*, vol. 12, fragment 2 [166]).

The kind of cheerfulness that for Nietzsche pervades *The Gay Science* is different from his previous conceptions and practices of cheerfulness in that it displays a reawakened faith in a tomorrow and the anticipation of a future (*GS* preface 1). This characteristic of his cheerfulness finds its clearest articulation in aphorism 343 from book 5 (1887), where he discusses the way in which the tremendous and gloomy event of the death of God can be positively received by fearless and strong free spirits, "born guessers of riddles" who are animated by the passion of knowledge and "posted between today and tomorrow, stretched between today and tomorrow." Cheerfulness here is closely connected not only with gratitude but also with premonitions and expectation. A new dawn may now shine on us: "[O]ur heart overflows with gratitude, amazement. . . . [A]ll the daring of the lover of knowledge is permitted again; the sea *our* sea lies open again; perhaps there has never yet been such an 'open sea'" (*GS* 343). Although Nietzsche considers false hope or wishful thinking "the worst of evils because it lengthens agony" (*HH* 72), it is undeniable that a belief in the future informs the texts of his middle period, especially starting with *Dawn* (see, e.g., *D* 575).[20] I show in chapter 6 below that this commitment to belief in the future forms an important part of Nietzsche philosophizing in *Thus Spoke Zarathustra*.

Cheerfulness and Hope

An important part of Nietzsche's cheerful mode of thinking and writing consists, in fact, in the communication of a hope in the possibility of new ways of thinking and living. In "Hope," aphorism 71 of *Human, All Too Human*, Nietzsche refers to Pandora's box, which is filled with evils and was given to humanity as a gift from the gods. Although characterized by the gods as a box of happiness, nothing but evils have flown forth from it, and the winged beings have been wandering about day and night doing harm to us. However, there is one single evil that remains in the box and that humankind takes for an amazing piece of treasure, some gold for which it can reach whenever the desire arises and that it thinks must be the greatest of worldly possessions. Its name, Nietzsche says, is *hope*, and he concludes the aphorism with a short parable: "For Zeus did not want human beings, however much tormented by the other evils they might be, to throw away their lives, but instead to continue letting themselves be tormented anew. Hence, he gives hope to humanity: it is in truth the worst of evils because it lengthens their agony" (*HH* 71).[21] This is hope in the sense of wishful thinking. In the second edition of *The Gay Science*, however, Nietzsche confesses to now being attacked by a feeling of hope as part of his conception of philosophizing as a visionary activity (*GS* preface 1). As a premature being of the coming century, he experiences, again he confesses, "a new and scarcely describable kind of light, happiness, relief, exhilaration, encouragement, dawn" (*GS* 343). And, in the closing sections of the second essay of *On the Genealogy of Morality* on debt and guilt, he refers to the redeeming human of the future who gives the earth a purpose and "humans their hope again" (*GM* 2.24). In the wake of the tremendous event of the death of God, humanity needs a new goal; it is to be one that will give meaning to the earth and express fidelity to it.

Although this too may be a case of wishful thinking when looked at from a severely realistic perspective, it is also the expression of a courageous hope. Pierre Hadot refers to what he calls "bold hope," which he locates in some of Goethe's poems and writings. "Hope," he writes, "is inherent in life and in action. To hope is to be alive, to be active" (2023, 124). This echoes Jean-Marie Guyau on the philosophy of hope: "One must thus know how to hope; hope is what carries us higher and farther. 'But it's an illusion!' What do you know of this? Should we not take a step for fear that one day the earth will slide away from under our feet? Looking far into the past or the future is not the only thing; one must look into oneself. One must see there the living forces that demand to be expended, and we must act"

(Guyau 1895). Hope, then, be it a blessing or a curse, is an integral part of the human animal's constitution as a creature of time and an essential feature of our being agents in the world.[22]

Nietzsche conceives of cheerfulness not only as a temperament but also as a style of thinking and writing and a way of communicating thoughts about grave problems. The result is a philosophical practice that involves intellectual courage, calmness, steadfastness, sobriety and coldness, liveliness, high spirits, gratitude, and hope and adopting a slow tempo in opposition to fanatic harshness and rashness. Cheerfulness is not merely a passive acceptance of things as they are; rather, it is the only mood that enables an active and transformative response to tragedy. Emerson writes: "But power dwells with cheerfulness; hope puts us in a working mood, whilst despair is no muse, and untunes the active powers. A man should make life and Nature happier to us, or he had better never been born" (2003, 138). In an unpublished draft of *Ecce Homo*, Nietzsche writes: "*Emerson*, with his Essays, has been a good friend and someone who has cheered me up even in dark times: he possesses so much skepsis, so many 'possibilities,' that with him even virtue becomes witty [*geistreich*]" (*KSA*, 14:476–77).[23] This is a telling disclosure by Nietzsche of what draws him, again and again, to Emerson. Virtue is typically taken to be something stiff and austere, so, when Nietzsche declares that virtue assumes the appearance of wittiness in Emerson, he is saying that in his case it is practiced with lightness and suppleness and as something genial and gay. One of the most important "possibilities" he finds in Emerson is the idea of a practical, hopeful cheerfulness that can cheer us up in times of existential difficulty.

For Nietzsche, Emerson is a man of taste who "lives instinctively on pure ambrosia and leaves behind the indigestible in things." Nietzsche identifies a specific kind of cheerfulness in Emerson, "the sort of kind and witty cheerfulness that discourages any seriousness": "His spirit always finds reasons to be satisfied and even grateful." Emerson's sense of gratitude is so profound that he now and then verges on "cheerful [*heitere*] transcendence"—although the potency of life may be lacking, the *lust for life* remains praiseworthy (*TI* "Reconnaissance Raids of an Untimely Man" 13). By way of contrast, Nietzsche finds in Carlyle's writings a figure who needed noise—by which he means he is a fundamentally reactive figure—and who displayed a "constant and passionate *dishonesty* with himself." He refers to Carlyle as a "rhetor" ("out of *need*") who was provoked by a longing for a strong faith but who knew he was incapable of it. Nietzsche adds that, if you are someone who *has* faith, as Emerson did, you can allow yourself "the fine luxury of scepticism" (*TI* "Reconnaissance Raids of an Untimely Man" 12; see also *AC* 54 [on "Carlylism"]).[24] As Nietzsche reports, Carlyle was one of the earliest critics to accuse Emerson of superficiality: "Carlyle really loved Emerson but still said that 'he doesn't give *us* enough to chew on'" (*TI* "Reconnaissance Raids of an Untimely Man" 13). Nietzsche, however, is keen to defend Emerson against Carlyle's accusation: although what he says might in fact be true, it does not reflect badly on Emerson. Note here that Nietzsche places the emphasis on "us": the fact that Emerson does not give *us* heavy thoughts on which to ruminate is not necessarily a flaw and might be one of his virtues. The sense in which this might be regarded as praiseworthy directly relates to Nietzsche's and Emerson's conception of a style of cheerfulness that knows how to triumph over black events (cf. Emerson 2002, 262).[25]

Although he takes thinking to be a serious business, Nietzsche wants to show in his writings that it does not need to culminate in an oppressive heaviness. When utilized to productive effect, seriousness can be part of a liberating, "joyful" science that is sustained by a cheerful mode of thinking that frees us from dogmatic and fanatic ways of thinking and in which questioning our self-assuredness becomes second nature. In addition, the seemingly wholly negative task of mining and undermining things may result in the discovery of new ways of thinking and feeling.

[CHAPTER TWO]

Honesty and the Passion of Knowledge

I no longer want any knowledge without danger: let there be, always, the treacherous sea or the merciless high mountains around the seeker of knowledge.

Nietzsche, note of 1881

I no longer wish to hear anything of all those things and questions that do not permit of experiment. This is the limit of my "truthfulness" and where courage loses its rights.

Nietzsche, *The Gay Science*, aphorism 51

We must *learn to think differently*—in order finally, perhaps very late, to attain even more: *to feel differently*.

Nietzsche, *Dawn*, aphorism 103

To stand amidst this *rerum concordia discors* and the whole marvellous uncertainty and ambiguity of existence *and not question*, not tremble with the desire and joy of questioning . . . this is what I feel to be *contemptible*, and it is this feeling that I first seek in everyone:—some kind of folly persuades me time after time that every human being has this feeling, as a human being. It is my kind of injustice.

Nietzsche, *The Gay Science*, aphorism 2

Know Thyself?

Nietzsche commences aphorism 335 of *The Gay Science*—"Long Live Physics!" on our becoming the ones that we are—by asking how many people know how to truly observe something, including themselves. As Christopher Janaway has pointed out, he is recommending not that to engage in self-discovery we literally do physics but rather that "there is a discipline and depth to the self-study which he finds it fruitful to see as *analogous* to a scientific approach" (2006, 338). At the start of the aphorism, Nietzsche invokes the famous pronouncement of the oracle at Delphi—to know thyself—which was addressed to human beings by a god, and he suggests we might want to consider it to be an almost malicious incitement. As Paul Bishop (2011, 219) recounts, this mistrust of the famous oracle was expressed by Goethe prior to Nietzsche.[1] The problem with the imperative, as Goethe interpreted it, is that it may well be a deception practiced by a secret order of priests to confuse human beings by placing impossible demands on them with a false, inner speculation and thus serving to divert attention from activity in the external world. The imperative makes sense, in fact, only when placed alongside the maxim of Pindar, which Nietzsche utilizes in his early and middle writings: "[*W*]*erde, der du bist!*" (Become the one that you are).

In aphorism 270 of *The Gay Science*, we read: "*What does your conscience say?* You shall become the one that you are." This is a conception of the self that Nietzsche first explores in the *Unfashionable Observations* of 1873–75. In the observation on history, he declares the task to be one of becoming "*human*," and it involves organizing the chaos within us by thinking back to our real needs. We are to be guided by honesty and truthfulness of character, and it is these qualities of character that will enable us to rebel against the state of things where we only repeat what we have heard, learn what is already known, and imitate what already exists. The chaos that we are is the result of our being a mixture of several influences and sources. Although this has a healthy aspect to it, there is always the danger of being overwhelmed by what is past and foreign, so there is a need to counter this by establishing one's own horizons.

In *Schopenhauer as Educator*, we encounter one of the first instances in Nietzsche's writing of the use of the word *probity* or *honesty*. The German word he uses is *Biederkeit*, which means "honesty," "sincerity," "uprightness," so that a *Biedermann* is a man of honor and his word. Typically, whenever Nietzsche puts probity or honesty to work in his later texts, he uses the word *Redlichkeit*. In the observation on Schopenhauer, *probity* or *honesty* denotes the qualities of the man of learning, such as the scholar with his attachment to dialectical investigation, which involves a search for truth in which the pleasure resides in the chase (*SE* 6). Probity is not highly valued at this stage in Nietzsche's development because he sees it as almost wholly tied to the convention whereby one typically tells the truth only in simple things and probity is distrustful of the innovator. The desire in this case is to employ probity to conserve the old wisdom and preserve established truths.

Nietzsche begins his observation on Schopenhauer as educator by noting that human beings are lazy and timid, preferring to hide themselves behind customs and opinions, and approaching life in the fashion of indolence and inertia. In truth, all human beings should be shocked into existence by the knowledge that, being unique, they will be in the world only once and that "no imaginable chance will gather into unity so strangely variegated an assortment it is for a second time" (*SE* 1).[2] The human being who does not wish to belong to the mass only needs to stop taking himself so easily and follow his conscience, which calls to him, "Be yourself!" And this means no longer being fettered by the chains of fear and convention. Without this liberation, life can be regarded only as something dismal and senseless. The fact that we live in this time, this here and now, must be the strongest incentive for us to live in accordance with our own laws and standards. We wish to be responsible to ourselves for our own existence and want to be the true helmsmen of this existence and refuse to allow our existence to resemble a mindless act of chance, which is what, in fact, it is.

For Nietzsche, one's true nature lies not concealed deep within but immeasurably high above, that is, above who it is we typically take ourselves to be. But it also something we carry within us as a potential: "Each of us bears a productive uniqueness within him as the core of his being; and when he becomes aware of it, there appears around him a strange penumbra which is the mark of his singularity." Nietzsche addresses the dangers of uniqueness. If we suppose that each individual bears within itself a productive uniqueness as the kernel of its being, then this means that a strange aura, "the aura of the unusual," surrounds it (*SE* 3). This uniqueness is taken to be unbearable by many people since attached to it is a chain of efforts and burdens. The individual finds that the desert and the cave are always within it and thus that solitude is given to it as a fate (*Loos*). Several dangers now confront the individual. First, there is the danger of pure science, in which one allows oneself to be educated by an inhuman abstraction and neglects the need for moral exemplars and models. Second, there is the danger of complexity: modern humans are so complex and many-sided that they become dishonest whenever they speak and try to act in accordance with their declarations. Third, there is the danger of leading a ghostly life, obliged to live without courage or trust, in denial and doubt, agitated and discontented, always expecting to be disappointed. Finally, there is the danger of petrifaction, where one is reduced to ruin by one's uniqueness and lives as an icy rock.

We need to try and ascertain how education can best preserve and nurture the vitality of life, knowing under what conditions maturation is a successful process as opposed to one that produces melancholy, apathy, or nausea, including a young person who is skeptical of all customs and concepts. Today, we are satisfied with too many things, and as a result we lose the sense of surprise and are no longer amazed at anything: "[T]he massive influx of impressions is so great . . . barbaric and violent things press so overpoweringly . . . in on the youthful soul; that it can save itself only by premeditated stupidity" (*HL* 7). A child can be too complete at too early an age. Moreover, education is being hijacked by the economic dictates of the modern world with the need for factories of scholarship ever increasing, utility is valued as a god, and a solid mediocrity is becoming only more and more mediocre. Today's educators behave as practical pessimists and thus are defeated by and resigned to what is fashionable in the present.

We should not underestimate the difficult nature of the task that lies before us as we seek to fashion our uniqueness: "[The human being] is a dark and veiled thing; and even if the hare has seven skins, the human being can shed seven times seventy skins and still not be able to say: 'This is really you, this is no longer outer shell.'" We need to recognize the dangers we will face when we dig down into ourselves: "How easy it is to do damage to yourself that no doctor can heal." Nietzsche recommends, therefore, pursuing a less hazardous strategy, advising that the young, perplexed soul should look back on its life with a question: "What have you up to now truly loved, what attracted your soul, what dominated it while simultaneously making it happy?" (*SE* 1). If we place before us a series of revered objects, then perhaps their nature and sequence may reveal to us the fundamental law of our authentic self (*eigentlichen Selbst*) (*SE* 1). We will surely need educators and cultivators to aid us in the task, and they will be our liberators.

Nietzsche continues to work with the notion of our becoming the ones that we are—unique, singular, incomparable—in *The Gay Science*. He argues that, if we suppose we can rely on our moral conscience to become acquainted with our singular self, we are, in fact, operating without real knowledge. In aphorism 308 of the book, we are invited to reflect on the history of our every day by considering the habits of which it is made up and ask, Are they the product of innumerable little acts cowardice and sloth or of courage and inventive reason on our part? In aphorism 319, Nietzsche speaks of making our experience a matter of conscience for our knowledge, which entails practicing a type of honesty (*Redlichkeit*) that is quite alien to founders of religion and moral systems. It requires being conscientious through knowledge: "What did I really experience? What was going on inside and around me? Was my reason bright enough?" Those who are thirsty for reasons and knowledge want to face their experiences as sternly as a scientific experiment, "hour by hour, day by day!" They want to be their own experiments and guinea pigs. However, we should not seek to posit valuations and ideals either in ignorance of what we discover to be lawful and necessary in the world or in contradiction to it. This compulsion to close observation places a constraint on self-creation, and what binds us to it is our sense of honesty. When we practice becoming the ones that we are in this way, we appeal to the voice of a superior form of conscience, one that is situated behind our conscience and that we can call our *intellectual conscience* (see also *GS* 2). We need to subject our claim to being sincere and upright to the scrutiny of a conscience that is informed by scientific reason and a training in it. When we do this, we are putting our claims to sincerity to the test, and in part this is what is meant by *physics* in the aphorism and learning about the physiognomy of moral judgment and evaluation.

Nietzsche invites us to consider the way in which we often declare ourselves to be good because we think we have judged a course of action to be right, which we then think entitles us to label the action that ensues *moral.* To justify that we have done the right action, we appeal to our conscience. But this is to assume that our conscience is infallible and that it always speaks morally or truthfully to us. Do we not, then, require another conscience to assess the adequacy of this belief, such as an intellectual conscience, which would be the conscience behind our conscience? Any judgment we make that "this is right" has a prehistory in our drives, inclinations, aversions, and experiences to date, including what we have *failed* to experience. As Nietzsche points out, there are many ways in which we can listen to our conscience, and the inadequate way lies in relying on the firmness of our moral judgment simply because this firmness could be evidence of our personal abjectness or lack of an individual personality. Moreover, our so-called moral strength might have its source in our stubbornness or in our inability to envisage new ideals. Furthermore, we can listen to the commands of conscience in numerous ways, for example: "[L]ike a good soldier who hears his officer's command. Or like a woman who loves the man who commands. Or like a flatterer and coward who is afraid of the commander" (*GS* 335). Our grand words, then, such as *conscience* and *duty*, need to be spoiled by knowledge of their actual sources, as opposed to what we like to believe of ourselves and our tendency to idealize ourselves.

Nietzsche contends that the reliance on an impersonal and universal law to acquire a firm moral judgment, as Kant's categorical imperative offers, shows that one has neither discovered oneself nor created for oneself one's own ideal: we subject ourselves to the Moloch of abstraction, as he puts it in a later text (*AC* 11).[3] Self-knowledge consists in coming to know that actions cannot all be the same; every act we perform is done in a unique and unrepeatable way, and all prescriptions of action cover only their rough exterior and so yield only a deceptive appearance of sameness. Nietzsche insists that, while our opinions and valuations constitute powerful levers in the machinery of our actions, the actual law of the mechanism of each action is unknowable, and it is here that knowledge reaches a limit. Nietzsche proposes a change in how we conceive ourselves and relate to others. This will involve purifying ourselves of our opinions and value judgments and creating our own new tables of good. These tasks are to become our new limit, leading to a situation where we cease to brood over the moral value of our actions and experience nausea when we hear people engaging in moral chatter about others; sitting in moral judgment will now offend our taste.

A note from the end of 1880 clarifies what Nietzsche has in mind concerning our becoming a self. He states that it is through practice and an exemplar, not knowledge, that we become ourselves. Knowledge certainly has value but only as means. Moreover, we will not find our genuine self by picking ourselves in an infinite regression. Rather: "The task is always that of a sculptor! A productive human being!" (*KSA*, vol. 9, fragment 7 [213]).

The Youngest Virtue

Nietzsche calls honesty (*Redlichkeit*) "our youngest virtue," a virtue that is still in the making and unaware of itself (*D* 456). As a core intellectual virtue, honesty plays a fundamental role in the thinker's development. Nietzsche confesses in his own case that he is not in a position "to acknowledge anything great which is not connected to *integrity towards oneself*; playacting towards oneself fills me with horror" (*KSA*, vol. 9, fragment 7 [53]).[4] He makes a comparison with Pascal: "[D]on't we, like him, also have our strength in beating ourselves into submission? He in aid of God, and we in aid of integrity?" (*KSA*, vol. 9, fragment 7 [262]).[5] To be honest with oneself requires bravery: "Never hold back or conceal from yourself anything that can be thought against your thoughts! Vow this to yourself! It is the first requirement for honesty of thought. Each and every day you must also conduct your campaign against yourself. A victory and a conquered bulwark are no longer your matter, what matters is the matter of truth—but your defeat is no longer your matter either!" (*D* 370). Honesty is declared to be our youngest virtue because it is taken to be "quite immature, still frequently mistaken and misconstrued, still barely aware of itself." There are many reasons we can find for our being untruthful with a good conscience, and among philosophers, Nietzsche maintains, nothing is rarer than intellectual integrity. Nietzsche contends that integrity or honesty does not appear among either the Socratic or the Christian virtues. The promises made by ancient philosophy, such as the unity of virtue and happiness, or by the Christian, such as seek the kingdom of God and all things shall be given to you, have not been made with complete integrity. Moreover, when we erroneously take ourselves to be selfless or to have attained a state of selflessness, we take truth less seriously and stand on a low rung of truthfulness.

Honesty, then, is a virtue that is still in the making and that "we can advance or retard, as we see fit" (*D* 456).

In a further note of 1880, Nietzsche writes of his task that it involves the sublimation (*sublimiren*) of the drives, and he refers to the drive for integrity toward himself and justice toward all things being so strong that the joy to be experienced outweighs the value of other forms of pleasure. He then adds: "True, there is no experience without involvement, it would be complete boredom. But the *gentlest* emotion would suffice" (*KSA*, vol. 9, fragment 6 [67]). In another note, he insists: "[The intellect is] the tool of our drives and nothing more, it is *never free*. It sharpens itself in the struggle with various drives and refines the activity of each individual drive thereby. The will to power, to the infallibility of our person, resides in our greatest justice and integrity: skepticism just applies to all authority, we do not want to be duped, not even by *our drives*! But what does not *want*? A drive, certainly!" (*KSA*, vol. 9, fragment 6 [130]; cf. *D* 109). So, although we cannot escape the drives in any absolute sense, we can gain a distance from them so that we are not duped by them. And, although we share drives with animals, our increase in integrity makes us less dependent on the stimulus of the drives (*KSA*, vol. 9, fragment 6 [234]).

Melissa Lane notes that Nietzsche's understanding of *Redlichkeit*, with its semantic overtones of frank speech, is "flavored both by his understanding of the flourishing of *parrhêsia* in the ancient world . . . and of its incarnation in the French classical moralists, above all in Montaigne" (2007, 27). She further suggests that what is essential to a Nietzschean conception of *Redlichkeit* is an honest acknowledgment of the unpleasant and inconvenient aspects of reality or nature (Lane 2007, 41). She then claims that Nietzsche favors a Stoic stance over an Epicurean one since the former is more honest, being cognitively "non-consolatory and non-delusional"; the Epicurean, she argues, commits to a strategy of cognitive self-constriction to preserve tranquility (Lane 2007, 27). However, this interpretation of Epicureanism fails to do its teaching justice and does not harmonize well with the reception of it we find Nietzsche. Tim O'Keefe has attempted to show that Epicurean arguments in physics are intended to establish "that their conclusions are true, not merely that believing them helps us feel good": "The pragmatic justification comes in, instead, to answer the question of why we should bother to engage in the activity of trying to understand the workings of the world in the first place" (2010, 135).

In "Why We Appear [*scheinen*] to Be Epicureans," aphorism 375 of *The Gay Science* (second edition), Nietzsche appeals to "an almost Epicurean bent for knowledge" that "will not easily let go of the questionable character of things; also an aversion to big moral words and gestures."[6] In this aphorism, Nietzsche expresses again his preference for being cautious with regard to having ultimate convictions: "Our mistrust lies in wait for the enchantments and deceptions of the conscience that are involved in every strong faith, in every unconditional Yes and No" (*GS* 375). He argues, also in book 5 of *The Gay Science*, that in science "convictions have no rights of citizenship" and should be accorded a certain value in the realm of knowledge only when they have "the modesty of hypotheses, of a provisional experimental point of view, a regulative fiction" and adds: "though always with the restriction that they remain under police supervision, under the police of mistrust" (*GS* 344). Indeed, in a note of 1884, he defines his philosophy "not as dogma, but as a provisional regulative of research" (*KSA*, vol. 11, fragment 26 [432]).

Patrick Wotling has ably demonstrated that appearing to be an Epicurean means rejecting philosophical fanaticism: "Excessive craving for knowledge exposes one to fall back into superstition under the pressure of the need to find a solution—any solution whatsoever—that would unravel the mysteries one is confronted with." He incisively identifies the remarkable wisdom Nietzsche finds in Epicurus when he adds: "It is better to accept the presence of riddles—better even, to learn to enjoy riddles—than to be the victim of the rancour instilled by the fanciful claim to absolute knowledge!" (2020, 167).[7] As Nietzsche writes in a note of 1885–86, what makes us good or wise philosophers is giving up the desire for absolute knowledge and cultivating instead "the Epicurean instinct of being the friend of riddles." We will become wise by cultivating a taste "that defends itself against all quadrangular opposites" and is more than content with the portion of uncertainty in things and has done away with crude opposites. We then become "a friend of intermediary colors, shadows, afternoon lights and infinite seas" (*KSA*, vol. 12, fragment 2 [162]; *SUP*, 16:380).

The wisdom Nietzsche locates in Epicurus's teaching centers on the theory of multiple explanations. In his middle writings, he draws on this teaching as a way of curing a human mind that he finds is prone to neurosis, to emotional and mental excess. In *The Wanderer and His Shadow*, for example, Epicurus is described as the soul soother of later antiquity who had the wonderful insight that to quiet our being it is not necessary to have resolved the ultimate and outermost theoretical questions (*WS* 7). To those who are tormented by the fear of the gods, one points out that, if the gods exist, they do not concern themselves with us and that it is unnecessary to engage in fruitless disputation over the ultimate question as to whether they exist. Furthermore, in response to the consideration of a hypothesis that half belongs to physics and half to ethics and that may cast gloom over our spirits, it is wise to refrain from refuting the hypothesis and instead offer a rival hypothesis, even a multiplicity of hypotheses. To someone who wishes to offer consolation—for example, to the unfortunate, to ill-doers, to hypochondriacs, and so on—one can call to mind two pacifying formulas of Epicurus that are capable of being applied to many questions: "[F]irstly, if that is how things are they do not concern us; secondly, things may be thus but they may also be otherwise" (*WS* 7). Epicurean teaching is helpful, then, since it serves to pacify a mind that is prone to all kinds of fanciful speculations and neurotic reflections.

Having the mistrust of which Nietzsche speaks in aphorism 375 of *The Gay Science* is the stance not simply of the burned child or the disappointed idealist but rather of a person superior to both, namely, "the jubilant curiosity of one who formerly stood in his corner and was driven to despair by his corner, and now delights and luxuriates in the opposite of a corner, in the boundless, in what is 'free as such.'" Indeed, Nietzsche locates in the old books of wisdom a great deal of childishness in the sense of the sages of old behaving like burned children who have shrunk from the fire of life: "Such people sit down to dinner and bring nothing with them, not even a good appetite—and now they say slanderously: 'All is vanity!' . . . But to eat and drink well, O my brothers, is truly no vain art!" (*Z* 3 "Of Old and New Law-Tables" 13). This "woeful wisdom" blossoms in darkness as a "night-shade wisdom" always sighing "all is vain!" and needs to be contested (*Z* 3 "Of the Three Evils" 2).

Nietzsche links curiosity and freedom, then, with an Epicurean-inspired predilection for wisdom about knowledge. Ultimately, his attitude toward Epicurus's teaching is best construed as an ambivalent one. In a note of 1876–77, he maintains that wisdom has "not gotten a single step beyond *Epicurus*" (*KSA*, vol. 8, fragment 23 [56]; *SUP*, 12:384). And, in a note of 1883, he writes, revealing his preference for beauty over sublimity: "Epicurus relates to the Stoics as beauty does to sublimity; but one would have to be a Stoic at the very least to catch sight of this beauty at all! To be able to be jealous of it!" (*KSA*, vol. 10, fragment 7 [151]).[8] However, Epicureanism is not a philosophy or teaching of power, and this is the case with respect to both mastery of the self and mastery over nature. The Epicureans can be admired for developing a fearlessness regarding the gods and nature; what they lack according to Nietzsche is, however, the ascetics' mastery over nature and the feeling of power that flows from it (*KSA*, vol. 9, fragment 4 [204]; *SUP*, 13:128–29). For the Epicureans, knowledge is seen not as "constructive" (*aufbauend*)—something that grants us the power to transform the natural world through human mastery—but rather as a project of "integration and quiet enjoyment" (*KSA*, vol. 9, fragment 4 [204]; *SUP*, 13:129 [translation modified]).[9]

The virtue of honesty continues to be lauded by Nietzsche in the writings after his middle period, including in *Beyond Good and Evil* and *The Anti-Christ*. In aphorism 227 of *Beyond Good and Evil*, he states that, supposing honesty is the key virtue of free spirits, then they can never cease from perfecting it with both love and malice. He also expresses an admiration for honest writers such as Stendhal (*BGE* 254).[10] In his autobiography, *The Life of Henry Brulard*, Stendhal confesses to the need to write with "perfect honesty" and out of an "adoration for the truth." Indeed, he refers at one point in the *Life* to the saying of the Delphic oracle *gnoti seauton* (know thyself) and comments that it inspires him not to write a history but rather to set down his recollections to ascertain what sort of man he has been: "stupid or witty, cowardly or brave, etc., etc." (1973, 225, 197).[11] Stendhal praises himself in these terms in the context of a criticism of what he regards as Rousseau's charlatanism (cf. Nietzsche on Rousseau in *HH* 617).[12] Nietzsche brings aphorism 227 of *Beyond Good and Evil* to a close by wisely signaling a danger concerning the free-spirited virtue of honesty, namely, that like every virtue it can become a piece of stupidity and even vanity since, if we adhere to it too strictly, we run the risk of turning ourselves into fanatics of mistrust. If free spirits are not careful, then, honesty will turn them into either holier-than-thou saints or serious bores. He draws the aphorism to a close on a witty note: "Is life not a hundred times too short—to be bored with it?" (*BGE* 227).

The Passion of Knowledge

In *Dawn*, Nietzsche speaks in glowing terms of certain philosophers—such as Plato and Aristotle from the ancients and Descartes and Spinoza from the early moderns—who found in knowledge—that is, "in the activity of a well-trained, inquisitive, and inventive understanding"—the highest happiness. Such thinkers, he surmises, "must have *enjoyed* knowledge!" (*D* 550). He is keen to contest the claims made by appeals to intuitive knowledge, especially the kind of intellectual intuition sought by the German idealists that purports to be able to see directly into the essence of things and of the world itself (*D* 544). What Nietzsche opposes here is the notion that through such intuition one is genuinely searching for knowledge. He asks the pertinent question, Let it be conceded that we are searching, but are we motivated by a philosophical drive or by a religious one? For him, the commitment to knowledge entails a commitment to laborious methods and procedures, and he allows for no shortcuts to knowledge either of the world or of ourselves.

There have been examples in the history of philosophy of thinkers motivated by a passion of knowledge and driven by an intellectual conscience. Montaigne and Hume are two who readily spring to mind.[13] Nietzsche holds that something more than curiosity is demanded from the thinker who lives in accordance with this passion. Seekers after knowledge, he stipulates, "must live continually in the thundercloud of the highest problems and the heaviest responsibilities," and this means they are no disinterested observers, "outside, indifferent, secure, and objective" (*GS* 351).[14] If we are to commit ourselves to knowledge, then we must pursue it as a passion and not simply as an ethos: the *amour-plaisir* or *amour-vanité* of knowledge is not sufficient; rather, something nobler and more heroic is required of us, including a willingness to develop and embrace knowledge that challenges human vanity (*GS* 123). Neither can we promote science in the hope that we will understand better God's presumed goodness and wisdom (as in Newton), or because we believe in the utility of knowledge with regard to a presumed intimate association of morals, knowledge, and happiness (as in Voltaire), or, finally, because we think we are valuing something harmless, self-sufficient, and innocent and beatific (as in Spinoza) (*GS* 37). In each example, we come to knowledge with an expectation and a human bias that can serve only to prejudice our inquiries.

Both Rousseau and Schopenhauer professed to dedicate their lives to truth, taking their inspiration from the motto found in Juvenal's *Satires*.[15] By contrast, Nietzsche encourages the thinker to dedicate truth to life. He contends that both Rousseau and Schopenhauer sought in knowledge only a mirror of their characters and suggests: "[K]nowledge would be in a sorry state if it were meted out to every thinker only as it suited his person! And thinkers would be in a sorry state if their vanity were so great that they could endure only this!" Rather, the most beautiful virtue of the thinker is the magnanimity with which, as a person of knowledge, he offers himself and his life in sacrifice, sometimes with the veiled smile of wisdom, and often with sublime taunting (*D* 459; see also *D* 547). Nietzsche thinks that we are now in a new situation regarding knowledge and that as a result we can conquer anew our courage for making mistakes, for experimentation, and for accepting things provisionally. Without the sanction of the old moralities and religions, individuals and entire generations "can now fix their eyes on tasks of a vastness that would to earlier ages have seemed madness and a toying with heaven and hell." Moreover, there is no longer the need to approach questions and experiments as if the solutions to them had to correspond to a typical human time span. The course of science is no longer being crossed by the accidental fact that people live to be approximately seventy years old. Indeed: "[P]reviously it would have meant blasphemy and the surrender of one's eternal salvation even to *have a presentiment* of the thoughts that precede our actions" (*D* 501). We are now free to take our time and go slowly: "To solve everything at one fell swoop, with one single word—that was the secret wish: this was the task one imagined in the image of the Gordian knot or of Columbus's egg; one did not doubt that in the realm of knowledge as well it was possible to reach one's goal after the manner of an Alexander or a Columbus and to solve all questions with *one* answer." The idea evolved that there was a riddle to solve for the philosopher and that the task was to compress the problem of the world into the simplest riddle form: "The boundless ambition and jubilation of being the 'unriddler of the world' were the stuff of thinker's dreams." Under such a schema of the task of thinking, philosophy assumed the guise of being a supreme struggle for the tyrannical rule of spirit reserved for a single individual. Nietzsche thinks that it is Schopenhauer who has most recently sought to assume this role. The lesson to be drawn from this inheritance is that the quest for knowledge has been retarded by the moral narrow-mindedness of its disciples. In the future, Nietzsche declares, it needs to be pursued with a higher and more magnanimous feeling: "'What do I matter!' stands over the door of the future thinker" (*D* 547).

Nietzsche regards the drive for knowledge as young and raw; when compared to the older and more richly developed drives, the knowledge drive appears to be ugly and offensive (which all drives have been at some point in their development). However, he confides that he wishes to treat it as a passion, "as something with which the individual soul can work side by side, so that it can look back on the world in a helpful and conciliatory fashion: in the meantime, we need a non-ascetic renunciation of the world again!" (*KSA*, vol. 9, fragment 7 [197]). The passion of knowledge can be placed in the service of a philosophical project that aims at disabusing humanity of its consoling fictions—for example, concerning the uniqueness of its origins and destiny—and encouraging it to pursue new truths and a new kind of philosophical wisdom. The passion gives humanity a right to engage in self-experimentation, replacing the dream of immortality with a new sobriety toward existence: "With regard to knowledge the most useful accomplishment is perhaps: that the belief in the immortality of the soul has been abandoned. Now humanity is allowed to wait; now it no longer needs to rush headlong into things and choke down half-examined ideas as formerly it was forced to do. For in those days the salvation of poor 'eternal souls' depended on the extent of their knowledge acquired during a short lifetime; they had to *decide* overnight—'knowledge' took on a dreadful importance" (*D* 501). The passion of knowledge is a curious passion that operates like an unrequited love. Our hearts may throb with expectation and we may even become miserable as a result of initial disappointments. We have the hope, though, that the bittersweet delicacies of the passion will enrich the world in the long run.

Nietzsche notes that science (*Wissenschaft*)—to be understood as denoting different forms and modes of knowledge that to varying degrees are informed and guided by scientific methods and procedures—can be promoted without the element of passion. In fact, this is how the modern state—and formerly the church—understands knowledge, that is, as "a mere condition or '*ethos*'" (*GS* 123). For scholars who need to make use of their leisure, the scientific impulse is merely a reflection of their boredom in which simple curiosity is felt to be sufficient for the pursuit of knowledge. Nietzsche, by contrast, does not conceive of knowledge as an idle activity or as a quantity that one acquires. Life, he writes, is to be treated as "an experiment of the seeker for knowledge," not as a duty, a calamity, or a piece of trickery (*GS* 324). For some, knowledge can be a diversion or a form of leisure, but, for the passionate seeker, it offers "a world of dangers and victories," one in which heroic feelings can find places to dance and play.

On reading Cicero, Augustine writes of his heart being "on fire with an incredible longing for the immortality of wisdom" (2019, 3.4.7 [see also 8.7.17]).[16] His first conversion was not to religion but rather to sagehood. He was led in the direction of wisdom by an encounter with Cicero's *Hortensius* (the original of which no longer exists) and its exhortation to philosophy. Of course, Augustine confesses that what was missing from his passionate longing for wisdom and what set him aflame was the name of Christ. Later in the book, Christ is presented as "a man of outstanding wisdom" in the sense of *the* way, *the* truth, and *the* life (2019, 7.18.24, 7.19.25). Augustine is keen to warn his readers against a specific kind of temptation, which is not the lust of flesh but something he regards as even more dangerous, namely, the "empty and inquisitive passion, not for enjoyment *in* the flesh, but for experience *through* the flesh, through the same bodily senses, a passion that disguises itself under the name of understanding and knowledge." He then refers to the "disease of curiosity," in which people seek to "pry into the mysteries of the nature that is outside of us" and that does us no good to know (2019, 10.35.54, 10.35.55). Elsewhere in the book (Augustine 2019, 1.15.23 [see also 2.6.13]), he admits that theology imposes a constraint on curiosity. It is obvious, however, and contra Augustine, that philosophy must reject any constraints placed on its inquiries and commitment to the search for knowledge.[17] One way in which Augustine's passion expresses itself is in his passion for God. In the history of thought, Nietzsche finds that this passion has assumed different forms. In the case of Luther, he finds that it assumes a "boorish, trusting, and obtrusive kind." In Augustine, it is "like that of a slave who has undeservedly been pardoned or promoted" and whose gestures and desires lack any sign of nobility (*BGE* 50).

Nietzsche cannot accept the prohibition on knowledge that Augustine wishes to place on it since it would stall humanity's attempts to develop itself and serve to ensure that we live in a never-ending state of fear, superstition, and ignorance.[18] Contra such prohibition, he writes: "The body purifies itself through knowledge; experimenting with knowledge it elevates itself: to the discerning human being all instincts are holy; the soul of the elevated human being grows joyful" (*Z* 1 "Of the Bestowing Virtue" 2). He is keen to show that Christianity is a religion unconcerned with truth; when it speaks of "truth," what is intended is faith. He then notes: "[*I*]*f* faith is needed above all else, then reason, knowledge, and inquiry have to be discredited: the path to truth becomes the *forbidden* path" (*AC* 23). Nietzsche deploys a skeptical practice in *Dawn*, often in connection with his criticism of the scribes and scholars of Christianity. An example is when he draws attention to the poor philology and art of interpretation to be found in their work. He argues that this work fails to foster the sense of integrity and justice necessary to the practice of good philology and replaces it with conjectures presented as dogmas. He alerts us to distortions and philological connivances on the part of the Christian founders, pointing out that they engaged in battles over interpretation in which "one thought about the enemy and not about honesty" (*D* 84). Christianity shows itself to be an enemy of truth when it declares doubt to be a sin: "Void of reason, one is supposed to be tossed into faith by a miracle and then to swim in it as if it were the clearest and most uncomplicated of elements. . . . What is wanted are blindness and delirium and an eternal psalm above the waves in which reason has drowned" (*D* 89).

Although some people find life unendurable without the idea of God, this says nothing as to the rational nature of such belief. It may simply be that we have grown so accustomed to such ideas that we cannot desire a life without them and that, while such ideas may seem to be necessary for people and their preservation, such a fact indicates nothing about the truth of the matter. As Nietzsche exclaims: "As if my preservation were something necessary!" (*D* 90). The problem with the concept of God is that it presumes to know something ultimate about the universe and how it supposedly came into being, about some supposed "all," when in fact it is question begging.[19] God and related concepts such as the immortality of the soul and the hereafter are childish notions, and, for anyone who is curious, dubious, and high-spirited, "God" is a "rough-and-ready answer" and a prohibition on thinking (*EH* "Why I Am So Clever" 1). In the aphorism "God's Honesty [*Redlichkeit*]," Nietzsche quizzes the idea of an omniscient and omnipotent God who does not bother to make his intentions understandable by the creatures he has supposedly created. If this is a God of goodness, we must ask why he has allowed innumerable doubts to persist for millennia as if these were without consequence for the welfare of humanity and with perhaps the most dreadful repercussions for mistaking the truth: "But perhaps he is a God of goodness after all—and he was *unable* to express himself more clearly! Did he perhaps lack the intelligence for it? Or the eloquence? So much the worse! Then perhaps he was also mistaken about what he labeled his 'Truth,' and he is himself not so very different from the 'poor deceived devil'!" (*D* 91).[20] In short, we are coming to the realization that God is not "Truth" but "the vanity, impatience, lust for power" and the "chilling and enchanting delusion of humankind" (*D* 93).

In a note from 1886–87, Nietzsche proposes that we get "rid of *the* universe" where it is conceived as a unity and refers to what is alleged to be unconditioned. He recommends this because we cannot avoid taking such a notion as the highest agency and naming it "God." Instead, he suggests that we splinter the universe and unlearn respect for it: "[W]hat we have given the unknown and the whole must be taken back and given to the closest, what's ours. Kant said, 'Two things remain forever worthy of admiration and awe' [the starry sky above us and the moral law within]—today, we would rather say; 'Digestion is more venerable.'" He concludes the note by offering a tremendous provocation: "The universe would always bring with it the old problems such as 'How is evil possible?' etc. Thus, *there is no universe, there is no great sensorium*, or inventory, or storehouse of forces" (*KSA*, vol. 12, fragment 7 [62]). This is one of Nietzsche's most brilliant and daring proposals, and it aims to set our minds free from the errors and tricks of theological thinking.

Skepticism plays an important role in the pursuit of knowledge since it serves to guard against the gullible and the overly enthusiastic. In a note from 1876/77, Nietzsche writes: "We must live through skeptical periods from time to time if indeed we want to have the right to call ourselves scientific personalities" (*KSA*, vol. 8, fragment 23 [38]; *SUP*, 12:379).[21] In the published writings, one might consider the following from *Zarathustra* as representative of the position to which he adheres: "The bold attempt, prolonged mistrust, the cruel No, satiety, the cutting into the living—how seldom do *these* come together! But from such seed is—truth begotten" (*Z* 3 "Of Old and New Law-Tables" 7).[22] However, he is critical of a skepticism that places arbitrary limits on knowledge and that serves to encourage obscurantism. He locates this kind of skepticism in Kant's critical philosophy, in which skepticism about knowledge and its limits seeks to give religious faith a good conscience. Here we have an example of excessive mental acuity—Kant's philosophy—encouraging thinkers to mistrust acuity. As a result, "the dark art" of obscurantism can appear "underneath a cloak of light" (*MOM* 27). This worry over Kant continues to express itself in Nietzsche's late writings. In *On the Genealogy of Morality*, for example, he argues that Kant's critique is not a genuine one and that its alleged success is merely the success of a theologian. After this critique, the metaphysical need can continue to satisfy itself with a good or clear conscience, and humanity is once again free to invest its energies in an unattainable beyond and thus satisfy its heart's desire or what it wishes to believe and feels the need to believe. It is thanks to an extremely canny skepticism on Kant's part that certain notions, such as God, the immortality of the soul, and freedom of the will, cannot be proved, but neither can they be refuted.[23] Kant's practical reason, for example, allows for the expression of a sublime command in the form of the categorical imperative and permits the play of beautiful feelings and moral convictions, which are, however, enemies of truth and of genuine knowledge. Here the philosopher is merely the continuer of the priestly type, that is, someone who falls for his own forgeries (*AC* 12). Indeed, German philosophy has a fundamentally priestly character.[24] As Nietzsche rhetorically puts it: "Why should a priest care about *science*? He is above all that!" (*AC* 12). The kind of thinking favored by Kant may make us feel sanctified by a task in which we feel part of a higher order of things, but we have also placed ourselves beyond any rational assessment of our ideas. With Kant, then, we find ourselves caught in a realm of impersonal and universal phantoms that, ultimately, can be seen to be expressions of decline and of the exhaustion of life.

Although Nietzsche makes use of skeptical practices of inquiry in both his middle and his late writings, he does not seek to promote total distrust about our ability to know or to discourage us from the task of developing knowledge.[25] "With his question 'what is truth?'" Pilate now serves as an advocate of Christ "in order to foster the suspicion that everything known and knowable is mere appearance and to raise the cross against the terrifying background of our inability to know" (*MOM* 8). Here he sees an extreme teaching—namely, Christ's—being used to justify a total way of life, one to be lived in blind faith in the face of a legitimate skepticism about existence and the world and our attempts to develop knowledge. A way of life based on blind faith is without warrant, and Christians should not be encouraged to think they have a legitimate basis for their desire to convert humanity to such a life. Neither should we allow hairsplitting metaphysicians to grant humanity free rein to satisfy its lamentable and enduring metaphysical need. Faced with people who boast about their metaphysics and claim that it has scientific credentials, all one can do, Nietzsche advises, is "to tug at the bundle that they hold rather timidly concealed behind their backs; if we do manage to open it, the results of such scientificity come to light, much to their embarrassment." The results will be "a cute little Lord God, a pleasing immortality, perhaps a little spiritism, and in any case, a completely tangled heap of poor sinners' misery and Pharisees' pride" (*MOM* 12).

In *Beyond Good and Evil*, Nietzsche is keen to show the merits of forging a distinction between weak and strong forms of skepticism since it enables us to see the dangers of a culture characterized by a paralysis of the will. The skeptic is said to be a delicate creature because his conscience "is trained to quiver at every No; indeed, even at a Yes that is decisive and hard" (*BGE* 208). The skeptic has an army of excuses to marshal against anyone who would demand a judgment from him, ranging from noble abstinence to Socratic wisdom and the wisdom of time itself.[26] By contrast, strong skepticism is identified by Nietzsche as a mode of skepticism that utilizes the critical tools of reason, such as doubt and suspicion, not to produce an epistemic deadlock or end in defeatism, such as the "what do I know?" associated with Montaigne or the dilatory figure of Hamlet, but rather to aid the productive investigations of knowledge.[27] This skepticism boldly attacks and functions neither to bolster human vanities nor to tolerate human stupidity.

In the *Human, All Too Human* aphorism "Age of Comparison," Nietzsche notes that in such an age the various worldviews, customs, and cultures of the earth can be compared and experienced side by side and that this is something new in history: "It is the age of comparison! That is its pride, but rightfully also its pain. Let us not be afraid of this pain!" In spite of the pain that we may experience in living in such an age, he wants us to welcome "the intermingling of humans" for the promotion of free-spirited ends, such as the liberation of human beings from the limits of local cultures where artistic styles and modes of thinking are restricted to particular times and places (*HH* 23). Come 1886, however, he is now deeply worried by "the great bloodsucker, the spider skepticism," and seeks to identify the cultural situation that gives rise to it. He makes two provocative claims. First, skepticism about life and values is an intellectual expression of a certain complex physiological condition—namely, weakness of the nerves and "sickliness"—that emerges "every time races and classes that have long been separated interbreed decisively and suddenly." Second, it leads to a degeneration of the will, even a doubting of "freedom of the will," and ultimately results in an almost complete paralysis of the will: "Our Europe of today, the showplace of an absurdly sudden mixing of radical class mixing and *consequently* race mixing [*Rassenmischung*], is therefore skeptical high and low" (*BGE* 208).

Nietzsche describes strong skepticism as a virile kind of skepticism and says he will comment on it in the form of a parable that is related especially for German ears since it concerns German history and especially the phenomenon of "Frederickianism," with the reference being to Frederick the Great and his "questionable, mad father," as he puts it. He locates in Frederick this "skepticism of audacious manliness," and that may well have been aided, he speculates, by the hatred he felt toward his stern and intolerant father as well as by the icy melancholy of a solitary will. It is worth noting that in the essay "Dissertation on the Innocence and Errors of the Mind," which assumes the form of a dialogue, Frederick himself makes a case for a certain Pyrrhonian skepticism as a way of being tolerant of error. He warns: "Reflect again that, if we were to banish error from the universe, we would need to exterminate the whole human race" (2021, 9). Where his father was intolerant, Frederick sees the value of being tolerant. What interests Nietzsche about a strong form of skepticism is that it has sublimated itself to a warlike distrust of soft and beautiful feelings, evident, he thinks, in the "strong and tough virility of the great German philologists and critical historians," who present "a *new* concept of the German spirit" and do so "in spite of all romanticism in music and philosophy." This gives such a spirit or intellect the courage of analysis and readiness to undertake "journeys of exploration." Nietzsche offers the following advice, directed at (moral) fanatics: the *gai saber* is to be worn as an amulet around people's hearts and necks to ward off a new style of bad taste that allows unmanly virtues, such as compassion and the cult of suffering, to reign: "'joyful science,' to put it in plain German" (*BGE* 293).

Interestingly, in aphorism 122 of *The Gay Science*, Nietzsche locates within Christianity an important contribution to skepticism. It has encouraged moral skepticism by destroying the faith human beings have in themselves as creatures of the virtues, accusing and embittering them and using patience and subtlety. Christianity has thus contributed to a culture of enlightenment, casting legitimate suspicion on paragons of virtue, such as the personalities of antiquity who considered themselves imbued with a faith in their own perfection. Nietzsche has in mind here Stoic sages such as Seneca and Epictetus. Anyone who has been trained in the Christian school of skepticism experiences, "a diverting sense of superiority" when encountering the moral treatises of these sages, feeling "full of secret insights and over-sights," feeling, in fact, "as embarrassed as if a child were talking before an old man, or an over-enthusiastic young beauty before La Rochefoucauld." They know better what virtue is, Nietzsche says. He closes the aphorism with a twist: "In the end, however, we have applied this same skepticism also to all *religious* states and processes, such as sin, repentance, grace, sanctification, and we have allowed the worm to dig so deep that now we have the same sense of subtle superiority and insight when we read any Christian book: we also know religious feelings better!" (*GS* 122).[28] Although Nietzsche applauds the contribution Christianity has made to human enlightenment, the skepticism it has promoted must in turn be applied to its own paralogical concepts, which serve to cultivate moral fanatics.

It is for good reasons, then, that Nietzsche places tremendous importance on the methods of science and how they train and discipline the intellect. Such a training cultivates a healthy mistrust and caution as well as wise moderation, and with its aid we can counter those who express opinions violently and are enemies of genuine inquiry. We need to attach ourselves to the pathos of searching for the truth, as opposed to indulging in the pathos that we fully possess the truth (*HH* 633). The scientific spirit consists in cultivating an instinctive distrust of misguided ways of thinking that typically display themselves in the form of a person having fanatically held convictions (*HH* 635; see also *AC* 54). Science provides us with knowledge of what is certain and probable, and it is part of its nature to promote distrust and find in the mendacious person something objectionable, even disgusting. The scientific spirit brings to maturity "the virtue of *cautious reserve*," which can be described as a wise moderation that is more familiar to us in the realm of practical life than in the realm of theoretical life (*HH* 631). In a similar vein, in an aphorism in *Dawn* Nietzsche stages in a minidramatic form a response to an exhortation from Luther that is designed to make us feel that a knife is at our throat and recommends instead the wisdom of withholding judgment with respect to some key existential matter as a way of freeing ourselves from "soul anxiety" (*D* 82). The taste for the unconditional is the worst of all tastes; it is a taste to which youths are especially prone, finding they cannot rest "until they have falsified people and things into such shape that they can vent themselves on them" (*BGE* 31). When the young soul becomes tortured by the disappointments of life, it then turns on itself with suspicion, "hot and wild" and with pangs of conscience, impatiently tearing itself apart and wanting to avenge itself for its self-blinding, as if this blindness was something voluntary. It now distrusts its feelings and tortures its enthusiasm with doubts, even feeling a good conscience to be a self-veiling. It takes sides against youth until a decade or more later; it then dawns on it that this too was *still* youth. Much better, Nietzsche suggests, is to learn the art of nuance since it constitutes the greatest benefit of life.

In pursuing experimental philosophizing, Nietzsche attempts several hypotheses and adopts a variety of perspectives. As Évelyne Grossman points out, in so doing he is contesting a tradition of metaphysical thinking that reasons with antinomies and rigid contradictions and ensnares us in the habits of dualistic thinking—good and evil, true and false, truth and error. In place of this wrongheaded metaphysics, he "pleads for subtle transitions, a sense of nuance" (2023, 87). Nietzsche puts it well himself when he describes the situation we face as follows: "An enormous amount of painfulness, arrogance, harshness, estrangement, frigidity has entered into human feelings because we think we see opposites instead of transitions" (*WS* 67). Unwittingly, we have in the process enslaved ourselves and rendered our existence sterile and impotent.

[CHAPTER THREE]

The Philosopher as a Wanderer

In Genoa, at the time of evening twilight, I heard a long chiming of bells from a tower: it refused to end and rang, as if insatiable for itself, above the noise of the streets and out into the evening sky and sea air, so horrible and at the same time so childlike, full of melancholy. Then I recalled the words of Plato and suddenly I felt them in my heart: *nothing human is worth taking very seriously: nevertheless.*

Nietzsche, *Human, All Too Human*, aphorism 628

Misanthropy and love.—One speaks of being sick of humans only when one can no longer digest them and yet has one's stomach full of them. Misanthropy comes of an all too greedy love of the human and "cannibalism"; but did anyone ask you to swallow humans like oysters, Prince Hamlet?

Nietzsche, *The Gay Science*, aphorism 167

What then are our experiences? Much *more* what we put in them than what is in them already! Or must we go so far as to claim: In and of themselves, there is nothing in them! To experience is to invent?

Nietzsche, *Dawn*, aphorism 119

Nietzsche and Philosophy

With *Mixed Opinions and Maxims* and *The Wanderer and His Shadow*, the two texts that make up the second volume of *Human, All Too Human*, Nietzsche aims to move philosophical education in a new direction through the book form. Today, he thinks, we are living in an age of self-education and peer education, and the task is to foster philosophical friendship through the appreciation of new kinds of books and writing (*WS* 180). Various conceptions of the ideal teacher and educator are played out in the texts. For example, in *Mixed Opinions and Maxims*, Nietzsche argues that what is needed is the blending together of knowledge and wisdom (*MOM* 180) and that the study of natural history is to be narrated from the vantage point of "spiritual-physical health and maturity," in which we can see the victories of "moral-spiritual force" over fear, indolence, and superstition (*MOM* 184). He advises us to take advantage of an intellectual nomadism in our efforts to learn and mature. The ineptest educator is the moral fanatic, and it is Rousseau he invariably has in mind when he depicts such a teacher (*WS* 70). In the case of the philosopher, we have, he thinks, a physician—the physician of culture—who must heal himself. This is because the philosopher must first become a thinker for himself before he can educate others. "As educators," he writes, "we should only speak of self-education" (*WS* 267). It is this role of physician that he assigns to the example of Zarathustra: "Physician, help yourself: in this way you will help your patients, too. Let this be the best way you can help them, letting them see with their own eyes someone healing himself" (*Z* 1 "Of the Bestowing Virtue" 2).

Perhaps Nietzsche's overriding concern as a philosophical educator is with self-cultivation, and this extends to the hopes he has for the development of a mature humanity.[1] Indeed, in his Basel lectures on the future of educational institutions, Nietzsche playfully engages in a search for philosophy, seeking to find out exactly what it is, and the answer he proffers in the opening lecture is that philosophizing is an activity centered on self-cultivation. This is an insight that he never abandons despite the significant developments his thinking undergoes in the 1870s and 1880s. Consider, for example, how in *Dawn* (from his middle writings) he criticizes what passes for a classical education. The following aphorism shows clearly that he favors an educational training of the individual that makes questions of value and the virtues central, along with instruction in ways of life:

> And now to look back on the course of our lives and to discover something that is no longer reparable: the squandering of our youth in which our educators failed to employ those inquisitive, impassioned thirsty years to lead us toward *knowledge* of things, but used them instead for the so-called "classical education." . . . And the classics! Did we learn any part of what these same ancients instructed their youth? Did we learn to speak like them, write like them? Did we practice unremittingly the fencing art of conversation, of dialectics? Did we learn to move beautifully and proudly like them, to wrestle, throw and box like them? Did we learn any part of the asceticism practiced by all Greek philosophers? . . . Wasn't our education altogether lacking in any reflection upon morality whatsoever, let alone in the only possible critique of it, that rigorous and courageous attempt to *live* within some morality or other? . . . Was the arrangement of the day and of life, along with life's goals, presented to us in the spirit of antiquity? (*D* 195; see also *EH* "Why I Am So Clever" 1)[2]

Nietzsche is not a slavish devotee of the tradition of self-cultivation. Indeed, he mounts a biting critique of *Bildung* in his writings, such as *Unfashionable Observations* and *Thus Spoke Zarathustra*. His critique is directed at the way in which, controlled by the greed of the state, modern educational and cultural institutions have tamed self-cultivation. To be cultivated today means, in fact, to conceal how wretched and base we have allowed ourselves to become (*SE* 6; see also *Z* prologue 5). Nietzsche laments: "No one dares to fulfil the law of philosophy in himself, no one lives philosophically." Modern philosophy, he adds, is today policed, "limited by governments, churches, academies, customs, and human cowardice to scholarly pretence" (*HL* 5).[3]

Nietzsche maintains that almost all philosophy to date shows a lack of knowledge about human beings, which he finds revealed in imprecise psychological analysis (*KSA*, vol. 8, fragment 22 [107]; *SUP*, 12:362). He turns to Montaigne and the French *moralistes* as sources of inspiration to correct what he sees as the lack of real knowledge and psychological analysis in German philosophy (*WS* 214). Furthermore, he seeks a new conception of the sage in which this figure from ancient times—who still has an important role to play in modern times—would occupy himself no longer solely with what is "amazing" and "divine" but rather with "what is small weak human illogical defective," and he does so because, he maintains, "we can become *wise* only through the most careful study of those very same things" (*KSA*, vol. 8, fragment 23 [5]; *SUP*, 12:368).[4] Although Nietzsche holds to the idea that the sage of modern times will give himself pleasure by *disturbing* the pleasure of human beings, he also wants readers of his aphorisms, with their probing psychological analyses, to derive a new and mature kind of pleasure from their tasting and assimilation.

In the literature on Nietzsche as an aphorist, the typical focus is on his debt to the French *moralistes* and the way in which under their inspiration he seeks to come up with a style of writing and thinking that is lucid, concise, and enigmatic. While important and instructive work has been done on this aspect of Nietzsche's philosophizing, what has been overlooked is the extent to which he is carrying on a quite fundamental program of philosophical training and education. This program centers on a reformation of the human mind, and the way he envisages this connects him in interesting and fruitful ways with ancient conceptions of the nature and tasks of philosophy such as we find in Epicurean teaching, where the overriding aim is to combat fear and superstition and help humans cultivate a new, beneficent relation to the world. In this respect, then, his thinking is consonant with ancient practices and techniques of philosophy: hence the positive references we find in *Mixed Opinions and Maxims* and *The Wanderer and His Shadow* to figures such as Epicurus and Epictetus. He admires them because they are figures in whom wisdom has assumed bodily form and manifests itself in how they comport themselves in the world (*MOM* 184).

The philosophy Nietzsche pursues in his middle writings, then, is one that has specific therapeutic ambitions, one that he finds pertinent to the needs of his age. In large part he conceives the art of the maxim in therapeutic terms. The modern age has forgotten the art of reflection or observation, in which it is possible to gather maxims "from the thorniest and least gratifying stretches of our lives" to make ourselves feel better, to give ourselves a lift and a tonic. We can return to life revivified rather than depressed from our encounter with thorny problems and with "presence of mind in difficult situations and amusement in tedious surroundings" (*HH* 38). Nietzsche is not, however, simply aping the work of the French *moralistes* but proposing a major reform of their practice and agenda. Such work now needs to become more rigorously scientific instead of being practiced in the spirit of a witty coquettishness. If the inquiry into the human, all too human is carried out in this way, Nietzsche hopes that it will come to be taken much more seriously than it is at the present time by the scientific person, who understandably professes a mistrust of the genre and its apparent lack of seriousness. But note that, although Nietzsche is appealing to the scientific community in this way, he does not lose sight of the fact that a scientifically minded philosophy has a therapeutic role to play in cooling down the human mind and transforming our sense of being in the world. He concedes that the new intellectual practice of this philosophy will have consequences for humanity that are at one and the same time frightful and fruitful: it will deflate human pretensions to significance while at the same time indicating that new ways of life are possible for us.

Nietzsche advises us to be wary of those who find nothing other than disillusionment in philosophy since they quickly turn against life and then seek to sell it off at the lowest price (*MOM* 1). Where a spiritual cure is required is in terms of administering to oneself an "anti-romantic" treatment as a way of countering the kind of Romantic pessimism that puffs up and interprets "individual personal experiences into general judgements" and even "world-condemnation" (*HH2* preface 2, 5). Philosophy for Nietzsche is not an activity that aims simply to secure personal serenity; rather, it aims to educate individuals in self-reliance and to transform human life. He does not aim to write for a narrow academic or professorial readership but for readers who have embarked on a journey of free-spiritedness. He is looking for friends. In a note of 1881, for example, he writes: "The loneliest of the lonely, the human being, no longer seeks a God, but a *companion*. This will be the *myth-building* drive of the future. He seeks the *friend of human beings*" (*KSA*, vol. 9, fragment 12 [23]; *SUP*, 6:425). We are delicate creatures, and both the artist and the thinker can teach us to feel respect for our deficiencies, our spiritual poverty, and our senseless delusions and passions. They do this most instructively when they show themselves as persons and so can inspire in us an enthusiastic (*schwärmerisch*) love of philosophy and art. In our inartistic and unphilosophical age, which we may have to endure for some time, this love can help us preserve our existence (*MOM* 148).[5]

Zarathustra chooses to teach us not the neighbor but rather the friend: "May the friend be to you a festival of the earth and a foretaste of the superhuman" (*Z* 1 "Of Love of One's Neighbour"). Nietzsche makes an interesting distinction: the ancients were profoundly concerned with friendship, whereas we moderns offer to the world idealized sexual love (*D* 503). He goes on to note that in antiquity the feeling of friendship was considered the highest feeling, "even higher than the most celebrated pride of the self-sufficient sage" (*GS* 61). Although Nietzsche readily acknowledges that there can be poor friendships—friendships lacking in trust, confidence, and genuine concern for the other—he sees it, at its best, as an effort at "fellow rejoicing" rather than "fellow suffering" (*HH* 499); it is the ability to "imagine the joy of others and rejoicing at it," which is a very rare human quality (*MOM* 62). Such is his esteem of friendship that he models marriage on it: "The best friend will probably acquire the best wife, because a good marriage is founded on the talent for friendship" (*HH* 378). Emerson seeks to understand what he calls the "laws of friendship." For him there are two elements that go into the composition of friendship, each sovereign, and one not superior to the other. One is truth as sincerity, and the other is tenderness: "A friend is a person with whom I may be sincere. Before him I may think aloud." The friend affords valuable opportunities for me to learn about myself and to become the one that I am: "A friend therefore is a sort of paradox in nature. I who alone am, I who see nothing in nature whose existence I can affirm with equal evidence to my own, behold now the semblances of my being, in all its height, variety, and curiosity, reiterated in foreign form; so that a friend may well be reckoned the masterpiece of nature." Emerson also anticipates Nietzsche in wanting the friend relation not to be one based on complacency, as when he writes: "Let him be to thee forever a beautiful enemy, untameable, devoutly revered, and not a trivial conveniency to be soon outgrown and cast aside" (2000, 207, 208, 211).

In "The Wanderer," the closing section of *Human, All Too Human*, Nietzsche alludes to "all those free spirits who are at home in mountains, woods, and solitude" and who "are wanderers and philosophers, in their now joyful, now thoughtful way" (*HH* 638). Unfettered from convention, custom, and tradition, the thinker picks his way along high mountain paths and seeks to lure others onto similarly slippery paths and down into similarly dark caverns (*D* 469; see also *HH* 137). These images connote the cognitive activity of those thinkers whose pursuit of knowledge is primarily a pursuit of self-knowledge. These self-reflective explorations entail the painstaking removal of long-entrenched errors and prejudices and are preparatory to the creation of new thoughts and feelings and new goals. Immediate self-observation is insufficient since history is needed for self-revelation since the past flows on through us and in a hundred waves. Moreover, when it comes to descending into the river of what seems to be our most individual and personal nature, Heraclitus's famous saying is applicable: we will never step into the same river twice. Furthermore, to understand history it is not sufficient to spend time in historical epochs other than our own; we must also travel and remove our civilized garments. Only in this way will we be able to "rediscover the travel adventures of this becoming and transformed ego in Egypt and Greece, Byzantium and Rome, France and Germany, in the age of nomadic or settled peoples, in the Renaissance and Reformation, at home and abroad, even in the sea, the woods, the plants and the mountains" (*MOM* 223).[6] We can never assume familiarity with ourselves when it comes to acquiring self-knowledge, and the hope that inspires us is that "self-determination and self-education" will become in the case of free and farsighted spirits "the determination of everything, with regard to all future humanity" (*MOM* 223). If this is not an insight into the actual figure of the superhuman that Nietzsche envisages in *Thus Spoke Zarathustra*, it may offer a valuable conception of the bridge humanity is to take to it.

The Wisdom of the Sages

In his early reflections, Nietzsche is keen to convey to us what the practice of philosophy as a form of free-spirited inquiry signifies: "The intellect must not only desire surreptitious delights; it must become completely free and celebrate Saturnalia. The released intellect surveys things, and now for the first time *mundane existence* [*Alltägliche*] appears to it *worthy of contemplation as a problem*" (*KGW*, 2, pt. 4; *PPP*, 6). There must be a taste for philosophy if it is to be prized as a mode of free-spirited inquiry. Philosophy is not necessary either for the individual or for a people since it requires an excess of intellect as well as key intellectual virtues, notably, courage and honesty. Nietzsche aims to show that the first philosophers are genuine discoverers who make the task easier for anyone who comes in their wake and wishes to traverse the path from myth to laws of nature, from image to concept, and from religion to philosophy.

We can identify a precise conception of wisdom in the beginnings of philosophy. Wisdom, Nietzsche reflects (quoting Aristotle), denotes scientific knowledge, and it means two things: first, being wise with regard not to any one single aspect of existence but rather to existence in general and, second, the cultivation of sharp knowledge as sharp taste or the exercise of judgment (*KGW*, 2, pt. 4:217–18; *PPP*, 8). The primary concern of philosophy is with questions of value and with discerning what is to be revered. It is because the philosopher has this concern that he can also be taken as a sage. In the earliest figures, the philosopher and the sage are combined, and being wise is not a matter of cleverness since being clever is simple and straightforward in comparison with having philosophical wisdom. Nietzsche suggests wittily that the Greeks were not, in fact, very clever, and this is one reason why the irony of Socrates created such a sensation among them (*PT*, 136). The earliest philosophical figures, by contrast, give themselves over to the excess of intellect and concern themselves with what is "out of the ordinary, miraculous, difficult, divine, but *useless*" (*PT*, 136).

Nietzsche provides three main paradigms by which we can learn about the ancient Greek thinkers: Pythagoras as the wise human as a religious reformer; Heraclitus as the wise one as a proud, solitary searcher after truth; and Socrates as the figure whose life symbolizes the eternal investigator of all things and self-cultivation as a way of life.[7] Although a typical moral reformer, Socrates distinguishes himself as a moralist with his attachment to self-knowledge as a means and path to virtue: "The struggle against desire, drives, anger, and so on directs itself against a deep-lying ignorance" (*PPP*, 145). It is on account of this struggle that Nietzsche describes Socrates as "the first philosopher of life" (*Lebensphilosoph*). The schools of philosophy that derive from him, such as the school of the Stoics, can also be said to be philosophies of life. It is on this issue that Nietzsche exclaims: "A life ruled by thought!" Where hitherto life had served thought and knowledge, we have now a philosophy in which thinking serves life. This development is a significant one since it means that philosophy is now conceived as "absolutely *practical*" and it assumes a hostile attitude to any knowledge that is not connected to ethical implications. Furthermore, it is "*for everyone* and *popular* because it holds that virtue may be taught." Where previously simple customs and religious prescriptions sufficed—for example, the philosophy of the Seven Sages "was merely the vitally practical morality . . . esteemed throughout Greece made into formulas"—we now have a philosophy that maintains: "Virtue is knowledge, the human sins only from ignorance." In Socratic philosophy, then, "knowledge and morality conjoin." Socrates's irony is not lost on Nietzsche: "Socrates claims the role of a learner, but he persuades his interlocutors of their own rashness" (*PPP*, 145; on the teacher as an ironist, see *HH* 372).

Although the lofty likes of Heraclitus, Empedocles, and Democritus breathed Hellenic morality, they did so according to a different form of ethics, and they did not expect people to conform to a single norm. With the emergence of Socrates, however, a moral flood now flows forth, and the philosopher assumes a prophetic and priestlike guise with a sense of mission. The result is that what we take to be human wisdom is revealed to be no wisdom at all. Socrates's wisdom is of a superior kind since it readily acknowledges that it does *not* know, and it is this experience that he repeats with politicians, orators, poets, and artists. Nietzsche writes on this transformation as follows: "The greatest happiness that a human being can achieve is daily discussion concerning virtue and others. Life without such conversation is not a life at all. He senses how everything sounds unbelievable and strange—knowledge as the path to virtue, yet [followed] not as a scholar but rather like a transporting god, wandering and testing. The search for wisdom appears in the form of the search for sages" (*PPP*, 147).

Nietzsche reflects on the image of the dying Socrates and its meaning throughout his writings, perhaps most notably in an aphorism in *The Gay Science* that immediately precedes the introduction in his corpus of the doctrine of the eternal recurrence of the same (*GS* 340; see also *TI* "The Problem of Socrates").[8] In his Basel lecture on Socrates, Nietzsche holds: "[He] knew what he had done; he wanted death." He wanted it because it enabled him to demonstrate to everyone and for all time "his domination of human fear and weakness and also the dignity of his divine mission": "The instincts are overcome; intellectual clarity rules life and chooses death." This is the ultimate exemplar of the sage known to us: Socrates as "the evoker of the fear of death" and "the wise man as the conqueror of the instincts by means of wisdom" (*PPP*, 150). In aphorism 340 of *The Gay Science* Nietzsche renews his profound admiration for "the courage and wisdom of Socrates in everything he said and did not say" but now expresses a deep concern about Socrates's final words: "Crito, we owe a cock to Asclepius; make this offering to him and do not forget" (Plato 1993 [*Phaedo* 118]). Nietzsche wonders: "Is it possible that a man like him, who had lived cheerfully and like a soldier in the sight of everyone, should have been a pessimist? He had merely kept a cheerful mien while concealing all his life long his ultimate judgment, his inmost feeling. Socrates, Socrates *suffered life*!" (*GS* 340; see also *WS* 322).

In the *Phaedo*, Socrates has no problem accepting his death and not being intimidated by it simply because he conceives the philosopher as one who lives in a state as close as possible to death. The true profession of the philosopher is, in fact, that of dying (*Phaedo* 67e). This is because the philosopher devotes his life to the attempt to free the soul from the body—from its loves, desires, fears, and fancies—and to divorce true knowledge from the deceptions of our sense perception. To devote oneself to philosophy consists in nothing other than preparing the self for dying. Asclepius was the Greek god of healing and medicine, and the customary way of expressing thanks to him for the curing of an illness would have been to offer a rooster. There have been several different interpretations of the meaning of Socrates's last words, for example, that they indicate that his soul has been healed or that he is presenting a challenge to the Pythagoreans he is addressing, Simmias and Cebes, who would have objected to any maltreatment of animals since their souls might be one's own ancestors. Socrates's challenge would consist in claiming that one is injuring only the body. Nietzsche, however, reads the last words of the dying Socrates as expressing a terrible complaint against life: life is one long illness, and death offers a release from it (see also *TI* "The Problem of Socrates" 12).[9] Although even in *The Gay Science* Nietzsche associates Socrates with cheerfulness, he is also casting suspicion on the authentic character of his cheerful appearance.

To this day, Socrates is taken to be the principal archetype of the philosopher when conceived as a skeptical ironist. His significance as a figure of the philosopher is captured well by Cicero in the *Tusculan Disputations* where he holds that Socrates was the first "to call philosophy down from the heavens and set her in the cities of men and bring her also into their homes and compel her to ask questions about life and morality and things good and evil" (1945, 435 [bk. 5]).[10] Socrates, he adds, is to be admired for his many-sided method of discussion and the varied nature of the subjects he wants philosophy to cover. Socrates shows in both his life and his death the radical opposition that exists between the habitual life of human beings and the life of the philosopher.[11] Indeed, Socrates's importance, Cicero states, is to have shown the value of living consistently, with wisdom, dignity, and courage.

In his early period, Nietzsche sees the problem of Socratic philosophy as twofold. First, an unbiased view of human nature eludes it, and this means it is unable to understand the irrationality and suffering of human existence. Second, it philosophizes with "horrible abstractions," such as "the good," "the just," and "the beautiful" (*PT*, 136). Although Nietzsche is complimentary about Socrates in several aphorisms in his middle texts (*WS* 86; *D* 9), he expresses a major concern he has with Socratic philosophy, namely, its deficient knowledge of human beings with its naive belief in good and evil as a black-and-white matter (*WS* 285).[12] In *Twilight of the Idols* (from the late period), he finds everything about Socrates to be "exaggerated, *buffo*, caricature" (*TI* "The Problem of Socrates" 4) and maintains that the moralism of Greek thinkers from Plato on is pathologically conditioned: "The fanaticism with which the whole of Greek thought throws itself on rationality betrays a crisis: they were in danger, they had just *one* choice: either perish or—be *absurdly rational*" (*TI* "The Problem of Socrates" 10). There is, then, something extreme about Socrates, and Nietzsche's criticism reminds us again of the stress he places on the need for nuance and measure. In spite of his criticism of Socrates and his wrestling with him, however, there remains an element of the Socratic philosopher in Nietzsche's conception of his own task, and this is evident in his attempt to show that we moderns presume what we have no right to presume when we think that we *know* what "morality" is and that it is beyond questioning (see *GS* 345 ["Morality as a Problem"]).[13] Like Socrates, Nietzsche, too, is an enemy of human rashness.

Key elements of Nietzsche appreciation of the earliest philosophers will change with the publication of *Human, All Too Human* in 1878. The change is evident both in this text and in the notebooks that lead to its publication. For example, whereas in his early writings he finds the ancient tragedies and philosophies as well as ancient poets and statesmen superior to the Epicureans and the Stoics (as well as Plato and Aristotle), in his notebooks of 1876–77 Nietzsche holds that wisdom has "not gotten a single step beyond *Epicurus*" (*KSA*, vol. 8, fragment 23 [56]; *SUP*, 12:384). In drawing on the wisdom of life to be found in the various Hellenistic schools of philosophy in his middle writings, however, Nietzsche does not invite his readers to make a "choice of existence" that would consist in following one school, such as Stoicism, Cynicism, or Epicureanism.[14] In a note of spring–summer 1878, he writes that he needs "the cans of ointment and flasks of medicine of *all* the ancient philosophers" (*KSA*, vol. 8, fragment 28 [41]; *HH2*, p. 318). On the level of praxis, he regards the ancient moral schools as sites of experimentation. Because several recipes in the wisdom of life (*Lebensklugheit*) have been practiced, we moderns are free to adopt the results of these experiments and make the experiences our own. Moreover, just because we have adopted a Stoic recipe does not mean we cannot also, in certain situations and circumstances, adopt Epicurean ones. The one-sided character of the ancient schools was useful and, in fact, necessary, he thinks, for establishing these experiments. He writes: "Stoicism, for example, showed that man was able to voluntarily give himself a harder skin and, as it were, a kind of nettle rash: from him I learned to say amid trouble and storm: 'What does it matter?' 'What does it matter to me?' From Epicureanism I took the willingness to enjoy and have the eye for everything where nature has set the table for us" (*KSA*, vol. 8, fragment 28 [41]; *HH2*, p. 318).

In his middle writings, Nietzsche expresses an affinity with aspects of Epicurean teaching and with the Stoic Epictetus. He confesses, for example, to having dwelled like Odysseus in the underworld and says that he will often be found there again; as a "sacrificer" who sacrifices to talk to the dead, he states that there are four pairs of thinkers from whom he will accept judgment, and Epicurus and Montaigne make up the first pair he mentions (*MOM* 408).[15] If a chief goal of philosophy is to temper mental and emotional excess, then Epicurean philosophy has a key role to play. Along with science in general, it serves to make us "colder and more skeptical," helping cool down "the fiery stream of belief in ultimate definitive truths," a stream that has grown so turbulent through Christianity (*HH* 244).

In Nietzsche, the reception of Epicurus has quite specific features. For example, he shows little interest in the ontological status of atomism and the problems of the theory of knowledge and much more interest in Epicurean cosmology, such as its distinction between world and universe. As one commentator has noted, this focus on the world and distrust of the idea of *the* universe, including the idea of the sum of all possible worlds, "allowed Nietzsche to collect the themes of Epicurean divinity, blessedness, friendship and philosophical regimen around the focus of the ancient science of this world of 'meteorology'" (Caygill 2006, 107).[16] As Liba Taub has expressed it, the Epicurean aim "was to demonstrate that the universe and various distant phenomena can be explained without reference to anything outside nature, or extraordinary." Informing Epicurean views on cosmology and meteorology was the desire to eliminate fear and anxiety, especially about the intervention of the gods in the world. Epicurus thus developed a strict materialist philosophy that was designed to provide natural explanations of phenomena that were often seen as being due to the activities of supernatural powers (Taub 2009, 124 [quote], 105). Although acknowledging the existence of an infinite number of worlds (*cosmoi*), Epicurus sought to account for the *meteōra*, such as the phenomenon of the sky and earthquakes, in terms of the natural workings of our local cosmos. Thus, the fundamental aims of Epicurean teaching, such as the alleviation of anxiety, are at the heart of its cosmological and meteorological explanations. Nietzsche is inspired by Epicurus's focus on the world, his redemption of nature from human projection and teleology, and his conception of philosophy as the art of living in which one lives the philosophical life and does not engage merely in theoretical discourses. Epicurus is a figure who was in his own way true to the earth, abandoning all hubristic conceptions of human significance, including exceptionalism, and taught that one should die as if one had never lived. As Nietzsche notes, never in the history of thought has the voluptuous appreciation of existence been so modest as we encounter it in Epicurus (*GS* 45).[17]

Nietzsche establishes a link between his existence as a philosophical wanderer and the wisdom of Epictetus. This wisdom finds no one blameworthy and wishes to assume responsibility for itself freely. It is wisdom of "the whispering of the solitary with himself in the crowded marketplace" (*MOM* 386). Nietzsche admires Epictetus for not being fanatic in the mode of life he cultivates for himself: "[H]e hates the showcasing and vainglory of our idealists." Nietzsche offers this portrait of the Epictetian as a point of contrast to the Christian. The Christian lives in hope and the consolation of unspeakable glories to come, expecting the best of life to come not from himself and his own resources but from divine love and grace. By contrast, Epictetus "does not hope and does allow his best to be given him—he possesses it, he holds it valiantly in his hand, and he would take on the whole world if it tries to rob him of it" (*D* 546).[18]

Nietzsche can fruitfully be conceived as a therapeutic naturalist. This naturalism is centered on the identification of real causes as opposed to imaginary ones, serving to free the mind from fear and superstition and from the menace of moral and religious phantasms. In the aphorism "Question of Conscience," Nietzsche articulates what he wishes to see changed: "We want to cease making causes into sinners and consequences into executioners" (*D* 208). In addition, and referring to the history of religion and metaphysics, he finds that it is under the most "scandalous quackery" that humanity has come to treat diseases of the soul: "[T]he human being's greatest diseases grew out of the battle against its diseases, and the apparent remedies have, in the long run, produced something much worse that what they were supposed to eliminate." Humanity has mistaken "the momentarily effective, anesthetizing, and intoxicating means, the so-called consolations, for the actual remedies" (*D* 52). There is, then, a clear therapeutic dimension to Nietzsche's philosophical practice with the focus on developing knowledge of the causes of human suffering and afflictions, and, in this respect, he has an affinity with figures in the history of philosophy such as Epicurus and Spinoza. However, although a therapeutic naturalism has an important role to play in liberating the human mind from fear and superstition, in Nietzsche philosophy does not stop at therapy and the attainment of (personal) serenity; rather, he wants to instill in his readers a desire for new possibilities of life that will serve to transform human existence on the individual level and ultimately on the level of culture too. His hope is that as we discover more and more about reality we will come to feel at home in its strangeness and otherness, inhabiting a less humanly fantasized world in which this involves a fundamental fear of life and an inability to accept the fact that humanity has no special destiny prescribed for it. Such an insight need not depress us and can, in fact, embolden us to become creators.

The Wanderer: Justice and Love

In *Mixed Opinions and Maxims*, Nietzsche identifies himself as an intellectual nomad (*MOM* 211), a figure he may well have borrowed from Emerson (2000, 122). He conceives such a nomad as a free-moving spirit in which freedom in thinking constitutes the strongest drive, one that stands in opposition to an intellect that takes a stubborn pride in being constrained and firmly rooted. In *Human, All Too Human*, Nietzsche has announced his preference for a state of being and living that consists in the desire "for a blissful, serene mobility," designating this way of life as "the artist's and philosopher's vision of happiness" (*HH* 611). The commitment to "modest and arduous travels" of the mind explains why he is resistant to the need for a philosophical system. All philosophical systems, he suggests, are like gleaming mirages that "with the magical power of illusion . . . show the solution to all riddles and the coolest drink of the true water of life to be near at hand" (*MOM* 31). It should not surprise us then when he acknowledges the limited character of his philosophizing in the middle writings. The task of painting what is casually called *the* picture of life as one set by both poets and philosophers is nonsensical. Philosophers need to show more modesty by showing that what they are doing is providing pictures and miniatures from a single life, from their own lives, "and nothing else is possible" (*MOM* 19). Expressed in an equally emphatic confessional manner, Nietzsche writes in *Dawn*: "Even great spirits have only their five-finger breadth of *experience*—just to the other side of it their contemplation ceases: and their begins their infinite empty space and their stupidity" (*D* 564).[19]

Existing in the world as a philosophical wanderer entails a reliance on intellectual virtues such as courage and prudence as well as enduring solitude and cultivating a spirit of cheerfulness or serenity (*MOM* 237). In addition, the thinker as wanderer who has this serenity needs to be open to disturbances and interruptions if he is to mature as a thinker (*WS* 342).[20] With respect to the use of the word *opinions* that appears in the title of the first book of volume two of *Human, All Too Human*, Nietzsche is keen to encourage his readers to become independent of general convictions and public opinions (*MOM* 325). Caution and prudence are required since one also needs to negotiate the way of the world intelligently and so ensure that one does not fall prey to the order of holy foolhardiness (*MOM* 338). In effect, this means that as an educator the philosopher needs to communicate his thoughts and opinions in a way that respects the demands of a critical intelligence. Moreover: "The wind in the valley and the opinions of today's marketplace signify nothing concerning what is to come, but only what has been" (*WS* 330). He applies this free-spirited manner of thinking to the social sphere when he favors employing science and wisdom to enlighten the malevolent forces that govern today's world and to counter "the now-reigning belief in numbers." This requires, he says, that the free spirit can have no truck with political parties: "[P]arties vote: and for every such vote there must be hundreds of people whose consciences are ashamed." There are also those who have been badly educated, those who are poor in judgment and perhaps not even capable of it, those who blindly follow the words of a leader, and those who are carried away by passion (*MOM* 318; see also *D* 183 and *GS* 174). He warns us against parties by noting that "their perpetual activity is counterfeiting" (*KSA*, vol. 8, fragment 2 [51]).

A commitment to justice serves as the strongest corrective to the mode of life led by free spirits, who exist "as noble *betrayers* of all the things that can ever be betrayed." The free spirit will "kneel down before justice as the only goddess that we acknowledge above ourselves." Justice, he adds, can be regarded as "the veiled Isis" of the lives of free spirits: "[W]ith shame we offer her our pain as penance and sacrifice whenever the fire attempts to burn and consume us" (*HH* 637). The worry today, however, is that modern human beings overestimate love at the expense of a commitment to justice. When a society allows itself to become overtaken by the emotion of love at the expense of justice, it will become weakened and ineffectual. We moderns, however, are in thrall to the love story (*D* 76). Love is a problem since it is "as impartial as the rain that, according to the Bible and experience, soaks to the skin not only the unjust, but in certain circumstances the just as well" (*HH* 69). Nietzsche notes how love "turns us into inveterate felons against truth and into people who habitually thieve and habitually receive stolen goods, who permit more to be true than seems true to us" (*D* 479). The language of romantic love typically speaks of forgetting oneself in love and of dissolving the self in another person. Here, however, Nietzsche observes, we are simply smashing the mirror, projecting ourselves "imaginatively upon a person whom we admire," and we then come to relish this new image of our self even though we call it by the name of the other person: "[A]nd this entire process is supposed *not* to involve self-deceit, *not* to involve egoism, you amazing people!" He closes with a witty and pointed reflection: "I think that those who conceal some of themselves *from themselves* and those who conceal themselves completely from themselves are alike in that they commit a *robbery* from the treasury of knowledge: from which it follows what crime the saying, 'Know thyself!' warns us against" (*MOM* 37).[21]

Contra the claims made for idealized romantic love, Nietzsche favors a mode of love where the two lovers do not become one but remain two and a duality is respected and allowed to flourish: "What then is love besides understanding and rejoicing in the fact that someone else lives, acts, and feels in a different and opposite way than we do? If love is to use joy to bridge over oppositions, it must not suspend or deny them.—Even love of self assumes an unalloyable duality (or multiplicity) within a *single* person as its precondition" (*MOM* 75).[22] The error of idealized love happens when the attempt is made "to spare the other to whom it consecrates itself every feeling of *being different*": "[C]onsequently, it is full of dissembling and a show of similarity; it deceives continually and playacts a sameness that in truth does not exist." A comedy of errors ensues: "[T]here exists no more no more complicated and impenetrable spectacle than when both are in the full throes of passion for one another and consequently relinquish themselves, feign sameness of the other and want to imitate the other and that other alone: and in the end neither knows any longer what one is imitating, why one is dissembling, who one is pretending to be. The beautiful madness of this spectacle is too good for this world and too subtle for human eyes" (*D* 532).

In the later *Beyond Good and Evil*, Nietzsche speculates whether beneath the sacred fable and disguise of Jesus's life we can discover "hidden one of the most painful cases of martyrdom of *knowledge about love*." This is the martyrdom of "the most innocent and desiring heart that could not get enough from any human love, that *demanded* love . . . with hardness, with madness, with terrible outbursts against those who denied him love" and who "had to invent a god who is all love, all *capacity* for love—who has mercy on human love because it is so utterly wretched, so ignorant!" Nietzsche concludes his speculation: "Whoever feels this way, whoever *knows* this much about love—*seeks* death" (*BGE* 269). Although this example may be a painful one for us to reflect on—we have become so wedded to the love story and continue to remain ignorant in matters of love—for the philosopher in search of knowledge about human beings it is necessary they do so.[23] Nietzsche continues with this line of honest thinking in his final texts. In Christianity, love has taken the form of a religion, a way of seeing the world or, rather, of *not* seeing it: "Love is the state in which human beings most see things as they are *not*. The power of illusion is at its height, likewise the power to sweeten and *transfigure*. One bears more in love than otherwise, one tolerates everything, . . . one has transcended the worst things in life—one no longer even sees it" (*AC* 23). As a virtue, love, along with faith and hope, can be regarded as one of the three Christian ingenuities (*Klugheiten*). Some people need such a religion of love to get through the worst in life, and Buddhism, Nietzsche thinks, is too mature and positivist—focused on physiological facts as opposed to moral concepts—to be ingenious (*klug*) in this manner.

The Wanderer's Shadow

When we think of the figure of the shadow, we perhaps think first of the role it plays in Jung's psychology where it is conceived as the personal unconscious and concerns the dark aspects of the personality that individuals struggle to acknowledge. D. H. Lawrence calls the shadow the "abstracted reality, the ego." For him it is the lesser reality, such as the "idea" or "concept" of a thing (1986, 329). Indeed, in Dostoevsky's "White Nights," the protagonist's story is presented as "the Memoirs of a Dreamer"; that is, the character lives his life as if in a fantasy world, an "inexhaustible fantasy" conceived as "the slave of a shadow, an idea" (1848/1999, 26). For Jung, the shadow personifies "everything that the subject refuses to acknowledge about himself and yet is always thrusting itself upon him directly or indirectly—for instance, inferior traits of character and other incompatible tendencies" (1983, 221).[24] Jung is keen to show that a close examination of the dark characteristics and aspects of the personality and what he calls "the inferiorities constituting the shadow" reveals their *emotional* nature, in which they are seen to have "a kind of autonomy," "an obsessive or, better, possessive quality." It is thus important, he argues, that we recognize that an emotion "is not an activity of the individual but something that happens to him" (1983, 91).[25] Moreover, affects usually occur when we are at our weakest in terms of our adaptation to life with our personality at a low level of development and maturation. It is not surprising that on this lower level we are the subject of uncontrolled or poorly controlled emotions, the passive victim of affects who is incapable of ethical discernment and judgment.

There are concerns about the self in Nietzsche's work that connect with Jung's conception of the shadow. In the discourse "Of the Tree on the Mountainside" in part 1 of *Thus Spoke Zarathustra*, for example, Zarathustra engages a young man who thinks that Zarathustra can uncover his soul, "downwards, into darkness, into the depths—into evil." The young man wishes to ascend to the heights and is willing to desire his own destruction in the process. The problem, however, Zarathustra tells him, is that he is still *searching* for freedom and, although his soul thirsts for the stars, so do his bad instincts thirst for freedom: "Your fierce dogs long for freedom; they bark for joy in their cellar when your spirit aspires to break open all prisons. To me you are still a prisoner who imagines freedom: ah, such prisoners of the soul become clever, but also deceitful and base. The free human being of the spirit, too, must still purify himself. Much of the prison and rottenness remain within him: his eye still has to become pure" (*Z* 1 "Of the Tree on the Mountainside").

Nietzsche ingeniously deploys the shadow in the prologue that frames *The Wanderer and His Shadow*, the second installment of volume 2 of *Human, All Too Human*. The shadow relates to darkness in Nietzsche, but it is a darkness that lets meaningful light in and more of it than humans typically experience. Nietzsche's introduction to the book is, in effect, about the art of conversing with oneself and with others, especially how this conversing needs to take place in a manner that esteems the pursuit of wisdom. For example, this is how the shadow responds to the wanderer near the start of the exchange between the two: "It is a good thing we are both considerate in the same way towards ourselves at moments when our reason stands still; thus, we won't become annoyed with each other while conversing, and won't out thumbscrews to the other right away, even if a word of his sounds incomprehensible. If we don't know how to reply at once, it is enough just to say something: that is the reasonable condition under which I will converse with someone. In any long conversation, even the wisest person is once a fool and thrice a simpleton."

The shadow encourages the wanderer not to approach the conversations they have as exercises in vanity, and for this to happen he needs to listen to the shadow and not be garrulous. Does not the vain person speak constantly? The wanderer understands this when he says that he loves the shadow as much as the light. In fact, we can go further: does not enlightenment happen precisely *because of* the shadow? Therefore, the wanderer declares: "In order for there to be beauty of visage, clarity of speech, goodness, and steadiness of character, shadow is as necessary as light." The shadow responds to this by disclosing that it loves humans precisely because they are disciples of light and not children of the night: "The shadow that all things display when the sunshine of knowledge falls upon them—I am that shadow too." The wanderer is confident he understands the shadow even if it expresses itself, he says, "in a shadowy way." Nietzsche's great wit is in evidence here and centers on illuminating in a subtle and delicate manner what is involved in the art of thinking for oneself and with the help of another. In fact, the wanderer understands the shadow extremely well. This is revealed when he speaks thus to the shadow: "But you were right: good friends now and then exchange an obscure word as the sign of mutual understanding, which should be a riddle for any third person. And we are good friends."

Nietzsche closes *The Wanderer and His Shadow* with a second and final exchange between the two figures, and this exchange seems to anticipate the role the figure of the shadow comes to play in the story of Zarathustra, as when the wanderer concedes: "Ah, you shadows are 'better humans' than we, I perceive" (*WS*, p. 293). In "On the Blessed Isles" in book 2 of the narrative, Zarathustra reveals: "[A] shadow came to me—the most silent, the lightest of all things once came to me! The beauty of the superhuman came to me as a shadow. Ah, my brothers! What are gods to me now!" This indicates that Zarathustra has no need of gods to help him climb to a higher level of existence since the ability to do so resides with his own will and reason.

The shadow continues to occupy Nietzsche's attention in subsequent texts, notably *Zarathustra* (*Z* 2 "On the Blessed Isles"; see also *Z* 3 "The Wanderer") and essay 3 of *On the Genealogy of Morality* (*GM* 3.8).[26] In *Beyond Good and Evil*, it is Dionysus who assumes the role of the shadow in Nietzsche's thinking and, as a friend of humans, is both canny and uncanny (*BGE* 295). In this penultimate aphorism in the book, in which Nietzsche takes his reader to be a friend, a genius of the heart is depicted that is possessed by "the great hidden one," the temper god and pied piper of human consciences that "knows how to descend into the underworld of every soul and smooth souls that are rough." Here, the teaching is centered not on feeling either blessed or burdened by the goods of others but on the desirability of becoming richer in oneself, maybe becoming more uncertain of oneself in the process of opening oneself, more delicate, fragile, and even broken, but also "full of hopes that have as yet no names." In the story of the genius of the heart, the tempter god has the virtues that Nietzsche prizes in his middle writings, notably, "courage as investigator and discoverer," "daring honesty" (*Redlichkeit*) and "truthfulness."

In his late writings Nietzsche's utilization of the Dionysian is quite different to the emphasis he places in his early writings on Dionysus as the god of intoxication whose worship leads to self-oblivion, notably in *The Birth of Tragedy*. Indeed, in his middle writings, he is severely critical of the idea that our true self is to be found in states of abandonment through intoxication (see *D* 50, "Belief in Intoxication [*Rausch*]").[27] Failure to take cognizance of this development in his conception has resulted in some far-fetched portraits of the Dionysian in Nietzsche. René Girard, for example, associates Dionysus with a cult of violence and the lynch mob: "Dionysus is the destructiveness at the heart of violent contagion" (2001, 120).[28] Note should be taken, however, of the wisdom offered by Zarathustra in the discourse "The Greeting" from part 4 of *Thus Spoke Zarathustra*: "Many a burden, many a memory weighs down your shoulders; many an evil dwarf crouches in your corners. And there is a hidden mob in you, too." Furthermore, we encounter this warning: "I count nothing more valuable and rarer today than honesty [*Redlichkeit*]. Does this today [*Heute*] not belong to the mob? The mob, however, does not know what is great or small, what is straight and honest: it is innocently crooked, it always lies" (*Z* 4 "Of the Higher Man" 8).[29]

In Praise of Solitude

> In solitude, the solitary person consumes himself; amid multitudes, he is consumed by many.
>
> Nietzsche, *Mixed Opinions and Maxims*, aphorism 348

> Loneliness is one thing, solitude another: you have learned *that*—now! And that among human beings you will always be wild and strange: wild and strange even when they love you: for above all they want to be *indulged*!
>
> Nietzsche, *Thus Spoke Zarathustra*, 3 "The Home-Coming"

> It is what one takes into solitude that grows there, including the beast within; and so, many should be discouraged from solitude.
>
> Nietzsche, *Thus Spoke Zarathustra*, 4 "Of the Higher Man" 13

Referring to the "weight of life," Nietzsche depicts human beings as more weights than humans (*GS* 107). Human beings find existence a heavy burden for various reasons, including the trials and tribulations of life, having a lovable-hateful ego, and needing control over life but experiencing only the lack of it. Nietzsche asks whether we find the weight of life too heavy, and he knows that we do. His advice to us is to increase the weight of our lives by freely assuming the burden, so becoming, he says, "a *hero*" (*MOM* 401). As a sufferer of life, we need to thirst for and seek out the river Lethe in Hades since only in this way can we be sure of finding it. In short, we need to desire wisdom, and at the center of the quest for wisdom we find ourselves. And, if we truly wish to become a hero, the snake must become a dragon; otherwise we are lacking our proper foe (*HH* 498). When we are heroic—doing something great or not doing something in a great way—we need not put ourselves in competition with others or in front of others: "[T]he hero always carries solitude and a sacred, restricted sanctuary around with him, wherever he may go" (*WS* 337; see also *WS* 347). In *Zarathustra*, Nietzsche introduces the figure of the "super-hero" (*Über-Held*) as a "secret of the soul." He does so to highlight an important aspect of the work of self-cultivation, namely, that it should not be a simple exercise in vanity: "Yes, you sublime one, you too shall one day be fair and hold the mirror before your own beauty. Then your soul will shudder with divine desires; and there will be worship even in your vanity!" (*Z* 2 "Of the Sublime Ones").

Several thinkers have written in praise of solitude, including Montaigne, Rousseau, Schopenhauer, Emerson, and Thoreau. Emerson, for example, construes solitude—and silence—as essential for the scholar and the student since it is only by means of them that we become acquainted with our thoughts and gain independence of spirit: "If he pines in a lonely place, hankering for the crowd, for display, he is not in the lonely place; his heart is in the market; he does not see; he does not hear; he does not think. . . . The poets that have lived in cities have been hermits still" (2012, 130). Schopenhauer recognizes that it is not possible to be truly ourselves as the characters we have without the endurance of solitude: "In solitude the wretched person feels his whole wretchedness and the great mind the full extent of its greatness; in short, everyone becomes aware of himself as what he is." Being a member of society involves mutual accommodation and feeling the pressure of displaying an agreeable temper. But as Schopenhauer astutely notes: "[W]hoever does not love solitude, also does not love freedom; for only when we are alone, are we free." Once society is recognized as something insidious, concealing behind an appearance of diversion, communication, and sociable pleasures "great and often irremediable evils," a major area of study for the young needs to be that of "*learning to tolerate solitude*" as a source of happiness and peace of mind (1851/2014, 369–70). It is, in fact, through the practice of solitude that we come to learn the value of self-reliance.[30] Schopenhauer cites Cicero on precisely this point: "'Whoever is completely on his own and relies on himself, cannot but be perfectly happy'" (1851/2014, 370). It is on account of our lack of self-reliance that we immerse ourselves in the rituals of society and undertake travel to foreign lands, and we do so as a way of hiding our inner emptiness and escaping the tedium of life (Schopenhauer 1851/2014, 471).[31] The love of solitude is not to be conceived as our natural state or as an original tendency since, when we enter the world, we do so with parents, siblings, and a community; rather, it develops as a result of experiences and reflection. Indeed, we might consider a love of solitude as signifying a mature state of mind.

Some of these insights of Schopenhauer's may have inspired Nietzsche when he thinks about solitude. In several aphorisms, he draws attention to the benefits of solitude. In an especially witty one, he writes: "'Only the solitary person is evil,' cried Diderot and immediately Rousseau felt mortally wounded. Consequently, he admitted to himself that Diderot was right. . . . Whoever is evil is at his most evil in solitude: also at his best—and consequently, to the eye of anyone who everywhere sees only playacting, also at his most beautiful" (*D* 499).[32] At the beginning of his second walk in the *Reveries of a Solitary Walker*, Rousseau states that his hours of solitude and meditation are ones during which he is fully himself without diversion. Rousseau values solitude because it affords a release from humankind. Toward the end of the first walk, he points out his difference from Montaigne with his retreat into the tower on his vineyard estate to write the *Essays*: "My enterprise is the same as Montaigne's, but my goal is the complete opposite of his: he wrote his *Essays* only for others, and I write my reveries only for myself." With his usual sense of high drama about his life, he declares: "Everything is finished for me on earth. People can no longer do me good or evil here. I have nothing more to hope for or fear in this world; and here I am, tranquil at the bottom of the abyss, a poor unfortunate mortal, but unperturbed, like God himself" (1782/2000, 8, 6).

Although Nietzsche esteems solitude in terms similar to Schopenhauer's, he also maintains that solitude can be practiced whether one finds oneself in the milling crowd or in a place of quietude (*D* 473).[33] In addition, he holds that solitude and the distance from things it affords us provides us with the perspectives we sometimes need to think well of things again (*D* 485). We go into solitude "so as not to drink out of everyone's cisterns": "Amid the many I live like the many and don't think as an I; after some time, I always feel then as if they wanted to ban me from myself and rob my soul—and I turn angry toward everyone and fear everyone. Then I need the desert to turn good again" (*D* 491; see also *D* 524).[34] Nietzsche echoes the concerns of Schopenhauer when he states that the most widespread deficiency in today's type of education and upbringing is that "no one learns, no one strives toward, no one teaches—*to learn to endure solitude*" (*D* 443). In the late writings, solitude is listed as one of the four main virtues that need to be mastered, along with courage, insight, and sympathy (*Mitgefühl*). Nietzsche discloses that he holds solitude to be a virtue since it amounts to "a sublime yearning and urge for cleanliness" in relation to the soiling that comes from unavoidable societal contact (*BGE* 284).[35]

The practice of solitude can be viewed as a component within the cultivation of a philosophy of spiritual health and recovery (*MOM* 356). It is not to be a solitude, however, "without friends, books, duties and passions" (*WS* 200). It is the sickly thinkers, Nietzsche suggests, who can best teach others the value of suffering simply because the one who is sick can develop a keen sense for what is healthy and sickly "in works and in action, his own and those of others . . . morning, sunshine, woods, and springs" (*MOM* 356). All kinds of advice can be offered to others when it comes to developing medicine for the soul, such as lying down quietly and thinking very little, and, when done with good will, becomes more pleasant to us hour by hour (*MOM* 361). Forgetting and letting go of things, including leaving some things, even many things, "in the Hades of half-conscious feeling," is also to be recommended. If we do not allow for this, then the things that bother us will, as thoughts and words, "become our demonic masters and clamor horribly for our blood" (*MOM* 374). Expecting perfection in life and even in oneself is not to be sought or prized: "It is not a matter of everything having been made equally well and perfectly: pride patches up the defective places" (*WS* 318). Furthermore, when we engage in criticism, including self-criticism, we need to realize the value of the affirmation contained within it. When we criticize something, this should not be viewed as an arbitrary or impersonal event; rather, it is "evidence of vital energies in us that are growing and shedding a skin." So, when we find ourselves practicing negation, this is "because something in us wants to live and affirm—something that we perhaps do not know or see as yet" (*GS* 307). We need also to beware of the fall of the night since it can be very persuasive about death. We can often feel ourselves at such a time of the day at a low ebb, weary and fatigued, and catch ourselves thinking excessively when it is unwise to do so. Thus, Nietzsche writes, we need to "perceive how living half of their lives veiled by darkness and deprivation of sunlight casts a pall upon the whole of humans' spiritual and psychic nature" (*WS* 8; see also *D* 317 and 539 and *Z* 2 "The Dance Song").[36]

Free spirits need to beware of the dangers of basing their lives on a too meager foundation of desire. If they renounce the joys that fellowship, sensual pleasures, the arts, and even everyday conveniences bring with them, they run the risk of becoming bored with life and making boredom rather than wisdom their neighbor (*MOM* 337; see also *MOM* 369). As Cioran (1972/2012, 139) notes, boredom amounts to a pure erosion, the imperceptible effect of which slowly transforms one into a ruin unnoticed by others and virtually unnoticed by oneself. There will inevitably be days of fatigue, days in which we may have to play patiently with our patience, days of welcome peace when we exist without a strong sense of purpose or end, even without need. In such hours of being, however, boredom is experienced as a brief pleasure. When it returns to us, "[w]ishing is a sign of convalescence and recovery" (*MOM* 349; see also *MOM* 369). Boredom, then, is paradoxically an experience of "the most refined and the most active animals" (*WS* 56), and it is, ultimately, unwise to shelter ourselves from it since, if we do, we are sheltering the self from itself and we will not "obtain the most powerfully refreshing drink" from our own "innermost fountain" (*WS* 200). What the free spirit needs is an education in needs, one in which essential needs are satisfied as much as possible, even if imperfectly, while allowing needs to proliferate, especially superfluous ones, only trains us in unfreedom (*WS* 318).

A Third Eye and Perceiving Cosmically

I want to draw this chapter to a close by considering how Nietzsche thinks we can extend knowledge beyond human megalomania and narcissism. In the aphorism "On Theater," he takes to task a modern culture that sees life as a business deal and art as mere entertainment, in which the enjoyment of elevated moods can be attained only with the aid of intoxicating substances and "idealistic lashes of the whip." He asks, If you are inspired, then what do you need of wine and narcotics? "Whoever is something of a Faust or Manfred, what does he care about the Fausts and Manfreds of the theater!" (*GS* 86). He locates intoxication and the desire for the stupefaction in those who are *incapable* of thinking and passion, and he writes against those who may even deploy thinking and passion as means to intoxication. He encourages his readers to cultivate instead their own third eye as a "theater-eye":[37]

> What? You still need the theater? Are you still so young? Wise up and look for tragedy and comedy where they are better acted! Where what transpires is more interesting and more interested! It's true, then it's not so easy to remain a mere spectator—but learn to! And in almost all situations that are difficult and painful for you, you will then have a little gateway to pleasure and a refuge, even when you are overcome by your own passions. Open your theater-eye, the great third eye that, through the other two, looks into the world! (*D* 509)

Instead of allowing our attention to be diverted from ourselves by observing what is happening on the stage, we are to make our own lives an object of interest. The third eye that Nietzsche invokes is intended to work in an eminently practical manner as part of one's exercises in self-cultivation. As he points out, although it does not come easily to us to be critical spectators of ourselves on account of the way the self-protective and self-defensive emotions stubbornly exert their influence and distort our view, it is necessary that we learn how to do so if our desire is for a deeper understanding of the self and a mature cultivation of it.[38]

In his middle writings, Nietzsche challenges the presumption that our identities are fixed. We unnecessarily limit our experience of life and our openness to it by assuming that there is such fixity: "[W]e take an attentive interest in the life and being of many things by not treating ourselves as fixed, stable, *single* individuals" (*HH* 618). When we observe closely, we discover that the individual is merely a sum of conscious perceptions, judgments, and errors, "a *belief*, a little piece of true life-system or many little pieces thought together and fabled together," in which a unity is not to be assumed or found. A wiser conception of ourselves comes into being when we see ourselves as buds on a single tree and concede that we do not know what can become of us in the interest of the tree. We need, then, to relinquish the sense we have of ourselves as a fantastic ego whereby we conceive ourselves as "if we wanted to be and should be *everything*, a fantasy of 'ego' and *everything* 'non-ego.'" Nietzsche concludes this note with a recommendation: "*Cease feeling ourselves to be such fantastical ego!* . . . Discover the errors of the ego! Realize *egoism as error*! Certainly, do not construe altruism as the opposite! That would be the love of *other reputed* individuals! No! Get **beyond** '*me*' and '*you*'! ***Perceive cosmically!*** [*Kosmisch empfinden!*]" (*KSA*, vol. 9, fragment 11 [7]; *SUP*, 6:307).

What exactly does it mean to perceive cosmically? The next note explains what Nietzsche in mind. Egoism in humans is an error, a delusion to be exposed, especially when it takes the form, as it typically does, of megalomania (*KSA*, vol. 9, fragment 11 [8]; *SUP*, 6:307). We learn this through the insight that what transpires in us is something quite different to what we think we know about ourselves. There is a need, then, for us to become better observers and learners of ourselves and, as Nietzsche puts it, to differentiate between "imagined individuals" and "true 'life-systems.'" Projecting "intent" and "morality" onto nature serves only to obfuscate what is taking place in the systems of life that characterize nature and that also characterize our own becoming—we are pieces of nature anyhow (*KSA*, vol. 9, fragment 11 [7]; *SUP*, 6:307). Instead of viewing everything from the perspective of our ego, which only encourages the mad animal or megalomaniac within us, we need to become more adept at "objective seeing" (*KSA*, vol. 9, fragment 11 [10]; *SUP*, 6:308).

In this note from 1881 on experiencing ourselves cosmically, Graham Parkes finds Nietzsche curiously adopting a Schopenhauerian-Buddhist stance toward the ego with a "remarkable outpouring of cosmic feeling" that "may have been occasioned by the recurrence of an access of mystical experience—perhaps prompted by immersion in the landscape around Sils-Maria," where Nietzsche spent his summers from 1881 on (Parkes 1994, 300).[39] If we examine the set of notes as a whole, however, it becomes clear that he is encouraging us to cultivate the practice of seeing objectively, that is, beyond a restrictive, egoistic relationship to things (*KSA*, vol. 9, fragment 11 [10]; *SUP*, 6:308). There is no need, then, to speculate about the return of some supposed mystical experience taking place in his life. Nietzsche is deeply suspicious of any appeal to such experiences in his middle writings and keen to avoid explanations that resort to mysticism since they reveal nothing: "Mystical explanations are considered profound; the truth is, they are not even superficial" (*GS* 126).[40] In one of the notes from 1881, he writes of "[w]anting to know things as they are—that alone is the *good* inclination: not looking over at others and seeing with other eyes—that would merely be a *change of place* of egoistic seeing!" And he stresses the need "to heal ourselves of the great fundamental madness *of measuring everything according to ourselves*" (*KSA*, vol. 9, fragment 11 [10]; *SUP*, 6:307). The same thought is expressed in an aphorism from book 5 of *Dawn*: "Why don't people see things? They themselves are standing in the way: they cover up things" (*D* 438). In seeking to free ourselves from the error of the ego, we should not then replace this with altruism as this only perpetuates the error; rather, we should approach things in terms of "multiplicities . . . and their laws": "Not 'for the sake of others,' but live 'for the sake of the true'!" (*KSA*, vol. 9, fragment 11 [21]; *SUP*, 6:313).

The task, then, is to cure ourselves of "the human-megalomania." Nietzsche does not pretend this is easy to carry out. Most of us see existence through a veil or cloak, and we may not, in fact, be suited for knowledge. Our minds may be too dull and our vision too crude to permit us access to knowledge. Nietzsche runs through the many subjective elements of our perception and vision of the world, for example, how we are on the lookout sometimes for something that affects us strongly and at other times for something that calms us because we are tired: "Always full of secret predeterminations as to *how* the truth would have to be constituted if you, precisely you, were able to accept it!" To attain superior perception and vision is hard for human beings—to be just toward something requires of us warmth and enthusiasm, and the lovable-hateful ego appears to be always present—and may in fact be attainable only in degrees. We may, then, have good reasons for living in fear of our own ghosts: "In the cavern of every type of knowledge, are you not afraid once more of running into your own ghost, the ghost that is the cloak in which truth has disguised itself from you?" (*D* 539).

Nietzsche thinks that human megalomania stems from fear and is an expression of our animal suffering (*KSA*, vol. 9, fragment 11 [10]; *SUP*, 6:308). In human history, the feeling of powerlessness has been extensive and is responsible for the creation of superstitious rituals and cultural forms such as religion and metaphysics (*D* 23). The feeling of fear and powerlessness has been in a state of perpetual excitation for so long a time that the actual feeling of power has developed to incredibly subtle degrees and levels and has, in fact, become our strongest inclination (*D* 23). We can safely say, Nietzsche thinks, that the methods discovered to enhance this feeling constitute the history of human culture. It is through moral, religious, and aesthetic demands, along with their blind inclination, passion, and fear and their reveling in habits of illogical thinking, that the world has become what it is for us, namely, something colorful, meaningful, and soulful, and we have been the colorists and continue to be so.

Nietzsche reflects on how the ancient Greeks viewed their nature through certain colors, having a blind eye for blue and green (colors that for Nietzsche dehumanize nature more than anything else), and seeing the former as deep brown and the latter as yellow (they used the same word to describe the color of dark hair, the cornflower, and the Mediterranean), with the result that nature was made to appear close to humankind "because in their view the color of human beings also predominated in nature," as if nature "swam in the atmospheric palette of humanity!" This partial coloring of the world is, however, not to be seen simply as a deficiency since it can serve as a metaphor for further inquiry: "Every thinker paints his world and every individual thing with fewer colors *than actually exist* and is blind to certain particular colors" (*D* 426; see also *GS* 152). Such blindness—amounting to approximation and simplification—enables the thinker to read into the things themselves color harmonies that then end up appealing to us and serving to enrich nature for us, even facilitating our learning how to take pleasure in existence. We need to be wary, though, of the melancholic poet and philosopher, considered as types for whom "the radiant luster of happiness is unattainable," and who present their appreciations of reality by coloring things several degrees darker than they are, thus leading to an exaggerated picture of reality, making use only of flames and lightning bolts, which serve to produce a glaring brilliance that confuses our eye, with even brightness employed only to increase the horror and make us think that things are more terrifying than they really are (*D* 561).

An important aim is to conquer human delusions and rid the world of the many types of false grandeur that have been bestowed on it. Nietzsche asks: "Have real things or imaginary things contributed more to human happiness? It is certain that the breadth of space between highest happiness and deepest despair has been established only with the aid of imaginary things. Accordingly, the influence of the sciences is constantly diminishing this type of spatial sense: just as science has taught and continues to teach us to experience the earth as small and the solar system even as a mere dot" (*D* 7). The astonishment afforded us by the sciences can be contrasted to the kind presented by the conjurer's art: where the conjurer disguises complex causality with simplicity, the sciences compel us "to relinquish our belief in simple causalities at the very moment when everything seems so self-explanatory, and we are being the fools of what is before our very eyes." The simplest things, Nietzsche wants us to understand, "are *very complicated*." And he remarks: "[O]ne can't marvel enough at that!" (*D* 6). As free-spirited inquirers who do not seek to practice wisdom in the mode of human vanity, we need to be open to this kind of surprise about the nature of the world and how things have evolved.

[CHAPTER FOUR]

The Passions

> Passions are the only thing that motivate human beings; they produce all the good, and they are all the evil, that we see on earth.
>
> Stendhal to his sister Pauline, January 29, 1803

> We live in the remnants of the sensations of our ancient ancestors; in fossils of feelings, as it were.
>
> Nietzsche, note of 1881

> *Under south winds.*—A: I no longer understand myself! Yesterday I still felt so turbulent inside and yet so warm, even sunny, and bright in the extreme. But today! Everything is now motionless, distant, mournful, somber, like the lagoon of Venice. I want nothing and draw a deep breath of release thereby, and I am secretly indignant with myself over this not wanting anything:—so do the waves leap back and forth in the lake of my melancholy.—B: You're describing here a pleasant little illness. The next northeast wind will sweep it right out of you!—A. But why!
>
> Nietzsche, *Dawn*, aphorism 492

Nietzsche and the Passions

In a study of the passions, Michel Meyer (2000, 1) notes that passion is a unique and enigmatic locus where people meet their animal nature and human nature encounters the forces of nature.[1] Passion is a hybrid entity that stems from our sensible appetites and the representations that they provoke but also from the urges and emotions that we feel from it. Nietzsche neatly captures an aspect of this insight when he writes: "In the outbursts of passion and in the fantasizing of dreams and madness a person rediscovers his own prehistory and that of humanity: *animality*, with its wild grimaces" (*D* 312). From Plato and the Stoics through to Kant, the wisdom of philosophy with respect to the passions has been, with a few notable exceptions, to seriously curtail and even cauterize them.[2] Typically, the attempt is made to oppose reason to the passions, and a classic modern source for this is Kant. In his *Anthropology from a Pragmatic Point of View*, Kant acknowledges that an inclination that can be conquered by reason only with difficulty or not at all is what we call *passion*. He adds: "To be subject to affects and passions is probably always an *illness of the mind*, because both affect and passion shut out the sovereignty of reason." Furthermore: "[N]o human being wishes to have passion. For who wants to have himself put in chains when he can be free?" (2006, 149, 151).[3]

Nietzsche attempts to develop a nuanced appreciation of the passions, noting that the affects "are one and all useful," whether directly or indirectly, and considered in economic terms the forces of nature are both useful and the sources of much terrible fatality (*KSA*, vol. 12, fragment 10 [133]). We both need to have and not to have our passions, knowing how to employ their stupidity as well as their fire (*BGE* 284). Indeed, as Meyer (2000, 2) notes, it is difficult on honest reflection to imagine what we humans would be like without the passions. Would not reason without passion amount to a ruination of the soul? The complex character of our passions, as well as the indispensable role they play in human life, is noted well by Paul Valéry when he writes: "Passions and emotions give us an intimate shock and affect us by surprise. Sometimes they release secret forces in us that suddenly disrupt the soul; sometimes they waste our energies in mad disordered impulses that are explicable only by the moment's overflow; at other times, they drive us to more or less reasonable and reasoned acts" (1958, 5). Meyer notes that passion is, above all, a form of sensitivity before being amorality or even immorality: "It is the sign of the contingent in human beings, that is to say, that which they wish to master. . . . [P]assion upsets, destabilizes, and disorients by reproducing the uncertainty of the world and the course of events" (2000, 5). Without the passions, Nietzsche himself notes, the world is reduced to simply "quantity and line and law and nonsense" (*KSA*, vol. 9, fragment 7 [226]). One reason why we might wish to value the passions, then, is because they prevent life from becoming automatic, predictable, regular, and tedious.

Robert Solomon (2003, 63) has argued that Nietzsche attacks philosophy's modern emphasis on epistemology and seeks to return philosophy to its true vocation as a doctrine of the passions.[4] However, this appreciation of Nietzsche as a "passionate defender of the passionate life"—a thinker, Solomon claims, who wanted to promote living with passion, who writes from the perspective of the passions and not from the supposedly objective perspective of reason and rationality, and who offers an *unrestrained* defense of them—requires a great deal of qualification since, as we shall see, his views on the passions are far subtler and more complex than this. Solomon's appreciation of Nietzsche is not in tune with the things he says about the passions, and as we shall see in the next chapter it cannot aid us in seeking to understand the ways in which he configures the role of the poet in his writings. Indeed, Nietzsche warns against turning passion into an argument for truth. Addressing "noble enthusiasts," he alerts us to the dangers involved when enthusiasm is allowed to develop to such a point that we come to hate criticism, science, and reason. Moreover, when we allow this to happen, we are happy to falsify history to make it bear witness on our behalf, and we deny certain intellectual virtues to prevent our idols and ideals being overshadowed. We have now placed ourselves beyond all doubt, and even more worryingly we intoxicate ourselves with our own self-righteousness. Nietzsche sees this mental state as amounting to a "*depravity of the intellect*"; it signals a quite despicable martyrdom where a person decrees: "[A]nyone who is not beside himself as we are cannot possibly know what and where truth lies!" (*D* 543). When it comes to injecting the emotions into the drama of life, Nietzsche recommends that we do so in a manner that is relevant to the needs of various life situations. For example, when we assume a wise, patient, and superior manner, we drip "with the oil of forbearance and fellow feeling" and become "absurdly fair" and "forgive everything." When this happens, Nietzsche recommends that we "should *cultivate* a little emotion [*Affekt*], a little vice of an emotion," in which "getting personal" assumes, curiously, "the virtue of the 'impersonal'" (*TI* "Reconnaissance Raids of an Untimely Man" 28).

In *The Gay Science*, Nietzsche is keen to revalue the "unreason or counterreason of passion" (*GS* 3). He makes a distinction between the common type of person and the noble type, noting how the former despises the latter, who is gripped by a passion for objects whose value appears as fantastic and arbitrary, and he gives the example of the passion for knowledge for which one is prepared to risk one's health and honor. He appears to be interested in not what he calls the "*coarser* eruptions and gestures of passion" but rather what he takes to be a "genuine passion" (*GS* 47). The contrast made here is between a convention of emotional behavior and a passion that is directed toward the pursuit of something rare and noble. Nietzsche also recognizes the need to provide the passions with an articulate discourse since in nature they find themselves poor in words, "embarrassed and all but mute." Even when they do find words, they become "irrational and ashamed" of themselves (*GS* 80). What needs resisting is the casting of an evil eye on the passions, in which we see the passions as "dirty, disfiguring, and heart-breaking"; this is an attitude that reveals an idealistic tendency that seeks to annihilate the passions. Nietzsche gives St. Paul as an example of this tendency, perhaps having in mind his cry in Romans: "[W]ith my mind, I serve the law of God, but with my flesh, the law of sin" (7:25). Contrary to this tendency, we can learn valuable lessons from two cultures: from that of the Greeks, who directed their own idealistic tendency toward the passions by loving, elevating, gilding, and deifying them, and from that of the Italians, who show us how the passions can be made to sing (*GS* 139, 80).

Nietzsche works with a specific conception of the passions and affects, involving letting ourselves go, not controlling ourselves, and giving free play to our wrath or our desires (*HH* 211). Although he often employs the word *Affekten*, for the most part he is using the German word *Leidenschaft*, meaning "passion," stemming from the verb *leiden*, meaning "to suffer." The word has several connotations worth taking note of. A passion takes hold of us and seeks to compel us to some action; it involves suffering precisely because it operates on the level of bodily and psychic feeling or affect, and this necessarily results in pain and hardship because of what one undergoes and must endure. Attached to a passion are feelings of pleasure and displeasure "so strong," Nietzsche observes, "that they reduce the intellect to silence or to servitude," and it is at the point where the heart replaces the head that we speak of passion (*Leidenschaft*) (*GS* 3).[5]

Nietzsche is acknowledging, then, that passions are powerful forces of nature that exert their seductions on us. Once we have experienced a passion, he observes, it leaves within us an obscure longing for it and so "[i]t must in fact have provided a sort of pleasure to be scourged with its whip" (*HH* 606). He is noticing how human beings prefer a more intense displeasure to a feeble pleasure. Indeed, he is keen for us to acknowledge that human beings strive for an *emotion in itself*, using other human beings only as a means, and that is most clearly evident in the example of cruelty. Human beings also derive a complex pleasure from what is tragic: "In the dramatic arts in general, a human being wants emotions [*Emotionen*], e.g., of compassion, without having to help." In the case of passionate peoples, it is possible to observe a delight "in the art of passion [*Leidenschaft*], of emotion in itself; without it, they are bored" (Nietzsche 2021b, 413). Nietzsche is aware, however, that human passions have evolved to the point where we can recognize: "Every emotion [*Regung*] has become intellectual. For example, what a person feels in love involves a great deal of their expectations of it, including 'all the metaphysics ever connected to it,' as well as the 'neighboring moods' that resonate along with it" (*KSA*, vol. 8, fragment 23 [80]; *SUP*, 12:392). We should not be tempted, then, to posit a dramatic split between feelings and the intellect. As Nietzsche notes: "Behind *hating* lies *fearing*, behind *loving* needing. Behind feeling and need lie experience (judging and memory)" (*KSA*, vol. 12, fragment 23 [186]; *SUP*, 12:426).

Nietzsche contests the idea that reason functions as an independent entity and instead construes it as "a system of relation between various passions and desires" in which every passion possesses its quantum of reason (*KSA*, vol. 13, fragment 11 [310]). Indeed, as Santayana (1967, 137) points out, viewed from a psychological angle reason can be seen to be an old, inherited passion itself, namely, a passion for consistency and order that likes to regard its own aims as alone important. Nietzsche is keen to draw attention to the need for human beings to educate themselves about the passions so that they can practice a genuine wisdom, one in which reason does not serve to oppose the passions or be permitted to rule over them tyrannically. Rather, the function of reason is to help human agents moderate the passions and learn how to cultivate them in mature and beneficial ways. We need reason, criticism, and science not to encourage us to dispense with the passions *tout court* but rather to aid us so that we do not intoxicate ourselves with passion and so exist beside ourselves.

The mindset to be avoided in seeking to become a master of one's passions is that of "melancholics and philosophical blind-worms" who can speak only of the dreadful character of the passions as a way of indicting the entire world (*WS* 37). What we find in this disparagement of the passions is a neglect of two things that are now of supreme importance to free spirits who are committed to psychological observation (*HH* 35): first, an attention to the detail of things, including nuances and subtleties, and, second, the practice of honest self-observation. If we are now gripped by terror whenever we hear the word *passion*, it is because we have allowed the passions to swell up into monstrosities. In an aphorism from *The Wanderer and His Shadow*, we are advised not to inflate our blunders into eternal fatalities but rather "to work together honestly at the task of transforming the passions of humanity [*Leidenschaften*] into joys [*Freudenschaften*]" (*WS* 37). I illuminate this recommendation in the final section of the chapter.

On the Greeks and Christianity

In *Dawn*, Nietzsche argues that in wanting to return to the affects "in their utmost grandeur and strength"—for example, as *love* of God, *fear* of God, fanatic *faith* in God, and so on—Christianity represents a popular protest against philosophy, and he appeals to the ancient sages against it since they advocated the triumph of reason over the affects (*D* 580).[6] For Nietzsche, then, much depends on the attitude we adopt with respect to the passions; he is keen to encourage us not to demonize the passions but rather to sublimate and cultivate them. As he notes in *Dawn*: "The passions become evil and malicious whenever they are viewed evilly and maliciously" (*D* 76). He is being quite serious when he contends that Christianity has sought to liberate humanity "from the burden of the demands of morality by pointing out a *shorter way to perfection*." Just as we cannot eschew the need for "laborious and tedious dialectics, as well as the collection of rigorously tested facts"—since there is no "'royal road to truth,'" he writes, echoing Hegel—so there is no easy path to self-perfection, and those who need such a path and purport to have found it are simply overweary ones "despairing in the wilderness" (*D* 59).

Nietzsche contends that the aim of Christianity is not, in fact, to make people ethically autonomous since it profits from encouraging them to hold themselves to be as sinful as possible. If in the world of antiquity ingenuity was expended to increase the joy in life through festivals and festive cults, then in the Christian era a huge amount of spirit has been spent on making people feel sinful in every way. Nietzsche speculates that such a stimulation and invigoration of the affects may well be the sign of an enervated and overcultivated age. Religious priests live on the narcotizing of human ills. The costs to the health of the body of a teaching of pure spirituality merit being highlighted. Such a teaching is excessive and, in the process, destroys much nervous energy, inciting one "to despise, ignore, or torment the body and, on account of all one's drives, to torment and despise oneself" (*D* 39).

Unsurprisingly, the teaching succeeds in producing human beings who feel melancholy and oppressed and conclude that the cause of their distress and anxiety must reside in the body, which continues to flourish. In such cases, it is in fact the body that registers a protest, and the irrational mode of existence in which spiritual excess results is made clear. "A pervasive, chronic hyper-excitability was eventually the lot of these virtuous pure spirits" since "the only pleasure they could muster was in the form of ecstasy and other harbingers of madness" (*D* 39). This mode of existence reaches an apogee when ecstasy is accepted as the highest goal in life and the standard by which all earthly pleasures are then judged and condemned. Nietzsche encourages humanity, then, to do away with the concepts of sin and punishment: "May these banished monsters henceforth live somewhere other than among human beings, if they want to go on living at all and do not perish of disgust with themselves!" (*D* 202). In another aphorism from *Dawn*, he notes that it is the most conscientious who suffer most dreadfully from the fears of hell: "Thus life has been made gloomy precisely for those who had need of cheerfulness and pleasant pictures" (*D* 53). Augustine offers penetrating psychological insight into how we enslave ourselves by not attaining mastery over our desires and passions, as when we allow them to form into habitual behavior and, ultimately, compulsions. Indeed, this is how he seeks to understand what he calls "the law of sin" (2019, 8.5.12).[7] Nietzsche, however, holds that the wisest understanding to cultivate is not the appeal to some godhead but rather the one taught by the Buddha, namely, the need for *self-redemption* (*D* 96). The teaching of India, he holds, is more rational and enlightened since it does away with the mediation of priests, and Europe would be wise to catch up with it.

Nietzsche's estimation of the ways in which the ancient Greeks approached the emotions or passions stands in sharp contrast with his valuation of Christianity's approach to them. Greek antiquity is to be esteemed on account of its moralistic broad-mindedness that in large part consists in having a keen sense for the real, that is, for what is typical and factual regarding everything human. The thinkers and writers of antiquity do not preach that we should strive for the complete annihilation of the passions; rather, according to Nietzsche, they "allowed for a moderate discharge of what was evil and questionable," including the "regressively bestial" elements they identified at the base of Greek nature (*MOM* 220). It is on account of having this sense for the real that Greek thinkers were able to become natural scientists, historians, geographers, and philosophers and so genuine masters and pioneers. Nietzsche thus praises the ancient Greeks for their ability to grasp the ambiguous character of many of our passions, for example, envy. For the Greeks, there was a good envy and a bad envy. The latter promotes wicked war and feuding and is cruel. The former, however, expresses itself in healthy, competitive ways, as in the case of the Greek *agon* (contest). We see this most obviously in sportsmen and -women, but we can find it also in evidence wherever we see human beings goaded into doing things and striving for excellence. In his middle writings, Nietzsche remains committed to the fundamental insight he had advanced in his early *Homer's Contest* (1872), namely, that, even "at the finest heights of his power," the human being is all nature, carrying within it nature's uncanny dual character: "His dreadful capabilities and those we count as inhuman are perhaps, indeed, fertile soil from which alone all humanity, in feelings, deeds and works, can grow forth" (Nietzsche 2017a, 177). (On the unintelligent character of the warmest heart, see also *HH* 235.)

Christianity has sought to transform the great passions and powers, such as Eros and Aphrodite, which are capable of positive idealization or spiritualization, into "infernal kobolds and phantoms of deceit," arousing in the conscience of the believer tremendous torments at the slightest sexual excitation (*D* 76). The result is to fill human beings with a feeling of dread at the sight of their natural animal conditions of existence, making necessary and regularly recurring sensations into a source of inner misery to the point where inner misery becomes a necessary and regularly recurring phenomenon in them. This may even be a misery that we keep secret and that is more deeply rooted than we care to admit (Nietzsche mentions in this regard Shakespeare's confession of Christian gloominess in the *Sonnets*). Christianity has contempt for the world and makes a new virtue of ignorance, namely, innocence, the most frequent result of which is the feeling of guilt and despair: "a virtue which leads to Heaven via the detour through Hell" (*D* 321). Furthermore, what is wanted by the Christian "are blindness and delirium and an eternal psalm above the waves in which reason has drowned" (*D* 89).

Nietzsche is keen to revalue sexual feelings by arguing that, as in the feeling of sympathy and the practice of worship, a pleasure is transferred from one person to another on the basis of giving oneself pleasure and that such a benevolent arrangement is all too rare in nature. Christianity, in contrast, has enjoined to them a guilty conscience and demonized Eros. As a result of this censorship, the church has succeeded only in making the erotic more interesting to people than all the saints and angels put together, and Nietzsche points out the comedic aspects of this: "[T]o this very day, the effect of such secretiveness has been that the *love story* became the only real interest that *all* circles have in common—and to an excess inconceivable in antiquity, an excess that will, at a later date, elicit laughter" (*D* 76). Christianity is to be regarded as a worrisome religion simply because it treats normal and necessary sensations as a source of inner misery and then seeks to make this misery the normal lot for every single human being. Christianity is a religion that stimulates the pathological excess of feeling: "[I]t wants to destroy, shatter, stun, intoxicate; there is only one thing it does not want: *measure*" (*HH* 114). It is also to be regarded as a presumptuous religion since it encourages only the atrophy of the human being, and on account of its lack of knowledge in psychological matters it is to be considered "the most disastrous kind of arrogance to date" (*BGE* 62). We can, therefore, learn valuable lessons from the Greeks of antiquity in terms of how to cultivate the passions in a healthier way than our Christian inheritance has bred into us. In their art and their culture in general, the Greeks felt "the outflow and overflow of their own well-being . . . and . . . loved to see their perfection *one more time* outside themselves": "[T]heir pleasure in themselves led them to art, but what leads these contemporaries of ours is: their annoyance with themselves" (*MOM* 169).

The overriding aim in the ancient Greek world, Nietzsche thinks, was to liberate the human from the passions so it can become a lawgiver. He notes that although for a thinker like Anaxagoras the world is fundamentally irrational it is nevertheless something measured and beautiful, and this, he says, is how human beings should be too (*PT*, 146). Even those who have become liberated and think they have no need of laws still require legislation or measure. This concern with measure persists in Nietzsche. One of the main concerns expressed in the late writings is with our plebeian curiosity that he finds evident in our lack of proportion and measure. What is genuinely noble in works and in human beings, Nietzsche maintains, is the "moment of smooth sea and halcyon self-sufficiency, the gold and coldness shown by all things that have perfected themselves." This is a taste and a love of which he thinks we moderns—we "semi-barbarians"—have largely lost sight. Today, "our thrill is this very thrill of the infinite, the unmeasured" (*BGE* 224). On these points, Nietzsche's thinking reconnects with his early concerns and his interest in the morality of antiquity where morality is conceived in terms of an ethics of character and self-discipline. Today, by contrast, too many things are treated medically with narcotics soothing our nerves, and in our lack of self-discipline we find revealed that our way of life is one "universal haste and *impotenia*" (*PT*, 106).

On Stoicism

> And the stoics, as we know, claim to be most like the gods. But give me a man who is a stoic three or four or if you like six hundred times over, and he too, even if he keeps his beard as a mark of wisdom, though he shares it with the goat, will have to swallow his pride, smooth out his frown, shake off his principles, and be fond and foolish for a while.
>
> Erasmus, *Praise of Folly* (1511)

While the mode of living of the Christian mindset involves pathological extremes of feeling, the Stoic way of living results in a petrified life devoid of movement and growth. In Nietzsche's writings, we encounter a mixed reception of Stoic teaching. There are places where Nietzsche will appeal to Stoic ideas as invaluable principles of living, while in other places he takes them to task for their teaching on the extirpation of the passions and their ideal of human invulnerability.[8] Martha Nussbaum has claimed that Nietzsche participates in a cult of Stoic strength and that as a result we see in his writings the depiction of "a fearful person, a person who is determined to seal himself off from risk, even at the cost of loss of love and value." Like the otherworldliness he abhors, the Stoicism he endorses is, she claims, a form of self-protection, expressing "a fear of this world and its contingencies" (1994, 160). A careful examination of Nietzsche's texts shows that nothing could be further from the truth. Nussbaum seriously distorts the character of Nietzsche's thinking and fails to acknowledge the powerful criticism of Stoicism we encounter in both the middle and the late writings. I shall, to begin with, provide two examples from the texts of the middle writings to demonstrate this.

First, let us consider aphorism 343 from *Dawn*. Nietzsche stresses the need for us to experience dissatisfaction with ourselves and assume the risk of experimenting in life, freely taking the journey through our wastelands, quagmires, and icy glaciers. The ones who do not take the risk of life will "never make the journey around the world (that [they themselves] are!) but will remain trapped within [themselves] like a knot on the log [they] were born to, a mere happenstance" (*D* 343). Nietzsche's commitment to the wisdom of taking risks in life and the need to experiment with modes of living could not be clearer. What this involves is made clear in *The Gay Science*, in which he acknowledges that, although the Stoic way of life—conceived in terms of building oneself up as a castle or an inner citadel—may contain greatness in it, it comes at a high price: that of closing oneself off to experience and from the instruction experiences afford, including not allowing the experience of "the beautiful fortuities" of one's soul (*GS* 305). Such people will become difficult to themselves and insufferable for others. In a related aphorism, though now speaking of the person of "great passion," Nietzsche writes of the benefits of our gazing out of the windows of our castle, which is our fortress, into "what is foreign, free, and *different*." This person of passion should be regarded as being very different from both the "excited, noisy, excited nervous" type of human being and the gregarious person always eager to please. Although such people may look outwardly impassive, appearing cold and indifferent, "a silent, dark fire" dwells within them and offers "a tempered, contemplative, composed friendliness" (*D* 471).

Admittedly, in one aphorism in *Beyond Good and Evil* Nietzsche does refer to himself and fellow free spirits as "we last Stoics" (*BGE* 227). However, this appellation is specific to the texts of his late writings and the way in which he polemically positions himself in them. He names himself a last Stoic because he thinks that the instincts of health can protect him against incipient decadence. In this context, then, he makes an appeal to a "brakeshoe morality" that is "stoical, hard, tyrannical" (*KSA*, vol. 13, fragment 15 [29]) and that denotes a union of a protracted will and knowledge that entails having respect for oneself (*KSA*, vol. 13, fragment 11 [297]; see also *KSA*, vol. 13, fragment 11 [375]). Self-control is required, then, to prevent clumsiness and sloppiness creeping in with regards to the tasks that confront the free spirit.

On occasion, Nietzsche expresses an affinity with the Stoics on the emotions. On their account, emotions are cognitive; that is, they are evaluative judgments, judgments of worth, where the objects being valued are external goods that lie beyond our control. Emotions are not, then, to be considered as mere impulses or simple feelings, except on the level of what the Stoics call *protopassions*. Nietzsche has a similar view when he claims that feelings are the products of judgments and beliefs. In short, emotions as beliefs or judgments typically take the form of false cognitions. As he puts it in *Dawn*: "'Trust your feelings!' But feelings are nothing final or original—behind feelings there stand judgements and evaluations which we inherit in the form of feelings" (*D* 35). If emotions are evaluative judgments, then the elimination of them also dissolves the emotion. Here, then, Nietzsche is adopting the Stoic view that every external event is a matter of indifference and so cannot be inherently good or bad. It is we ourselves who give external events their value by applying to them evaluative predicates, and, when we do this, we bind our *eudaimonia* to things over which we have very little control. Implicit in Nietzsche's account of this Stoic doctrine is the idea that assenting to things is within our control; that is, whether we apply these value predicates to things is a matter of election or choice. In and of themselves, external events have no intrinsic value and are indifferent unless we assent to such value judgments.[9]

Nietzsche is keen to utilize these insights to counsel his readers in the art of life. When we suffer a terrible misfortune, such as the death of a loved one, we need to recall how we viewed such an experience when we observed someone else bearing the same adversity. We need to see and judge our own experiences as we see and judge such experiences when they happen to others since this enables us to see events in an objective fashion, that is, without the exaggeration and excess of the ego standpoint. By seeing things in this manner, we may eventually free ourselves from the negative passions, such as anger and self-pity.

Typically, Nietzsche's consideration of the Stoic is a critical one. He describes the Stoic as someone who prepares himself for the worst, training himself to swallow stones and worms, "slivers of glass and scorpions without nausea" (*GS* 306). Stoicism prepares one only for petrifaction: "[A] certain *heavy pressure* and *indolence* is intensified to the extreme, in order to sense pain only slightly: *rigidity* and *coldness* are the trick, in other words anaesthetics." Nietzsche confesses to finding the Stoic way of thinking repugnant since it underestimates the value of pain as well as the value of excitement and passion. We can imagine the Stoic telling himself, Everything is fine with me as it comes, I want nothing else: "[H]e no longer *eliminates any emergencies* because he has killed the sensitivity for emergencies" (*KSA* vol. 9, fragment 15 [55]; *SUP*, 6:492). Moreover: "For those with whom fate solicits improvisations, such as those that live in violent ages and depend on sudden and mercurial people, Stoicism is probably advisable; but for those who can foresee that fate permits them to spin *a long thread* they do well to make Epicurean arrangements. That is what all those have always done whose work is of the spirit" (*GS* 306). The Stoic way of life is a religious one in that the task is to live in complete accord with the actions and wishes of the deity. Stoics are to be taken to task for the delusion of believing they are acting in accordance with the putative *Logos* of the cosmos, failing to acknowledge the pleasure they derive from their exercises in self-mastery: "There is a serenity the Stoic possesses whenever he feels constricted by the duties he has prescribed for his way of life: he takes pleasure in himself as the ruler" (*D* 251). Moreover, why make a virtue of what one is? "If the Stoic achieves the condition that he wants to have—*usually he brings this with him*, and this is why he chooses *this* philosophy!" (*KSA*, vol. 9, fragment 15 [55], pp. 652–53; *SUP*, 6:492).

Nietzsche rejects the Stoic identification of full human flourishing with the attainment of freedom from emotional turmoil and disturbance.[10] He draws attention to the value of displeasure and pain because experience of them ultimately affords access to "subtle pleasures and joys that have been rarely relished yet," indeed, entire "galaxies of joy" (*GS* 12). As Aurelia Armstrong (2013, 14) notes, Nietzsche's objection to the Stoics is a quite specific one. He does not object to their therapy on the grounds that it works to deaden painful affects since he recognizes that this can often be a useful strategy when dealing with suffering that becomes unbearable or a passion that becomes extremely debilitating, such as fear. Sometimes the preservation of one's life and one's strength requires that one acts something like a Stoic would. The mistake in the Stoic conception of life is to turn a potentially useful strategy for dealing with debilitating passions into an ideal of human flourishing. This approach to life fails to recognize that we can learn the value of our bitternesses by knowing that it is possible to drop sweetnesses on them and that we can find "remedies in our courage and sublimity." Moral preachers who teach us to silence the will and annihilate passion thus tell us lies because they seriously underestimate our strength to endure life and fashion for ourselves new galaxies of joy (*GS* 326; see also *GS* 338).

In aphorism 9 of *Beyond Good and Evil*, Nietzsche conceives philosophy as the most spiritual will to power. He outlines this conception in the context of a critique of Stoicism as a form of self-tyranny. Although he considers the Stoics to be noble types in their endeavor to live according to nature, he questions whether the Stoic way of life is coherent and advisable. If nature is taken to be in character something that is wasteful without measure and indifferent without measure, without purpose, mercy, justice, and so on, then how could a mere mortal human being live according to this power of indifference? Does this not suggest, in fact, that living entails wanting to be different than this indifferent nature and that this involves assessing, having preferences, being unjust and limited? If the Stoics agreed with this conception of life, Nietzsche wants to know why they should wish to make a principle out of what they are anyhow. In essence, he accuses Stoics of being actors and self-deceivers. They have an unacknowledged pride in prescribing their morality onto nature, demanding that it be "according to the Stoa," and, most damningly of all, they want to make all existence conform to their own images of existence, "as a monstrous eternal glorification and universalization of Stoicism!" (*BGE* 9). The Stoic is an actor for Nietzsche because he sets up an ideal of life that in addition to being excessively tyrannical proves unlivable. As a way of life, Stoicism is riddled with serious levels of self-deception, for example, in the Stoic person's denial that there is any pleasure involved in living the life of virtue (see also *D* 251 and *GS* 122).[11] And it is lamentable when this way of life is conceived as universalizable since here we find neither knowledge nor wisdom (see *BGE* 197, 198).

The Passions and Self-Cultivation

When we consider the mastery of the passions in relation to our efforts at self-cultivation as well as in the context of the endurance of the power of life, it is possible to conceive our passions as sources of delight and joy. Self-discipline is obviously an important part of the effort since the disorganized mass of passions requires organization if our master passion is to achieve its goals. As T. L. S. Sprigge points out: "This is different from the appearance of self-control on the part of the weak who refrain from doing anything much with their lives from timidity" (1984, 105). That the task of becoming a master of oneself is one of Nietzsche's chief concerns as an educator is clear when we take cognizance of the following aphorism from *The Wanderer and His Shadow*: "A person who does not want to become master of his temper, of his jaundice and vengefulness, of his sensual pleasures, and who attempts to become master somewhere else, is as dumb as the farmer who lays out his field beside a mountain torrent without protecting himself against it" (*WS* 65).

In his reflections on the passions and how to cultivate them wisely, Nietzsche is combatting two things: first, the presumption that there is a *single* moral-making morality (*D* 164) and, second, any system of morality that teaches renunciation as the chief task and goal of the ethical work we conduct on ourselves. With regard to the first point, his advice is that we refrain from assuming that what is "higher" and "lower" in morality is to be measured by some moral yardstick: "[T]here is no absolute morality. So, take your rule from somewhere else—and now beware!" (*D* 139). No morality or ethical practice should presume to have a monopoly over us, and we should not, therefore, permit a single morality to assume dominance in human life.

When we think about morality in this way, we only impoverish ourselves by diminishing our sense of the multiple ways it is possible to conduct and discipline ourselves. Humanity has suffered for too long from teachers of morality who wanted too much all at once and sought to lay down precepts for everyone (*D* 194). In the future, care will need to be given to the most personal questions and time created for them (*D* 196).

Nietzsche makes clear his opposition to a moral code that advocates strict renunciation as the way to self-contentment and self-mastery when he announces that he abhors "all those moralities which say: 'Do not do this! Renounce! Overcome yourself!'" (*GS* 304). The morality he prefers is one that goads us to do something and to do it again, from morning until evening, but with the encouragement that we are to do it well and as well as we alone can do it. Only by doing things for ourselves can we do something well and learn what this might mean for our own development without hatred or aversion (*GS* 304). In short, we should aim to live without negative virtues when it comes to cultivating our passions. Moralists who command human beings to, above all, gain control of themselves in some severe fashion and with an austere teaching succeed only in afflicting us with the disease of constant irritability in the face of natural stirrings and inclinations. As Huxley notes in "Personality and the Discontinuity of the Mind," it is a delusion to think that the emotions can be simply outlawed: "[U]nco-ordinated instincts and emotions do not thereby cease to exist; they live on, but apart, and as it were autonomously. The rationalizing Stoic leads his barbarous one-sided life of reason, and every now and then the outlaw breaks in on him" (Huxley 2000, 273).

In Nietzsche, we encounter a wisdom of the passions centered on the recognition of the need for us to discharge them in culturally healthy ways and to master them as sources of felt joy. He does not want us to aspire to a state of beatitude, at least not as a permanent state and not as the highest state we can attain, and hence his critical remark that he finds Spinoza's intellectual love of God—which signals we have attained a state of supreme beatitude—as "bloodless" (*GS* 372).[12] Nietzsche values being open to experience, and this for him necessarily entails profiting from experiences of pain. He thinks we simply cannot do without pain as an essential element in human life: "There is as much wisdom in pain as there is in pleasure: both belong among the factors that contribute the most to the preservation of the species. If pain did not, it would have perished long ago; that it hurts is no argument against it but its essence" (*GS* 318).

Nietzsche draws attention to the importance of being rich in opposition and advises that to remain young we should not seek peace of the soul (*TI* "Morality as Anti-Nature" 3).[13] He thus sees the goal of philosophy as something quite different from the attainment of either Epicurean ataraxia or Spinozist beatitude. Indeed, he refers to Spinoza's philosophy as, for example, the "conceptual cobwebbery of a hermit," and this echoes the critical point he makes in *Beyond Good and Evil* that Spinoza disguised and armored his philosophy in the "hocus-pocus of mathematical form." The masquerade of the hermit betrays the timidity and vulnerability of Spinoza as a philosopher (*TI* "Reconnaissance Raids of an Untimely Man" 23; *BGE* 5). The problem with modes of philosophical therapy that seek to counter the strength of our passions, such as the therapy of the Stoics or the therapy of Spinoza, is that they generalize where generalization is inadvisable. We are dealing here not with science or even with wisdom but rather with prudence mingled with stupidity: "whether it be that indifference and statuesque coldness towards the passionate folly of the affects [*Affekte*] which the Stoics advised and applied; or that no-more laughing and no-more weeping of Spinoza, that destruction of the affects through analysis and vivisection which he advocated so naively" (*BGE* 188).

Spinoza famously holds to the view that the study of human actions and appetites can be approached "as if it were an investigation into lines, planes, or bodies" (1992, 103 [pt. 3, preface]). However, as Santayana notes, Spinoza does violence to physics and natural history in the very starting point of his philosophy, namely, with self-preservation held to be the principle of life and the root of all feelings or affects. Strictly speaking, he argues, such a principle is not illustrated in nature, where all is in flux and habits destructive to the body are just as conspicuous as protective instincts. As a result, he can develop his ethics of the passions only by explaining the changes in life in terms of a "crystallised posture" of what life might be at a single instant (Santayana 2016, 82). In the account Spinoza provides, then, a passion's history was to be the history of what would have been its expression if it had had no history at all.

Nietzsche too encourages us to approach emotions, feelings, and moods in a quite different way to Spinoza's. In the aphorism "Resonances," he argues that these phenomena should be treated as "complexes" and not simply as unities since "the unity of the world guarantees nothing about the unity of the thing"; they are "streams with a hundred sources and tributaries." Any strong mood we experience will bring with it a "resonance of related sensations and moods . . . [that] churn up our memory, as it were" (*HH* 14). Because of the way habitual associations of feelings and thoughts are formed, following each other with lightning speed, we no longer sense them as the complexes they are. We allow ourselves to be led astray by our feelings in another way, for example, believing that profound feelings somehow enable us to "draw near to the heart of nature." Such a belief rests on a deeply rooted error encouraged by philosophers, namely, that the world is to be understood in terms of an "inside" and an "outside" with a distinction drawn between "essence" and "appearance." Nietzsche continues:

> But these feelings are profound only insofar as, almost unnoticeably, certain complicated groups of ideas that we call profound are regularly aroused along with them; a feeling is profound because we take the accompanying thought for profound. But a profound thought can nevertheless be very far from the truth, as is for example every metaphysical one; if we subtract from the profound feeling the intermingled elements of thought, what remains is the *strength* of feeling, and this guarantees nothing with respect to knowledge except its own strength, just as a strong belief demonstrates only its strength, not the truth of what is believed. (*HH* 15)

A truth we may find difficult to stomach is to be found in the insight that what has made metaphysical assumptions about the world something valuable, pleasurable, and terrible are error, self-deception, and passion. It is these, "the worst of methods of knowledge," that have taught us to believe in them, and moral and religious feelings are completely bound up with them (*HH* 9). Nietzsche argues that, while it is human pride that to date has impeded a proper understanding of these feelings, we can remove this brake by appealing to a new pride, notably, the pride to be taken in securing honest knowledge (*D* 32).

In the discourse "Of Joys and Passions" in *Thus Spoke Zarathustra*, which builds on the basic idea expressed in aphorism 37 of *The Wanderer and His Shadow*, Nietzsche acknowledges that the passions belong to a dark underworld and require transmutation: "You laid your highest aim in the heart of these passions: then they became your virtues and joys. . . . At last all your passions have become virtues and all your devils angels. Once you had fierce dogs in your cellar: but they changed at last into birds and sweet singers" (*Z* 1 "Of Joys and Passions"). In this discourse, virtues are presented as sublimated forms of primitive passions and are in need of cultivation if human beings are to free themselves "from the race of the hot-tempered or of the lustful or of the fanatical or of the vindictive." However, Nietzsche does not seek to advise that we simply dispense with the passions since this "would result in the deepest atrophy" (*KSA*, vol. 9, fragment 11 [73]; *SUP*, 6:329).[14] All great human beings have been great through the strength of their affects: "Even health is worthless if it is not equal of great affects, indeed if it doesn't need them." The affects do this, Nietzsche thinks, by concentrating and holding power in a state of productive tension. Even for cognition, he suggests, we need all our drives, the good as well as the evil, for example, approaching a problem suspiciously, cunningly, and by dissembling. He thus opposes our current morality, which wants only "amiable and credit-worthy payers and borrowers," which is a life without risk and experiment (*KSA*, vol. 9, fragment 11 [73]; *SUP*, 6:329). He has announced in *Dawn* that we *are* experiments or can view ourselves as such and that the task is to *want* to be such (*D* 453). What he has in mind is the creation in the individual of "*his own existential possibility*," which is to be conceived in terms a "*re*arrangement and assimilation excretion of drives" (*KSA*, vol. 9, fragment 11 [182]; *SUP*, 6:365).[15]

Virtue and the Passions

> I love those people who are transparent water and who also, to speak with Pope, "do not hide from view the turbid bottom of their stream." Even for them, however, there remains one vanity, one to be sure of a rare and sublimated sort: some of them want us to see only just the turbidity and ignore the water's transparency, which makes seeing the former possible. No less a person than Gautama Buddha came up with vanity of the few in the formula: "let your sins be seen before people and hide your virtues." But this amounts to presenting to the world a lousy spectacle—and it is a sin against good taste.
>
> Nietzsche, *Dawn*, aphorism 558

The discourse "Of Joys and Passions" in *Zarathustra* is important for understanding how Nietzsche conceives the relation between virtue and the passions and what he thinks a virtue is. Put at its simplest, *virtue* denotes an ethically admirable disposition of character and involves more than the exercise of skills since a virtue also entails "characteristic patterns of desire and motivation," as Bernard Williams (1985, 9) puts it.[16] Nietzsche understands virtue in two main ways. On the one hand, when virtue emerges out of our socialization, he takes it to denote a consistent principle of action that helps foster a habitual and regular mode of behavior, ensuring conformity to social norms. On the other hand, when his focus is on self-cultivation, it denotes a kind of human excellence. As Robert Solomon rightly notes, the emphasis on excellence is important simply because not any good trait will prove adequate: "[N]o virtue is good 'in itself,' but only as it contributes to something else of value, such as personal style and character" (2003, 140).

Nietzsche commences "Of Joys and Passions" in a provocative manner by declaring that one's virtue needs to be singularly one's own and not shared with any other person. This opening statement is in accord with his teaching on the virtues in his middle writings—and, indeed, throughout his writings—namely, that there is a vital need for each one of us to cultivate our virtues in a singular fashion: "A virtue needs to be our *own* invention, our *own* most personal need and self-defence: in any other sense, a virtue is just dangerous" (*AC* 11). Nietzsche states wittily in "Of Joys and Passions" that we will want to provide our virtue with a name if only to pull its ears and caress it, but in doing this we run the risk of having the name of our virtue held in common with the people and the herd. Instead, he suggests, it would be much better to say that it is the unutterable and nameless that both torments and delights my soul and that is the hunger of my belly. In short, what propels me forward in life is something that is uniquely my own and is neither a law of God nor a human statue, let alone a signpost to "super earths and paradises." For Nietzsche, then, our virtue is to be considered "too exalted for the familiarity of names," and, if we feel compelled to speak of it, then we should stammer it: "Thus say and stammer: 'This is *my* good, this I love, just thus do I like it, only thus do *I* wish the good.'" He places the emphasis on stammering simply because in learning to prize our virtue in a singular fashion we are struggling to speak in our own voice and to speak of our will or desire. He lays down an important condition for the healthy cultivation of our virtue, namely, that it be an earthly virtue.

Nietzsche now introduces into "Of Joys and Passions" the passions that represent for him our original human animal endowment. We once had only passions, and we called them evil; now, however, we have only our virtues, which have grown out of these original passions. Nietzsche is acknowledging the roots of the passions, namely, that they emanate from the worst aspects of human nature. The passions, then, and without achieving a sublimated character, are to be guarded against simply because they can unleash such dangerous sentiments, such as the thirst for revenge. In the process of sublimating the passions, Nietzsche maintains that individuals purify themselves of previous opinions and valuations, to the extent that no evil now comes from us. The only evil that should come out of us is that which comes from the conflict of our virtues. Although he regards it as a healthy condition for the self to engage in the conflict of its virtues, Nietzsche also recognizes in "Of Joys and Passions" the hazards that come with having more than one virtue and, in fact, states that it may be wise for the self to cultivate the one virtue since it may then go over the bridge to the superhuman more easily: "To have many virtues is to be distinguished, but it is a hard fate." It is such because one can so easily tire of being a battleground between different competing virtues. From this insight, however, Nietzsche does not go on to disavow the importance of battling with oneself in an agonistic manner, and he has Zarathustra raise the question whether war and battle must always be regarded as something only evil. He seeks to challenge such a perspective: "But this evil is necessary, envy and mistrust and calumny among your virtues is necessary."

Nietzsche draws "Of Joys and Passions" to a close by writing about the virtues in a way that resonates with what he had already attempted to show in aphorism 21 of *The Gay Science*. Each of our virtues desires the highest or most exalted place in the economy of our affective life. Each thus wants, he says, to take hold of our entire spirit so that our spirit may be its herald: "[I] t wants your entire strength in anger, hate, and love. Every virtue is jealous of the others, and jealousy is a terrible thing. Even virtues can be destroyed through jealousy." Nietzsche is keen to indicate just what it entails to be under the rule of a virtue: "When you have a virtue, a real, whole virtue (and not merely a mini-instinct for some virtue), you are its *victim*" (*GS* 21).

In "Of Joys and Passions," Nietzsche seeks to show the character of a virtue when it is socially inculcated. For example, it begins with him noting that a person's virtues are called *good* because of the probable consequences they hold not for him but rather for the rest of us and for society, and this means that hitherto the praise of virtues has not at all been selfless. Virtues such as obedience, chastity, filial piety, and even justice are typically of great harm for the individuals that possess them. This is because they are, in effect, instincts "that dominate them violently and covetously and resist the efforts of reason to keep them in balance with their other instincts." This is why Nietzsche adheres to the view that to have a virtue in this social sense is to be its victim. This praise of virtue is, then, praise for something that is privately harmful and deleterious for individuals and their self-cultivation. It is "the praise of drives that deprive a human being of his noblest selfishness and the strength for the highest achievement of oneself" (*GS* 21; see also *Z* 1 "Of the Bestowing Virtue" 1). Socialization likes to make it appear that virtue and private advantage are sisters, and, although a relationship of some kind as this may well exist, even to the point where a healthy industriousness can cure boredom and the blind raging of the passions, education remains silent about the extreme dangers of this inculcation of habits and virtues: "That is how education always proceeds: one tries to condition an individual by various attractions and advantages to adopt a way of thinking and behaving that, once it has become a habit, instinct, and passion, will dominate him *to his own ultimate disadvantage* but 'for the general good.'" There are several dangers here. First, while industriousness can create wealth and reap honors, it can also deprive the organs of their subtlety, and that would allow for the enjoyment of this wealth and these honors. Second, by subjecting ourselves to industrious socialization, we run the risk of becoming dull creatures of routine and habit. Industriousness becomes its own end with the endless pursuit of only more industry and more money:

"[T]his chief antidote to boredom and the passions . . . blunts the senses and leads the spirit to resist new attractions" (*GS* 21).

My insights into this discourse on passions and virtues are largely in accord with the reading provided by Leo Strauss. Strauss notes that the passions denote the way in which we are affected and in which we can be both pleased and pained in life. On a basic level, *virtue* denotes the ways in which we take a stand toward these affections. Nietzsche departs from the philosophical tradition in not construing passion and virtue as radically different. "In the Platonic simile," Strauss shows, "the passions would be like the horses, noble or base, of a chariot; virtue is the character of the charioteer" (2017, 43). He suggests that Nietzsche is best seen as following a more modern tradition, which he dates to the seventeenth century and associates with the likes of Spinoza, Montesquieu, and Rousseau, in which virtue is the good passion that defeats the bad passion. Nietzsche radicalizes this tradition in the sense that, while virtue is itself a passion and the highest passion, there is inseparable kinship between the highest and the lowest.

Strauss notes a further important point. This is the insight that for Nietzsche virtues are deeply and intimately related to the unique character of one's self and one's efforts to fashion this self or to become what one is. "Virtue has some character of the self," he writes, "because if it were merely a character of the ego it would only be a surface phenomenon, but since this self is characterized by uniqueness, the virtues are something different in every different human being" (2017, 44). An aphorism from *Dawn* may help clarify the distinction Strauss is making here between the "self" and the "ego." That aphorism is "Pseudo-Egotism," and it is notable for the way in which Nietzsche draws a distinction between one's phantom ego and what he calls one's "self-established, genuine ego." The former is a pallid fiction produced by internalizing the view of oneself that is formed in the heads of those around us and then communicated to us and to the extent that we live "in a fog of impersonal, half-personal opinions" and arbitrary "fictitious evaluations." This is to dwell in a strange world of phantasms that nonetheless dons a sensible appearance. The result of this process is the establishment of "general opinions about 'the human being'": "[A]ll these humans who do not even know one another believe in the bloodless abstraction of 'human being,' in a fiction" (*D* 105).[17] One's highest goal is something original to one's self-established ego and necessarily involves self-cultivation.

We can understand virtue, then, in terms of sublimated passion.[18] As Strauss rightly notes, *sublimation* was Nietzsche's term before it became Freud's. In Nietzsche, sublimation is connected to the sublime, that is, to attaining states of elevation and even exaltation, and this is a key element in the transfiguration of the passions, that is, in the activity of turning our passions into joys. Passions become virtues, then, when we dedicate them to our highest goal, and, in this way, we contribute to the creation of the superhuman. Strauss maintains, however, that the connection between sublimation and the sublime is peculiar to Nietzsche and not part of Freudian vocabulary. This, however, is mistaken since the connection between the two is made in highly instructive terms in psychoanalysis. In his study of sublimation, for example, Hans Loewald observes that the etymology of the word *sublime* suggests "rising to a limit or upper threshold and proceeding on a slope." When deployed in a figurative sense, *sublimation* denotes the elevation to a higher state of existence, "transmutation into something higher, purer, or more sublime." In both chemical and psychoanalytic senses, sublimation, then, denotes a transmutation from the lower to the higher, to a purified mode of existence. Loewald insists that we should not think automatically of this transmutation as a simple form of progression, say, from a coarse state to a more refined and advanced one in which the crude state is completely left behind. Rather, we need to see the highest and the lowest as enveloped within one another and within "an original, unitary experience" (1988, 12–13).

This insight helps us understand Nietzsche's lesson on the transmutation of the passions into joys: the passions are not to be regarded simply as crude modes of being that are to be left behind as one pursues the task of becoming what one is. Although purification is involved in the tasks of self-cultivation, the aim is not to attain some pure moral condition in which we would say farewell to the amoral or immoral passions.[19] Indeed, in the entry on *Zarathustra* in *Ecce Homo*, Nietzsche reveals that his aim in the book is to pay careful attention to both the highest and the lowest powers of human nature, in which "that which is sweetest, airiest, and most fearsome pours forth from a single spring" (*EH* "Zarathustra" 6).

[CHAPTER FIVE]

The Poets

> You must have eyes of science to see the seed in its modes; you must have the vivacity of the poet to perceive in the thought its futurities.
>
> Emerson, "Poetry and Imagination"

> He is the true Orpheus who writes his ode, not with syllables, but men.
>
> Emerson, "Poetry and Imagination"

> I give you hopes; but what will you hear and see of them if you have not experienced splendor, ardor, and dawns in your own souls? I can only remind you; more I cannot do. To move stones, to turn animals into human beings—is that what you want from me? Oh, if you are still stones and animals, then better look for your Orpheus.
>
> Nietzsche, *The Gay Science*, aphorism 286

The Poet as Seer

Although Nietzsche is often presented by commentators as a poet-philosopher, such an appellation reveals very little about his conception of the task of the poet or about his interpretation of modern poets. Both Walter Kaufmann (1980) and Erich Heller (1988) wrote fine essays on Nietzsche and poetry, including essays on Nietzsche and Rilke, but they considered the relevant issues, such as the task of the poet and the nature of the relation between philosophy and poetry, in abstraction from how Nietzsche conceives them. More recently, Michael Robertson (2012) has sought to provide a fresh illumination of Nietzsche's ideal of the poet-philosopher, and, although he utilizes material from middle texts such as *The Gay Science* and has interesting things to say, once again we are given a consideration that is divorced from an appreciation of the specific details of what Nietzsche says and argues for and makes no reference to key aphorisms we find in middle texts such as *Mixed Opinions and Maxims* (1879) and *The Wanderer and His Shadow* (1880).[1] These texts are typically overlooked by commentators who may operate with the assumption that they are merely transitional or casual texts, little more than a loose collection of aphorisms, and so not crucial to an understanding of Nietzsche's project. In my view, this is an error of judgment, and it is thus not surprising that appreciations of Nietzsche as a so-called poet-philosopher end up being developed in terms that are often vague and general as well as insufficiently informative and unnecessarily speculative. The German word for poet Nietzsche uses is *Dichter*, which literally means "composer," someone who brings together in an artistic form images, symbols, ideas, thoughts, and meditations. Many of the writers he admires were prose writers and storytellers as well as poets.[2] His attention is focused on the idea of a poetry of the future, which he posits in a specific manner. A number of writers after Nietzsche concerned themselves with a poetry of the future or with the poet yet to come, such as Rilke (2011), D. H. Lawrence (2019), and Virginia Woolf (2008), and some of their concerns resonate with Nietzsche's.[3] He appeals to the poets to assume the task of providing signposts to the future in the context of the specific concern he has with the cultivation of human beings.[4]

The nature of Nietzsche's conception of cultivation will be brought out as my analysis proceeds, but several points are worth noting at the outset. The first point is to stress the need to take cognizance of the fact that Nietzsche advances his conception in the context of his response to social and political developments taking place in the nineteenth century as he perceives these developments. The second point is the need to take cognizance of the fact that the cultivation of the human being, which in large part centers on a doctrine of the passions, is Nietzsche's abiding concern. Nietzsche conceives of philosophy as a practice of a sober mind that cools down a human mind prone to neurosis. Philosophy, in concert with science, has the task of tempering emotional and mental excess. Indeed, Nietzsche defines the philosopher as a human being who speaks "from a cool, invigorating resting place" (*WS* 171). Nietzsche favors a project of sobriety that supposes philosophical moderation to combat human neurosis and a sentimental, self-intoxicating worldview, which he associates with Rousseau and his influence (see *HH* 463; *WS* 216, 221). He notes his century's proximity to madness where the "overstimulation of the nervous and intellectual powers is a universal danger" and "the cultivated classes in European countries are thoroughly neurotic." And he lives in hope of a new Renaissance, noting that we "have Christianity, the philosophers, poets, and musicians to thank for an overabundance of deeply moving sensations" and that that can be combated only with the spirit of science that cools us down and makes us wise skeptics (*HH* 244). In terms of the nineteenth-century developments, Nietzsche is responding to a range of events, including "national wars," "ultramundane martyrdom," and "socialist alarm." In terms of art, he is responding most critically to Wagnerism, which he describes as "the *last of all* reactionary military campaigns against the spirit of the Enlightenment" (*MOM* 171).

For Schopenhauer (1818/2010), the poet is the universal human being and the mirror of humanity that brings to consciousness what it feels and does. For Nietzsche, by contrast, the task of the poet is to assume the role of a seer. He appeals to poets to once again have the desire to become what they were once held to be "*seers*, who recounted to us something of the *possible*!": "If only they wanted to let us experience in advance something of *future virtues*! Or of virtues that will never exist on earth, although they could exist somewhere in the world—of purple-glowing galaxies and whole Milky Ways of the beautiful! Where are you, you astronomers of the ideal?" (*D* 551). This conception of the poet as a seer (*Seher*) is not simply that of the poet as the one who pushes beyond observations accessible to everyone—Nietzsche is not making a literal reference to eyesight—since the stress is on prefiguring new ways of thinking, feeling, and living.[5] The contrast with Schopenhauer reveals an important difference between the two thinkers and highlights a distinctive feature of Nietzsche's thinking, namely, its concern with the future. Schopenhauer infamously has no hope or belief in the future. The response to the problem of existence is aesthetic contemplation and ascetic renunciation. Georg Simmel astutely noted that Schopenhauer's pessimism is not drawn from positive pain so much as it is derived from ennui, including the dulling monotony of days and years. Moreover: "It is the absence of the idea of evolution which condemns the world and mankind to always being the same, without solace" (1986, 8–9). For Nietzsche, by contrast, there are "possibilities of life" to be discovered (*HH* 261), and the human being remains the undetermined animal (*BGE* 62).[6]

Although Nietzsche is highly critical of the poets of his time, he does esteem the poet as an artist and educator. In a note from the autumn of 1880, for example, he places the poet in a higher order of artists and thinkers than the musician. Musicians do not know, he argues, the refraction and color of a feeling in the flash of thought but rather coarsen all states by translating them back into the inhuman as if thoughts and words had not yet been invented. Music seems to provide us with the return of primal nature, and we may be attracted to it for this reason. Nietzsche, however, prefers an aesthetics centered on the whole human being:

> Music has little sound for the delights of the spirit; if it wants to reproduce the state of Faust and Hamlet and Manfred, it omits the spirit and paints states of mind that are extremely unpleasant, without spirit.... [I]t coarsens and paints the displeasure and misery, perhaps with a musical spirit;

> but how terrible is this art when it paints the ugly without selection: what tortures are inherent in the tones, the obtrusive tones! . . . The poet stands higher than the musician, he makes higher demands, namely, to the whole human being: and the thinker makes even higher demands: he wants all the fresh energy he has collected and calls not for enjoyment but for wrestling and the deepest renunciation of all personal drives. (*KSA*, vol. 9, fragment 6 [39], pp. 203–4)

He contests the idea that music "is in itself profound and meaningful" by somehow speaking, for example, of the will (to life) and the thing-in-itself, or, more simply, our inner being. Rather, it is the intellect that places significance in sounds (*HH* 215).

In the course of our evolution, we have developed the unique skill of seeking to understand the feelings of other people, something that we constantly deploy when we are in their presence. Sometimes we do attempt to understand the emotions and moods of another through recourse to reason, such as asking ourselves, Why is this person feeling depressed? More commonly, however, we seek to produce the feelings of another in ourselves according to the effects these feelings exhibit in the physical movements of this other person, such as the expression of the eyes and the gait. It is music that illustrates best for us this process of how we have become masters in "the rapid and subtle deciphering of feelings" that constitutes the art of empathy (*Mitempfindung*, lit. "feeling with"): "[M]usic is, namely, an imitation of an imitation of feelings and yet, despite this remoteness and indefiniteness, it often enough still makes us partake of those emotions to the degree that, like complete fools, we grow mournful without the slight est cause for mourning merely because we hear tones and rhythms that somehow remind us of the voice or movement of mourners or even of their customary practices." We can develop an evolutionary explanation of this skill we have developed to reproduce in ourselves the feelings of others, to the point that it has become second nature for us. Nietzsche's explanation is that the human being is the most timorous of all creatures, and so it is on account of our subtle and fragile nature that we have been instructed in empathy: "For millennia upon millennia he saw in everything alien and alive a danger: with each appearance he immediately reproduced the expression of features and bearing and formed his conclusion about the type of malevolent intent behind them. Humans have even applied this interpretation of all movements and lineaments as *emanating from intentions* to the nature of inanimate things—in the delusion that nothing inanimate exists" (*D* 142).

In short, then, it is fear that has served for us as the "instructress of understanding." For example, when we speak of our having a "feeling for nature"—as when we view "sky, field, cliff, forest, storm, stars, sea landscape, springtime," and so on—it is the age-old operation of fear that explains how our sentiments provide our experiences with a second, ulterior meaning. This then allows us to experience other emotions: "Joy and agreeable amazement, and finally a feeling for the ridiculous are . . . empathy's later-born children and fear's much younger siblings." The example Nietzsche gives of music to illustrate how empathy works is an effective one since it shows how our emotions can work on us: "[T]he state of feeling into which music moves us is almost always in contradiction to the blatant reality of our actual situation and to reason, which recognizes this actual situation and its causes" (*D* 142).

One major shift that takes place in Nietzsche's thinking in the middle writings and needs to be taken account of is his changed attitude toward art. For example, whereas in *The Birth of Tragedy* (1872) and the four *Unfashionable Observations* (1873–75) it is art that dominates his thinking about culture, be it an artist's metaphysics ("only as an aesthetic phenomenon are existence and the world justified to eternity" [*BT* 7]) or the need to will illusion, in the middle writings it is the passion of knowledge that now governs his thinking, and this necessarily means that art is now valued by him in a way different to the views we encounter in his early writings. In *Human, All Too Human*, Nietzsche lets it be known that he maintains that there has not yet been any philosopher who has not eventually looked down on the philosophy he invented in his youth with disdain or at least with suspicion (*HH* 253). In an unpublished note from 1877, he discloses that he has abandoned the metaphysical-artistic views of his early writings (*KSA*, vol. 8, fragment 23 [159]). In particular, he wants to overcome what he calls the "deliberate holding on to illusion" as a foundation of culture (*KSA*, vol. 10, fragment 16 [23]).[7] He is seeking to overcome what he calls *Jesuitism*, which he located in his predecessors in German philosophy and himself. In the words of one commentator, this means not allowing the uncovering of the limits of human knowledge to be conducted in such a way that the task also gives free rein to the metaphysical need, which is the need to ask the grand questions concerning the first and last things, a need that fails to recognize that where there is darkness the human mind succeeds only in making things even murkier (Montinari 2003, 60). Where it has not been possible to establish certainties of any kind in our efforts to penetrate this dark region, an entire moral-metaphysical world has been displaced into it, the fantasies of which posterity is then asked to take seriously and for truth (*WS* 16). In making this point, Nietzsche is close to Hume. For Hume, we need to curtail our imagination since it is "naturally sublime" and so "delighted with whatever is remote and extraordinary" (1999, 208). Nietzsche proposes that a mature humanity would be one that weaned itself off its need of metaphysics since it is based on error and a failure of the intellect. The need is not the origin of religions, as Schopenhauer supposed, but rather a "religious after-shoot" (*GS* 151).[8] Santayana nicely pinpoints the core error: "an abuse that occurs whenever logical, moral, or psychological figments are turned into substances or powers placed beneath or behind the material world, to create, govern, or explain it" (1940, 274). Nietzsche advises us to practice indifference toward supposed knowledge with respect to the first and last things and become instead good neighbors of the nearest things. Our task is to focus on what is tangible and sensible and not gaze beyond the closest things as we have hitherto contemptuously done, living in clouds, and conversing with monsters of the night.

In his self-criticism of 1886, written as a preface to *The Birth of Tragedy*, Nietzsche shows himself to be an astute critic of his own writings. He looks back on his youthful first book and finds it "an impossible book . . . image-mazed and image-crazed," hinting at the fact that there is a distinct lack of clarity in its usage of concepts. He writes perspicaciously of its lack of "logical cleanliness." It is, he says, "sugary to the point of effeminacy" and "too arrogant to prove its assertions"; in short, it manifests bad philosophy. This does not mean it is not posing some important questions, such as asking whether pessimism is necessarily a sign of weakness, of decline and decay, and whether there might be a pessimism of strength that would consist in having an intellectual predilection for the hard, gruesome, and problematic aspects of existence and stem from an overall feeling of well-being.

In the *Gay Science* aphorism "Our Ultimate Gratitude to Art," Nietzsche credits art with having "the *good* will to appearance [*Schein*]" (*GS* 107). It makes existence bearable for us by providing us with ways of taking a rest from ourselves, gaining an artistic distance, and so enabling us to laugh and weep at ourselves. Because we are such grave and serious creatures—"more weights than human beings"—it helps if we can "discover the *hero* no less than the *fool* in our passion of knowledge." Although the passion may be foolhardy in some respects—since we do not know exactly where it will lead us and human narcissism will be challenged in all kinds of ways—we may also find that we discover new truths about ourselves and that such knowledge then encourages us to create new values and virtues. Art exists to help us endure existence as we pursue the passion of knowledge and experience ourselves as both fools and heroes. Although we honor truth on account of its tremendous power, we must guard against it assuming a tyrannical status in our lives. A dedication solely to truth will make our existence tasteless, powerless, and boring. It is thus necessary to be in a position from time to time to recuperate in forms of untruth (*D*

507).[9] It is these insights that guide aspects of Nietzsche's thinking about art in his middle writings.

Suspicions about the Poets

Nietzsche expresses several suspicions about the poets. For example, he is keen to expose what he sees as the mythological sensibility that informs our appreciation of art and refers to a science of art that will now contradict the illusions we have about it and point out "the erroneous reasoning and self-indulgence that lead the intellect into the artist's net" (*HH* 145). He points out that when it comes to the apprehension of truths the artist has a "weaker morality" than the thinker and so cannot be relied on. This is because the artist is so committed to his brilliant and meaningful interpretations of life that he will not allow the sober, simple methods and results of science to impinge on them. Instead, in struggling for his vision of "the higher dignity and meaning of humanity," the artist is devoted to presuppositions that prove so effectual for his art and craft, namely, "what is fantastic, mythical, uncertain, extreme" and executed with a "sense for the symbolic, the overestimation of his own person, the belief that there is something miraculous in genius" (*HH* 146).

Nietzsche construes artists as figures who juvenilize humanity. This is both their glory and their limitation. They cannot, therefore, be said to stand in the forefront of a new Enlightenment and the progressive maturation of humanity (*HH* 147). Indeed, Nietzsche contends that the artists of all ages "are the glorifiers of the religious and philosophical errors of humanity" and mentions in this regard Dante's *Divine Comedy*, the paintings of Raphael, the frescoes of Michelangelo, and Gothic cathedrals (*HH* 220). Philosophy fares little better for Nietzsche. In *Dawn*, he cannot conceal his irritation with philosophy when it sets its sight on getting behind the veil of appearance and accessing either divine being (Plato and dialectics) or the horror of the world (Schopenhauer and the opposite of dialectics): "[T]he thing to which they want to show us the way does not *exist* at all.—And up until now haven't all of humanity's great passions been just such passions for nothing? And all their solemnities—solemnities about nothing?" (*D* 474).[10]

Nietzsche further contends that the poets exist to soothe and heal life, but they do so only temporarily and even "keep people from working toward genuine improvement of their circumstances," palliating the discharge of the passion that would impel them to act (*HH* 148). Moreover, he holds that the images the artist creates for himself and presents to others, including images of the human being and images of life, can have validity only for a certain time "because humanity as a whole has come to be and is changeable, and even the individual human being is neither fixed nor enduring." Art can teach us well about the need to take pleasure in existence without too fervent engagement with it. It can also teach us the importance of viewing human life as a piece of nature, as an object whose development is governed by laws. However, Nietzsche thinks that this latter teaching now expresses itself in us as an omnipotent need to know, and, in this respect, it is possible to appreciate that the scientific human being represents a further development of the artistic one (*HH* 222).

In an unpublished sketch of 1875, "On the Poet," and anticipating what he will go on to argue in the volumes of *Human, All Too Human*, Nietzsche approaches the poet as a deceiver who "*imitates being a knower*" and argues: "Sleep and dream for the head—that is what the artist is for human beings. He makes things *more valuable*: because people *believe* that what seems more valuable is *truer*, more real. Even today, poetic people (for example, Emerson or Lipiner) prefer to seek the limits of knowledge, indeed, skepticism, in order to withdraw from the path of logic. They want uncertainty because then the magician, intuition and great effects upon the soul become possible once again."[11] Nietzsche's criticism of Emerson is questionable. Emerson himself insists, for example, on poetry's "science" and on the poet as a "truer logician." Indeed, he names poetry "the *gai science*." He conceives of poetry in these terms because, he thinks, the "poet is enamored of thoughts and laws" (2010a, 20, 19, 22).[12] In "Poetry and Imagination," Emerson several times appeals to poetry as a species of sanity, and he means this in two senses: first, in the sense of showing "that life should not be mean" and with the aid of it, although we may lose our wit, we gain our reason, and, second, in the sense that the poetry that elevates us will dissipate the dreams under which we reel and stagger, bringing in new thoughts and a sense of the heroic, showing us that "[t]he grandeur of our life exists in spite of us" (2020, 30, 42).

Nietzsche's development as a poet-philosopher after this moment in his intellectual evolution is a complex affair. I shall probe it more in the next chapter, devoted to *Thus Spoke Zarathustra*. By the time of *The Gay Science*, Nietzsche has assumed a philosophical persona like Emerson's, a professor of the joyous science, as the title of the work indicates. In his notebooks of 1881, there are two devoted to Emerson, the second one taking the form of excerpts from Emerson's *Essays*. This is significant since it reveals that in the middle of working out the project of "la gaya scienza" he is reading Emerson intensively and is inspired by his ideas.[13]

Nietzsche continues to express suspicions about the poets in *Mixed Opinions and Maxims* with the claim that they tend to disparage reality, transforming it in the process into "something uncertain, apparent, counterfeit, full of sin, sorrow, and deceit." He even goes so far as to suggest that they aim at this and are secretly conscious of it as part of their power over human minds and so indulge in "every skeptical extravagance in order to spread the crumbled veil of uncertainty over things" (*MOM* 32). This would not be so dangerous to future human health and well-being were it not for the fact that so many poets spread obscurity and exercise their sorcery and magic as a way of enticing people into believing that they are offering the way to the true truth and the real reality. We should not be surprised, then, as many readers of Nietzsche might be, when he expresses a deep interest in "Plato's great question concerning the moral influence of art" (*HH* 212). In *The Wanderer and His Shadow*, he argues that the thoughts of poets are not worth as much as we think: "[W]e are not only paying for them, but also for the veil and our own curiosity" (*WS* 105). In *The Gay Science*, he refers to the saying credited to Homer: "'Many lies tell the poets'" (*GS* 84).[14] In this aphorism on the origin of poetry, Nietzsche challenges the view that holds that the wild and beautiful irrationality of poetry is of value because it is beyond utility. When poetry came into existence in ancient times, he argues, the aim was "a very great utility," and "the utility in question was *superstitious*." Rhythm, for example, was intended to impress the gods more deeply with some human petition, with the poets noticing that human beings remember verse much better than they do ordinary speech: poetry was thrown at the gods, then, "like a magical snare." Nietzsche concludes this long aphorism by suggesting we ought to find it amusing to this day that the most earnest philosophers, "however strict they may be in questions of certainty, still call on what poets have said in order to lend their ideas force and credibility." Is it not, he concludes, and just before referring to Homer, "more dangerous for a truth when a poet agrees than when he contradicts it"? (*GS* 84). Echoing Nietzsche, the Mexican poet and essayist Octavio Paz notes in his study *The Bow and the Lyre*: "The tale and its representation are inseparable. Both are already in the rhythm, which is drama and dance, myth and rite, story and ceremony. The twofold reality of the myth and the rite rests on the rhythm, which contains them." Moreover, he notes: "The poet's process is no different from conjuration, enchantment, and other magical procedures. And the poet's attitude is very similar to the magician's. . . . [B]oth act for utilitarian and immediate ends: they do not ask themselves what language or nature is but use them for their own purposes" (1973, 47, 42). Paz is not saying that the poet is a magician but rather noting that like the magician the poet utilizes rhythm as a means of seduction.

In expressing interest in Plato on the quarrel between philosophy and poetry, Nietzsche is not endorsing Plato's view that the poets—storytellers—should be banished from the *polis*. Rather, his aim is to raise a suspicion about art and to argue that unless it attaches itself to a specific noble task, such as being an educator and cultivating the self, art will lose sight of its true vocation and become little more than a medium for giving vent to barbarizing impulses. As Santayana notes, although Plato's judgment on the arts and poetry has been generally condemned by philosophers, it is eminently rational, "justified by the simplest principles of morals" (2009, 272).[15] In addition, we may note that in the *Apology* Socrates criticizes the poets as a strict philosopher, that is, as a questioning skeptic: "I decided that it was not wisdom that enabled them to write their poetry, but a kind of instinct or inspiration, such as you find in seers and prophets who deliver all their sublime messages without knowing in the least what they mean" (Plato 1993, 45 [*Apology* 22c]). Moreover, as one reader notes, Plato's great worry is that poets—including ones of a certain stature and authority, such as Homer and Sophocles[16]—pander to the audience's lowest self even as they purport to address the highest and most important matters, such as the nature of excellence, and so disable audiences from understanding what justice is, one of philosophy's chief concerns (Crotty 2009, 118). Aspects of Plato's worry find an echo in the suspicions Nietzsche raises about the poets.

The issue of the poets telling lies is a complex one in Nietzsche. Cognizance needs to be taken of observations we find in his early notebooks that assume an especially dramatic form in the story of Zarathustra (*Z* 2 "Of the Poets"; *Z* 4 "The Song of Melancholy" and "Of Science") and that I consider in the next chapter. In the unpublished essay "On Truth and Lies in an Extra-Moral Sense" from 1873, Nietzsche notes how the human animal allows itself to be deceived and becomes "enchanted with happiness when the rhapsodist tells him epic fables as if they were true" (*PT*, 89). In the notes for his planned *Philosophenbuch* from the early 1870s, he writes: "Now, however, what is rare and unaccustomed is *more attractive*: the lie is felt as a stimulus. Poetry" (*PT*, 51).[17] As Charles Kahn (1979, 11) notes, it was part of a popular tradition in ancient times for the bards to be accused of telling many a lie. In their defense, the poets felt justified in the art of telling lies—the lie as an expression of imaginative powers and inventive thinking—by assuming the right to correct their predecessors and rejecting or reshaping a familiar story. In a note from 1876–87, Nietzsche readily acknowledges that storytelling is an essential feature of the human animal conceived as the interpretive animal in need of meaning: "Anyone who wants to give the deepest meaning to life entangles the world in fables; we are all still deeply tangled up in it, however free-minded we may seem to ourselves" (*KSA*, vol. 8, fragment 23 [133]; *SUP*, 12:409). The question for us moderns is what kind of story about the meaning of the earth we now choose to tell. Humans have a poeticizing drive (*dichterische Trieb*), and after the event of the death of God its cultivation needs to work in ways that do not nourish the human capacity for fantasy since this only encourages the "human being as the animal gone mad" that lives in "pure delusion" (*KSA*, vol. 9, fragment 11 [77]; *SUP*, 6:330).

On Shakespeare and Corneille

Nietzsche suggests, with reference to Homer describing Achilles, that a real writer is one who gives words to the affects and experiences of others. Artists are not themselves persons of great passion, he thinks, although they often present themselves as such. Furthermore, although artists may exist as unbridled individuals, it is not in their mode of living that they are artists and cultivate their craft (*HH* 211). In the aphorism "The Revolution in Poetry," he argues that the task of the artist is to freely limit himself or herself in the most severe, even arbitrary way and to do so to ensure that "naturalizing impulses" are conquered (*HH* 221; cf. *BGE* 188). If we trace the history of music, for example, what we observe is how musicians learned artistic grace, so bringing "the highest suppleness in movement." The situation, he contends, is different in the case of modern poetry, where there has taken place a "leap into naturalism" (*HH* 221). Goethe inspires us, Nietzsche notes, insofar as he made the effort to bind himself in ever new and varied ways, but even he could go only as far as continual experimentation permits.

In the aphorism "The Revolution in Poetry," it is Voltaire and his aesthetic moderation that Nietzsche prizes. Voltaire is a dramatist who deployed Greek moderation to "restrain a polymorphic soul that could encompass the greatest tragic thunderstorms"; Nietzsche holds that he had a Greek ear and a Greek aesthetic conscientiousness in his handling of prose discourse.[18] Indeed, he will declare the possession of an aesthetic conscience to be a sine qua non for being an artist since it is the only thing that can prevent the artist and the writer from becoming the fanatic of an artistic faction (*MOM* 133). He compares Voltaire's freedom of spirit and unrevolutionary disposition with the woeful predicament of the modern spirit characterized by restlessness and a hatred of moderation and restraint. He even follows Voltaire in conceiving Shakespeare as "the 'great barbarian'" (*HH* 221).[19] Furthermore, whenever we encounter a great artist or poet, we ought to ask ourselves, What is the new constraint this artist or poet has imposed on himself or herself? Nietzsche adds: "For what we call 'invention' (with respect to meter, for example), is always this sort of self-imposed fetter." The creative artist or poet, then, is always "dancing in chains." In Homer, for example, it is possible to perceive an abundance of formulas and rules for epic narration "*within* which he had to dance." At the same time, the poet created a set of new conventions for poets who came after him (*WS* 140). Nietzsche is keen to stress that the clarity, simplicity, and order we associate with ancient Greek art, such as tragedy or the epigram, was not given to the Greeks as a gift and that we deceive ourselves if we think otherwise. Although periodically subject to "a dark, overflowing flood of mystical impulses, elementary savagery, and gloom," the Greeks succeeded in returning to the light as good swimmers and divers, "the people of Odysseus" (*MOM* 219).

What are we to make of Nietzsche's endorsement of the reception of Shakespeare as the barbarian? Santayana's definition of the barbarian may be relevant since it focuses on an issue that is at the heart of Nietzsche's consideration of the poets: "For the barbarian is the man who regards his passions as their own excuse for being; who does not domesticate them either by understanding their cause or by conceiving their ideal goal" (1900/1989, 108).[20] In reading Shakespeare as a moralist, in the sense of the French tradition that he greatly admires and that runs from Montaigne through to Chamfort, Nietzsche argues that, although Shakespeare may have reflected a great deal on the passions and possessed a temperament that gave him access to many of them, he was not capable like Montaigne of speaking about them but instead "placed observations *about*" them in the mouths of several impassioned figures. The result, he claims, is that Shakespeare's dramas are full of ideas to the point "that they make all others seem empty and easily arouse a general antipathy against them" (*HH* 176).[21]

Like Nietzsche, Coleridge takes Shakespeare to be a moralist but one who does not promulgate "any party tenets." If he must have a name, Coleridge writes, he is best styled as a "philosophical aristocrat." Indeed, Coleridge locates Shakespeare's maturity as a poet in the way he portrays intensely individualized characters: "He had virtually surveyed all the great component powers and impulses of human nature—had seen that their different combinations and subordinations were in fact the individualizers of men, and showed how their harmony was produced by reciprocal disproportions of excess or deficiency" (Coleridge 1969, 228). In short, the manner in which Shakespeare portrays the passions is best seen in the context of his attempt to present his audience with such highly individualized characters. And it should be noted that in reflecting on "the poetry of barbarism," where he considers the examples of Whitman and Robert Browning, Santayana does not conceive Shakespeare as a barbarian. Although not a philosopher, Shakespeare, he argues, thinks "far above the passionate experience" and "on the plane of universal reason." He further argues in a superb insight: "When we read the maxims of Iago, Falstaff, or Hamlet, we are delighted if the thought strikes us as true, but we are not less delighted if the thought strikes us as false. These characters are not presented to us in order to enlarge our capacities of passion nor in order to justify themselves as processes of redemption; they are there, clothed in poetry and imbedded in plot, to entertain us with their imaginable feelings and their interesting errors" (1900/1989, 116).

In the chapter "Nietzsche's Shakespeare," Andreas Höfele claims to investigate, "for the first time, Nietzsche's relation to Shakespeare in its entire development" (Höfele 2016). However, except for a discussion of *GS* 98, he offers no coverage of Nietzsche's reception of Shakespeare in the middle writings. Aphorism 98 of *The Gay Science* is entitled "In Praise of Shakespeare," and the way Nietzsche concludes it is highly telling since it reveals, once again, the problems he has with the poets: "Before the whole figure and virtue of Brutus, Shakespeare prostrated himself, feeling unworthy and remote. His witness of this is written in the tragedy. Twice he brings in a poet, and twice he pours such an impatient and ultimate contempt over him and it sounds like a cry—the cry of self-contempt. Brutus, even Brutus, loses patience as the poet enters—conceited, pompous, obtrusive, as poets often are—apparently overflowing with greatness, including moral greatness, although in the philosophy of his deeds and his life he rarely attains even ordinary integrity" (*GS* 98). In his notes for this aphorism, Nietzsche, citing dialogue from the play to support his interpretation, understands Brutus to embody "philosophy," someone who "loses patience when the poet approaches with his wisdom and importunity." The tragedy, he thinks, is about having belief in great human beings: "How highly Shakespeare thought of Brutus is shown by the way he drew Caesar, 'Brutus's best friend'—such a genius, and a glorious one at that, but the one who adorns the world must be destroyed if he proves detrimental to freedom" (*KSA*, 14:251). In the published aphorism, Nietzsche makes it clear, however, that he thinks that it was something more than the cause of political freedom that drove Shakespeare to sympathize with Brutus, something that involves an adventure of the poet's own soul, something about which he chose to speak in signs: "What is all Hamlet-melancholy compared to the melancholy of Brutus!" (*GS* 98).[22] Nietzsche is suggesting that Shakespeare may well have identified with Brutus because he too had his gloomy hour and evil angel. This does not stop Shakespeare, he continues, from feeling unworthy before someone of the stature and virtue of Brutus.

In what proved to be his final work, Harold Bloom reads Nietzsche as "[d]esiring to *be* Shakespeare," but failing this, he suggests, he rested content with becoming "a Shakespearean tragic protagonist" (2020, 5). This is to overlook, however, the complex character of Nietzsche's appreciation of the bard. In *Ecce Homo*, he discloses that his "artistic taste stands up for the names of Molière, Corneille, and Racine, not without indignation against a wild genius like Shakespeare" (*EH* "Why I Am So Clever" 3). In this artistic taste, Nietzsche departs from the preferences of one of his intellectual heroes, namely, Stendhal (*BGE* 39; see also *EH* "The Case of Wagner" 3). Stendhal favors Shakespearean drama over the seventeenth-century French drama of Racine and company because in "Racinian tragedy . . . there is never any development of the passions": "Either I am mistaken, or these changes of the passions in the human heart are the most magnificent thing that poetry can hold up to be viewed by the eyes of human beings, whom it at once moves and instructs" (1962, 38). Stendhal gives the example of Macbeth, who, he says, begins as a good man and becomes a bloody monster. For Stendhal (1962, 12), Shakespeare is to be championed over Racine as a tragedian owing to the fact that, as he sees it, the former can better inspire plays that will vitally interest nineteenth-century audiences by giving them dramatic pleasures and not merely epic ones. He holds that a century of troubles, civil wars, and countless acts of treason and torture had well prepared the subjects of Elizabeth's reign for this kind of tragedy, and he sees parallels with the France of his own time dominated by factions, tortures, and plots (Stendhal 1962, 37).[23]

Like Poe before him, Nietzsche holds that in depicting his characters Shakespeare draws on his own reality. Poe draws attention to Shakespeare's "marvellous power of *identification* with humanity at large" and how this accounts for "his magical influence upon mankind": "He wrote of Hamlet as if Hamlet he were; and having, in the first instance, imagined his hero excited to partial insanity by the disclosures of the ghost—he (the poet) *felt* that it was natural he should be impelled to exaggerate the insanity" (1989, 429).[24] Similarly, Nietzsche writes: "I know of no more heart-rending reading-matter than Shakespeare: what must a person have suffered if he needs to be a clown that badly!—Is Hamlet *understood*?" (*EH* "Why I Am So Clever" 4).[25] Although the early Nietzsche presents "Dionysian man" as like Hamlet—the human being who has insight into "the terrible truth" and has developed the wisdom that knowledge kills action (*BT* 7)—subsequent depictions show that he abandons this appreciation because of its metaphysical character. "Dionysian man" is a complete abstraction and exists only in what appears to be a metaphysical moment, a trick of the mind in which our perception of the world and our own existence is utterly static. As his writings develop, Nietzsche comes more and more to read the figure of Hamlet in terms of his critical interest in modern pessimism and melancholy. This is especially evident in his notebooks (see, e.g., *KSA*, vol. 9, fragment 13 [4]; *SUP*, 6:460–61; and *KSA*, vol. 13, fragment 11 [296], p. 119).[26]

Nietzsche is keen to defend tragedy, including Shakespearean tragedy, against the expectation of offering the audience moral lessons (as in moralizing), in which the tragic poet would supply an audience with images of life that seek to turn them against life, when what they need to show is that "'[i]t is an *adventure* to live'" (*D* 240).[27] However, he detects a gloominess in Shakespeare and holds that too many poets reveal an impatience with themselves and become gloomy on account of their desire to take flight from themselves (he mentions the likes of Byron and Musset): they "resemble stampeding horses, who glean from their own creative work only a short-lived joy and ardor that virtually explodes their veins before falling into so wintery a desolation and woebegoneness." Poets thirst to dissolve, typically into an "outside" or into God, and become completely one with him, or, as in the case of Shakespeare, Nietzsche adds, "into images of the most passionate life" (*D* 549). The poet might even thirst for deeds as a way of diverting the self from itself, as Nietzsche finds in the case of Byron.[28] This suggests to him that, in the most extreme examples we encounter of people disclosing in their behavior this drive for action at any price and to the point of recklessness, we need to consult the knowledge and experience of the psychiatrist.

An aphorism in *Dawn* enables us to secure a grasp on how Nietzsche's artistic taste informs both his appreciation of tragedy (and the arts in general) and the stress he places on the cultivation of the passions. The aphorism in question bears the ironic and witty title "*Better People!*" It centers on how a modern humanity experiences art and frames an encounter with this experience in the following instructive terms:

> Everyone says to me that our art is directed toward the greedy, insatiable, unrestrained, disgusted, harassed people of today and opens up for them an image of bliss, loftiness, and otherworldliness next to their own image of a dissolute wasteland: such that they can for once forget and breathe a sigh of relief, indeed, perhaps they bring back from that forgetting an impulse toward flight and toward turning back. Poor artists with such a public as this! With ulterior motives of such a half-priestly, half-psychiatric bent! How much happier and more fortunate was "our great Corneille," as Madame de Sévigné exclaims with the inflection of a woman in the presence of a complete *man*.

Nietzsche goes on in the aphorism to refer to the images of "valiant virtues," "magnanimous sacrifice," and "heroic self-restraint" that Corneille employed to elevate his audience. As he brings the aphorism to a close, we get a glimpse of the model of self-cultivation that is informing his treatment of the passions:

> How differently did he and they love existence, not out of a blind dissolute "will" that one curses because one is unable to kill it, but as a place instead where greatness and humanity are *possible* side by side and where even the strictest constraint of forms, subjugation to princely and priestly arbitrariness, is able to suppress neither pride, nor valor, nor grace, nor the spirit of each individual; on the contrary, it is experienced much more as an *antithetical stimulus and spur* toward innate self-sovereignty [*angeboren Selbstherrlichkeit*] and nobility, to an inherited power of the will and passion! [*Macht des Wollens und der Leidenschaft*]. (*D* 191)

Living a passionate existence for Nietzsche does not mean giving free and spontaneous rein to destructive egocentric energy. As John Cairncross notes, Corneille's characters, such as Rodrigo, Horace, and Augustus, all display a readiness to be faithful to the virtue of *générosité* or nobility of soul: "[T]hey are ready to devote all their inner resources to the task of incarnating their sublime image of themselves. Will-power, self-control, courage, and judgment, all these enhance man's powers and his greatness" (Corneille 1975, 13 [introduction]). Nobility of soul should be equated not with bombast but with the essence of the Roman spirit: "gravity, sobriety and resoluteness" (Corneille 1975, 115 [preface to *Cinna*]).[29] As Maximus implores Emilia in *Cinna* (4.5.1345): "Recall, recall your heroism sublime" (Corneille 1975). The characters in Corneille's plays are neither sublime automata nor unhesitatingly sublime. This is because their task is to become masters of themselves and the world. As Cairncross puts it: "The tragic element in Corneille, then, is not to be sought in the pathetic helplessness of the characters but in the harrowing circumstances in which a wicked fate has placed them." In short, they are implicated in a tragedy of circumstances over which as heroes they must rise superior by relying on their own resources: "People are not born heroes, they become heroes. Corneille's Theatre is, in the literal sense of the phrase, 'a school of moral greatness'" (Corneille 1975, 14 [introduction]).[30]

Nietzsche seeks alternatives to the atavism of vanity.[31] Like Spinoza, he regards self-esteem as a noble virtue and more estimable than either pride or vanity.[32] When we turn our gaze to the modern age and the democratic order of things, we find that the originally noble and rare urge to "'think well' of oneself" and to accord value freely and spontaneously to oneself is being increasingly encouraged and propagated (*BGE* 261). This laudable development is, however, constantly being opposed and mastered by an older and more deeply ingrained urge that manifests itself in the phenomenon of envy and represents the slave in the blood of the vain human being.[33] In several of his texts, Nietzsche endeavors to provide modern human beings with examples of a noble selfishness: "the soul that loves itself the most, in which all things have their streaming and counter-streaming and ebb and flood" (*EH* "Zarathustra" 6).[34] He is keen to remind his readers what it means to practice self-control and proud composure (*BGE* 283–84), to be a master of one's virtues (*BGE* 284), and to have self-respect (*BGE* 287). And it is the noble virtue of generosity of spirit that enables us to conceive of a positive selfishness (see *Z* 3 "Of the Three Evils" 2).

Nietzsche is also keen to spell out what it means to be a creator of value, an aspect of his thinking that is often reduced to caricature. Historians of morality, he thinks, commit a crass error when they begin with the question, "Why do we praise an empathetic action?" Contrary to the assumptions informing this question, he argues: "The noble kind of human being feels *itself* to be value-determining . . . knows itself to be that which imparts honor to things in the first place." Such a human being does not solicit approval but has a "feeling of fullness, of power that wants to overflow . . . the consciousness of wealth that would bestow and give of itself." The noble human being acts from an urge produced by an excess of power: "[B]elief in oneself, pride in oneself, a fundamental hostility and irony toward 'selflessness' belong just as surely to noble morality as a mild disdain and caution toward sympathy and a 'warm heart'" (*BGE* 260). It is in the sense of self-worth, then, which includes understanding how to honor, that Nietzsche speaks of being able to create and determine value as an art and a realm of invention.

Beautiful Human Beings: Nietzsche and Adalbert Stifter

Nietzsche laments the fact that poets are no longer teachers: "However strange it may seem to our age: there were once poets and artists whose souls were beyond the passions, with their convulsions and raptures, and who therefore took pleasure in purer materials, worthier human beings, more delicate combinations and solutions." Today, he reflects, all the talk among artists is on unchaining the will, liberating life, and smashing things. In previous ages, however, the artist was conceived as a tamer of the will, a transformer of animals, and a creator and sculptor of human beings. Whereas the ancient Greeks saw the poet as a teacher of adults, as someone who himself "became a good poem or a beautiful creation," today we are presented with art that is the reflection, even celebration, of little more than "a cave of desires, ruinously overgrown with flowers, prickly plants and poisonous weeds," so presenting the thinker with an object for melancholy reflection because the "most noble and most precious now grow up already in ruins" (*MOM* 172).

A quite specific conception of the role of art in human life informs Nietzsche's consideration of the poet. He contests the idea that the artwork of the artist is the real thing and is all that matters. Against this modern idea he wants us to see and appreciate the artwork as an *appendage of life*. One aim of art is to embellish life, aiding the task of making ourselves tolerable to ourselves and pleasing to others: "[W]ith this task before its eyes, it restrains and reins us in, creates forms for social intercourse, binds ill-bred people to the laws of propriety, purity, politeness, of speaking and keeping silent at the right time." Furthermore, art needs to focus its energy on concealing and reinterpreting everything ugly, "those painful, frightening, disgusting things that will, despite all our efforts, break out again and again in accordance with the descent of human nature." Art needs to address the problems presented by human passions, including "the soul's pains and fears and allow the *meaning* behind whatever is unavoidably or insurmountably ugly to shine through." A human being, therefore, who feels within himself or herself a surplus of "embellishing, concealing, and reinterpreting energies" will "seek to discharge this surplus in artworks" (*MOM* 174). In one aphorism, Nietzsche discloses his interest in the perfecting of the human animal, and, after considering the possibility of a Phidias (a Greek sculptor and poet) in our own time, only to doubt it, he continues:[35] "Even the wish for a poetic Claude Lorrain is at present presumptuous, however much someone commands his heart to yearn for it.—Representing the *last* human, *that is, the simplest and at the same time most complete*, is something of which no artist has yet been capable; but it is perhaps the Greeks who, *in the ideal of Athena*, cast their gaze the farthest of any human being thus far" (*MOM* 177). The nature of the appeal made here to the female warrior Athena is perhaps obvious. She represents for Nietzsche a figure of unity, namely, the unity of culture involving justice, wisdom, and the arts.[36] In aphorism 173 of *Mixed Opinions and Maxims*, Nietzsche conceives of art as the energetic surplus of a wise and harmonious individual. Once again, we see in this commitment to harmony and integration evidence of his concern about the barbaric that is such a feature of modern culture: "*Forward and backward glance*. An art as it flows forth from Homer, Sophocles, Theocritus, Calderón, Racine, Goethe as the *surplus* of a wise and harmonious mode of life—that is the right sort of art, toward which we finally learn to reach when we have ourselves become wiser and more harmonious, not the barbaric, however delightful bubbling over of heated and brightly colored things from an untamed, chaotic soul, which we had earlier, as youths, understood to be art" (*MOM* 173).[37]

In *Human, All Too Human*, poets are said to exist to ease life, and their gaze is typically directed backward toward the past. Nietzsche suggests we can employ them "as bridges to far away times and ideas, to dying or deceased religions and cultures": "They are, in fact, always and necessarily *epigones*" (*HH* 148) In seeking to make our lives easier, poets either turn our gaze away from the toilsome present or aid the present by shining a light on it from the past. It is this preoccupation with the past and bygone times, however, that turns them into deeply melancholic figures or reveals that they are such types. It is only in the second volume of *Human, All Too Human* that Nietzsche enunciates his expectation of the poets of today, assigning to them the specific task of intimating the future and a new cultivation of human beings. The composing of beautiful human beings is not, however, envisaged as an easy task, especially when we consider what he says in aphorism 111 of *Mixed Opinions and Maxims*, chiefly, that today's poets live in too close a proximity to "the sewers of the big cities." This theme is continued in *The Gay Science* where, echoing the preparatory task he assigns to the poets, he writes of the need for preparatory human beings who cannot emerge out of "the sand and slime of present-day civilization and metropolitanism" but rather must exist patiently and cheerfully like shy deer in the forests (*GS* 283).[38] The poet's task is clearly not that of an imaginative political scientist who seeks to anticipate in images more favorable social and cultural conditions that might then give rise to new human beings. Rather, poets need to take their lead from artists of earlier times who sought to compose and recompose images of divine human beings. Now, however, the task is to create images of beautiful human beings, sniffing out cases where, in the midst of the modern world, the beautiful and great spirit can be found. If poets commit themselves to this task, they will help create the future and be distinguished "by seeing to be closed off from and protected against the breath and heat of the *passions*" (*MOM* 99).

Nietzsche spells out why he holds to these views. If the poets focus on "smashing the entire human frame," they will be overburdened by such a task and may well end up producing little more than "mocking laughter" and "gnashing their teeth," simply because they will be dealing with "everything tragic and comic in the usual old sense." In short, the danger of the poets who pursue the task in this way will be one of promoting despair and thus encouraging a mood of profound melancholy to take root in human souls. Instead, Nietzsche encourages poets to develop the sense of moderation, along with strength and mildness, cultivating "a level ground that gives rest and pleasure to the foot, a shining heaven mirrored in faces and events" in which knowledge and art flow together into a new unity. What is needed from the poets is "the grace of seriousness" and not "the impatience of division." Nietzsche ends the aphorism by referring to this art of the poets as being informed by an "inclusive, general, golden background" on which, for the first time, "the delicate *differences* among embodied ideals would make up the actual *painting*—that of an ever-increasing majesty." Although several paths lead to this poetry of the future from the example of Goethe, the need remains for many more good pathfinders and a greater power than can be found in today's poets, who are little more than "inoffensive depicters of semi-animals and of an immaturity and immoderation that they confuse with force and nature." The poets will help build the future by composing images of beautiful and great spirits that will stimulate envy and imitation. Such spirits will be shown embodying themselves "in harmonious, well-proportioned circumstances," revealing "visibility, durability, and exemplarity" (*MOM* 99). In a note from 1881, Nietzsche appeals to "*beautiful, joyful* humans" to lead the way and construct society on a foundation of integrity (*Redlichkeit*) (*KSA*, vol. 9, fragment 6 [203]).

The ideas Nietzsche puts into play in his middle writings continue to resonate in his subsequent and later texts, for example, in the critique he offers of the sublime human beings in *Zarathustra* who return gloomily from the forest of knowledge, having failed to learn the lessons of beauty, and are depicted by him as tense, wild beasts. Beauty is to be equated with gracefulness and a nonviolent will: "When power grows gracious and descends into the visible: I call such descending beauty" (*Z* 2 "Of the Sublime Ones"). The discourse on the sublime ones in *Zarathustra* clarifies Nietzsche's sense of beauty, though much remains teasingly enigmatic. We remain merely sublime when we continue to hide our playful monsters, ultimately presenting ourselves as something ugly.[39] Like Emerson, Nietzsche subscribes to the view that beauty is, in Emerson's words, "the most enduring quality," bound up with "the grace of movement" (2003, 154–55).[40]

In his remarkable study of Nietzsche, Ernst Bertram (1918/2009, 208) suggested that the main inspiration for Nietzsche's conception of beautiful human beings comes from the writings of the Austrian poet and storyteller Adalbert Stifter, especially his novel of 1857, *Indian Summer*.[41] In the literature on Stifter, there is a long-standing debate about the relation of *Indian Summer* to conceptions of utopia, including the paradise of the blessed isles.[42] Bertram sees Nietzsche being drawn to Stifter's novel in terms of a pedagogical utopia, and this insight helps explain, at least in part, his great interest in it.[43] In "Upon the Blessed Isles," where it is said to be autumn all around with a pure sky and afternoon, Zarathustra gives expression to his fundamental desire, which is to see humanity's creative will come into being: "Behold, what abundance is around us! And it is fine to gaze out upon distant seas from the midst of superfluity [*Überfluss*]. Once you said 'God' when you gazed upon distant seas; but now I have taught you to say 'superhuman'" (*Z* 2 "Upon the Blessed Isles"). It is on reading Stifter's novel that Nietzsche becomes inspired by the thought that the poet needs to persuade others that a rich harvest awaits and that all may not yet be lost to us.

In a November 5, 1879, letter to Ida Overbeck in Basel, Nietzsche requests that his copy of Stifter's novel be specially bound and then well wrapped and sent to him in Venice (*KSB* 5, p. 462). In an April 28, 1881, letter to Franz Overbeck, he reminisces about the experience of reading the novel the previous year with him (*KSB* 6, p. 88). And, finally, in an April 19, 1887, letter to Peter Gast, he confides that he finds Gast's lion music "as refreshing, healing, heartfelt, cheerful [*heiter*]" and "transfigured" as Goethe's *Löwennovelle* and Stifter's *Nachsommer* (*KSB* 8, pp. 60–61). Bertram is correct to note that Nietzsche's love of Stifter is not an early attachment on his part, one that he would disavow in later years, like his love of Schumann. Rather, it is a love of the mature Nietzsche, ripening and ripened, "directed solely at the autumnal poet who wrote *Der Nachsommer*" (1918/2009, 203).[44]

Nietzsche expresses his admiration of Stifter in his middle writings. If we leave to one side the writings of Goethe, especially the conversations with Eckermann and "the best German book that exists," only four German books remain that merit being read again and again: "Lichtenberg's aphorisms, the first book of Jung-Stilling's biography, Adalbert Stifter's *Nachsommer* and Gottfried Keller's *Leute von Seldwyla*" (*WS* 109). Nietzsche's admiration of Stifter is also revealed in the notebooks of the late period. For example, in reflecting on what is born in the nineteenth century from relative plenitude, and revealing a self-confidence, he remarks: "[A]mong poets, e.g., Stifter and Gottfried Keller are signs of greater strength, inner well-being" (*KSA*, vol. 12, fragment 10 [2], p. 454; *WP* 1021). In a note from October–November 1888, Nietzsche discloses that *Indian Summer* is the only German book after Goethe that has magic for him (*KSA*, vol. 13, fragment 24 [10], p. 634). The Indian summer in Stifter's novel, completed when he was fifty-two years old, is the blossoming time of one's life, the time when the roses cultivated through many hard years of toil burst forth in full bloom. It is this time to which Nietzsche is referring when in the note of October–November 1888 he writes of an autumnal mood of the soul, "golden and sweetening," telling of an October sun of profound serenity. In *The Wanderer and His Shadow*, he writes of the "constantly sunny October air" as an atmosphere where Italy and Finland "have come together in union, in a place that seems to be home to all the silvery tints of nature:—how happy is he who can say: 'There is certainly much that is greater and more beautiful in nature, but *this* I find to be intimate and familiar to me, related by blood, indeed, even more than that'" (*WS* 338; see also *WS* 109). Nietzsche depicts this mood and experience in "Upon the Blessed Isles" in *Zarathustra*: "Thus, like figs do these teachings fall to you, my friends: now drink their juice and eat their sweet flesh! It is autumn all around and pure sky and afternoon."

In *Indian Summer*, Nietzsche would have found references to several poets of interest to him, including Homer, Shakespeare,[45] and Goethe, along with discussions between the main characters on a range of topics that we can surmise resonated deeply with him, including reflections on life in the city contrasted with life in the country, a stress on the need to approach the study of the human animal and its history through the lens of the natural sciences, and reflections on the importance of beauty in life, on the need to become a master of the emotions, and on the role of the poets. Indeed, in the chapter of Stifter's *Indian Summer* entitled "Die Erweiterung," the poets are referred to as the greatest benefactors of mankind, indeed, as "the priests of the beautiful" (Stifter 2005, 334; and Stifter 2009, 196; see also Stifter 1994, 7; and Stifter 2021, 3). According to one commentator (Gump 1974, 99–100), love of beauty, including nature, the human body, art, and human relations, is the basic theme of the novel. As Bertram (1918/2009, 204) asked, why did Nietzsche so much love a book by a poet so unlike himself? The answer is that he saw in it the possibility of "an entire world of beauty," as he confides in a letter of 1887 to Peter Gast (*KSB* 8, pp. 60–61). Stifter saw himself not as a Goethe but simply as one of his kin. From his writings, so he hopes, "the seed of the pure, noble, simple goes out to men's hearts" to direct their minds and lives away from the "odious, disgusting nihilism" that surrounds them (Stifter quoted in Bruford 1975, 130). As one commentator has noted: "Science and Art are the two educative factors of most importance in *Der Nachsommer* and they synthesize in the garden of the 'Rosenhaus'" (Blackhall 1948, 319). Indeed, in the novel the main character, a young man named Heinrich Drendorf, a student of the natural sciences, confides that it is the history of the earth that represents the most stimulating and promising history there is, "where man is only an interpolation, who knows how small a one, and can be superseded by other histories of perhaps higher beings" (Stifter 2005, 328; Stifter 2009, 192).[46] In the chapter "*Die Erweiterung*," Drendorf distances himself from bombastic writers who fail to "portray Nature as it is within and outside the human" but instead "make it more beautiful, seeking to elicit certain effects": "In natural science I had gotten used to observing the characteristics of things, to value those qualities and pay homage to their essential nature. I found no qualities whatsoever amongst the authors of bombast." He concludes: "[I]t seemed the height of ridiculousness that someone who had learned nothing was trying to create something" (Stifter 2005, 329; Stifter 2009, 193). Indeed, in the novel it is clearly stated that the sublimity (*Erhabenheit*) of the books we read should be drawn into our earthly needs (Stifter 2005, 217; Stifter 2009, 129).

Hannah Arendt identifies Stifter's greatness as a writer in the way he brings out into the open "the last implications of the philosophy of man that underlies the German educational novel." Stifter, she suggests, is "the true heir of Goethe's prose," someone for whom *Wilhelm Meister* "probably was the always-present model." She describes Stifter as the greatest landscape painter in literature, even greater than Goethe: "someone who possesses the magic wand to transform all visible things into words and all visible movements—the movement of the horse as well as that of the river or the road—into sentences" (2007b, 110–11). Although Arendt provides a rich appreciation of Stifter, his novel can be too hastily interpreted in terms of the tradition of the bildungsroman. Margaret Gump (1974,93) has it right, I think, when she argues that *Indian Summer* is best approached in terms of its uniqueness and not simply as an entwicklungsroman or a bildungsroman. The education of the hero, who is already educated at the start of the novel, is not staged in terms of trial, error, and guilt.[47] As one commentator has noted, Heinrich is prepared to probe the nature of existence "to the very frontier of death and meaninglessness": "Though terrified of the void, he resists the seduction of despair by summoning up the forms he has come to love" (Sjögren 1972, 89). Rilke had a wise appreciation of the novel as "one of the most unhurried, harmonious, tranquil books in the world" (quoted in Gump 1974, 94).[48]

In a recent appreciation, Samuel Frederick shows how Stifter sets his novel apart from two prominent genres of his time, the tendentious novel of current times (*Tendenzroman* or *Zeitroman*) and the trivial or entertainment novel (*Unterhaltungsroman*). In these genres, the novelist aims for an effect outside the integrity of the form of the novel, directed either at social and political change or at the reader's satisfaction. Moreover, Stifter's aim of undermining the narrative conventions of the novel as well as the expectations of the reader represents on his part an attempt to tell a story without a story, "a story that would not just convey, but *enact* beauty and truth, without succumbing to plot's constricting devices, which only play into the public's predilection for base pleasures." Such a rich appreciation of the novel as an experiment in postnarrative allows Frederick to develop a thought-provoking insight into the utopia that is presented in the novel, and his insight may well be close to the one that informed Nietzsche's appreciation of the novel concerning the need for an education in harmonious self-cultivation: "[I]ts story can only be told by enacting the end of tellable stories, by creating a narrative that is at once a reflection of this timeless utopian space as well as a sad reminder of our intraversable distance from it" (2012, 163, 167). This recent appreciation of the novel complements an earlier one offered by J. P. Stern, who, in an astute description, noted that the journey undertaken by the hero of the novel is not, strictly speaking, a journey but a composition: "a still life; that is, an assembling of the diverse elements of *Bildung*—moral, spiritual, and emotional as well as scientific and aesthetic—into a unified whole" (1971, 120). And W. H. Bruford astutely notes the heathen sentiments that inform the novel: "Instead of the hope of salvation, the inhabitants of the world of *Der Nachsommer* have before them the ideal of a truly civilized life on earth, a life fashioned to match their disciplined human desires" (1975, 145).

New Dawns

> *Poet and bird.*—The bird Phoenix showed the poet a flaming scroll turning into ashes. "Do not be terrified!" it said, "it is your work! It does not possess the spirit of the times and still less the spirit of those who are against the times: consequently, it must be burned. But this is a good sign. There are many types of dawn."
>
> Nietzsche, *Dawn*, aphorism 568

In *A Week on the Concord and Merrimack Rivers*, Thoreau imagines himself a dweller "in the dazzling halls of Aurora . . . playing with the rosy fingers of the Dawn." He is keen to ensure that what he calls the "matutine intellect of the poet," which dwells in this auroral atmosphere, keeps itself "in advance of the glare of philosophy" (Thoreau 1998, 151, 49–50). By contrast, Nietzsche bestows on both the philosopher and the poet the task of heralding and prefiguring an era of new dawns. In his preface to *Human, All Too Human*, he contends that in any case it is always the future that regulates our today. He further notes that poets can artificially compel the future to appear to us and thus invent and forge it for humanity's consideration (*HH* preface 1).

What role, then, is philosophy to play in this heralding of the future? Nietzsche addresses this issue in several aphorisms in book 5 of *Dawn*. In one, he draws a comparison with the rococo horticulture that arose from the feeling that nature is ugly, savage, and boring and thus that the aim was to beautify it. This is now what philosophy does with science or scholarship, beautifying what strikes us as ugly, dry, cheerless, and laborious (*D* 427).

Nietzsche speaks of philosophy enabling us to wander in science as in wild nature, without effort or boredom. We can take our inspiration from Rousseau's discovery of a feeling for beauty while walking in the Alps and the desert of human existence: where once humans lived in fear of certain regions of nature, we moderns now feel at home in the dimensions of wild nature and the contemplation of a godless universe.[49] In *Dawn*, Nietzsche refers to the realism of contemporary artists and suggests that today our happiness may reside in what is realistic, "in having the most acute senses possible . . . not therefore *in* reality but *in knowing about reality*": "Science has gained such a profound and widespread effect that artists of this century . . . have already become the true glorifiers of scientific 'ecstasies'!" (*D* 433).[50] He wants us to learn to appreciate that knowledge of the ugliest reality can itself be beautiful (*D* 550; see also *TI* "Reconnaissance Raids of an Untimely Man" 19, 20). The realm of beauty is thus getting bigger for us moderns (*D* 468), and we may even come to appreciate that those who pursue knowledge serve to increase the amount of beauty in the world: "[K]nowledge places its beauty not merely around things but, in the long run, into things—may future humanity bear witness to this proposition!" (*D* 550).

Nietzsche calls on thinkers and poets, then, to develop a new aesthetic education of humanity. If we once believed a god takes pleasure in beholding the world, we have now come to understand that it is humans who fashion the world through "*their* aesthetics" (*KSA*, vol. 9, fragment 12 [29]; *SUP*, 6:426). Through a new aesthetic education, we can "reclaim all the beauty and sublimity that we have conferred on things real and imagined as the *property and productivity of human beings* and as their most beautiful ornamentation, most beautiful apology. The human being as poet, as thinker, as god, as power, as compassion" (*KSA*, vol. 9, fragment 12 [34]; *SUP*, 6:427). The beauty and sublimity of nature before which the human appears small "was first *imposed* on nature by us—consequently humankind has been *deprived* of this portion": "It will have to atone for it" (*KSA*, vol. 9, fragment 12 [38]; *SUP*, 6:428). For this aesthetic education to take root we need to know ourselves as poets and creators of our lives. Being neither simply actors nor mere spectators, we invent by always being able to fashion something that was not there before, including "the whole eternally growing world of valuations, colors, accents, perspectives, scales, affirmations, and negations." When human beings fail to recognize what is their best power—the capacity to invent and create—they end up being "*neither as proud nor as happy*" as they might be (*GS* 301).

The discourse "Of Immaculate Perception" in *Thus Spoke Zarathustra* is consonant with these insights. It commences with a reference to the moon rising the day before and Zarathustra expecting it to give birth to a sun, so pregnant does it seem. This is a clear reference to cold knowledge—the kind of knowledge that strips our minds of illusions and delusions—that may contain within it the seeds of new ways of thinking and feeling (see chapter 1 above). However, Zarathustra has allowed himself to be deceived by the moon, and there is more of man in it than there is woman. This is not much of a man, however, since he reveals himself to be a "timid night-reveller"; he is "catlike" and "without honesty." This is a parable that Zarathustra narrates to "sentimental hypocrites of 'pure knowledge.'" Although the seekers of pure knowledge love the earth and all things earthly, they have a bad conscience in their love and are just like the moon. Their love of things of the earth is combined with a healthy contempt of earthly things too, but this does not then express itself as a desire for transforming the earth. Rather, they want to love the earth only as the moon does, touching its beauty "with the eyes alone." They wish, in short, only to gaze and not to create: "And let this be called by me my *immaculate perception* of all things: that I desire nothing of things, except that I may lie down before them like a mirror with a hundred eyes." To this Zarathustra sternly replies: "Truly, you do not love the earth as creators, begetters, humans joyful at entering upon a new existence!" Zarathustra then makes an appeal to a courageous will where one must will with all one's will, including where the will welcomes its own perishing, so that "an image may not remain merely an image" (*Z* 2 "Of Immaculate Perception"). In begetting, then, we can feel the delight of our creative will.

In this discourse, we encounter an oblique set of references to the image of the sun in Plato and how we are expected to emerge from the cave to contemplate the eternal form of the Good represented by the sun (Aristotle too esteems contemplation as the highest end of philosophy). Clearly, the sun is operating quite differently in Nietzsche, signaling the arrival of new life and new dawns—in short, possibilities of life—that cannot be stared at in contemplation but must be fashioned and cultivated:

> But I *approached* you: then day dawned for me—and now it dawns for you—the moon's love affair had come to an end!
>
> Just look! There it stands, pale and detected—before the dawn!
>
> For already it is coming, the glowing sun—*its* love of the earth is coming! All sun-love is innocence and creative desire!
>
> Just look how it comes impatiently over the sea! . . . It wants to suck at the sea and drink the sea's depths up to its height. . . . It *wants* to be kissed and sucked by the sun's thirst, it *wants* to become air and height and light's footpath and light itself!
>
> Truly, like the sun do I love life and all deep seas.
>
> And this *I* call knowledge: all that is deep shall rise up—to my height! (*Z* 2 "Of Immaculate Perception")

Although we are not the originating sources of the world itself, we can recognize ourselves as the creators of value in the world. The world is to be formed in our image as enlightened humans, informed by our reason, our will, and our love.

Once we recognize that there is no absolute truth, we are free to let go of all demands for the absolute (*KSA*, vol. 9, fragment 11 [79]; *SUP*, 6:331). The possession of absolute truth is not simply an accident beyond the range of our minds but incompatible with being alive. As Santayana puts it: "[T]he absolute truth is undiscoverable just because it is not a perspective" (1942, xiii).[51] Our task now is to deanthropomorphize nature after poeticizing ourselves for so long into it and then to "*poeticize* more *into*" ourselves so that in place of simply seeking our ideals of life in philosophies and artworks we fashion ideals of ourselves and for ourselves (*KSA*, vol. 9, fragment 11 [238]; *SUP*, 6:383; see also *KSA*, vol. 9, fragment 11 [276]; *SUP*, 6:397). The goal is "to plant the love for life, for *one's own* life": "*Whatever* each individual devises *for this*, others will let it stand, and will have to acquire a great new tolerance for it: as often as it runs counter to his taste when the individual really increases his joy in his own life!" (*KSA*, vol. 9, fragment 11 [183]; *SUP*, 6:366). And the pertinent question is posed: "How do we give weight to the inner life without it making it evil and fanatic toward those who think differently?" (*KSA*, vol. 9, fragment 11 [172]; *SUP*, 6:361).

[CHAPTER SIX]

Only a Fool, Only a Poet

The Passion of Zarathustra

> [T]he knowledge of nature is only half the task of the poet; he must be acquainted likewise with all the modes of life.... He must write as an interpreter of nature, and the legislator of mankind, and consider himself as presiding over the thoughts and manner of future generations; as being superior to time and place.
>
> Samuel Johnson, *The History of Rasselas Prince of Abissinia*, chapter 10

> God is dead—then who *killed* him? This feeling *of having killed the most sacred and most powerful* needs to strike *individual* human beings—now, though, it is too early! too weak! Murder of murders! We awaken as murderers! How does someone like this console himself? Cleanse himself? *Must he not himself become the most omnipotent and sacred poet?*
>
> Nietzsche, note of 1881

The Passion of Zarathustra

In *Ecce Homo*, Nietzsche writes about the passion that led to the creation of *Thus Spoke Zarathustra: A Book for All and None*,[1] which he composed in four parts between 1883 and 1885 (*EH* "Zarathustra" 6).[2] Indeed, the book can be interpreted as an exemplification of Nietzsche's pedagogical passion. Although Michel Serres does not mention Nietzsche, what he says about the great pedagogues applies well to him: "How can one be surprised that bodies gifted with this completeness would have been seized with the passion of pedagogy? Those who loved their own begetting like to beget. Model of models, Plato, Aristotle, Montaigne, or Rabelais sow their culture with all the knowledge of the time, to model, with this combination, the man to come" (1997, 54). It is also in *Ecce Homo* that Nietzsche writes of his dedication to the art of the grand style and rhythm that expresses the rise and fall of sublime (*sublim*), superhuman passion (*EH* "Why I Write Such Good Books" 4). T. E. Lawrence regarded *Zarathustra*, along with *The Brothers Karamazov* and *Moby-Dick*, as one of those "Titanic books" distinguished by greatness of spirit and sublimity as defined as Longinus (see Steiner 1967, 24). The title of the treatise by Longinus, of uncertain date but typically ascribed to the first century CE, *Peri hypsous,* translated as *On the Sublime, On Greatness,* or *On Eloquence,* literally means "on the height," and the text is concerned with showing how our natural gifts can be led to states of elevation. The "true sublime," says Longinus, which is to be found in "the grand style" of poetry and literature, "uplifts our souls," filling us with "proud exaltation" and a sense of "vaunting joy" (1965, 107).[3] The word *sublime* is derived from the Latin *sublimis,* which is a combination of *sub* (under) and *limen* (a lintel or the top piece of a door, suggesting threshold); thus, in the *Oxford English Dictionary, sublime* is defined as "set high up or raised aloft." The main German word for *the sublime, das Erhabene,* linked to the adverb *erhaben* (raised, elevated), captures well the sense of elevation beyond the ordinary and the familiar that is at work in Nietzsche's utilization of the word. For Nietzsche, it is not so much a question of the sublime providing us with access to some ideal of a rational and universal moral humanity, as in Kant (1989) and Schiller (2001), as it is of certain privileged and superior insights and perceptions manifesting themselves to us, often in special and tremendous moments. Nietzsche wants the reader to experience these moments of sublime perceptions in their encounter with the narrative of *Zarathustra.* Arthur Ransome was insightful when he characterized the book as the "Ossianic poem of a hero of thought" (1913, 122).

Nietzsche immodestly advises the reader who chooses to engage with *Zarathustra* to leave the poets of old aside since "absolutely nothing has ever been achieved, perhaps, from a comparable surfeit of strength" (*EH* "Zarathustra" 6). The thinker is a poet in a broad sense: a creator or an inventor and a stylist of dithyrambs and songs for whom the music of life is not heard simply as the song of the sirens.[4] Nietzsche contends that having wax in one's ears has long been a condition of philosophizing: "[A] real philosopher no longer listened to life insofar as life is music; he *denied* the music of life—it is an ancient philosopher's superstition that all music is sirens' music" (*GS* 372). (See also the final aphorism of *Dawn,* where Nietzsche poses the question whether it is the lot of those in search of new lands to shipwreck on infinity: "Or else, my brothers? Or else?" [*D* 575].) Pursuing this insight further, he claims that philosophers of old were heartless, with their philosophizing operating as a kind of vampirism; ideas live on the blood of the philosopher and consume his senses. With their anemic appearance, our ideas assume a curious existence, and as a way of provoking us to think about the issue Nietzsche gives the example of Spinoza with his idea of the *intellectual* love of God (*amor intellectualis dei*): "Don't you sense a long-concealed vampire in the background who begins with the senses and in the end is left with, and leaves, mere bones, mere clatter? I mean categories, formulas, *words*. . . . What is *amor*, what is *deus*, if there is not a drop of blood in them?" (*GS* 372). When seen in the context of this criticism of philosophy as vampirism, the meaning of Zarathustra's appeal to writing with blood becomes intelligible: "Of all writings I love only that which is written with blood. Write with blood and you will find out that blood is spirit" (*Z* 1 "Of Reading and Writing").[5]

In *Ecce Homo*, Nietzsche opines that as a whole *Zarathustra* "may perhaps be counted as music" and adds that a rebirth of the art of listening is a prerequisite for relating to it (*EH* "Zarathustra" 1).[6] In a draft of the book from the spring–autumn of 1881 entitled "Indications toward a New Life," he outlines its four parts as four movements with, for example, the first book to be written in the style of the first movement of Beethoven's Ninth Symphony and the fourth book to be "dithyrambically comprehensive" (*KSA*, vol. 9, fragment 11 [195–97], pp. 519–20; *SUP*, 6:372–73). It is with the dithyramb that Nietzsche aims to fly "a thousand miles beyond what had hitherto been called poetry" (*EH* "Why I Write Such Good Books" 4; see also *EH* "Zarathustra" 7). Nietzsche also writes of the inspiration that he experienced in writing *Zarathustra* and highlights the importance of "the need for a rhythm with a *wide span*" as "practically the measure of the power of the inspiration, a kind of compensation for its pressure and tension." In a condition of inspiration, the poet experiences revelations where things not ordinarily seen or heard suddenly become visible and audible: "You hear, you don't search; you take, you don't ask who is giving." Although as philosophers we must be distrustful of "truths" that purport to be disclosed by means of inspiration, Nietzsche reveals his true aim as a poet-philosopher when he writes that he wants to make fundamental concepts dance and sing: "'On every allegory you ride here to every truth. Here the words and word-shrines of all Being spring open for you; all Being wants to become word here, all Becoming wants to learn from you how to talk'" (*EH* "Zarathustra" 3). (Nietzsche is quoting himself, with some modification, from *Z* 3 "The Home-Coming.") One way we can give concepts existential meaning and significance, including the most abstract ones such as being and becoming, is by incorporating them and relating them to our experiences of life.

Nietzsche also writes of *Zarathustra*'s wisdom, suggesting that we do not know what truth is until both the highest and the lowest powers of human nature have been comprehended. This is because what we find "sweetest, airiest, and most fearsome" about the human animal "pours forth from a single spring with immortal assuredness" (*EH* "Zarathustra" 6). In *Ecce Homo*, he seeks to illuminate the kind of wisdom offered in *Zarathustra*: "Here speaks no 'prophet,' none of the gruesome hybrids of sickness and will to power called founders of religions." He renounces not only the title of the saint but also that of the sage, if we take *sage* to name someone who wants believers and devoted followers. And he insists that to be receptive to the book's wisdom we "have to *hear* properly" the *halcyon* tone of Zarathustra's speeches, which is the exact opposite of the tone of the fanatic, who seeks to preach and demands faith (*EH* foreword 4). Zarathustra aims to charm the turbulent human mind into quietude so that it may better think and reflect and learn to be honest about its will and desire: "'It is the stillest words that bring on the storm; thoughts that come on doves' feet direct the world'" (*EH* foreword 4, citing *Z* 2 "The Stillest Hour").[7] Nietzsche acknowledges that his book has "the value estimations of a couple of millennia against it," and he worries that modern ears will not have the time to invest in it properly, "to hear the ringing of its overall tone," and meet the challenge of the philological demands it places on readers, such as the need for slow reading (*KSA*, vol. 11, fragment 38 [15]; *SUP*, 16:173).[8]

Zarathustra in Relation to Nietzsche's Middle Writings

In an essay on the drama of Zarathustra, Hans-Georg Gadamer (1998, 220) argues that because *Zarathustra* is a literary work of art it is incorrect to identify the figure of Zarathustra with Nietzsche and Zarathustra's speeches with his philosophy.[9] This does not correspond to Nietzsche's own understanding of the book. Although a distinctive moment in his corpus, the philosophizing we encounter in *Zarathustra* is an important component of the mature philosophy Nietzsche has been developing since the publication of the volumes of *Human, All Too Human* (1878–80). Most commentators assume—on the basis of a remark he makes—that *Thus Spoke Zarathustra* is most closely linked in his corpus to *Beyond Good and Evil*. This is when he states in a letter to his friend Franz Overbeck that the latter text says the same things as the former but in a very different manner (*KSB* 7, p. 223; Middleton 1996, 255). However, reflecting in the mid-1880s on his middle writings after finishing the composition of *Zarathustra*, he wittily discloses to Overbeck that he had written the commentary on the text *before* the text itself (*KSB* 6, p. 496; Middleton 1996, 221–23). This alone indicates just how important it is to work through the middle writings. Indeed, there is much in the text that echoes the key motifs Nietzsche has put into play in them. For example, the imagery of dawn and heralding of new dawns features prominently in the text (*Z* 3 "Of Old and New Law-Tables" 3), and the intellectual virtues he has stated in the middle writings as being of special importance for the development of free spirits, including "one of the youngest virtues," namely, honesty (*Redlichkeit*), are given prominence (*Z* 1 "On Hinterworlders"). Enlightened free spirits are said to feel at home neither in the incomprehensible nor in the irrational. Furthermore, all the conceptions of classical metaphysics, such as "the one," "the perfect," "the unmoved," and "the intransitory," are regarded as misanthropic (*Z* 2 "Of the Blessed Isles"). Such notions do not work in favor of human health—of sanity and serenity—and flourishing, and indeed they lead our vision astray, away from the earth. In taking cognizance of the commitment Nietzsche has in the book to remaining true to the earth and discovering a new earth, we should bear in mind the advice he gives to those keen to promote free-spiritedness in *The Wanderer and His Shadow*, namely, that they "*look directly at* the great task of *preparing* the earth for a growth in the greatest and happiest fertility" (*WS* 189).The discourse "The Famous Wise Ones," featured in part 2 of *Zarathustra*, reveals that Nietzsche conceives the free-spirited philosopher as a figure who is "the enemy of fetters" and "the non-worshipper" and dwells in a particular domain, namely, the forests. This echoes what he has indicated to his readers in the middle writings, such as the way he describes preparatory human beings in *The Gay Science* (*GS* 283). Although it is not without a degree of exaggeration, we would be wise to pay attention to what Nietzsche discloses in a letter to his friend Carl von Gersdorff: "Do not be deceived by this booklet having a legendary air: behind all the simple and strange words stands my *deepest seriousness* and my *whole philosophy*" (*KSB* 6, p. 386; Middleton 1996, 213).

In *Thus Spoke Zarathustra*, Nietzsche assumes the role of the poet as seer we have seen him call for in the middle writings. This development in his thinking should not be taken to mean that he now simply jettisons the concern with truthfulness and assumes the guise of a straightforward liar. Cognizance needs to be taken of how he portrays Zarathustra in *Ecce Homo*, as when he describes him as a thinker who "considers truthfulness to be the highest virtue" and, as such, is said to have "more courage in his body than all thinkers put together." His distinctive virtue, he claims, is "to speak the truth and *shoot well with an arrow*" (*EH* "Destiny" 3). To maintain a fidelity to truthfulness means being courageous in the face of reality, including the full reality of the human being, and not a coward like the idealist who flees from it. Nietzsche has Zarathustra lament the fact that he is a poet since, as a suitor of truth, he relies on metaphors and teaches with the aid of parables. In the earlier *The Wanderer and His Shadow*, he had already noted that, although it is possible to persuade with images and similes, it is impossible to *prove* anything with them (*WS* 145). The task of the poet-philosopher, however, is a specific one: to provide a new meaning for the earth and offer it to humanity as a recommendation and provocation. In addition, with the teaching that we need to remain true to the earth, Zarathustra sets himself apart from the poet as a figure who seeks to draw humanity upward to cloudland, where humans "set out motley puppets on the clouds and then call them gods and supermen." Although Zarathustra observes—in a nod to Hamlet's famous lines, "There are more things in heaven and earth, Horatio, than are dreamt of in your philosophy" (*Hamlet*, 1.5. 166–67)—that poets dream about the things that lie between heaven and earth, he contends that the poets are too attached to heavenly images, even supraheavenly ones. Hence his exclamation that he is weary "of all the unattainable that is supposed to be reality": "Alas, how weary I am of the poets! . . . I cast my net into their sea and sought to catch good fish; but I always drew forth the head of some ancient god" (*Z* 2 "Of Poets").[10] Nietzsche's problem with the poet, then, is not that he is a fool who tells lies, since a lie can serve as a stimulus, but rather with the fact that the poet is too often a figure whose messages to humanity encourage it to invest its energy and hopes in supraterrestrial fantasies.

Zarathustra confides that he would not know how to live if he were not a seer of that which must come, and this is the principal role Nietzsche accords the poet in his writings. He has Zarathustra readily acknowledge, however, the immense problem the teacher of humankind faces as he walks among humans as among fragments and limbs of humans: "When my eye flees from the present to the past, it always discovers the same thing: fragments and limbs and dreadful chances—but no human beings!" (*Z* 2 "Of Redemption"; on this theme see also Lawrence 1931/1974, chap. 23). The task is clear, then, and it consists in cultivating complete human beings.

A Book for All and None

The teaching of *Zarathustra* is offered to everyone and no one: all humans are addressed insofar as they are prepared to incarnate a task of self-overcoming, with the "no-one" in the book's subtitle referring to those who do not wish to question themselves or existence and are merely satisfied with established opinions and comfortable with accepted wisdom about life.[11] We may be tempted to declare, echoing the book of Ecclesiastes, that in the case of the human animal all is vanity and all is in vain. Nietzsche knows well that this idea holds a grip on humanity, serving to cast a cloud of pessimism over the human animal and a sense of futility about its possible future development.[12] In *Zarathustra*, he takes to task this moldy old wisdom of life, finding that it is cheaply bought and brings nothing to the table:

"What's the point of living? All is vanity! Life is—threshing straw; life is—getting burned and still not getting warm."

This kind of ancient drivel is still regarded as "wisdom"; but the fact that it is old and smells moldy *is the reason* it is more admired. Even mustiness ennobles things.—

Children were allowed to talk like this: they are twice *shy* because one time they were burned! There is a lot of childishness in the ancient books of wisdom.

And those who are always "threshing straw," how should they be allowed to slander the act of threshing! Fools like this should really be forced to shut up!

Fools like this sit down at the table and contribute nothing, not even a healthy appetite:—and now they utter this blasphemy, "All is vanity!"

But to eat and drink well, oh my brothers, this is certainly no mean skill! Take these tablets of those who are never happy and smash them, smash them for me!

(*Z* 3 "Of Old and New Law-Tables" 13)

In thinking about the significance of the subtitle Nietzsche gave to *Zarathustra*, we can also consider Carlyle's conception of the poet as a seer and a prophet. In a lecture on the hero as poet, delivered on May 12, 1840, Carlyle argues that, although the hero as prophet is a notion that belongs to the old ages not to be repeated in the new, in some ancient languages the titles *poet* and *prophet* are synonymous, enjoying "much kindred of meaning" (1841/1983, 97). In particular, he suggests, both the poet and the prophet have penetrated the mystery of the universe or what Goethe called "the open secret," which is open to *all* but seen by *none*. This mystery concerns the heady realities of the universe, which do not readily lend themselves to common eyes. In seeing into the secret, the vision of the poet makes hidden things become clear.

In German, the word *Geheimnis* covers both "mystery" and "secret." Nietzsche was, of course, familiar with Goethe's conception of the open secret as well as ancient mysteries such as the Eleusinian ones. In *Twilight of the Idols*, he refers to the Dionysian experience as "this world of secret states" (*TI* "What I Owe the Ancients" 4). In opening the Dionysian secret for our view, he contends: "*Goethe did not understand the Greeks.*" Why? Because, he claims, Goethe did not understand the basic fact of the Hellenic instinct expressed in the psychology of the Dionysian state: "its 'will to life.'"[13] He elaborates on the character of this will as follows: "*Eternal* life, the eternal return of life; the future heralded and consecrated in the past; the triumphant yes to life over and above death and change; *true* life as the totality living on through procreation, through the mysteries of sexuality" (*TI* "What I Owe the Ancients" 4).

Eleusis derives from *Elauno* (I come); hence the mysteries are focused on "coming into being." Cicero viewed the mysteries as concerned more with natural science than with religion, "a recognition of the powers of Nature rather than the power of God" (1972, 118 [bk. 1]).[14] In a consideration of the Eleusinian mysteries, Unamuno (1912/1962, 74) notes that Nietzsche's idea of eternal recurrence is an Orphic one but also that the immortality of the soul is not a philosophical principle. Indeed, Nietzsche has no truck with the Orphic doctrine that the human being must free itself from the fetters of the body to release itself from an imprisoned existence. In *The Tragic Sense of Life*, Unamuno (1912/1962, 187) maintains that we do not hope because we believe; rather, we believe on account of our hope, and this hope for him is belief in a God who guarantees the eternity of consciousness and the human desire for immortal life. If, *pace* Spinoza, it is of the actual essence of a thing to want to persist in its own being, then the essence of the thing we call the *human* is to want to be forever. As Amalia Elguera puts it in her introduction to Unamuno's text, "'Know thyself' comes specifically qualified as 'Know thyself to want to be immortal.'" Unamuno maintains that, like Spinoza, Nietzsche is a rationalist and, furthermore, that, like him, he had "a mad hunger for eternity, for immortality" (1912/1962, 9, 111).[15] In the Christian doctrine of the salvation of the soul through the so-called gift of eternal life, however, Nietzsche sees individual egoism taken to its furthest extreme.[16] In the "enormous lie of personal immortality," he reflects, we see the destruction "of all reason," and "everything natural in the instincts," including their beneficial and life-enhancing qualities, now arouses mistrust: "To live *in this* way, so that there is no *point* to life any more, *this* now becomes the 'meaning' of life" (*AC* 43).

Unanmuno holds that it is my health and strength that urge me to want to perpetuate myself and that only the feeble resign themselves to final death and seek to "substitute some other desire for the longing of personal immortality" (1912/1962, 65).[17] Nietzsche's doctrine of eternal recurrence, he argues, is a counterfeit doctrine of immortality and one for weaklings. Such a standpoint, however, ignores the wisdom of Epicurean teaching and the reasons for Nietzsche's attachment to it: "Read Lucretius to understand *what* Epicurus fought against, *not* paganism, but 'Christianity,' the corruption of souls through the guilt and ideas of punishment and immortality.— He fought against *subterranean* cults, the entire latent Christianity—to deny immortality at that time was already an actual *redemption*" (*AC* 58; see also *D* 72). The Epicurean teaching on death is aimed at an intellectually mature humanity, one that wishes to remain true to the earth.[18] As Nietzsche points out, as a religion Christianity owes its victory to the "miserable flattery of personal vanity": "'Salvation of the soul'—in plain language—'the world revolves around *me*'" (*AC* 43).

In the discourses that close parts 3 and 4 of *Zarathustra*, we hear the refrain that "all joy wants eternity, deep, deep eternity!" (*Z* 3 "The Second Dance Song" 3; *Z* 4 "The Intoxicated Song"). Indeed, the lust at play in the book is the lust for eternity and the ring of recurrence: "Never yet did I find the woman by whom I wanted children, unless it be this woman, whom I love: for I love you, O Eternity. *For I love you, O Eternity!*" (*Z* 3 "The Seven Seals" 7). These expressions of lust centered on joy, however, do not reveal a desire for personal immortality. Such a desire would not be one that was true to the earth and attuned to the laws of nature (*AC* 43). Rather, it is part of the definition of joy and of what constitutes its experience that it *wants* eternity.[19] The "want" is an expression of the desire in the very experience of joy and reveals to us what the experience feels like as well as something important about the character of our desire. Peter Durno Murray expresses it well when he notes that the blessed isles in Nietzsche serve as a metaphor for a place where the spirit of the Dionysian continues to affect humanity in spite of centuries of antinaturalism, encouraging us to form new allegories and symbols of time and becoming and to renounce "those associated with everlasting transcendence of nature and personal immortality" (2018, 233).

Nietzsche and Heraclitus

Nietzsche notes that Heraclitus has no truck with the Eleusinian mysteries, seeing in Dionysian excitement only "an invitation to ill-bred drives by way of hot-blooded festivals of desire" (*PTAG*, 56). Furthermore, as Nietzsche notes, he holds a special contempt for creators of popular mythology such as Homer and Hesiod. Heraclitus writes: "If learning were a path of wisdom, those most learned about myth would not believe, with Hesiod, that Pallas in her wisdom gloats over the noise of battle." This is all part of the disdain Heraclitus has toward the superstitious practices of the masses, such as purification rituals, the honoring of the gods, and the cult of the mysteries. However, Heraclitus writes: "Now that we can travel anywhere, we need no longer take the poets and mythmakers for sure witnesses about disputed facts" (2001, fragments 16, 14).[20]

Heraclitus's thinking embraces two things: first, the multicolored changing world that crowds in on us in all our experiences and, second, the conditions that make our experience of the world possible. The fundamental conditions are time and space, including their pure, empty forms: "For they may be perceived intuitively, even without a definite content, independent of all experience, purely in themselves" (*PTAG*, 52). As Walter Pater (2018, 218) noted, philosophy for Heraclitus means being susceptible to mobility and versatility so that we may follow "the subtle movement of things" as the secret wisdom and true knowledge of them, in contrast to Plato's philosophy, where motion is the token of the unreality in things and the falsity of our thinking about them. For Heraclitus, every moment exists only insofar as it has consumed the preceding one and in its turn is immediately consumed likewise. The present is but the durationless and dimensionless borderline between the two consuming times of past and future. If all coexists in space and time, this means that all that exists has only a relative existence in which each thing exists through and for another that is like it and is just as relative. It is difficult to reach such an insight, Nietzsche notes, by way of a concept of reason. Once we accept this, we must reach the following remarkable conclusion: reality (*Wirklichkeit*) lies in its acts (*Wirken*), and this is the only "being" there is. The world forever makes itself and unmakes itself *in every moment*. Is this not a terrible, paralyzing thought? Does it not mean that everything that is actual is impermanent? We can compare the impact of the thought to the sensation one would have in response to an earthquake in which one loses one's familiar confidence in a firmly grounded earth. Although our confidence in life is tested, a superior confidence is now free to come into being. It means we must regard the world as like a mixed drink that requires constant stirring, containing in one and the same moment opposites (light and dark, bitter and sweet). This is a contest or strife of the powers of life that endures into eternity. Nietzsche notes that what was a blessed phenomenon for Heraclitus is now in modern times expressed in Schopenhauer in very different tones: as menacing, gloomy, and frightful.

Heraclitus is a significant figure according to Nietzsche because he presents us with not a theodicy but a cosmodicy in which passing away is not conceived as a punishment. Rather, in Heraclitus the world is seen in terms of the play of the child, the game of Aeon; in other words, the world is seen as an aesthetic phenomenon and not in terms of a moralistic calculation. Neither is there any teleology allowed in Heraclitus's conception of the world. Nietzsche describes this cosmodicy as *sublime*. He means this in the sense of having an experience of the uncanny and as something that decenters us. Ultimately, we are elevated to a different and higher level of insight into the character of the world. If everything is implicated in becoming, this means that predicates cannot adhere to a thing but rather must be in its flow (*PPP*, 65). Nietzsche notes that the game of Aeon is not to be conceived as the best of all possible worlds, and he also adds that there is no necessity that compels us as human beings to acknowledge the *Logos* since it is a matter of superhuman perception. For Heraclitus, the significance of doing natural philosophy is that it allows one to see that the pattern of human life and the pattern of cosmic order are one and the same, and this means two things: first, that, when you go in search of yourself, you should develop knowledge of the workings of the cosmos and, second, that wisdom needs to become an actual practice of life in which one lives by this pattern. In Heraclitus, Charles Kahn argues, wisdom is a form of mastery, denoting both a form of knowledge and a plan of action, and it has become a notion that is offered "as a norm for human thinking in general" (1979, 171–72 [see also 9–25]). This notion of wisdom as a form of mastery is captured well in Heraclitus's maxim that declares: "Wisdom is the oneness of mind that guides and permeates all things" (2001, 13 [fragment 19]).

Nietzsche presents Heraclitus as a daunting figure who inspires and alienates in equal measure. He has the arrogance of the typical philosopher, seeing what exists outside himself as error, illusion, and the absence of knowledge. Moreover, there is nothing in his mode of comportment that binds or connects him with his fellow human beings. We find in him "no overpowering feeling of sympathetic stirring." No desire to help, to heal, or to redeem comes forth from him. Furthermore: "We must conceive of such a grand, solitary, and inspired human being as placed in an isolated sanctum: he simply cannot live among his fellow man—at best he could still interact with children" (*PTAG*, 55). Heraclitus is a figure who sees himself offering the proudest response possible to the Delphic oracle ("know thyself") since he locates all learning within himself, as when he declares, "I have searched myself," in which learning from others amounts to nonwisdom. Heraclitus is something extremely rare: "Among human beings, Heraclitus as a human being was unbelievable" (*PTAG*, 67). The kind of solitude that marked his life is something we ourselves can intuit only when freezing on wild, desolate mountains of our own.

However, while for Heraclitus the natural philosopher eclipses the age of the poets, for Nietzsche the time of the poets is not yet over, including the time of the poet-philosopher of the future. One important reason why Nietzsche is not, strictly speaking, Heraclitean as a philosopher is because he does wish to provide humankind with a teaching of redemption—to be conceived neither as salvation nor as retribution but as liberation.[21] Although he expresses in his late writings an affinity with royal hermits of the spirit such as Heraclitus, Nietzsche is never so aloof as to be without care for humanity and its fate. He creates the figure of Zarathustra on account of his commitment to a task of redemption: "For *that man may be freed from the bonds of revenge*: that is the bridge to my highest hope and a rainbow after protracted storms" (*Z* 2 "Of the Tarantulas"). The principal way human revenge manifests itself is as an antipathy toward time's desire and time's "it was." The fact that human beings are so afflicted by time's essential pastness has cast a curse on the whole of humankind (*Z* 2 "Of Redemption"; see also *GM* 2.24). However, only a new action and having the will of a creator can ultimately "redeem" the past.[22]

Power: An Open Secret

Nietzsche's sense of the open secret is not so much that of the inaccessible as that of the unnoticed. As Michael Bell has noted, *Zarathustra* is "centrally focused on the problem of the will." In terms of its organic needs, the human will does not "have the simple goals of purely animal life" (2007, 147). Zarathustra, in fact, proclaims to teach humankind "a new will: to desire this path that humans have followed blindly, and to call it good and no more to creep aside from it, like the sick and the dying!" (*Z* 1 "On Hinterworlders"). Moreover, the will that wants to command all things needs to be "the will of a lover." We are to recognize that we are willers of a single will—the will to power—and that this "turning of all need" to "will" amounts to necessity for us and is the source of our virtue (*Z* 1 "Of the Bestowing Virtue" 1). This turning, then, from "need" to "will" captures Nietzsche's hope that humankind will no longer live blindly but pursue life more knowingly. As Bell rightly notes: "The will to power, then, is for Nietzsche the supreme open secret." This will, he adds, is "closer to the ancient Greek ideal of flourishing but with a modern naturalistic edge countering the moral idealisms which modernity has also inherited" (2007, 152).[23] This open secret is no longer that of Goethe's "Nature"; rather, it speaks of "Life," which is to be understood "in a qualitative rather than simply a biological sense" (Bell 2007, 152).[24] Paul Tillich provides one of the best descriptions of Nietzsche's compound formulation of "will to power" I know of when he conceives it in terms of the self-affirmation of life as life, encompassing both self-preservation and growth. Understood correctly, it means that the will does not strive for something it does not have and for some object outside itself but rather wills itself in the double sense of preserving and surpassing itself. "This is its power," he writes, and "its power over itself" (1962, 36). If we think of will to power in terms of a "will" that wants something it lacks, namely, "power," we are not hearing Nietzsche well.

Nietzsche posits a natural aim of life, but unlike Epicurus, whose naturalistic teaching inspires him in this regard, he conceives the goal as not one of pleasure but rather one of power.[25] As the goal of life's activity, it is to be conceived, as Tillich suggests, as immanent to life's will or desire. There are two key insights: first, that pleasure and displeasure are consequences and mere epiphenomena since what every organism strives after is an increase of power and pleasure and displeasure follow from this goal of power enhancement and, second, that displeasure, which we can posit as an obstacle to an organism's will to power, is to be considered a typical fact within any organic event. In the case of the human being, displeasure plays a highly productive role in growth and development, with the result that we are in continual need of it: "[E]very victory, every feeling of pleasure, every event, presupposes a resistance overcome" (*KSA*, vol. 13, fragment 14 [174]; *WP* 702). For Nietzsche, activity is associated with pleasure because all doing is an overcoming and a becoming master; it increases the feeling of power, and we take pleasure in creating and in what we have created (*KSA*, vol. 12, fragment 7 [2], pp. 252–53; *WP* 661). Moreover, then: "[B]rave and creative human beings *never* consider pleasure and pain as ultimate values—they are epiphenomena: one must *desire* both if one is to achieve anything" (*KSA*, vol. 12, fragment 8 [2], pp. 327–28; *WP* 579).[26] Nietzsche is granting a role to pleasure in life, then, but he does not conceive it as the main goal. Pleasure is the result not of the satisfaction of the will but rather of "the will's forward thrust . . . and becoming master over that which stands in its way" (*KSA*, vol. 13, fragment 11 [75], pp. 37–38; *WP* 696). He posits this conception of life against the simpleminded ideal of "the happy human" and as the ideal of the herd. The dissatisfaction of our drives, therefore, does not denote anything depressing but is an agitation of the feeling of life, with the result that far from making us disgusted with life dissatisfaction can serve as a tremendous stimulus.[27]

Nietzsche thinks that this insight takes him well beyond Schopenhauer's conception of the character of the will to life and the reasons we have for adhering to the hopelessness of life in the dimension of the will. Indeed, he calls this "a weakly and sentimental way of thinking." His criticism is equally directed at hedonism: "The 'predominance of suffering over pleasure' or the opposite (*hedonism*): these two doctrines are already signposts to nihilism" (*KSA* 12, fragment 9 [107], pp. 397–98; *WP* 35). In a note from 1881, he refers to Schopenhauer's doctrine of the will as signifying in its attempt to penetrate directly into the heart of things a reaction against Cartesian rationalism and English skepticism. As such, it appeals to "noble idlers" as well as "dreamers, mystics, artists, three-fourths Christians, political obscurantists and metaphysical concept-spiders." It has only the pretense of profundity. Nietzsche makes it clear he has no time for either the "pantheistic vapors" of Hegel and Schelling or the mystical, life-negating gnosis of Schopenhauer (*KSA*, vol. 11, fragment 38 [7]; *SUP*, 16:163–64).

The criticisms that he develops in these notes echo what he had already warned against in an aphorism in *Dawn* in which he exposes the delusional character of "good-natured, silver-lined idealism" that wants "nobly affected gestures and nobly affected voices, a thing as presumptuous as it is naive, animated by a most sincere aversion to 'cold' or 'dry' reality, to anatomy, to undiluted passions, to every type of philosophical temperance and skepticism." He advises us to be skeptical of "the passionate demand for boneless brilliant generalities combined with an intentional 'beautifying vision'" (*D* 190), and he wants us to resist the idea of positing either a divine or a diabolical nature, suffusing nature with the kind of ethical and symbolic significance that we find in Schopenhauer's metaphysics and that leads us so badly astray (*D* 197).

Zarathustra the Poet

In *Thus Spoke Zarathustra*, we encounter a frank admittance: "What did Zarathustra once say to you? That the poets lie too much? But Zarathustra too is a poet" (*Z* 2 "Of Poets"). Zarathustra goes on to say in this discourse that he has grown weary of the poets since they have not thought deeply enough and have not plumbed the depths. The spirit of the poet is too often captured by vanity. However, Zarathustra has hope since he has "seen penitents of the spirit appearing: they grew out of the poets" (*Z* 2 "Of Poets"). Although he is frustrated at still having to be a poet, Zarathustra draws inspiration from the possibility of a new future: "out into the distant future, which no dream has yet seen, into warmer Souths than artists have ever dreamed of" (*Z* 3 "Of Old and New Law-Tables" 2). As Michael Bell (2007, 142) has noted, Nietzsche often presents himself, as he does here, as a philosophical time lord living in the present only as a visitor from afar.

In the discourse "The Song of Melancholy" in part 4 of *Zarathustra*, Nietzsche depicts Zarathustra's melancholy devil as the evil spirit of deceit and sorcery that attacks him, and this is the ghost of the poet haunting him. The parable depicted in this discourse is the story of an old sorcerer who torments Zarathustra with the thought that he is only a fool and only a poet and, moreover, that it is impossible for him to be anything other than this. Zarathustra may well like to think of himself as a passionate seeker of knowledge who can discover truth, but, so the old sorcerer wishes to tell him, the only truth he needs to be prepared to acknowledge is that, and for all time, he is "banished from all truth" (*Z* 4 "The Song of Melancholy" 3).

We can also note what is said in "Of the Priests" in part 2 of the text: "[H]e who lives in their neighbourhood lives in the neighbourhood of black pools, from out of which the toad, that prophet of evil, sings its song with sweet melancholy" (*Z* 2 "Of the Priests"). The old sorcerer, then, tries to persuade Zarathustra to accept that he is banished from the domain of truth and, even more damning, that he is an enemy to "statutes of truth" (*Z* 4 "The Song of Melancholy" 3).

The danger facing Zarathustra if he accepts the words of the old sorcerer is that he will give up on his truth as a poet-philosopher and come to accept that there is only one truth, the truth of science. If he does this in his daytime longings, he will grow "weary of day and sick with light" and become, like the sorcerer, "scorched and thirsty" (*Z* 4 "The Song of Melancholy" 3). We know that Zarathustra wants not believers but only companions and fellow creators. However, in *Zarathustra*, Nietzsche also seeks to grant a legitimate role to belief in the future as an important part of philosophy's intellectual perception. In "The Song of Melancholy," the spirit of evening melancholy comes to Zarathustra naked and asks him to open his senses. This spirit is that of the driest and most tedious of empiricists.[28] In the discourse "Of the Land of Culture," Zarathustra seeks to fly far into the future, but he is assailed by his contemporaries. The contemporaries with which he now contends are presented as complete realists and said to be without belief or superstition. He confronts them by instructing them: "You are walking refutations of belief itself and the fracture of all thought. *Unworthy of belief*: that is what *I* call you, you realists!" The realists fail to realize that even they, who wish to see reality and themselves naked and unadorned, "are paintings of all that has ever been believed!" (*Z* 2 "Of the Land of Culture").[29] Zarathustra knows that he cannot argue with them. Instead, he chooses to engage them in a pithy and teasing manner: "You are unfruitful: *therefore*, you lack belief. But he who had to create always had his prophetic dreams and star-auguries—and he believed in belief!" (*Z* 2 "Of the Land of Culture").

Nietzsche is well-known for holding to the view that belief in things—for example, belief in God—counts for little. And we have seen that Zarathustra has no interest in gathering believers around him but rather seeks fellow creators and fellow rejoicers. The belief in the future to which he is appealing is of a special or unique kind. We might call it a *bedrock* belief in life and the insight that it has possibilities. The future is unknown (as well as uncertain), and a task we can set ourselves, in terms of the conduct of life, is to make ourselves worthy of the belief in it by becoming "fruitful," that is, pregnant with possibilities ourselves. When Zarathustra declares that the one who has grown wise concerning old origins will ultimately seek new origins and new springs of the future—"it will not be long before *new peoples* shall arise and new springs rush down into new depths" (*Z* 3 "Of Old and New Law-Tables" 25)—and when at the denouement to the second essay of *On the Genealogy of Morality* Nietzsche says that the antinihilist "must come one day" and appeals to "Zarathustra the Godless" (*GM* 2.24, 25), he is expressing his commitment to the future.[30]

Zarathustra, then, is a fool and a poet as well as a philosopher and truth seeker because he has belief and hope, affirming the importance of a will to truth (establishing and esteeming what is knowable), and recognizing the need for a will to untruth (accepting a degree of risk and uncertainty in the creation of the future as something new). We wish to value sobriety, but not to the point that we become sterile (*KSA*, vol. 9, fragment 11 [68]; *SUP*, 6:327). The following note from 1885 may serve to clarify his position. He writes as an advocate of the passion of knowledge and the will to truth: "Just as Napoleon, to the astonishment of Talleyrand, allowed his anger to bark and roar at the chosen time and then later, just as suddenly silenced it, so too the strong spirit must do with his wild dogs: at the chosen time, no matter how urgent the will to truth is in him—it is his wildest dog—he must *be able* to be the incarnate will to untruth, the will to uncertainty, the will to ignorance, above all to foolishness" (*KSA*, vol. 11, fragment 38 [20]). On Nietzsche's understanding, free spirits find themselves thrust into the future as "into the distance, into adventures . . . into the boundless, the untried, and the undiscovered." He holds that there can be a legitimate appeal to the future even if we "do not yet know the 'wither' toward which we are driven once we have detached ourselves from our old soil" (*KSA*, vol. 12, fragment 2 [207]; *WP* 405). In "Of the Tree on the Mountainside" in part 1 of *Zarathustra*, an important contrast is made between the noble and the good human being, with the former wanting to create new things and a new virtue, the latter committed only to preserving the old things and old ways. Nietzsche then alerts his readers to several dangers that face the noble human being. They include becoming a mere destroyer and an impudent one at that, losing their highest hope to the point where they slander all high hopes, becoming cynics or losing themselves in brief pleasures with no aims beyond the current fashions of the day.

Évelyne Grossman provides us with an important insight into Nietzsche's philosophical practice when she notes that since he assumes neither the role of the priest nor the classical figure of the sage the teaching of Zarathustra is the very opposite of all doctrine; it says to us: "[D]eliver us from the certainties brandished by the priests and masters and we will have a chance, perhaps, of becoming creators" (2023, 89).

Zarathustra the Fool

There are several figurations of the fool in *Zarathustra*. The so-called wise man is depicted by Nietzsche as a fool in the second discourse of part 1 of the book (*Z* 1 "Of the Professorial Chairs of Virtue") and then again in the final part of the book (*Z* 4 "The Awakening"). In the critical encounter with the last human in the prologue to the book—the human that blinks because it has found happiness, is now simply content, and has no wish for life any longer to be a task—Zarathustra counsels that one must traverse warily in one's travels and adventures since "sickness and mistrust" are regarded as sins by the last humans. He then adds: "He is a fool who still stumbles over stones and over humans!" (*Z* prologue, 5).[31]

One of the most important depictions of the fool in the book takes place in the discourse "Of Passing By" in part 3. Here, "Zarathustra's monkey"—as he is called by the people—is depicted as the fool that foams at the mouth. (Zarathustra also calls him his *grunting swine*.) He is called the *monkey* of Zarathustra because he adopts some of the phrasing and cadence of Zarathustra's speech and professes to borrow from the pearls of Zarathustra's wisdom. The monkey, however, is a misanthrope and presented by Nietzsche as a fool in this guise. Zarathustra finds himself at the gate of a great city where his path is blocked by this fool, his monkey. The monkey tries to warn him that he is wasting his time and will find nothing in the city and that, in fact, he has everything to lose there:

> Why would you want to wade through this slime? Take pity on your feet, will you! Better to spit on the city gate and—turn back!
>
> This place is hell for a hermit's thoughts: this place is where great thoughts are boiled alive and cooked until they shrivel.
>
> This place is where great feelings rot away: only little feelings with feeble rattles are allowed to rattle here! (*Z* 3 "Of Passing By")

The monkey has witnessed the worst on earth, the full stomach-churning baseness of human beings, as when he asks Zarathustra: "Do you not smell already the slaughterhouses and rendering plants of the spirit? Does the city not reek of the fumes of slaughtered spirits? Do you not see the souls hanging like limp dirty rags?—And they also make newspapers from these rags!" (*Z* 3 "Of Passing By").[32] Zarathustra ultimately interrupts the speech of the monkey—depicted as such to represent the figure who holds that humans can never go beyond themselves and their base animal roots to anything superior, such as the superhuman—and declares himself to be disgusted by him and calls him a *frothing fool.* Zarathustra quizzes the monkey, wondering why he has not pursued options other than the path of misanthropy, such as returning to the forests or ploughing the earth in search of new green islands.[33] Zarathustra reveals that he despises the monkey's contempt and maintains that his contempt for humankind is of a different nature since it comes not from the swamp but from love alone. As a frothing fool, who is really a grunting pig, the monkey finds reasons to be miserable and thinks it can identify causes for its grunting, including causes for revenge, the deadliest of the passions: "For all your frothing, you vain fool, is revenge; I have divined you well!" (*Z 3* "Of Passing By").

Zarathustra seeks to humor the monkey: "[B]y grunting you are undoing even my praise of folly." Not only is the monkey devoid of hope for the future and without any belief in it, but his constant moaning also makes a claim to knowledge about human existence—"to know everything that has ever happened" (*Z* prologue 5)—and even expects to receive flattery for exposing its filthy nature. Zarathustra, however, detects in this frothing fool only spite and revenge. In the prologue, Zarathustra challenges us: "Where is the lightning to lick you with its tongue? Where is the madness, with which you should be cleansed? Behold, I teach you the superhuman: he is this lightning, he is this madness (*Wahnsinn*)! . . . I want to teach humans the meaning of their existence: which is the superhuman, the lightning from the dark cloud man" (*Z* prologue 3, 7). What is this madness? Gide helps here when he notes that perhaps a certain madness is necessary to make people say and see certain things for the first time, and he adds: "[M]aybe Nietzsche felt it" (1927, 180). In Plato's *Phaedrus*, Socrates reminds his interlocutor: "The people who designed our language in the old days never thought of madness as something to be ashamed of or worthy of blame; otherwise they would not have used the word 'manic' for the finest experts of all—the ones who tell the future—thereby weaving insanity into prophecy" (1995, 244c). Although Nietzsche is not simply weaving insanity into prophecy in his writings, including *Zarathustra,* he recognizes that the idea of the superhuman will inevitably appear to humans as a kind of madness or craziness.[34]

As Stanley Rosen rightly points out, the fool is in some respects a caricature of Zarathustra, a grotesque one at that, and not entirely without bite: "Zarathustra's rhetoric is sufficiently perfervid to give rise to this sort of imitation. And this is no doubt why Zarathustra is so furious with the foaming fool" (2004, 191). He suggests that the satire of humanity's condition offered by the frothing fool has irritated Zarathustra because it is not entirely without a point. Indeed, in the discourse, Zarathustra confides to the fool that its foolish teaching is harmful to him, "even when you are right!" He adds: "And if Zarathustra's teaching *were* a hundred times justified, *you* would still—*use* my teaching falsely!" (*Z* 3 "Of Passing By"). Toward the end of the discourse, Zarathustra exclaims an exasperated woe to the great city, and advises the frothing fool to pass by where one can no longer love, but also expresses the wish to witness the pillars of fire that will consume the city. Rosen sees this wish as being dangerously close to the spirit of revenge, but it is, in fact, an expression of (Zarathustra's) disgust, a disgust that must give rise to a more creative desire. In contrast to those who dwell on the filthy aspects of human existence, Zarathustra remains undaunted and appeals to the positive effects of the emotion of disgust: "That is why the fanatics and hypocrites with bowed heads whose hearts too are bowed down preach: 'The world itself is a filthy monster.' . . . There is much filth in the world: *so much* is true! But the world itself is not yet a filthy monster on that account! There is wisdom in the fact that much in the world smells ill: disgust itself creates wings and water-divining powers!" (*Z* 3 "Of Old and New Law-Tables" 14; see also *Z* prologue 3; and *Z* 3 "The Convalescent" 2).

The Mask

In Nietzsche's poem "Only a Fool! Only a Poet" in *Dithyrambs of Dionysus*, even the wooer of truth is said by his accusers—those who appear most keen to expose him as a mere poet—to be uttering "gaudy nonsense from a fool's mask [*Narrenlarven*]" (*DD*, 23). As David Napier notes: "Masks [expose us] to an awareness of the ambiguities of appearance and to a tendency toward paradox characteristic of transitional states. They provide . . . a means of investigating the problem that appearances pose in the experience of change" (1986, xiii).[35] For example, we can ask, Is Zarathustra really a fool? Is he adopting the role of a fool to show humans the value of being unwise, that is, of not acting with total knowledge and complete wisdom, because he sees the positive side of living impudently? Is this how he wants to appear to us? Or does he think it is a projection that others project onto him so as not to take him seriously? Zarathustra is barred from the truth in a quite specific sense. As a philosopher of the future, he is providing a teaching that is uncertain simply because the future is uncharted. When Nietzsche takes the poets to task for glorifying the uncertain, as we saw in the previous chapter, he is expressing his impatience with writers who are content to leave us in a state of befuddlement and bewitchment. The two different senses of the uncertain need to be cognized and kept distinct.[36]

For Nietzsche, every profound spirit requires a mask. Even more, however, a mask continually grows around the profound spirit owing to the false and shallow interpretations of every word and sign of life this spirit gives and emits (*BGE* 40). In *The Gay Science*, he suggests that the spirit of the ancients consists in the delight they took in the mask, and this is what we can love about them; they had a good conscience "in using any kind of mask [*Maske*]" (*GS* 77). Furthermore, he maintains that everything that is profound loves a mask, "having a hatred of images and likenesses," and he provides a range of examples to illustrate his insight. A fair number of them are far from the obvious ones that might be selected to highlight the extensive nature of mask wearing (*BGE* 40). For example, he presents Epicureanism as a subtle form of disguise since it displays to the world a "courageousness of taste that takes suffering lightly and resists everything sad and profound" (*BGE* 270). There are, then, so-called cheerful people who use cheerfulness precisely to be misunderstood. Or take the case of Hamlet, as Nietzsche understands him: "There are free and impudent spirits who would like to conceal and deny that they are at bottom broken incurable hearts—it is the case of Hamlet: and then foolishness itself can be the mask for an ill-fated, all-too certain knowledge" (*CW* "The Psychologist Has His Say" 3).[37] From these examples, we can extract a valuable lesson: "[P]art of a refined humanity is having respect 'for the mask' and not practicing psychology and curiosity in the wrong place" (*BGE* 270).[38] This does not mean, however, that we should not be suspicious of the mask and refrain from posing critical questions when we are confronted with a disguise that conceals something that troubles us and needs exposing. This for Nietzsche is the case when confronted with the mask of the scholar and modern critic. This will be examined in the next chapter.

We also need to be on guard when confronted with actors of the spirit.[39] Nietzsche seeks to draw our attention to the way humanity frequently allows the actor type the freedom to govern and rule over the earth. In *Zarathustra*, for example, he laments the fact that "the people and the glory revolve around the actor" as "'the way of the world.'" The actor who takes to the world stage believes only in things with which he most powerfully produces belief, including, and perhaps especially, belief in himself. He has a capricious temperament and believes only in gods who make a great noise. These individuals, heroes of the hour, are "inflexible and oppressive human beings" and, as such, menacing (*Z* 1 "Of the Flies of the Marketplace"). In *Zarathustra*, the character of the magician is addressed as an "enchanter" and an "actor from the heart," the "peacock of peacocks," and an "ocean of vanity." The magician responds to Zarathustra's admonishments by revealing that it has taken Zarathustra a long time to see through his trickery and lies (*Z* 4 "The Magician" 2). The magician, whom Zarathustra acknowledges is something of a penitent of the spirit, has sought greatness, but this has been exposed as a sham since it is all pomp and ceremony. There is plenty of evidence to suggest from the language employed in this discourse that the figure in question corresponds to Nietzsche's image of Wagner (see Santaniello 2005, 29ff.).

In *Zarathustra*, Nietzsche advises us not to will beyond our powers (*Vermögen*) lest we deceive ourselves that we are creators when, in fact, we are merely actors, false to ourselves and "cloaked with clever words, with pretended virtues, with glittering, false deeds" (*Z* 4 "Of the Higher Man" 8). In an essay on Nietzsche and Diderot, James Porter has argued that for Nietzsche we can never remove the mask of life and thus that life "just is a theater and a masquerade, however unconscious we may be of this fact, and however much we deny it" (2023, 165).[40] When he also argues that for Nietzsche acting is the very condition of life, he fails adequately to negotiate the ways in which the problem of the actor is dealt with in his writings and note his aversion to playacting. In *Twilight of the Idols*, Nietzsche challenges us by presenting us with a disconcerting question: "Are you genuine? Or just a play-actor?" (*TI* "Maxims and Barbs" 38). Porter underestimates the desire Nietzsche has for genuine life and for mature love. Ernst Bertram observes that Nietzsche felt so acutely his disappointment over the encounters with Lou Salomé in the years 1882 and 1883 because he fell "victim to the actor at precisely the place where he looked for and thought he beheld the most living person, to see through the mask where he yearned to believe in a face" (1918/2009, 140). In two notes of 1884, Nietzsche writes tellingly: "[S]earching for love—and always the *mask*, I must find the accursed *mask* and *crush it to pieces*!" Also: "Love is what tells me to go along, Love keenly desired!" (*KSA*, vol. 10, fragment 28 [12–13], pp. 303–4; *SUP*, 15:282). In his published writings Nietzsche typically uses the phrase *die Maske*, but in this note he uses the archaic word for *mask*, *die Larve* (larva): the immature or juvenile form of an insect or animal.

Nietzsche and the Superhuman

> Once upon a time I projected my delusion beyond human beings in this way, as all hinterworlders do. . . . Alas, my brothers, this god that I created was the work of human beings and the madness of human beings, just like all gods!
>
> This god was human, and only a poor excuse for a human being and an I: this ghost, it came to me out of my own ashes and glowing coals, and truly! He did not come to me from beyond!
>
> What then happened, my brothers? I overcame myself, a human being who was suffering, I carried my own ashes to the mountain, I invented a brighter flame for myself. And behold! Then the ghost *abandoned* me. . . . [B]elieving in such ghosts now would make me suffer and would be humiliating. This is what I say to the hinterworlders.

> It was suffering and impotence that created all the hinterworlds; and that brief moment of madness that comes with happiness, which is experienced only by those who suffer the most.
>
> Weariness that wants to reach the end in one leap, in one leap to the death, a pathetic and ignorant weariness that doesn't even want to will anymore: this is what created all gods and hinterworlds.
>
> Nietzsche, *Thus Spoke Zarathustra* 1 "Of the Hinterworlders"

Zarathustra declares that the *Übermensch* is his paramount and sole concern: "not man—and not the neighbour, not the poorest, not the most ailing, and neither the best" (*Z* 4 "Of the Higher Man" 3). And in *Ecce Homo* Nietzsche stresses that *Übermensch* is intended to be a "very thought-provoking word" (*EH* "Why I Write Such Good Books" 1). The word *superhuman* was well established in Nietzsche's time, and he would have been familiar, for example, with the word *hyperanthropos* found in the writings of Lucian in the second century AD and aware of its usage in the writings of modern literary figures such as Goethe and Byron. There are several figurations of the superhuman in the texts of the middle period. In *Human, All Too Human*, it denotes that which is taken to be more or higher than the human, a sanctified virtue such as superhuman goodness or justice, the value of belief in superhuman passions, or the way of life of the saint and the mind of the genius (*HH* 143, 441; *WS* 190; *D* 27, 548). Typically, we construe it as bound up with the divine, as when we speak of a *divine humanity*, or as denoting the popular faith people have of something higher than the human, such as the miracle or the redeeming god (*D* 60; *GS* 358).[41] The first use we find in Nietzsche of the superhuman as a substantive is in aphorism 143 of *The Gay Science*, where he speaks of *Übermenschen* along with gods and heroes and of *Nebenmenschen* and *Untermenschen*, such as dwarfs, fairies, and satyrs and demons. Human beings find themselves surrounded by creatures that stand alongside, below, and above them. The *Übermensch* also denotes the repudiation of conformity to a single norm and the rebellion against mediocrity and stagnation in the closed society of the morality of custom. (In this aphorism, we also find the earliest appearance in his writings on the contrast between the morality of custom and the sovereign or self-determining individual [see GM 2.1–2].)[42]

As Paul Loeb and David Tinsley (*SUP*, 14:754) point out, the etymology of the noun *Übermensch* shows how Nietzsche took a word that had been in common usage since the Reformation and reshaped it for his own purposes. Indeed, this is in accord with Nietzsche's view: "[The philosopher] has to interpret in a quite individual way even the words he has inherited. His interpretation of a formula at least is personal, even if he does not create a formula: as an interpreter he is still creative" (*KSA*, vol. 10, fragment 24 [33]; *WP* 767). Loeb and Tinsley, whose advice I am adopting in this chapter, find *superhuman* to be a better choice than *overhuman* because "it corresponds to current standard English usage in its word field and because it is part of a tradition of translating *Übermensch* that extends back to the beginning of the sixteenth century" (*SUP*, 14:754).[43]

Conceived as a gift to humanity and the hope that is highest, Nietzsche's teaching of the superhuman is not without its mythic dimensions and cannot be. It must be posited as an ideal because there has never yet been such a being and, therefore, we do not know how this being would live, think, and feel, in short, what its actual reality would be (*Z* 2 "Of the Priests"). Santayana understandably asked: "How could so fantastic an ideal impose on a keen satirist like Nietzsche and a sincere lover of excellence?" And he suggests we regard the superhuman as more of a protest than a possibility (Santayana 1916/1939, 120 [quote], 124). Although the teaching of the superhuman is not without fantastic aspects, it emerges quite naturally out of Nietzsche's probing of the human animal and his commitment to its future development. The teaching is best construed, then, as a continuation and an extension of Nietzsche's concern with self-cultivation that characterizes his thinking from first to last.[44] Several discourses in the text center on this idea, including "Of Joys and Passions," "Of the Way of the Creator," "Of Child and Marriage," "Of Self-Overcoming," and so on.[45] It is also connected to the invocation of new peoples and a new earth to come, notably in the discourse "Of Old and New Law-Tables," which Nietzsche regards as the crucial part of book 3 of the text (*EH* "Zarathustra" 4). Zarathustra presents his readers with the challenge of a rare and special art, encouraging them to compose into one and unify what is but fragment and dreadful chance in the human. He also declares himself to be a poet and reader of riddles who encourages human beings to "create the future, and to redeem by creating—all that *was past*." If life has in a sense promised us, then we need to keep a promise to life itself. It is not a question of wanting or expecting to live gratis. What is needed, above all, Zarathustra teaches, is a new nobility and to "oppose all mob-rule and all despotism and to write anew upon new law-tables the word: 'Noble'" (*Z* 3 "Of Old and New Law-Tables" 3, 4, 11). With this teaching, Nietzsche aims to combat the putative wisdom of gloomy sages (*Z* 3 "Of Old and New Law-Tables" 2) and show that once you start to discover the country of the human you also at the same time discover the country of the human future (*Z* 3 "Of Old and New Law-Tables" 28). Although it is the case that "much ignorance and error has become body in us," with the madness of millennia breaking out in us, the land of the human remains to be discovered (*Z* 1 "Of the Bestowing Virtue" 2).

The emphasis Nietzsche places in *Thus Spoke Zarathustra* on the plural—the creation of new peoples—should be noted. In their translation of the *Zarathustra-Nachlass*, Loeb and Tinsley have shown that for Nietzsche the goal of superior human beings is to foster superhumans. They cite various passages from the *Nachlass* that support their interpretation that hitherto these human beings have failed in this task because they have been "diverted and perverted into religious and metaphysical speculation" (*SUP*, 15:515). The problem with religious and metaphysical teachers, such as the Brahmins and Plato, is that they have always sought to flee into some hereafter, into, as Nietzsche says, "striving for a divine form of existence *beyond what is human*—beyond space, time, multiplicity, etc." (*KSA*, vol. 11, fragment 26 [203]). Now is the time, then, for concentrating human energies on the goal of building an earthly superhuman future: "It is time for man to plant the seed of his highest hope" (*Z* prologue 5).

Nietzsche knows well that his thinking has undergone a significant development from the time he published *Human, All Too Human* (1878), which was born of a major intellectual crisis (*EH* "Human, All Too Human" 1). *Thus Spoke Zarathustra* can, however, be interpreted as a response to a problem he had highlighted in aphorism 33 of *Human, All Too Human*. The problem is that of humanity having no goal. It is an extraordinary aphorism, one in which Nietzsche suggests that our belief in the value and worthiness of life rests on defective thinking and that it is for this reason that sympathy with the general life and suffering of mankind is so imperfectly developed in us as individuals. We fail to think beyond ourselves: "[Although we] endure life without any great protest, and believe, to this extent, in the value of existence, this is because each individual decides and determines alone, and never comes out of his own personality. . . . [E]verything outside of the personal has no existence for them or at the utmost is observed as but a faint shadow." We lack both imagination and the ability to enter the feelings of beings other than ourselves, and as a result our sympathy with their fate and suffering is of the slightest possible description. If we really could sympathize, however, we may well come to doubt the value of life:

> [W]ere it possible for him to sum up and to feel in himself the total consciousness of humankind, he would collapse with a malediction against existence,—for humankind is, in the mass, without a goal, and hence man cannot find, in the contemplation of his whole course, anything to serve him as a mainstay and a comfort, but rather a reason to despair. If he looks beyond the things that immediately engage him to the final aimlessness of humanity, his own conduct assumes in his eyes the character of a frittering away. To feel oneself, however, as humanity (not alone as an individual)

> frittered away exactly as we see the stray leaves frittered away by nature, is a feeling transcending all feeling. But who is capable of it? Only a poet, certainly: and poets always know how to console themselves. (*HH* 33)

Having, by the time of *Thus Spoke Zarathustra*, traversed the pathways opened in the subsequent middle writings, Nietzsche envisages a different kind of poet, one whose task is not simply to console but to help create a new earth and new peoples. In *Mixed Opinions and Maxims* (1879), as we saw in chapter 3 above, he is keen to inculcate in his readers an enthusiastic love of philosophy and art in which the focus is on encouraging human beings to cultivate respect for their defects, their spiritual poverty, and their senseless delusions and passions (*MOM* 148). Although an attentiveness to the troubling aspects of human nature remains in *Zarathustra*, another and much more dramatic visionary aspect of Nietzsche's thinking comes to the fore, one centered on the teaching of the superhuman. In *Ecce Homo*, he reveals that the "ravenous hunger" he experiences in his knowledge means that he cannot be satisfied with present-day humanity (*EH* "Zarathustra" 2).

However, a key aspect of the teaching of the superhuman must be acknowledged, and this is the fact that it can be posited only as the goal of a *human* passion. Santayana writes: "I must think humanly or I cannot think at all" (1940, 279). Indeed, in *Zarathustra*, Nietzsche has Zarathustra acknowledge a point we would be wise not to overlook: "[T]he belly of being does not speak to man, except as man" (*Z* 1 "On Hinterworlders"). The desire in the book remains for the terrestrial conditions of human existence where we affirm the body,[46] the senses,[47] transitoriness, change, becoming, and so on: "Lead, as I do, the flown-away virtue back to earth—yes, back to body and life: that it may give the earth its meaning, a human meaning!" (*Z* 1 "Of the Bestowing Virtue" 2). Moreover, although Nietzsche is appealing to the superhuman, he is also clearly stating that this form of life—one that will remain true to the earth—has to be thought of in terms that are humanly thinkable and tangible, and this requirement acts as a constraint on our conception of it: "[M]ay the will to truth mean this to you: everything shall be transformed into the humanly-conceivable, the humanly-visible, the humanly-palpable [*Menschen-Denkbares, Menschen-Sichtbares, Menschen-Fühlbares*]! You should follow your own senses to the end!" Furthermore:

> And what you used to call "world," this has yet to be created by you: what you called "world" must itself become your reason, your image, your will, your love! And truly, created for your bliss, you who know!

And how could you want to endure life devoid of this hope, you who know? You could not have been born into that which is incomprehensible nor into that which is irrational.

But to open my heart to you completely, you friends: *if* there were gods, how could I stand not being a god! *Therefore*, there are no gods.

Yes, I drew this conclusion; now it's drawing me.—

God is a conjecture: but who would drink in all the torment of this conjecture without dying? Must those who create be robbed of their faith and must the eagle be robbed of its ability to soar off into eagles' distances?

God is a thought which causes everything that is straight to become crooked and everything that is standing still to rotate. What's that? You're saying that time would vanish and everything that is impermanent would just be a lie?

To think like this causes our human bones to whirl and become dizzy and turns our stomach even now: truly, making conjectures like this is what I call vertigo.

I call this evil and misanthropic: all these doctrines about unity and perfection and immovability and self-sufficiency and permanence!

Everything permanent—this is only a symbol; and poets lie too much.—

But the best symbols must speak of time and becoming: they must praise and justify all transitoriness!

To create—this is the great redemption from suffering, and this is life becoming less burdensome. But the fact that there are people who create, this itself requires suffering and much transformation.

Yes, there must be much bitter dying in your lives, you who create! Therefore, you are advocates and defenders of all impermanence. . . .

All feelings turn to sorrow when they relate to me and become repressed: but my willing always comes to me as my liberator and as that which brings me joy.

Willing liberates: this is the true doctrine of will and freedom—this is what Zarathustra is teaching you.

. . . [M]y will drives me toward human beings over and over again, my burning will to create; in this way it drives the hammer toward the stone.

(*Z* 2 "Upon the Blessed Isles")

Zarathustra is no misanthropist conceived as someone who seeks revenge against life owing to feeling resentful toward the limits of its conditions, and sight should not be lost of the central role played by the human in the drama of his teaching, chiefly, that a new meaning of the earth is required.[48] The issue of the human works on two main levels in the book. First, and as we have seen, it is the human that is to inform and shape our conception of the superhuman as a new goal. Second, the problem of the human and its psychological formation and deformation as an animal with a deep past is to be worked through on an individual level prior to the transition to a superior humanity. Although our souls may thirst for the stars, it is our bad instincts that thirst for freedom. Prisoners of the soul who aspire to nobility can also be deceitful and base; all human beings conceal within themselves monsters and a hidden mob. The question that we need to ask of ourselves is not "free from what?" but rather "free *for* what?" (*Z* 1 "Of the Way of the Creator").

Nietzsche and Dostoevsky

The often-drawn similarities of Nietzsche's new human to the doctrine of the "man-god" expounded by the remarkable character Kirillov in Dostoevsky's novel *The Devils* and stressed by major literary figures such as Camus are in my view ultimately superficial. As Gide (1923/1967, 161) notes, it is Kirillov who carries the whole plot of the novel on his shoulders.[49] Kirillov conceives the act of suicide as the sign of our supreme freedom and a symbol of our "self-will," which is the doctrine he espouses in the novel:

> A new man will come, happy and proud. To whom it won't matter whether he lives or not. He'll be the new man! He who conquers pain and fear will himself be a god. And that other God will not be. . . . Man will be god. He will be physically transformed. And the world, too, will be transformed, and things will be transformed, and thoughts and all feelings. . . . Everyone who desires supreme freedom must dare to kill himself. He who dares to kill himself is a god. Now everyone can make it so there shall be no God and there shall be nothing. (Dostoevsky 1872/1971, 126 [pt. 1: 3, sec. 8], p. 126; see also Dostoevsky 1872/1971, 610–21 [pt. 3: 6, sec. 2])[50]

Camus puts it well in *The Myth of Sisyphus* (1942/2004, 580) when he describes Kirillov as imbued with "evangelical melancholy," while in his remarkable writings on Dostoevsky Gide brings out well why Kirillov is portrayed by him as a Christ-like savior and redeemer figure.[51] Although Kirillov's words and pedagogical suicide will strike the reader's ears as blasphemous, we need to "rest assured that Dostoevsky, in drawing his figure, was possessed by the idea of Christ, by the necessity of the Crucifixion as a sacrifice to redeem mankind": "If Christ had saved Himself, mankind would have been lost: to save it, He surrendered His own life." Gide goes on to cite from an essay of Dostoevsky's where he makes it clear that for him voluntary sacrifice that is "offered consciously and without constraint" and entails the individual's sacrifice for the greater good of humankind is "the mark of personality in its noblest and highest development, of perfect self-control" and "the absolute expression of free will" (1923/1967, 169). In Camus's language, Kirillov's fatal logic reveals the secret of the absurd and does so in all its purity, where it is no longer a question of revenge but one of revolt: "The reasoning is classic in its clarity. If God does not exist, Kirillov must kill himself. Kirillov must therefore kill himself to become god. That logic is absurd, but it is what is needed" (1942/2004, 579).

Nietzsche copies key declarations made in the novel by the characters Stavrogin and Kirillov in his notebook of early February and late March 1888, and he does so in the context of research he is conducting into the psychology of nihilism and the logic of atheism (*KSA*, vol. 13, fragment 11 [331–35]).[52] Although the characters of Dostoevsky's novel clearly fascinate and intrigue Nietzsche, there is no indication in his notebooks that he identifies with them. Gide (1923/1967, 139) notes that Dostoevsky's philosophy ultimately leads to a sort of Buddhism and to quietism, and Paolo Stellino (2015, 2010–12) has also noted the mystical and Buddhistic character of Kirillov's conception of self-deification as symbolized in the figure of the "man-god." This is utterly different to Nietzsche's teaching and the warnings he gives his readers in his late writings about an emerging new European Buddhism that reflects our tiredness over the human (*GM* preface 5; *GM* 3.27). Miller (1975, 187) is also astute in showing that Kirillov's annihilation of God does not represent liberation to a Dionysian affirmation of the body and the earth but is rather the assertion of a supposed total freedom that transcends death by, in effect, negating life.

Gide is to be especially applauded for resisting the too easily accepted view that Nietzsche's superhuman is the same as Dostoevsky's, whether in the Raskolnikov version or the more plausible Kirillov one. As he astutely notes, in Nietzsche, the superhuman figure is ruthless not to others but to himself, and the humanity he seeks to outstrip is his own. Gide rightly maintains that to one and the same problem—the event of the death of God—Nietzsche and Dostoevsky propose radically opposed solutions: "Nietzsche advocates the affirmation of the personality—for him it is the one possible aim in life; Dostoevsky postulates its surrender. Nietzsche presupposes the heights of achievement where Dostoevsky prophesises utter ruin" (1923/1967, 157).

While the theory of the new human that Kirillov expounds in the novel appears to anticipate aspects of Nietzsche's "death of God" atheism, we should not lose sight of the fact that Nietzsche construes this atheism in terms of a project of knowledge and a task of experimentation. The "temptational ideal" (*versucherisches Ideal*), as he describes the *Übermensch* (Miller 1975, 166), is not a matter of simple heroic self-affirmation but rather involves all the work that is attached to the passion of knowledge that will make it something real, including developing new knowledge about the body and the senses: "Be like me, guide back to earth the virtue that has flown away—yes, guide it back to the body and to life: so that it may give to the earth the meaning that belongs to it, a human meaning! . . . The body knowingly cleanses itself; it uses knowledge in an attempt to make itself superior; for those who know, all drives become holy; for those who have become superior, the soul becomes joyful" (*Z* 1 "Of the Bestowing Virtue" 2).

In *Thus Spoke Zarathustra*, Nietzsche has Zarathustra declare that he is gentle with the sick, adding that he is not even angry at their manner of consolation or their ingratitude toward life: "May they become convalescents and overcome themselves and create superior bodies for themselves!" Religious or metaphysical convalescents are advised to glance tenderly at their illusions as they creep around the grave of their God at midnight, knowing that their tears speak only of sickness and a sick body. We can make an appeal to the healthy body that is purer and more honest of speech and wishes to speak of the meaning (*Sinn*) of the earth:

> Those nations who compose poetry and are addicted to gods have always included many diseased peoples; enraged, they hate those who know and that newest of virtues called: honesty.
>
> . . . It's better to listen to me, my brothers, to the voice of a healthy body: it has a more honest and a purer tone.
>
> A healthy body speaks more honestly and with a purer tone, a perfectly proportioned body: and it speaks of the meaning of the earth. (*Z* 1 "Of the Hinterworlders")

While Dostoevsky is obsessed with the issue of God's existence, Nietzsche's instinct is always in favor of atheism, simply because for him "God" represents a prohibition on thinking, being nothing more than "a rough-and-ready answer" (*EH* "Why I Am So Clever" 1). Only the atheist possesses the intellectual modesty and commitment to honesty required to pursue knowledge as a passion. It is Dostoevsky's obsession with God that is extreme, not Nietzsche's honest atheism. When looked at from the perspective of Nietzsche's middle writings and the work conducted in them, it is evident that his philosophy does not envisage some miraculous process of self-transformation involving curious acts of self-will. With respect to a significant transformation of human life, we need to think of a process involving transitional stages and lasting for millennia. For example, Nietzsche advises that the new life heralded with the teaching of eternal recurrence is not to be taught "like a sudden religion" but needs to be allowed to seep in slowly with entire generations building on it and making it fertile "so that they become a great tree that provides shade for all future humankind": "What are the couple of millennia in which Christianity has sustained itself! For the mightiest thought many millennia are needed" (*KSA*, vol. 9, fragment 11 [158]; *SUP*, 6:358).

"Between Gilded Ice and Pure Blue Sky"

In *The Wanderer and His Shadow* (1880), Nietzsche presents an imaginary exchange between the ancient skeptic Pyrrho and an old man. Pyrrho is portrayed as a fanatic of mistrust whose stance of mistrust nevertheless contains wisdom within it too and encourages us to cultivate modest seeds of truth: "Of mistrust, as it has never yet existed in the world, of mistrust against anything and everything. It is the only path to truth. . . . Do not believe that it leads to fruit trees and beautiful meadows. You will find small, hard seeds upon it—those are the truths" (*WS* 213). By 1881, Nietzsche has discovered a beautiful meadow for himself. In a note from the spring–autumn of that year he writes: "Are you now *prepared*? You must have lived through every degree of skepticism and have bathed lasciviously in ice-cold streams—otherwise you have no right to this thought." The thought in question is that of eternal recurrence, which, Nietzsche says, "should be the religion of the freest most cheerful [*heitersten*] and most sublime [*erhabensten*] souls—a lovely stretch of meadow between gilded ice and pure blue sky!" (*KSA*, vol. 9, fragment 11 [339]; *SUP*, 6:419). This radiant thought signals the dawning of a new way of life, making of life something truly and deeply affirmative, and providing an existential impetus that encourages fidelity to the earth and with it the cultivation of earthbound wisdom.

The doctrine of eternal recurrence—to which Nietzsche devotes two discourses in part 3 of *Zarathustra* ("Of the Vision and the Riddle" and "The Convalescent")—maintains that whatever state this world can attain it must have attained not just once but countless times. We are invited to reflect on *this* moment, the moment we are experiencing right now, and to recognize that it has already taken place once and multiple times and that it will return, again and again, exactly as it is now: "Man! Your whole life will be turned over like an hourglass time and again, and time again it will run out—one vast minute of time in between, until all the conditions that produced you, in the world's circular course, come together again." Nietzsche concludes this sketch on a portentous note: "The ring, in which you are a tiny grain, shines again and again. And in every ring of human existence altogether there is always an hour when—first for one, then for many, then for all—the most powerful thought surfaces, the thought of the eternal recurrence of all things: each time it is for humanity the hour of midday" (*KSA*, vol. 9, fragment 11 [148]; *SUP*, 6:354).

In this notebook of 1881, the doctrine is presented as a new thought of thoughts, a thought that can supervene in our other thoughts as a way of providing existence with a new comportment and orientation (*KSA*, vol. 9, fragment 11 [143]; *SUP*, 6:352). Nietzsche also expresses the hope of developing a new education on its basis (*KSA*, vol. 9, fragment 11 [145]; *SUP*, 6:353) as well as the expectation of a new future history leading to a mode of existence that to date no utopian has reached (*KSA*, vol. 9, fragment 11 [338]; *SUP*, 6:419). The teaching encourages us to impress the image of eternity on our lives: "Whoever does not believe has a *fleeting* life in his consciousness" (*KSA*, vol. 9, fragment 11 [160]; *SUP*, 6:358). The ethical character of the thought can be clearly discerned in this note. "[This] most powerful thought," Nietzsche writes, "creates new laws of movement for energy, but no new energy [*Kraft*]. Therein lies the possibility, however, of determining and ordering the affects of human beings anew" (*KSA*, vol. 9, fragment 11 [220]; *SUP*, 6:379).

This notebook also contains several outlines of what are taken by Nietzsche to be the scientific presuppositions of eternal recurrence. A notably succinct one runs as follows: "Formerly one thought that infinite activity in time required an *infinite* force that no consumption could exhaust. Now one thinks of force as constantly equal, and it no longer needs to become *infinitely great*. It is eternally active, but it can no longer create infinite cases, it must repeat itself: this is *my* conclusion" (*KSA*, vol. 9, fragment 11 [269]; *SUP*, 6: 39). This idea is clarified further in a note of 1885 when Nietzsche argues that there is no capacity in the world for eternal novelty since a divine creative force or an infinite transformational force does not exist: the concept of an *infinite* force is incompatible with the notion of force (*KSA*, vol. 11, fragment 36 [15]; *SUP*, 16:121–22).[53]

To say that Nietzsche has great expectations of the thought of eternal recurrence is an understatement. Whether the doctrine—conceived as a "truth" that rests on a credible cosmology—can withstand skeptical scrutiny is clearly open to debate. One questionable assumption we find in Nietzsche's thinking on the necessity of recurrence is that there is a correspondence between the becoming of the cosmos and the evolution of life. The evolution of biological life on earth, however, may be quite different to the cycles of recurrence he thinks we can attribute to the forces that make up the physical universe. The claim is not that life is a miracle but rather that it is something uniquely contingent with respect to its occurrence and the evolutionary pathways it has taken. Furthermore, even if we decide to accept eternal recurrence as cosmologically true—which in the absence of firm empirical support for the theory entails making an incautious intellectual leap—nothing on the ethical and social levels follows from this by natural-scientific necessity. Any schemes with which we come up on its basis for the further cultivation of humankind are acts of creative imagining on the part of the thinker who posits it.

Michael Bell rightly notes that what Zarathustra teaches is not strictly the eternal recurrence but *willing* recurrence. In *Zarathustra*, eternal recurrence "is presented as a stupendous thought, in which the willing of its truth is the highest test of character" (2007, 150–51; compare Yeats 1925/2008, 142, 173). It is not difficult to comprehend why the thought mattered to Nietzsche. He hoped it would compel humankind to become serious about its existence and reach a new stage in its maturation. This seriousness about existence refers to the need to assume responsibility for the future development of humankind, in which for the first time in our history we might become masters of our lives and custodians of the earth who have renounced supraterrestrial desires and hopes. We can surely sympathize, however, with Valéry's admittance: "I could never conceive why this vast and violent mind could never leave the unprovable alone" (1968, 260). Does it matter, However, whether Nietzsche's doctrine of recurrence is true? Over the decades, numerous commentators have wrestled with this issue, but their differing efforts to make the thought a credible one run into serious problems and in my view are all unconvincing.

Philip Kain, for example, has argued that Nietzsche's doctrine of eternal recurrence can be defended against skeptical criticism by recognizing that it is not to be taken as true but simply a belief in oneself in which one has a "godlike self-confidence" in oneself as the source of values. He attributes to Nietzsche the view that to depend on something independent of us as the ground of truth or belief involves "a lower level of existence." He concludes his essay as follows: "Nietzsche says 'the Revolution made Napoleon possible; that is its justification.' We might say that the concepts of will to power and eternal recurrence make the overman possible; that is their only justification!" (1983, 386, 387).[54] Although his interpretation frees us at once from the need to take seriously the cosmology of recurrence, it encourages us to cultivate a delusional conception of the world and is thus out of sync with the attempts we encounter in Nietzsche's writings to expose the errors of a delusional mind. Nietzsche's recommendation to us does not seem to be one in which we become self-creators through acts of fantasy, acting *as if* the universe corresponded to our existential desire. That way surely lies the philosophy of the lunatic.

Paul Loeb (2013, 2018b) is one commentator who is acutely aware of the problem of fantasy and unwilling to rest content with attributing to Nietzsche the kind of position Kain settles for. He has attempted to demonstrate the cosmological character of recurrence by showing how its "truth" is disclosed to Zarathustra through the media of precognitive dreams, reveries, experiences of déjà vu and especially the prevision of prospective memory.[55] However, in my view this attempt fails to convince since it invites us to give credence to the claims of personal testimony, including the alleged experiences of prospective memory of Zarathustra that Loeb discerns at work in Nietzsche's text and holds provide us with mnemonic evidence of recurrence. The media appealed to here are unreliable sources of robust knowledge and cannot be relied on to disclose to us anything about the nature of the cosmos. Bergson (1919/2007, 132–33) offers a plausible explanation of paramnesia or the *illusion* of déjà vu in which there is a recollection of the present contemporaneous with the present itself. The illusion, he suggests, is generated from thinking that we are actually undergoing an experience we have already lived through when in fact what is taking place is the perception of the duplication of time into two aspects we do not normally perceive, involving an actual perception and the formation of virtual memory (*virtual* because it is unconscious and inactive, i.e., unrelated as a recollection to action). There is, then, a memory of the present in the actual moment itself. I cannot predict what is going to happen, but I feel as if I can, and what I foresee is that I am going to have known it. I thus experience what can be described as a "recognition to come" in which I gain an awareness of the formation of a memory of the present. If we could stall the movement of time into the future, this experience would be much more common for us.

Interestingly, an attempt to show that precognitive dreams provide us with access to aspects of the future was made by J. W. Dunne in *An Experiment with Time*. At points in the book, he feels compelled to engage with Bergson on duration and his view that future events do not exist in any shape or form (Dunne 1927/2023, chaps. 8, 19). It is only in a later edition of the book that Dunne mentions Nietzsche. He refers to his rendition of eternal recurrence as "glib nonsense," the theory of someone "completely ignorant of science" who "did not know that the Second Law of Thermodynamics expressly forbids any such repetition of the past state of the material world" (Dunne 2023, 138 ["Replies to Critics"]). Indeed, we know that Nietzsche was far more interested in the first law of thermodynamics (concerning the conservation of energy) than he was in the second law (concerning entropy): "The law of the conservation of energy [*Energie*] demands *eternal recurrence*" (*KSA*, vol. 12, fragment 5 [54]; *WP* 1063).

Jorge Luis Borges is astute in identifying Dunne's error, namely, that he "is an illustrious victim of that bad intellectual habit—denounced by Bergson—of conceiving time as the fourth dimension of space." Dunne's postulation that the future—as that toward which we must move—already exists simply converts it into space and requires a second time and then a third time and so on to infinity. Dunne proposes infinite dimensions of time, but as Borges point out any such dimensions are spatial: "For Dunne, real time is the unattainable final boundary of an infinite series" (2000, 219). The human mind finds it difficult to break with the habit of spatializing time, typically by conceiving reality in terms of discrete forces and objects. We see this at work in Nietzsche's thinking too. Although his conception of a great dice game of existence—in which the world conceived as a definite quantity of force is held to pass through a fine and calculable number of combinations—rejects the notion of the atom as a piece of passive matter and (under the influence of Boscovich and Faraday) substitutes for it the concept of dynamic centers of force, Nietzsche's thinking continues to adhere to the view of matter as consisting of discrete and persistent entities. He supposes that because they are finite in number such entities can enter into only a finite number of combinations, of which there is an eventual reoccurrence (see Čapek 1983, 143).

In the face of all these difficulties with Nietzsche's doctrine, then, we might wish to reflect on Santayana's penetrating insight that, when viewed from a sufficient distance, all systems or programs of philosophy can be seen "to be personal, temperamental, accidental, and premature." In a word, they are *human heresies* that "confuse the grammar of human expression, in language, logic, or moral estimation, with the substantial structure of things" (1936, 71).

[CHAPTER SEVEN]

The Philosopher's Vision

> A philosopher: that is a human being who constantly experiences, sees, hears, suspects, hopes and dreams of extraordinary things. . . . A philosopher: oh, a being that often runs away from himself and is often afraid of himself—but who is also too curious not to "return to himself" again and again.
>
> Nietzsche, *Beyond Good and Evil*, aphorism 292

> The sage as an astronomer.—As long as you still feel the stars as something "above you," you lack the vision of a knower.
>
> Nietzsche, *Beyond Good and Evil*, aphorism 71

Introduction

In this chapter, I examine several key features of the late Nietzsche with a focus on his conceptions of philosophy and the philosopher, the discussion largely centered on *Beyond Good and Evil* (1886). I seek to illuminate his criticism of our modern attachment to "objectivity" in two ways: first, understanding his objections to the literary criticism of Sainte-Beuve and, second, understanding his discontent with the "Parisian decadents" such as Flaubert and his ideas about the novel. Nietzsche sees himself addressing a noisy and plebeian age (*BGE* 282), and in both *Beyond Good and Evil* and book 5 of *The Gay Science* (1887) he presents himself as a solitary spirit with a hermit's conscience. In his late writings, he is keen to lay bare what he sees as the general malaise and weakness of modern culture. In the aphorism "Leisure and Idleness" in the first edition of *The Gay Science* (1882), Nietzsche had already observed: "one is [today] ashamed of resting, and prolonged reflection almost gives people a bad conscience. One thinks with a watch in one's hand, even as one eats one's midday meal while reading the latest news of the stock market; one lives as if one always 'might miss out on something.'" What we are losing, he adds, are culture and good taste, the feeling for form, and the ear and eye for the melody of movement. There is now a demand for "*gross obviousness*." Furthermore: "Living in a constant chase after gain compels people to expend their spirit to the point of exhaustion in continual pretence and overreaching and anticipating others. Virtue has come to consist in doing something in less time than someone else. Hours in which honesty is *permitted* have become rare." We have become frugal regarding joy, even suspicious of it: "More and more, *work* enlists all good conscience on its side; and the desire for joy already calls itself a 'need to recuperate' and is beginning to be ashamed of itself" (*GS* 329). It is hard to imagine Nietzsche being able to endure more than a single day of noisy human life if he were to live on planet Earth today. As Italo Calvino points out, the so-called vitality of our times, "noisy, aggressive, revving and roaring," belongs, in fact, "to the realm of death, like a cemetery for rusty old cars" (1996, 12).

In *Ecce Homo*, Nietzsche discloses that "in all essentials" *Beyond Good and Evil* amounts to a "*critique of modernity*," including modern art, the modern sciences, and modern politics. It also offers, he says, "pointers towards an opposing type, as unmodern as possible, a noble yes-saying type" (*EH* "Beyond Good and Evil" 2).[1] The book offers, he discloses, "*a school for the gentilhomme*," where this concept of the refined person of taste and culture is to be understood "more spiritually *and more radically* than ever before" (*EH* "Beyond Good and Evil" 2).[2] To endure its schooling one needs, he states, courage in one's body, and one must have learned not to live in fear.[3] Nietzsche's "gentleman" is neither the vain and snobbish aristocrat nor the bourgeois gentleman portrayed by Molière. Rather, he is a noble figure who dares to be an intellectual marksman of distinction, a solitary who wishes to speak truthfully and shoot arrows well. Nietzsche holds that the absence of "royal and magnificent hermits of the spirit" is a deficiency in the modern age, and he refers in this regard to Heraclitus, Empedocles, and Plato (*BGE* 204). The value of the hermit lies in the fact that his reflections on existence come from dwelling in a world of solitude and silence where he has conversed day and night with his soul; royal hermits speak from caves, labyrinths, and possibly gold mines.[4] It is not that the philosopher wants isolation. Rather, he is aware that the majority in society regard him with deep suspicion and wish only to rescue him from himself. As a result, prudence is called for: "[C]unning and disguise will be needed today for such a human being to sustain himself, to hold himself *up* amidst the sweeping, dangerous rapids of the times . . . and he might marvel at the hidden wisdom of his nature" (*KSA*, vol. 11, fragment 38 [11]; *SUP*, 16:168).

The hermits of the spirit offer not thoughts that aim to console but ones that seek to provoke and challenge and may well blow a chill on passersby (*BGE* 289). The supposition that a philosopher is entitled to holding ultimate opinions is questionable since the thought can be entertained that it is always possible to dig deeper. The free-spirited philosopher considers himself to be a jealous friend of solitude who has his subtlety and, like Epicurus, his garden. In aphorism 25 of *Beyond Good and Evil* Nietzsche offers important advice to philosophers and friends of knowledge about their comportment. Let me cite him at some length:

> After such a cheerful entrance a serious word does not wish to go unheard: it is directed at the most serious. Watch out . . . and beware of martyrdom! Of suffering "for the sake of truth"! Even of defending yourselves! It will ruin all the innocence and delicate neutrality of your conscience, it will make you stiff-necked against objections and red flags, it will stupefy, animalize and brutalize you when in struggling with danger, slander, suspicion, expulsion and even cruder consequences of animosity you have to pose as a defender of truth on earth. . . . In the end you know well enough that it is not supposed to matter whether *you* are right; and likewise that until now no philosopher has been right, and that a more praiseworthy truth could be in every little question mark you put behind your choice words and favorite doctrines. . . . Rather step aside! Go into hiding! And have your mask and subtlety so that you will be mistaken for something or feared a little! And do not forget the garden, the garden with golden trelliswork! And have people around you who are like a garden—or like music over waters at evening time, when the day fades into memories:—choose the *good* solitude, the free, mischievous, light solitude that also gives you the right in some sense to remain good yourselves![5]

Not only is Nietzsche seeking in this aphorism to provide wise counsel for philosophers who are engaged in a serious activity with all kinds of hazards; he is also displaying his qualities as a thinker, such as his integrity and his tact. We also understand why he thinks that, as a protector of truth and advocate of knowledge with an attachment to question marks, the philosopher must don the mask, to wit, wanting to resist the temptation to react and to be a friendly riddler.

The Problem with "Objectivity": Sainte-Beuve and the Scholar

Having demoted philosophy in significance, relative to science, in the first book of his free-spirit writings, *Human, All Too Human*, in *Beyond Good and Evil* Nietzsche is now keen to defend it as a unique mode of vision or perception. Indeed, philosophy is now defined as intellectual vision (*geistige Blick*) (*BGE* 252), a style of perception, which in *Twilight of the Idols* is clarified as "the *power* [*Macht*] of philosophical vision [*Blick*]," which can judge in all the most important matters and does not hide under the mask of objectivity. Nietzsche criticizes the French critic Sainte-Beuve precisely for holding up objectivity as a mask. What the mask conceals in this case is the critic eschewing the task of judging in any matter of importance. Nietzsche identifies in the criticism conducted by Sainte-Beuve "a petty rage against any manly sort of spirit," and he accuses Sainte-Beuve of being "plebeian in the lowest instincts," "related to Rousseau's *ressentiment*," a critic "with the tongue of a cosmopolitan *libertin* for many things, but without the courage to confess even to libertinage" (*TI* "Reconnaissance Raids of an Untimely Man" 3). We saw in chapter 3 above that Nietzsche favors "objective seeing" over ego megalomania, and in his late texts he continues to think of novel ways in which the objectivity of our perception can be enhanced and enriched without castrating the human intellect (see, e.g., *GM* 3.12). In attacking the mask of objectivity in his late texts, he directs his critical focus toward the limits of the scholar who shows a serious lack of discerning taste.

A letter Nietzsche writes to Peter Gast dated November 10, 1887, clearly indicates that he regards Sainte-Beuve as a skeptical critic. He groups him with various literary and scientific figures as belonging to "the most witty and skeptical gang of Parisian minds of the time"—he mentions, among others, Flaubert, Hippolyte Taine, Ernest Renan—and finds in these writers "exasperated pessimism, cynicism, nihilism, alternating with lots of exuberance and good humor," concluding that he knows "these gentlemen by heart," and adding that he is "fed up with them": "One must be more radical" (*KSB* 8, p. 192). Furthermore, in a note of 1885, he refers to Renan and Sainte-Beuve as "both insecure and skeptical down to the bottom of their hearts." Sainte-Beuve is said to have no foothold in philosophy, lacking "genuine *solid* taste" in arts and letters, and turning this lack into "a kind of principle and method of neutrality" (*KSA*, vol. 11, fragment 38 [5], p. 599; *SUP*, 16:159).[6] If one does not have this proper foothold, along with the need for this kind of "solid taste," one will be prone to exaggerated forms of cynicism, pessimism, and nihilism, devoid of nuance and of measure.

Although stylistically, and in terms of the aesthetics of the novel, Flaubert brings "resounding and colorful French" to a pinnacle, Nietzsche finds him to be like Renan and Sainte-Beuve, lacking philosophical self-discipline and "a genuine knowledge of scientific procedures" (*KSA*, vol. 11, fragment 38 [5], p. 600; *SUP*, 16:160). We get a keen sense of Flaubert's tremendous pessimism from his unfinished and posthumously published novel of 1881, *Bouvard and Pécuchet*.[7] Borges writes about it: "[I]f universal history is the history of Bouvard and Pécuchet, everything it consists of is ridiculous and insignificant" (2000, 389). Ernst Bertram advances an astute insight when he argues that Nietzsche displays in his work a "determined overcoming" of the kind of "skeptical fanaticism" that, if followed to its conclusion, leads to "the gruesome Don Quixoteism of Bouvard and Pécuchet," in which "the final communal-human ties are severed by words of utmost nihilistic irony" (1918/2009, 306). The association made here is an interesting one. In his closing meditation on Quixote, Ortega y Gasset reflects on the previous century as one of positivism and pessimism and notes that already in Cervantes's novel the balance of poetic sensibility was tipping toward the side of bitterness while "the nineteenth century, our parent, has felt a perverse delight in pessimism." It has, in fact, "wallowed in it," blowing a gust of animosity onto the next generation. He concludes ominously: "One night Bouvard and Pécuchet buried poetry in the Cemetery of Père Lachaise—in honor of verisimilitude and determinism" (Ortega y Gasset 1914/1961, 165).[8] The concern Ortega y Gasset is expressing is that, with an intellectual commitment to determinism and under the influence of positivism, the natural sciences have imprisoned life within physical necessity, with human actions being conceived simply and only as reactions and enjoying no freedom or originality. He depicts the situation dramatically: "Adaptation is submission and renunciation. Darwin sweeps heroes off the face of the earth" (Ortega y Gasset 1914/1961, 164).[9]

It is possible to conceive much of Nietzsche's thinking in his late writings as a rebellion against positivistic-minded science and its influence on the thinking of his century. This is especially evident in texts such as *Beyond Good and Evil* and *On the Genealogy of Morality*—for example, the attack on Buckle in treatise 1 of the *Genealogy*, which I shall discuss shortly, and the attempt in treatise 2 of the book to contest the primacy accorded to adaptation in thinking about life (*GM* 2.12). And, as we saw in chapter 5 above, much of his attack on the poets of his time is directed at their indulgent pessimism and what Nietzsche calls their "leap into naturalism." There are no references to Flaubert's *Bouvard and Pécuchet* in Nietzsche's corpus. There are, however, interesting and revealing insights into Don Quixotism. In a note of 1875, for example, Nietzsche describes Cervantes's epic novel as "one of the most harmful books" (*KSA*, vol. 8, fragment 8 [7]; *SUP*, 12:104), and in a note of 1876/77 he argues that Cervantes is part of the decadence of Spanish culture and a national misfortune: "[H]e made all of Spain, including all the idiots, laugh and seem wise to themselves" (*KSA*, vol. 8, fragment 23 [140]; *SUP*, 12:412).[10] He regards Cervantes as a contemptuous writer, more cold than cruel. He, of course, appeals to contempt in *Zarathustra* and in his late writings, such as book 5 of *The Gay Science*, as a spur to greatness through self-overcoming, but the contempt he locates in Cervantes is of a distinctly nihilistic kind.[11]

Nietzsche identifies neutrality and an attachment to objectivity in the work of scholars. The task of the genuine philosopher, however, is to grant importance to questions of value. In his early period, Nietzsche holds to the view that the primary concern of philosophy is with the question of the value of existence and with making judgments of taste about what is to be revered: "For science there is nothing great and nothing small—but for philosophy! The value of science is measured in terms of this statement" (*KSA*, vol. 7, fragment 19 [33]; *SUP*, 11:11). As the love of wisdom, philosophy is concerned not only with the domain of truth but equally with the domain of value, enabling us to esteem what is rare, extraordinary, noble, great, and so on. Drawing on Aristotle's distinction between *phronesis* (prudence) and *sophia* (wisdom), in which the former is concerned with common human goods and the latter with knowledge of what is most precious, the early Nietzsche pointed out to his students at Basel University that the Greek word *sophos* does not simply denote "wise" in the usual sense but is related etymologically to *sapio*, "to taste." Suggesting nothing of quietude or asceticism, the wise human being is the one who has sharp taste as sharp knowledge in which the aim is to know not how conclusions follow from principles but which forms of knowledge contain those principles most worthy of knowledge (*KGW*, 2, pt. 4:217–18; Nietzsche 2001, 8).[12] This suggests the need for a discriminating taste, and Nietzsche argues that while philosophical thinking is of the same kind as scientific thinking, it differs from it in that it directs itself "toward *great* things and possibilities." He duly notes that the concept of greatness is amorphous, being partly aesthetic and partly moral. The *great* names that which departs from the normal and the customary and refers to the things we come to venerate (*KSA*, vol. 7, fragment 19 [80]; *SUP*, 11:30). Nietzsche repeats the lesson on taste in his subsequent writings. For example, in *Mixed Opinions and Maxims*, he holds that taste makes one not only blessed but also wise: "which is why the Greeks, who were very subtle in such things, designated the wise man with a word that signifies the *human of taste*, and called wisdom, artistic and practical as well as theoretical and intellectual, simply 'taste' [*Sophia*]" (*MOM* 170).[13] We can accord significance to the philosopher, then, since he or she is the figure whose peculiar task is to be the lawgiver of "the measure, mint, and weight of things" (*SE* 3). In the late writings, Nietzsche seeks to show that the character of the genuine philosopher consists in being a creator and a legislator of value (*BGE* 211).

In *Beyond Good and Evil*, Nietzsche speaks out against a shift he sees taking place in his time in the respective ranks of science and philosophy, one that is in the process of becoming established with a good conscience (*BGE* 204). We are witnessing in the present age, he contends, the growing independence of the scholars and their emancipation from true philosophy. He regards this as one of the more refined effects of the democratic order, in which freedom from all masters—the rabble instinct par excellence—is sought. Once science liberates itself from theology, whose handmaiden it once was, it seeks to play master over philosophy and lay down laws for it. Nietzsche does express admiration, however, for one aspect of the lives of his "scholarly friends," which is their despising of "men of letters" and "culture parasites." The scholar is to be applauded for not knowing how "to make a business of the spirit" and for having opinions that cannot readily be translated into financial values. His worry, however, is over their bookish character and the fact that they produce only "oppressive books," books that do not enliven the spirit but serve only to deaden and depress it and that it comes as a relief to finish: "Cramped intestines betray themselves . . . no less than closet air, closet ceilings, closet narrowness. . . . Our first questions about the value of a book, of a human being, or a musical composition are: Can they walk? Even more, can they dance?" (*GS* 366).

Nietzsche observes on the part of scholars a disdain toward genuine philosophy. A utility principle on the part of modern scholarship serves to make it blind to the value of philosophy, with the result that philosophy is seen as little more than a series of "*refuted* systems" and a "prodigal effort" that benefits nobody. Or, he muses, the lack of respect shown to philosophy today might be the result of the bad aftereffect of some philosophers (he gives the example of Schopenhauer). He goes on to note a deeper reason for philosophy's woeful state in the present age, and this has to do with its own self-image and practice—where it has become timid, reduced to little more than the theory of knowledge—and this can be taken as a signal that philosophy is in its last throes. He thinks philosophy has today lost the will to be master, that is, to have the will to direct other inquiries and surmount them by determining the "whither" or "where to?" of humanity. He reminds readers of philosophy's past glories and of the royal hermits of the spirit, whom he contrasts with today's "hodgepodge philosophers," positivists and philosophers of reality who embody today's "*unbelief* in the masterly task and masterfulness of philosophy." In *On the Genealogy of Morality*, he maintains that modern philosophers of reality are simply bad musicians in whom the abyss of scientific conscience does not reveal itself, and thus the fact that the will to truth may conceal a will to death goes unrecognized. After addressing the industry of the best scholars, he challenges his readers in the following way: "Science as a means of self-anaesthetic: *do you know that?*" (*GM* 3.23).

Much of the polemic of the text of *On the Genealogy of Morality* (1887) is directed at the "*plebeianism* of the modern spirit," the erupting force of which is like a "volcano of mud" (*GM* 1.4). Nietzsche associates this plebeian spirit with various modern writers, including the naturalistic historian Henry Thomas Buckle (1821–62). Buckle was the author of the multivolume *History of Civilization in England* and a pioneer of the statistical approach to history, in which human actions are held to be governed by laws as fixed and as regular as those we find in the physical world. The approach Nietzsche adopts in the *Genealogy* is in stark contrast to that of a historian like Buckle, for whom individual efforts are insignificant in the story of history; indeed, for him, the great human being represents only a force of disturbance and is nothing more than a creature of its time. Nietzsche comments on this approach in a note of 1888 and argues that an "agitator of the mob" like Buckle is incapable of comprehending the concept of a "higher nature" (*KSA*, vol. 13, fragment 16 [39], pp. 497–98; *WP* 876).[14] Nietzsche feels compelled to contest the claim that our modern morality represents the end of history in the sense of its fulfillment. As he makes clear in the preface to the *Genealogy*, "morality," as we moderns understand it, can be regarded as the "danger of dangers" because it makes the present live at the expense of the future. The aim is to combat the "degeneration and diminution of man into a perfect herd animal" (*BGE* 203). This requires that we recognize "that man is the *animal that has not yet been established*" and that it is possible for man to be something other than a "sublime miscarriage" (*BGE* 62).

The Novel and "Objectivity": Flaubert

In *The Case of Wagner*, Nietzsche connects the problems that characterize Wagner's art and its mythical content to the problems that interest those he calls "the little Parisian decadents" and states with biting wit: "Always five steps away from the hospital! Entirely modern, entirely *metropolitan* problems! Don't doubt it" (*CW* 9). He typically interprets literary figures such as Baudelaire and Flaubert as writers who display pessimistic attitudes.[15] He regards Baudelaire as "just as German as Parisian": "[H]is poetry has something of what in Germany is called *Gemüt* or 'endless melody' and sometimes also 'caterwauling.' . . . There is much Wagner in Baudelaire" (*KSA*, vol. 11, fragment 38 [5], p. 601; *SUP*, 16:160).[16] As a critic and poet, Baudelaire, Nietzsche claims, had ruined but also sharp taste that was sure of itself, with which "he tyrannize[d] the insecure of today" (*KSA*, vol. 11, fragment 38 [5], p. 601; *SUP*, 16:160).[17] Nietzsche opens the long section of aphorisms in *Twilight of the Idols* entitled "Reconnaissance Raids of an Untimely Man" with a list of his "impossibles," with each philosophical and literary figure mentioned referred to in witty terms, such as "*Carlyle*: or pessimism as lunch revisited" and Zola as "or 'the joy of stinking,'" offered as a pun on Zola's novel of 1885, *The Joy of Living* (*TI* "Reconnaissance Raids of an Untimely Man" 1).[18] In a note from 1887–88, Zola with his literary naturalism is unsurprisingly listed as belonging to the French literary tradition of pessimism (*KSA*, vol. 13, fragment 11 [158]), and in another note from the same period he is said to have emerged from a skeptical milieu (*KSA*, vol. 13, fragment 11 [56]). More substantially, in a note from the autumn of 1887, Nietzsche outlines his objections to what he sees as the brutalism of modern art. He identifies in the likes of Zola a "crude and strongly exaggerated logic of delineation" in which motifs are simplified to the point of formulas and the formula is allowed to tyrannize, with little more than a brutality of colors and desires presented (*KSA*, vol. 12, fragment 10 [37]; *WP* 827). Ultimately, Nietzsche will question whether there is such a thing as genuinely pessimistic art, as Schopenhauer espoused: "Tragedy does not teach 'resignation'—To represent terrible and questionable things is in itself an instinct for power and magnificence in an artist: he does not fear them.... Art affirms. Job affirms.—But Zola?" Nietzsche's critical insight is that, even when an artist like Zola displays ugliness and a fascination with it, he is taking "*pleasure in the ugly*," and to think otherwise is to deceive oneself. He also notes in this regard: "How liberating [*erlösend*] is Dostoevsky!" (*KSA*, vol. 13, fragment 14 [47]; *WP* 821).

Writing against the romanticism of passion, Nietzsche argues that the task facing art is not to play with artistic formulas but to "remodel life so that afterward it *has* to formulate itself" (*KSA*, vol. 13, fragment 11 [312], p. 132; *WP* 849). Art can be the consequence of a soul dissatisfied with reality, as is evident in the romantic pessimism of a great deal of modern art, but it can also be "an expression of *gratitude for happiness enjoyed*" (*KSA*, vol. 12, fragment 2 [114]; *WP* 845). Nietzsche identifies the former with romanticism and the latter with aureole (*Glorien-schein*) and dithyramb, and in connection with this blissful and graceful "art of apotheosis" he mentions the likes of Rubens, Hafiz, and Goethe.[19] He contrasts this "blissful" and "graceful" art of eternalization with its opposite, which is governed by the tyrannical will of the great sufferer from life who forges "what is most personal, individual, and narrow ... in his suffering, into a binding law and compulsion, taking revenge on all things, as it were, by impressing, forcing, and branding into them his image, the image of his torture" (*WP* 846; see also *GS* 370).

The suspicions about modern poets that Nietzsche has in his middle writings continue then into his late ones. In aphorism 269 of *Beyond Good and Evil*, for example, he reflects on what appears to be the rule when it comes to the souls of the stranger human types, namely, the fact that they are so prone to self-destruction and corruption, and he refers to the likes of Byron, Musset, Poe, Leopardi, Kleist, and Gogol. Such great poets, he suggests, "often take revenge on their works for an inner contamination ... often lost in the mud and in love with it, until they become like the will-o'-the-wisps around the swamps and *pretend* to be like stars" (*BGE* 269). His impatience with them is well expressed in this note from 1885: "Against false idealism, where exaggerated subtlety alienates the best natures in the world. What a pity that the whole of southern Europe has lost the inheritance of that bound sensuality through the abstinence of the clergy! And it's fair that such Shelleys, Hölderlins, Leopardis perish, I don't think much of such people. It amuses me to think of the revenge that the rough naturalness of nature takes in such people, e.g., when I hear that Leopardi used to masturbate and later became impotent" (*KSA*, vol. 11, fragment 34 [95], p. 451). Nietzsche, it can be noted, writes in favor of a relative chastity, which he conceives as a "fundamental and prudent caution against eroticism even in thought" that can, he adds, "belong to the great sense of life even in richly endowed and whole natures": "This principle applies especially to artists, it belongs to their best wisdom" (*KSA*, vol. 13, fragment 23 [2]; *WP* 815). This practice of relative chastity constitutes an ethics of life, which is why Nietzsche rails against Wagner's preaching of chastity as "an incitement to perversion": "I despise anyone who does not regard *Parsifal* as an attempt to assassinate ethics" (*NCW* "Wagner as Apostle of Chastity" 3; see also *KSA*, vol. 12, fragment 2 [22]).[20]

In Flaubert, Nietzsche locates the hatred of life as an instinctive judgment: "He tortured himself when he wrote, just as Pascal tortured himself when he thought—they both felt unegoistic. . . . 'Selflessness'—that principle of decadence, the will to the end in art as in morality" (*NCW* "We Antipodes"). To want to flee from oneself in this way through the medium of art is to want to flee from life itself (*D* 549). (See also the criticism of "belief in intoxication" in *D* 50.) Decadence for Nietzsche is the art par excellence of modern metropolitan existence. As one commentator notes, however, decadence for Nietzsche is more complicated than a simple weakening of the will since it also involves an overrefinement characterized in terms of "a hypertrophy of the delicate sense of values and subtlety which civilization brings" (William 1952, 154). Nietzsche conceives literary decadence as a situation where "[t]he whole does not live at all anymore: it is cobbled together, calculated, synthetic, and artifact" (*CW* 7). Here, he is utilizing Paul Bourget's definition in his *Essais de psychologie contemporaine*: "A decadent style is one in which the unity of the book falls apart, replaced by the independence of the sentence (*phrase*), and the sentence makes way for the word" (1883/1993, 14).[21] As an issue of style, then, decadence amounts to "a dangerous erosion of the classical proportion of part to whole" (Baudelaire 2022, 64 [introduction]).[22] Nietzsche may also have encountered in his reading this pertinent appraisal of decadence by the Austrian poet and storyteller Adalbert Stifter, whose work, as we saw in chapter 5 above on the poets, he esteemed: "Declining peoples first lose their sense of moderation. They strive for isolated particulars, they fling themselves shortsightedly on narrow and trifling things, they raise the conditional above the universal. . . . [T]heir art depicts what is one-sided what is valid from one perspective only, then what is disjointed dissonant bizarre, eventually what excites and tantalizes the senses. . . . [T] he individual scorns the whole, pursuing his pleasure and his ruin" (Stifter 1994, 13; Stifter 2021, 8).

Nietzsche has several objections to Flaubert and to French writers. He contends that what motivates them is self-loathing and a fatalism that provides a certain peace in the face of this self-loathing. We see, then, in their existence "a flight from the self and forming ideals, making things *better*, through seeking to know how things have *gotten* this way" (*KSA*, vol. 11, fragment 25 [164]; *SUP*, 15:48). Nietzsche's position on fatalism is a complex one. On the one hand, he applauds Goethe for his "joyful and *trusting* fatalism" in which what is singular or separate (*Einzelne*) finds itself reprehensible and "everything is redeemed and affirmed in the whole" (*TI* "Reconnaissance Raids of an Untimely Man" 49).[23] On the other hand, he is keen to challenge the fatalism and weariness of the modern spirit, including "positivistic systems" of thought and the wisdom of leaving things to some supposed providential law (see *GS* 277, 347). These modes of thought display an attitude of resignation that Nietzsche finds contemptible. In a note of autumn 1887, he writes: "[T]he disastrous belief in *divine Providence* continues to exist—that most paralysing belief for hand and mind there's ever been. . . . That absurd trust in the course of things, in 'life,' in the 'life instinct.'" He has just referred to what he sees lying behind the formulas of "progress," "perfectibility," and "Darwinism." He concludes: "Even fatalism, our present-day form of philosophical sensibility, is a consequence of that *longest-held* belief in divine dispensation, an unconscious consequence: as if it were not precisely up to *us* how everything turned out (—as if we could let things run as they run: each *individual* himself merely a mode of absolute reality—)" (*KSA*, vol. 12, fragment 10 [7]). Indeed, he criticizes "naturalism" on the grounds that it eliminates "the choosing, judging, interpreting subject as a principle." When conceived as mechanism or the view that everything can be accounted for in terms of "the calculable rigidity of the mechanical process," this naturalism is but another example of a "fatalistic submission to matters of fact" (*KSA*, vol. 12, fragment 9 [178], p. 442; *WP* 95).

In seeking to lose themselves in art, writers like Flaubert achieve only "a scientific approach or photography," which Nietzsche describes as "description without perspective" with "nothing but foreground and everything cluttered" (*KSA*, vol. 11, fragment 25 [164]; *SUP*, 15:48).[24] Moreover, the French novelists describe only exceptions, and, although these are taken from all circles of society, it is the bourgeois that is hated equally by each one of them (*KSA*, vol. 11, fragment 25 [164]; *SUP*, 15:48).[25] Flaubert, Nietzsche observes, was "sick and tired of himself as 'bourgeois'" (*KSA*, vol. 11, fragment 25 [181]; *SUP*, 15:53), and his much-lauded "objectivity" is nothing more than a modern means of freeing oneself from scorn (*KSA*, vol. 11, fragment 25 [216]; *SUP*, 15:60; see also *KSA*, vol. 11, fragment 26 [458]; *SUP*, 15:252; *BGE* 218; *TI* "Maxims and Barbs" 34; and *CW* 9).[26]

In *Ecce Homo*, Nietzsche refers to another pessimist, Maupassant, as one of the most delicate psychologists based in Paris and reveals that he is especially fond of him as a writer (*EH* "Why I Am So Clever" 3).[27] Although he does not expand on this, and despite the fact that no further references to the novelist are to be found in the corpus, what Maupassant says about the psychological novel in the preface to his novel *Pierre and Jean* (1888) resonates with Nietzsche's criticism of photographic objectivity: "The realist, if he is an artist, will try not to show us a commonplace photograph of life, but to give us a more complete view of it, more striking, more convincing than reality itself." In the preface, Maupassant takes aim at "partisans of objectivity" who expect the novelist to provide an exact representation of what takes place in life (1888/2008, 26, 28). (Compare Nietzsche on the "lie" of objectivity in *BGE* 208.)[28] The picture that emerges of Nietzsche's interest in the French pessimists and Parisian decadents is a complicated one since it was Flaubert who served as Maupassant's mentor in the art of the novel and the objective method. Nietzsche's criticism of Flaubert, however, is a specific one focused on what he discerns as a lack of genuine independence with respect to humanity's condition and the fact that as a writer he does not express his true feelings.

Koenraad Swart (1964, 112) argues that, while Flaubert sought to illustrate the dangers of Romantic idealism in his novels—for example, in *Madame Bovary* and *Sentimental Education*—he belonged to a group of self-styled realists who did not fully overcome Romanticism and admitted themselves that they suffered from the nervous exhaustion and the irritability of a decadent era.[29] Christopher Isherwood noted that the atmosphere of Paris was the native element of Baudelaire's inspiration and cites him on his attraction to "the religious intoxication of the great cities" (1969, 41).[30] Indeed, Nietzsche holds that in the last analysis the French novelists and poets "can never rid themselves of Paris" (*KSA*, vol. 11, fragment 25 [164]; *SUP*, 15:48).[31]

Hashish and Satanism: Baudelaire and Wagnerism

In a note from 1888, Nietzsche reflects on Wagner as an artist and suggests that, under the spell of a "pathological sexuality that was the curse of his life," Wagner "knew only too well what an artist loses when he loses freedom and respect for himself": "[The artist] is condemned to be an actor. His art itself becomes for him a constant attempt to escape, a means of forgetting himself, of numbing himself." He then adds: "Such a 'slave' needs a hashish world, strange, heavy, enveloping vapors, all kinds of exoticism and symbolism of the ideal, just to get rid of his reality for once—he needs Wagnerian music." He concludes this note by linking Baudelaire, Poe, and Wagner: "A certain catholicity of the ideal above all in an artist is almost proof of the 'swamp' of self-contempt: the case of Baudelaire in France, the case of Edgar Allan Poe in America, the case of Wagner in Germany" (*KSA*, vol. 13, fragment 23 [2]).

Baudelaire discusses in a clear-eyed manner the effects of opium and hashish in his essay "The Poem of Hashish." He refers to Poe as "that incomparable poet and unrefuted philosopher, who should always be quoted on all the mysterious maladies of the soul," including "the sombre and compelling splendours of opium!" In reflecting on the experience of consuming hashish, Baudelaire is keen to expose the conquering monomania that grips the smoker under its effects, delighting himself with the thought that he is "the most virtuous of all men," and bringing him daily ever "nearer to the glittering abyss in which he will gaze upon the face of Narcissus." He adds, wittily (referring to Rousseau): "Jean-Jacques managed to intoxicate himself without hashish" (1950, 106, 117). Baudelaire is especially interested in exploring the effects of hashish on the personality of the human being of sensibility or the misunderstood genius of the Romantics, the type stigmatized in his own time as *an original.*

Nietzsche utilizes his own experience smoking opium and hashish in an epistemic manner, seeking to enhance his understanding of mental processes and aid his research into different states of consciousness, including the experience of time: "Enjoying hashish and dreaming teach us that the *speed of mental processes* is enormous. Apparently, we don't *deal* with most of them, they don't enter our consciousness. There must be a great deal of consciousness and willing in every complex organic being: our highest level of consciousness usually keeps the other levels shut down" (*KSA*, vol. 11, fragment 25 [401]; *SUP*, 15:103). In a note of 1884, he observes: "When smoking hashish, space [is] much more extended because we see much more in the same time frame than usual. *Sense of space dependent on time*"

(*KSA*, vol. 11, fragment 25 [306]; *SUP*, 15:98 [emphasis added]). Unlike Baudelaire, Nietzsche appears not to have been familiar with Thomas De Quincey, who, in *Confessions of an English Opium Eater*, discloses how taking opium affected his sense of space and time, which was "amplified to an extent of unutterable infinity," with his sense of time undergoing a vast expansion: "I sometimes seemed to have lived for 70 or 100 years in one night; nay, sometimes had feelings of representatives of a millennium passed in that time, or, however, of a duration far beyond the limits of any human experience" (1821/1971, 103–4).[32]

Nietzsche sees Baudelaire's creativity as bound up with the satanic and holds that it does not free itself from it.[33] In a February 26, 1888, letter to Gast, he discloses excitedly that he has been thumbing through a recently published volume of Baudelaire's *Oeuvres posthume* and has found in it, along with some "invaluable psychological observations relating to *decadence*," an unpublished letter of Wagner's that has caught his eye. The letter in question was intended for Baudelaire and contains an effusive response to an essay he published in the *Revue européene* that Wagner had read. "A thousand thanks for your beneficence," Wagner planned to reply to Baudelaire (see n. 16). This find confirms for Nietzsche what he had suspected for some time but until this discovery had no proof of. Citing himself on a previous occasion, he addresses Gast as follows: "'[W]ho was most ready for Wagner? who was most naturally and inwardly Wagnerian, in spite of and without Wagner?' For a long time, I had been telling myself: it was that bizarre, three-quarters lunatic [*Narr*] Baudelaire, the poet of *Les Fleurs du Mal*" (*KSB* 8, pp. 262–65, 263; Middleton 1996, 287). He then admits to being disappointed that "this kindred spirit of Wagner's had not during his lifetime discovered him," only to now learn that Baudelaire had more than discovered Wagner. In Baudelaire's poems, he reveals to Gast, he had found "a sort of Wagnerian *sensibility*," and he goes on to describe him as "a *libertine*, mystical, 'satanic,' but, above all, Wagnerian" (*KSB* 8, pp. 263; Middleton 1996, 287).[34]

T. S. Eliot argues that Baudelaire was exposed to both the follies and the inventions of his time.[35] He explicitly refers to his satanism but notes that now the prevailing tendency is to present him as a serious Catholic Christian. However, he argues that, when not simply an affectation, satanism is an attempt "to get into Christianity by the back door": "It is a way of affirming belief" (Eliot 1930/2015, 157).[36] Despite the morbidity of his temperament, Baudelaire is to be understood as a theological innocent who is discovering Christianity for himself. Thus: "[T]he true claim of Baudelaire as an artist is not that he found a superficial form, but that he was searching for a form of life." Although the satanism of the Black Mass was in the air at the time, Eliot maintains that Baudelaire redeemed it by making it mean something different: "Baudelaire is concerned, not with demons, black masses, romantic blasphemy but with the real problem of good and evil. . . . Baudelaire perceived that what really matters is Sin and Redemption" (Eliot 1930/2015, 158, 161).[37]

Eliot provides an intelligent interpretation of Baudelaire as an artist and locates in him a genuine discipline of thought and life. For Nietzsche, however, Baudelaire is a questionable mystic. The attachment to mysticism is evident in how he reflects on the significance of Wagner's music. He writes, for example, of how this ardent despotic music recaptures for the listener "the vertiginous imaginings of the opium smoker," with the overture to *Lohengrin* expressing "the ardour of mysticism, the yearnings of the spirit towards God and the incommunicable" (Baudelaire 2006, 332, 342).

When commentators write on Nietzsche's musical taste, they typically cite his preference for Bizet over Wagner, in accordance with what Nietzsche says himself in *The Case of Wagner*. Perhaps a better counterpoint, however, is to be found in his liking of Chopin. He admires Chopin for liberating music from German influences and the tendency to be ugly, gloomy, petty bourgeois, and self-important and for expressing in his music beauty, noble cheerfulness, exuberance, and splendor of the soul. Even Beethoven is to be regarded as a semibarbaric creature since his great soul never learned to distinguish the sublime from the adventurous, the simple from the mediocre and insipid. His worry about Chopin is that the "strong Slav" lived too close to the dangerous current in the French spirit and allowed himself to be influenced by the narcotics of an overrefined culture (see *EH* "Why I Am So Clever" 7; *KSA*, vol. 9, fragment 21 [2], pp. 681–82; and *KSA*, vol. 11, fragment 28 [10], p. 302; *SUP*, 15:281). In *The Wanderer and His Shadow*, he writes about Chopin's *Barcarolle* in connection with the insight that all circumstances and ways of life contain a blissful moment: "*That* is what good artists know how to fish out. . . . [I]n the *Barcarolle*, Chopin brought this blissful moment into music in such a way that even gods could desire to spend lengthy summer evenings lying in a boat" (*WS* 160).[38]

As a musician, Wagner shows, Nietzsche contends, that he has the instincts of a great actor. Wagner's art makes music a means to the ends of drama with the whole spectacle becoming a theatrical one, "a mere occasion for many dramatic poses." Nietzsche finds dishonesty at work in the theater: "In the theater one is honest only in the mass; as an individual one lies; one lies to oneself. One leaves oneself at home when ones goes to the theater, one renounces the right to one's own tongue and choice, to one's taste, even to one's courage as one has it and exercises it between one's own four walls against both God and man." In contrast to the theatrical poses that govern

Wagner's music, the body, he holds, is always central to our enjoyment of music and being persuaded by it. *His* body seeks from music, he reveals, "its own *ease*," in which the animal functions are "quickened by easy, bold, exuberant, self-assured rhythms; as if iron, leaden life should be gilded by golden and tender harmonies." Moreover: "My melancholy [*Schwermut*, lit. 'heavy mood'] wants to rest in the hiding places and abysses of *perfection*: that is why I need music" (*GS* 368).

In *Nietzsche contra Wagner*, Nietzsche finesses the insight into the vanity of artists he had offered in *The Gay Science* and depicts the artist as "the Orpheus of all secret misery" who has incorporated into art things that seemed unworthy of it and incapable of being expressed in music, so giving speech to dumb animals, to depressed and tormented souls, and who can be admired for this (*NCW* "Where I Admire"; see also *GS* 87). Wagner, he writes, is someone who has suffered deeply, and therein lies "his *superiority* to other musicians." Nietzsche has in mind here "very small and microscopic features of the soul." He admits, then, that he does admire Wagner, notably "wherever he has set *himself* to music," but maintains that he did not know what he could do best as an artist. It was his vanity that led Wagner to focus on something prouder and louder than the "small plants" considered as something "new, strange, and beautiful" (*NCW* "Where I Admire"; see also *KSA*, vol. 9, fragment 15 [51]; *SUP*, 6:491; and *KSA*, vol. 11, fragment 28 [10], pp. 302–3; *SUP*, 15:281).

The Observations of the Psychologist

Nietzsche issues a set of warnings for anyone who wishes to be a psychologist. It should not be a matter of observing merely for the sake of observing since such a contrived observation may well give us a false squint by making our observations forced and exaggerated. We should also not seek to look at ourselves in the middle of any experience since our eye may well turn into an evil eye. We project all kinds of phantasms on what it is we are seeing and observing; and the evil eye is an eye that does not trust itself but allows itself to be led astray by distractions and unimportant little facts. Like the painter, the good psychologist, Nietzsche advises, does not simply work from nature but trusts his instincts, his *camera obscura*, and sifts through and expresses the case, the nature, or the thing experienced (*TI* "Reconnaissance Raids of an Untimely Man" 7).[39] When looked at from the perspective of the undisciplined eye, nature is merely chance. This explains why Nietzsche insists that studies from nature are a bad sign, showing "subjugation, weakness, fatalism" (*TI* "Reconnaissance Raids of an Untimely Man" 7).

In *An Essay on Criticism* (1711), Alexander Pope writes of the poet as someone who copies from nature:

> First follow NATURE, and your judgment frame
> By her just standard, which is still the same:
> *Unerring Nature*, still divinely bright,
> One *clear*, *unchang'd*, and *Universal* Light,
> Life, Force, and Beauty must to all impart,
> At once the *Source*, and *End*, and *Test* of Art.
> (Pope 1969, 40)[40]

In a draft sketch of *The Gay Science* 290, an aphorism on the need to give style to one's character, Nietzsche refers to Pope and admits to understanding his weariness with excessive artificiality. He makes it clear, however, that he favors a stylized nature: "The deep passion of wanting is relieved at the sight of stylized nature: the beautiful bondage and perfection in compulsion is its ideal" (*KSA*, 14:265). In aphorism 290 of *The Gay Science*, the emphasis is on strong natures who "enjoy their finest gaiety in such constraint and perfection under a law of their own; the passion of their tremendous will that relents in the face of all stylized nature, of all conquered and serving nature": "Even when they have to build palaces and design gardens, they demur at giving nature freedom" (*GS* 290; see also *D* 560). The criticism Nietzsche makes of regarding oneself as a piece of free nature and the stress he places on the need to stylize nature through compulsion, where constraint is conceived as a form of training and discipline, is a key aspect of his thinking about self-cultivation. In aphorism 188 of *Beyond Good and Evil*, for example, he argues: "What is essential and inestimable in every morality is that it is a long compulsion. . . . [W]e need to recall the compulsion under which so far every language has achieved strength and freedom—the compulsion of meter, the tyranny of rhyme and rhythm" (*BGE* 188).

When he addresses the question of just who the philosopher is, Nietzsche highlights the importance of having a clear perception of things. In aphorism 39 of *Beyond Good and Evil*, he quotes from Stendhal, whom at this time he considers Europe's last great psychologist: "To be a good philosopher you must be dry, clear, and without illusion. A banker who has made a fortune has part of the character required to make discoveries in philosophy, that is, to see clearly into what is." Nietzsche cites Stendhal in the context of attempting to specify the conditions favorable to the emergence of strong, independent spirits. He wants his readers to reflect on the fact that these conditions may well include "hardness and cunning" and not, as idealists who gush about the true, the good, and the beautiful like to think, gentle and overrefined good-naturedness. In a long note from 1885 on French literature, he praises Stendhal for his free-spiritedness along these lines, referring to him as a writer "gifted with subtle and daring senses, curious to the point of cynicism, a logician nearly from disgust, riddle guesser and friend of the sphinx" (*KSA*, vol. 11, fragment 38 [5]; *SUP*, 16:158).[41]

With the previous reference to the pessimism and cynicism of writers such as Flaubert and Renan and now this reference to cynicism in Stendhal, we see the extent to which for Nietzsche intellectual dispositions can assume both crude and refined forms. When Nietzsche refers to cynicism in a positive manner as opposed to a pejorative one, he has in mind, as in the case of a writer like Stendhal, the way problems need to be tackled with *both* "delicate fingers" and "the bravest fists" (*EH* "Why I Write Such Good Books" 3).[42] In *Beyond Good and Evil*, he notes with great acuity how cynicism "is the only form in which vulgar souls come in contact with what honesty [*Redlichkeit*] is," adding: "[T]he higher human being has to open his ears to every cruder and finer cynicism and congratulate himself each time the shameless jester or the scientific satyr speaks up right in front of him" (*BGE* 26).[43]

Here, Nietzsche is taking *cynics* to denote those who acknowledge the animal and the vulgarity in themselves and at the same time have a degree of spirituality that allows them to talk about themselves and their kind "*in front of witnesses*:—sometimes they will even wallow in books as if in their own filth." We can approach the scientific head, then, knowing that it is a head mounted on an ape's body, which gives us "a subtle, exceptional understanding on a base soul—especially not a rare occurrence among doctors and physiologists of morals" (*BGE* 26).[44] In this aphorism, Nietzsche's attention is focused on how human beings who feel predestined for knowledge of humanity, including both its reality and its possibilities, need to comport themselves in the world once they realize they cannot remain in their fortress, where they endeavor to avoid the crowd and the many. The danger to which they then expose themselves is becoming not gloomy and despondent by the encounter with human beings but rather contaminated by misanthropy and the turning against humanity. Nietzsche advises the lover of knowledge to be wary of those who speak badly—not wickedly, he adds—of humanity and with indignation, seeing only baseness in the human animal: "For the indignant person, and whoever tears and mangles himself (or, as a substitute, the world, God, or society) with his own teeth may indeed be higher morally speaking than the laughing and self-satisfied satyr, but in every other sense he is the more ordinary, more indifferent and less instructive case. And nobody *lies* as much as the indignant" (*BGE* 26). In short, nothing is more ordinary and in fact nothing is easier than speaking ill or badly of humanity, and doing so offers little in the way of instruction or knowledge. The cynics are to be valued but not overvalued. They abbreviate and alleviate the task of the lover of the passion of knowledge, but on account of their baseness they must be reckoned to be unreliable guides to humanity and its possibilities.

When addressing the topic of the scholar, Nietzsche makes it clear that he is speaking from his own memory as someone who was trained as one. As an old philologist, he has the experience of the scholar's training, and philologists are said to be the most learned and conceited of all scholars. The scholar is trained to be a specialist and a nook dweller, an educated person who must resist any kind of synthetic enterprise and talent. At the same as he extolls the virtues of philosophy as the mastery of life, Nietzsche also draws attention to the current dangers facing the maturation of the philosopher today. He notes that they are so manifold that it is far from clear whether such a fruit can, in fact, ripen. For example, there is the fact that the construction of the various sciences has grown to an enormous size, and this may, during his apprenticeship, make the philosopher weary and, as a result, choose to become a specialist. When this happens, the philosopher does not attain what Nietzsche calls his *proper level*, which he construes as the height for a comprehensive look. Or, if he does attain it, he attains it too late, when his most favorable time and strength are spent; or he could be delayed on account of the severity of his intellectual conscience such is his fear of becoming a dilettante, "an insect with a thousand antennae." If the philosopher loses his former self-respect, he knows it is impossible for him to lead and command in the realm of knowledge—unless, Nietzsche notes, he is willing "to become a great actor, a philosophical Cagliostro and pied piper, in short, a seducer" (*BGE* 204). It is the second reference Nietzsche makes in the book to Cagliostro (see also *BGE* 194), who stands for the archetype of a human being whose power and influence is founded on deception.[45]

A further problem that Nietzsche notes is that the philosopher demands from himself a judgment, a yes or a no, not about the sciences, but about the value of things, yet he is reluctant to believe that he has such a right or even a duty to such a lofty judgment. The path to such a judgment—one based on experiences—is perilous, and the philosopher frequently hesitates and doubts and may even lapse into silence. It is perhaps not surprising, Nietzsche notes, that the crowd misjudges the philosopher, taking him for an ideal scholar or religiously elevated and enthusiast of God or the divine. Nietzsche notes that there are good reasons to welcome up to a point a spirit that weds itself to objectivity. The danger comes when we exaggerate the importance of the depersonalization of the spirit as if this was the goal of existence. The objective spirit sees itself as a mirror of reality, simply submitting before whatever it is that is to be known and providing a mirror to it. The scholar allows himself to be used as an instrument and seeks to do everything possible to remove what is accidental and arbitrary from his perception of the world. Nietzsche notes there is a high price to be paid for this depersonalization being for the sake of attaining the ideal scholar: one loses seriousness for oneself. The scholar may be cheerful, but his cheerfulness shows not a lack of distress but a neglect of his own needs. The irony of the scholar's taste, then, is that it results in a lack of concern with the need for taste and judgment (see *HH* preface 6–7). The scholar thinks he can only attain authenticity by being strictly objective, and, if love and hate are wanted from him, he will do what he can and give what he can, but it will not be much; rather, it will be something "inauthentic, fragile, questionable, and worm-eaten." Nietzsche contrasts the scholar with the philosopher, whom he describes in this section as "the Caesarian cultivator and cultural dynamo." The objective man is a pure instrument and, as such, "the most sublime type of slave" who weds himself to a cause that has no aim or goal other than detachment from life. Such a human being is a *formal* man, "without substance and content," a "'selfless' man," neither a begetter nor a sunrise. The modern scholar type, he argues, belongs to the intellectual middle class, and this is a class that is simply unable to catch sight of the truly great problems and profound question marks (*GS* 373).

The Philosopher as Legislator

In his early writings, Nietzsche conceives the philosopher as primarily a name giver who seeks to elevate the human being and the legislation of the ancient philosophers as consisting primarily in this naming (*KSA*, vol. 7, fragment 19 [83]; *SUP*, 11:31).[46] In *Beyond Good and Evil*, he once again presents the philosopher as a legislator, but this time as a meaning maker and creator, that is, as a figure who posits tasks and sets goals for humanity and declares "thus it shall be!" (*BGE* 211). In *Human, All Too Human*, he had reflected on the first Greek philosophers—figures such as Parmenides, Pythagoras, and Empedocles—and presented them as spiritual tyrants who had "a robust faith in themselves and in their 'truth.'" As a statesman and poet, Solon is said to be an exception inasmuch as he sought not personal tyranny but the setting down of laws in which law giving is a sublimated form of tyranny. In Plato, we find "the incarnate desire to become the supreme philosophical legislator and founder of states": "[H]e seems to have suffered terribly from the nonfulfillment of his nature, and toward the end his soul was filled with the blackest bile" (translation modified). Although Nietzsche expresses in this aphorism tremendous admiration for these philosophers—just as he does in his lecture course on the pre-Platonic philosophers in the early 1870s, locating in them supreme possibilities of life, and lamenting Plato falling prey to Socratic enchantment, which was then followed by "the loquacious hordes of the Socratic schools"—he maintains in this text from 1878 that the time of these tyrants of the spirit is over and is no longer ours. If our commitment is to a higher culture, then we must realize that some form of mastery of one's soul and of life is necessary. Today, Nietzsche advises, such mastery needs to lie in the hands of ones he calls "the *oligarchs of the spirit*": "The spiritual superiority that previously produced division and enmity now tends to *unite*" (*HH* 261).

There appears to be a marked difference between how Nietzsche conceives these spiritual tyrants in 1878 (*Human, All Too Human*) and how he conceives them in 1886 (*Beyond Good and Evil*). In contrast to the posited unity of new oligarchs of the spirit that we find him advocating in the middle writings—united in their commitment to the cause of creating a higher culture through free-spirited enlightenment—in his late writings his focus is on the philosopher as a hermit of the spirit. The philosopher has to be genuinely free-spirited in relation to the ideals of modernity. He is keen to articulate the difference between free spirits who harm their time and its reigning stupidities and freethinkers, *libres-penseurs*, who cannot see the impending decadence because they are too wedded to the fashionable ideals and creeds of the present age. He calls them "loquacious scribbling slaves of democratic taste and its 'modern ideas' . . . people without their own solitude, clumsy nice fellows whose courage and respectable morals [*Sitte*] are not to be denied, only they are quite unfree and laughably superficial, above all with their fundamental tendency to more or less identify the cause of *all* human misery and failure in the forms of the previous old society: which amounts to happily standing truth on its head!" What is now being sought is "security, freedom from danger, comfort, and easy living for everyone" (*BGE* 44).[47] This may suggest that Nietzsche thinks he is the only genuine philosopher of the modern age, and it is highly likely that he did conceive himself this way. This is perhaps why in *Ecce Homo* (1888) he appeals to the Persian virtue of telling the truth and shooting arrows well, informing his readers: "I am by far the most terrifying human being there has ever been." But this does not prevent him, he holds, "from being the most benevolent in the future" (*EH* "Why I Am a Destiny" 2, 3). As Peter Sloterdijk (2013, 32–33) points out, Nietzsche saw himself as, quite probably, the most independent thinker in Europe. He thinks what human beings have wanted to date and what most of us still want is not truth but *faith*, and faith, he duly notes, "is created by methods antithetical to the methods of research" (*KSA*, vol. 13, fragment 15 [58]; *WP* 455).

At the end of the "Defence of Poetry"—written in 1821 and published in 1844—Shelley (2003, 701) declares poets to be the unacknowledged legislators of the world.[48] Although Shelley places the emphasis on poetic experience as "visionary" and "transformative" as well as a "meliorative force" that works on human social and psychological relations, suggesting an affinity with Nietzsche, I do not think he is an influence on Nietzsche's conception of the philosopher, or poet-philosopher, as a legislator; rather, the influence comes from two quite different sources.[49] The first is Helvétius, and the second is Emerson. We know that he admired the work of Helvétius, to whom he refers in *Beyond Good and Evil* as a "dangerous human being" (*BGE* 228).[50] In *The Wanderer and His Shadow*, he depicts Helvétius as a good moralist whose contribution to human understanding is abused in Germany: "What is all of German moral philosophy, counting from Kant onward, along with its French, English, and Italian offshoots and sidelines? A half-theological assault upon Helvétius, a rejection of the laboriously acquired clear views or indications of the right path, which he did in the end articulate and bring together well" (*WS* 216). Examining Helvétius's ideas on legislation in *The Ethics of Epicurus*, Guyau—a thinker whose work Nietzsche very much admired—writes: "Education is, therefore, strictly linked to legislation, and from the art of governing human beings to the art of forming them" (1878/2021, 214).[51] It is this conception of education as cultivation or formation that is informing Nietzsche's thinking about the role of the philosopher, as legislator, in *Beyond Good and Evil*. In *Schopenhauer as Educator*, he is greatly inspired by Emerson's essay "Circles," and he cites from it at the end of the essay. He does so in the context of an attack on the cultured state (*Kulturstaat*) and what he regards as the lamentable contemporary condition of philosophy: "[T]he emergence of a philosopher on earth is more important than the continued existence of a state or a university." A few sentences later he advises professors of philosophy and possessors of scholarly wisdom in Germany to listen to an American who will tell them "about the significance of a great thinker who arrives upon this earth as the center of tremendous powers" (*SE* 8). He then cites from Emerson's essay: "Beware when the great God lets loose a thinker on this planet. Then all things are at risk" (Emerson 2000, 255–56).[52] In "Prudence," an essay that Nietzsche knew well, Emerson advances the notion of wisdom as amounting to "spiritual perception" *and* the notion of the poet as a lawgiver whose task is not to chide but to announce and lead (2000, 216 and 220).

In *Ecce Homo*, Nietzsche informs his readers that with his unfashionable observations he wanted to do something different from psychology. He refers to "an unparalleled problem of education" and calls for "a new concept of *self-discipline* . . . to the point of harshness." With respect to *Schopenhauer as Educator*, this observation, he confides, bears his "innermost history," with his "*becoming*" inscribed in it (*EH* "The Untimelies" 3). The meditation or observation contains a pledge Nietzsche made to himself, and this centers, at least in part, on his concern with the future and the arrival on earth of a true philosophical educator. Philosopher-legislators, he now states in *Beyond Good and Evil*, are "genuine commanders and legislators" (*BGE* 211). We might ask, however, How is this conception compatible with the stress Nietzsche places on the modesty of the philosopher in book 5 of *The Gay Science* (see esp. *GS* 351)? The answer is that it is compatible once we grasp that the philosopher as legislator is *both* wise and unwise, being an experimenter, risk-taker, and taskmaster all at once and willing to play the wicked game of life. He does not, then, presume to be in possession of final knowledge and ultimate wisdom; rather, he prides himself on being an experimenter.

One thing the philosophers of the future will aim not to be, however, is dogmatists and fanatics (*BGE* 43; see also *BGE* preface). Although there are many things that can be achieved only by way of having convictions, in the hands of human beings of faith convictions are the expression of having "pathologically conditioned optics," which readily turns them into fanatics (*AC* 54; see also *HH* 483).[53] Fanatics, Nietzsche writes, are picturesque; "humanity would rather see gestures than listen to *reasons*," and fanatics are "partisan through and through," unable to be free on any single point (*AC* 54). The faith in question here refers to the need for an unconditional yes and no and is required by those who can neither posit themselves as a goal nor posit goals from out of themselves. They are *dependent* people. In *Ecce Homo*, Nietzsche prides himself on his unfanatic nature: "[Y]ou will not find a trace of fanaticism in my being." To clarify this self-declaration, he adds: "There is not one moment in my life where you will find any evidence of a presumptuous or histrionic attitude" (*EH* "Why I Am So Clever" 10).[54] By *fanaticism* here is meant a strength of will but one that the weak and insecure can secure for themselves only by "a sort of hypnotism of the whole system of the senses and the intellect for the benefit of an excessive nourishment (hypertrophy) of a single point of view and feeling" (*GS* 347).

As opposed to simply having convictions and stubbornly holding on to them, it is more important to have the courage to overcome one's convictions. Nietzsche takes *conviction* to denote the belief that "we possess the absolute truth about some specific point of knowledge." The presupposition of all believers, whatever their persuasion, is that they cannot be refuted. In the face of strong objections, they malign reason and may even appeal to the *credo quia absurdum est* (I believe because it is absurd) "as the banner of the most extreme fanaticism" (*HH* 630). The violence in history is due not to the conflict of opinions but rather to the conflict of *belief* in opinions, that is, of convictions. In Nietzsche's mind, the free spirit par excellence would be a person who could take leave of all faith—conceived as adhering to a single dominant point of view—and every need for certainty, "being practiced in maintaining himself on insubstantial ropes and possibilities and dancing even near abysses" (*GS* 347).

Nietzsche states that the philosophers of the future may well have to be skeptics, even critics, but they will also be human beings of experiments. Indeed, he declares that their passion for knowledge compels them to go further with experiments than the "effeminate taste of a democratic century" approves of (*BGE* 210). These coming philosophers have several traits, including genuine independence in relation to prevailing valuations and opinions. Throughout his writings, Nietzsche stresses the need for the thinker to gain distance from his time to truly address it, to be out of sync with his time to the point where his birth will be posthumous. For him, the philosopher is "*of necessity* a man of tomorrow and the day after tomorrow," a figure who is compelled to find himself in contradiction to his today (*BGE* 212). Indeed, the greatness of the philosopher's task requires that he assume the guise of the bad conscience of his age and to do so to harm stupidity. Perhaps of necessity, then, the philosopher is at odds with his own time and appears as a foolish figure, dangerous and disagreeable.

In aphorism 379 of *The Gay Science* (1887), "The Fool Interrupts," Nietzsche informs his reader that he does not write as a misanthrope and stresses that contempt is quite different from hatred. If you hate humanity, then you have renounced contempt and humanity with it (see also *GS* 167). Moreover, in hatred, there is an ample element of fear. By way of contrast, Nietzsche appeals to the fearless ones who do not fear because they are more spiritual, that is, they have the loftiness of vision or perception that can look beyond the present. And, because the modern age loves the spirit, he argues, it needs these spiritual human beings who have contempt for humanity because secretly these beings love humanity and seek its further development and enhancement. Because these spiritual ones have this refined contempt, they can be considered "the most modern of moderns" (*GS* 379; see also *GS* preface 1).[55] I take Nietzsche to mean that human beings rich in the spirit are able to discern what merits a critique and an overcoming. Nietzsche, however, alas, has too much confidence in the modern age and its need for spirit, as when he states that the fearless, free-spirited ones, who endeavor to comport themselves in a manner that is mild, patient, congenial, and polite, will not face exile or imprisonment and their books will not be banned or burned.

Philosophers of the future derive their pleasure from saying no and from taking things apart, and, by the standards of modern humaneness, they will be judged to be hard. The dedication to truth is so severe that it must have little truck with beautiful feelings, enthusiasms, and idealism in general since the chief task is to aim for "cleanliness and severity in matters of the spirit."[56] Despite this cultivation of a disciplined critique, Nietzsche does not wish philosophers of the future to be labeled mere critics, such as the ones who draw boundaries and establish the limits of knowledge. Critics, including great ones such as Kant, are important but serve primarily as instruments of the philosopher. Nietzsche once again takes issue with positivist-minded philosophers for whom the label *critic* would be the highest sign of the philosopher's strength and distinction. It is fatal if philosophical laborers and scientific human beings are confused with genuine philosophers. The task of the true philosopher is to create values, and to attain this he will have to pass through the range of human values and value feelings to attain the requisite level of comprehensiveness, being at different turns critic, skeptic, historian, poet, and solver of riddles. All these identities are preconditions of his task.

The needs of our time, then, require that an important distinction is made between the two main types of philosophers. On the one hand, we have the philosophical laborers—Kant and Hegel can be taken as exemplary models of this type—who "press into formulas . . . some great data of valuations" or "former *positings* of values." This task is an important one since it enables us to conquer the past: everything long, including time itself, is abbreviated and rendered serviceable for life, including our digestion and comprehension. On the other hand, however, there are the true philosophers who are "*commanders and legislators*" since they declare of things and existence, "'*thus it shall be!*'" With the preliminary labor of the philosophical workers at their disposal, the true philosophers can determine "The Whither and For What of the human." Nietzsche maintains that the "knowing" of such philosophers is a "*creating*," that "their creating is a legislation, their will to truth is—will to *power*" (*BGE* 211). He further holds that the philosopher wishes to find greatness in man's "range and multiplicity," that is, the fact that he is whole only to the extent that he is multiple: "He would even determine value and rank in accordance with how much and how many things one could bear and take upon himself, how *far* one could extend his responsibility." The taste of today, however, is in favor of weakness of the will. This is lamentable since what is needed is the capacity for long-range decisions. In the face of the war that modern ideology is waging on behalf of equality of rights and hence against everything "that is rare, strange, privileged," including the nobler duties and responsibilities held by higher types of humans, the concept of greatness entails wanting to be different, wanting to stand alone, being beyond good and evil and a master of one's virtues.

Spiritual Caesarism

Nietzsche has been thinking about the philosopher as a Caesar-type figure for some time before expressly articulating his view in *Beyond Good and Evil*. In a note of 1881, for example, he refers to the "spiritual Caesarism" that hovers over the striving of philosophers and merchants. This form of Caesarism is appealed to in the context of the observation that, owing to the whole world now wanting and coveting the sensual gratification that prosperity and comfortable living bring with them, humankind is approaching "a *spiritual slavery* that has never before existed" (*KSA*, vol. 9, fragment 11 [294]; *SUP*, 6:403).[57] In a long aphorism on cultural and moral decay in *The Gay Science*, Nietzsche reflects on how tyrants emerge as "precocious harbingers of *individuals*," with the final tyrant, the Caesar, appearing to put "an end to the weary struggle for sole rule—by putting weariness to work for himself." It is the Caesar figure, then, who allows for individuals to emerge simply because he can tolerate the rights of the individual and even abet a bolder private morality: "The times of corruption are those when the apples fall from the tree: I mean the individuals, the seed-bearers of the future and the authors of the spiritual colonization and renewal [*Neubildung*] of states and societies" (*GS* 23).

In *Ecce Homo* of 1888, Nietzsche identifies himself with the "higher type" of Caesar. This identification is best seen in the context of the conception of the philosopher as a cultural dynamo as he articulates it in *Beyond Good and Evil* (*EH* "Why I Am So Wise" 3; see also *EH* "Why I Am So Clever" 4). It is also in *Beyond Good and Evil* that Nietzsche once again addresses the issue of how a type becomes strong through a long struggle with essentially unfavorable conditions. In moments of cultural decay and corruption: "[T] he greater, more diverse, more comprehensive life *lives over and beyond* the old morality; the 'individual' now stands there, compelled to a legislation of his own, creating his own arts and wiles of self-preservation, self-enhancement, self-redemption" (*BGE* 262). We can also consider in this regard the discussion of freedom in *Twilight of the Idols* where Nietzsche makes the interesting point that liberal institutions cease being liberal once they have been established. Then they "undermine the will to power," leveling becomes a morality, and things are made "petty, cowardly, and hedonistic" (cf. Santayana 1922/1967, 178–90 ["The Irony of Liberalism"]). Nietzsche favors a freedom in which one assumes the will to be responsible to oneself and is indifferent toward hardship. He writes: "The highest type of free human beings would need to be sought in the place where the greatest resistance is constantly being overcome: a short step away from tyranny, right on the threshold of the danger of servitude. This is psychologically true, if one understands here by 'tyrants' pitiless and terrible instincts which require the maximum of authority and discipline to deal with them—finest type Julius Caesar—and it is also politically true, if one simply takes a walk through history" (*TI* "Reconnaissance Raids of an Untimely Man" 38; see also *TI* "Reconnaissance Raids of an Untimely Man" 45).

Camus cites Nietzsche's note on spiritual Caesarism in his classic study on human revolt *The Rebel* (1951/1971, 71).[58] His engagement with Nietzsche in this part of the book is one of the most disquieting I have encountered in relation to how to respond to his possible legacy in a manner that is not glib. Let me cite him at some length:

> "How can one make the best of crime?" asks Nietzsche, a good professor faithful to his system. Caesar must answer: by multiplying it. "When the ends are great," Nietzsche wrote to his own detriment, "humanity employs other standards and no longer judges crime as such even if it resorts to the most frightful means." He died in 1900, at the beginning of the century in which that statement was to become fatal. It was in vain that he exclaimed in his hour of lucidity, "It is easy to talk about all sorts of immoral acts; but would one have the courage to carry them through? For example, I could not bear to break my word or to kill; I should languish, and eventually I should die as a result—that would be my fate." From the moment that assent was given to the totality of human experience, the way was open to others, far from languishing, to gather strength from lies and murder. (1951/1971, 68–69)

Although Camus's concern should make us pause for some serious reflection, it is far from clear that Nietzsche is ascribing a murderously tyrannical role to the philosopher when he conceives him as a cultural dynamo since his estimation of Caesar is not equivalent to advocating political Caesarism, at least not in the sense of desiring a powerful Caesarean state. This is a desire Nietzsche associates with socialism, which he conceives as "the visionary younger brother of an almost decrepit despotism whose heir it wants to be." Because it can no longer rely on the old religious piety and indeed must work to abolish it to maintain its ideological stranglehold over individuals, socialism will find itself compelled to resort to manipulative modes of control and social policing, even "extreme terrorism" (*HH* 473).

In contrast to this kind of political Caesarism, then, Nietzsche employs the type *Caesar* as an emblem of the rarity and precariousness of the emergence of the higher type (Holzer 2009, 382). Such a type for Nietzsche is not the result of either evolutionary or historical progress, which in part explains why he opposes attempts to conceive his figuration of the *Übermensch* in Darwinian terms (*EH* "Why I Write Such Good Books" 1). The higher type can occur at any time and place and may still do so, as a stroke of luck (Holzer 2009, 383). In attaching himself to the "type" *Caesar,* then, Nietzsche is deliberately opposing himself to *the* type, in which the type is something transmitted by heredity and is neither an extreme nor a stroke of luck (*KSA*, vol. 13, fragment 14 [133], p. 317). As part of his attempt to dissociate himself from a racial blood identity or genealogy, he declares in *Ecce Homo* that Julius Caesar—or Alexander the Great—could be his father (*EH* "Why I Am So Wise" 3). It is in these terms, then, that we should conceive Nietzsche's conception of the true philosopher, the philosopher as creator and legislator, as a Caesar-inspired cultural dynamo. The possibility of such a philosopher emerging again, even in our decadent times, cannot be ruled out.[59] It becomes clear from the way he portrays himself to Georg Brandes, in a letter dated October 20, 1888, that Nietzsche conceives himself as an intellectual criminal. He refers to his books as being considered "'dangerous to public morals'" and says of his forthcoming *Twilight of the Idols*: "This work is my philosophy in a nutshell—radical to the point of crime" (*KSB* 8, p. 457; Middleton 1996, 317). In attacking human verities and encouraging intellectual fearlessness, Nietzsche knows that he must assume the role of a philosophical criminal and that society will perceive him as such.

Angela Holzer (2009, 388) argues that Nietzsche esteemed Caesar primarily not as a military and political tyrant but rather, and as in *Zarathustra,* as a convalescent: "a figure that unites creativity and clemency," an independent and courageous human being like, she quotes Nietzsche, "the hero, the prophet, the Caesar, the redeemer, or the shepherd" (citing from *KSA*, vol. 12, fragment 9 [145], p. 149). And it is indeed the case that in his notebook of summer–autumn 1884 Nietzsche develops a conception of the Roman Caesar with the soul of Christ, and he does so in the context of an attempt to think about the education that is needed in the rulers' virtues that makes it possible to master one's benevolence and compassion (*KSA*, vol. 11, fragment 27 [60]; *WP* 983).

In *Ecce Homo*, and in the context of reflecting on Shakespeare's depictions of Caesar and Hamlet, as well as making the claim that Francis Bacon "is the originator, the animal self-tormentor of this uncanniest kind of literature," Nietzsche holds that having "the strength to achieve the most powerful realization of one's vision is not only compatible with the most powerful strength to act, to act monstrously, to commit crime—*it most powerfully requires it*" (*EH* "Why I Am So Clever" 4). Here, Nietzsche is drawing on the account of Bacon's impeachment provided by Schopenhauer. Bacon was thrown out of the House of Lords and confined to the Tower of London for accepting bribes and gifts in civil proceedings in his role as lord high chancellor under the regime of James I. Schopenhauer cites Pope on Bacon in his *Essay on Man*: "the wisest, brightest, meanest of mankind" (1844/2018, 241 [chap. 19]). Neither Schopenhauer nor Nietzsche, however, show any real understanding of Bacon's actual situation, including the details of his short-lived confinement or the complex political circumstances of the time. The "crime" to which Nietzsche refers is, in effect, much ado about nothing and reveals little about Bacon's character.

Cioran mocks Nietzsche for holding to the view that Bacon lurks behind Shakespeare and describes Bacon as "the least *poet* of the philosophers!" (1972/2012, 158).[60] However, the matter of Bacon's philosophical identity is more complex than Cioran supposes, especially once one considers Bacon as the author of the *Essays* and his explications of classical myths and fables in *The Wisdom of the Ancients*. Carlyle (1841/1983, 126–27), another acerbic writer, is happy to accept the view that the understanding shown in Shakespeare's dramas is equal to what we encounter in Bacon's *Novum Organum* but maintains that Bacon's intellect is of a secondary order and poor in comparison. Chesterton (1935/2012, esp. 288–94 [but see chap. 8 generally]) also wittily dismisses the attribution of Shakespeare's plays to Bacon. The attribution begins in the 1830s with the American writer Delia Bacon, who believed herself to be distantly related to him. Emerson, who had no small intellectual investment in Shakespeare as, in his words, a "cheerful poet," visited her and recognized that a great deal was at stake in her theory. However, he remained skeptical since no decisive evidence was forthcoming, and he was ultimately of the view that the mask of the poet could not be penetrated.

In "Shakespeare; or, The Poet," Emerson refers to "the wise Shakespeare and his book of life." For Emerson, Shakespeare is the figure who writes "the airs for all our modern music" and "the text of modern life" (1996, 120–21). Despite the inevitable flaws in his thinking, with readers such as Eliot finding a confusion of thought, emotion, and vision in his writings, notably in *Zarathustra* (Eliot 1951, 322), something similar can be said about Nietzsche as a poet-philosopher, but in a much more portentous manner since his words must be received as both ominous and hopeful and as those of a true singing master of the longing of our earthly souls.

Coda

Umana commedia

> [W]ill you not tolerate one or two solitary voices . . . speaking for thoughts and principles not marketable or perishable? Soon these improvements and mechanical inventions will be superseded; these modes of living lost out of memory; these cities rotted, ruined by war, by new inventions . . . or the geologic changes:—all gone, like the shells which sprinkle the beach with a white colony to-day, forever to be renewed forever destroyed. But the thoughts which a few hermits strove to proclaim by silence as well as by speech, not only by what they did, but by what they forbore to do, shall abide in beauty and strength, to reorganize themselves in nature, to invest themselves anew in other, perhaps higher endowed and happier mixed clay than ours, in fuller union with the surrounding system.
>
> Emerson, "The Transcendentalist"

> Shakespeare puts "the lunatic, the lover, and the poet" together, as being "of imagination all compact." The problem is to keep the lover and the poet, without the lunatic.
>
> Bertrand Russell, "On the Value of Scepticism"

In what proved to be his last published text, *Ecce Homo* (1888), Nietzsche states that he would rather be considered a buffoon than a saint and offers himself as a destiny: "I know my lot. Someday my name will be linked to the memory of something monstrous, of a crisis yet unprecedented on earth, the most profound collision of consciences, a decision conjured up *against* everything hitherto believed, demanded, hallowed. I am not a man, I am dynamite. . . . [T]he truth speaks from me.—But my truth is *terrifying*, for *lies* were called truth so far." He goes on to state that, when truth confronts the lies of millennia, there will be "upheavals, a spasm of earthquakes, a removal of mountain and valley such as has never been dreamed of." Moreover, the "notion of politics will then completely dissolve into a spiritual war" (*EH* "Why I Am a Destiny" 1). The notion of great politics that is being invoked here refers to a politics that thinks beyond the petty politics of nation, class, and race, and it is meant to capture the idea of a planetary governance and so is not a politics in any conventional sense. When Nietzsche predicts in the closing section of *Ecce Homo* that "there will be wars such as there have never yet been on earth," we should not assume that he is being especially prescient about the actual wars of the twentieth century. The wars to which he is looking ahead involve "heroism in knowledge" and are to be conducted "for the sake of ideas and their consequences" (*GS* 283). He has in mind the noblest ideas we can conceive about the future of humanity, focused on the need for an intellectual mastery of ourselves. How do we now want to live, and how can we most fruitfully cultivate humanity and our earthbound existence, in the wake of the death of God?

Nietzsche speculated about the new intellectual wars of the future in 1888, and, although he was acutely aware of the dangers posed by the burgeoning European nationalism and militarism of his time and provided warnings, the wars to which he appealed are not the world wars that unfolded and assumed reality in the twentieth century. These are wars of the kind that he argued against (in a discarded draft of an attack on the Germans): "If we could dispense with wars, so much the better. I can imagine more profitable uses for the twelve billion now paid annually for the armed peace we have in Europe; there are other means of winning respect for physiology than field hospitals.—Good, very good even: since the old God is abolished, I am prepared *to rule the world*" (Kaufmann 1967, 344). In *Ecce Homo*, Nietzsche is leaping ahead of himself, understandably allowing his enthusiasm for a new earth to get the better of him. The coming into being of the "great politics" for which he calls assumes that the world has gone beyond human tribalism, but we know that this was far from being the case in his time, and it is also manifestly not the case, alas, in our time. Still, it remains the case that Nietzsche honors the name of the philosopher throughout his work and reinvents philosophy as a way of life for us moderns, making it something more vital and much more significant than a mere academic discipline. While humanity chokes on the miasmas of the past and the present, the philosopher endeavors to think beyond the local and the momentary, to protect neither the interests of a profession nor the interests of a party, to venture new modes of perception, and to provide pathways to the sublime.

When he is at his most patient, Nietzsche knows that there is no quick fix to our ills and defects, and the emphasis is placed on tasks and the need to regard ourselves as experiments and wisely administer small doses and slow cures. In staging an encounter with Nietzsche, several points are worth taking stock of. First, we know that he is not a thinker who advocates revolution as a way of transforming society. Although a revolution can be a source of vital energy for a humanity that has grown feeble, it is not an organizer, an artist, and a perfecter of human nature and resurrects "the most savage energies in the form of long-buried horrors and excesses of the most distant ages" (*HH* 463). Second, he is not sure that the genuine philosopher—the philosopher as legislator who aspires to a comprehensive vision of humanity's development—is possible today. His hesitation centers on the enormous realms of knowledge that need to be mastered today and that may well lie beyond the capabilities of a single philosopher, including the philosopher who wishes to be a cultural dynamo. Third, he recognizes that, in positing a goal for humanity, one that will give a new meaning to the earth such as the superhuman, there is still lacking humanity itself (*Z* 1 "Of the Thousand and One Goals"). There is, then, a great deal of work to be carried out by philosophers and other educators in our "fragile, broken time of transition" (*GS* 377).

We should not be surprised that, as an experimental philosophy of the future, Nietzsche's thinking frequently assumes a speculative and provisional character. This is an aspect of his thought that we should not overlook or seek to downplay since it is what gives his philosophizing its strength and boldness. Often, he is making recommendations, not prescriptions, and he knows that this is all he is entitled to (*D* 108, 449). It is not a question for him of a philosophy ever being proved right, and as he notes to date no philosophy has, in fact, been proved right. Moreover, the little question marks that the conscientious philosopher places at the end of his mottoes and doctrines have more value for truth than all the dignified gestures he might display before plaintiffs and courts of law (*BGE* 25). He is acutely aware that we moderns are living in a fertile yet fragile period of human development, a time of transition that is an age of anarchy but also an age of the most spiritual and freest individuals and an age of genius from which he has the hope that a more independent species of human may emerge (*KSA*, vol. 9, fragment 11 [27]; *SUP*, 6:315). Given that there is no definite time line to his recommendations, it is not necessary to privilege any single text or set of texts from his corpus in the period 1878–88 on which I have focused attention in this study. Rather, all remain pertinent to us in terms of the tasks that they set and that we can make our own.

The transformation of the human that Nietzsche wants us to imagine is an existential one, and he writes as an existential pioneer. Throughout his writings, we find the emphasis placed on modes of self-cultivation and self-surpassing that involve new ways of thinking and feeling. It is clear, I think, that he wants—at least initially and perhaps for some considerable period—only certain individuals to cultivate the new life and assume the role of pioneers. Although the existential dimension clearly remains vitally important to the concern we have with the continued development of the human, today humanity faces ecological challenges and transhuman possibilities that Nietzsche could never have imagined, at least not of the order of magnitude and realm of possibility we are now witnessing.

We find only isolated insights on technics in his corpus, as when he reflects on a machine culture and the machine as teacher. As we might expect, the insights he offers are perceptive and thought-provoking and consonant with the concerns expressed by several nineteenth-century thinkers and writers about the modern capitalist dynamic and its deleterious effects on our mental habits and potentialities, such as Marx, John Ruskin, and Walter Pater. The machine, Nietzsche notes, "releases an immense quantity of energy that would otherwise lie dormant, it is true, but it does not provide any incentive to ascend higher, to make things better, or to become artistic." On the contrary, he maintains, it makes people *uniform* (*WS* 220). Humanity, he further reflects, makes pitiless use of individuals "as material for heating its great machines." He then asks: "[B]ut what are the machines for, if all the individuals (that is, humanity) serve only to keep them going? Machines that are their own purpose—is that the *umana commedia*?" (*HH* 585).

Various thinkers and storytellers writing in the wake of Nietzsche who shared his concerns about impending decadence and nihilism have endeavored to alert us to the dangers caused by the brave new world of rapid technological progress that creates not a new species of superhumans but tranquilized subhumans.[1] Nietzsche himself sought to show that as the consumption of humankind becomes more and more economical, with the "machinery" of interests and services intricately integrated, a countermovement is needed. He designates this as "*the secretion of a luxury surplus of humankind*," which would aim "to bring to light a *stronger* species, a higher type that arises and preserves itself under different conditions from those of the average human." His concept and symbol for this type, he discloses, is the word *Übermensch* (*KSA*, vol. 12, fragment 10 [17], p. 462; *WP* 866). As we ourselves today witness human life becoming ever more tightly integrated into one vast megamachine, involving new, subtle forms of control and manipulation as well as widespread conformist and reactive behavior, with the human animal encouraged to play the mad animal, Nietzsche's appeal to a stronger species and an independent form of life becomes more and more intelligible—and laudable.

The pressing questions facing us at this point in our development include, Do we wish the desire for the superhuman, supposing we still have it, to be congruent with a love of the earth that would be in accord with a powerful new consciousness focused on life and its renewal, teaching both a care of self and a care of life? Would this love renew and intensify the desire to remain true to the earth conceived as the place of our material and existential dwelling? Is our desire that we become posthuman and forge a new contract between ourselves and nonhuman life? Or is our desire for the transhuman, and is this anything other than the desire of a megalomaniac monkey? Nietzsche's exhortation to remain true to the earth is an inspiring and necessary one (the stars are not simply above us). As we seek to cultivate a new earth, and create new worlds for ourselves, we would be wise to keep in mind Nietzsche's words:

> O human, who has been consumed by lust, don't forget—you are the stone, the desert, you are death . . .[2]

Acknowledgments

I am grateful to Kyle Wagner, the philosophy editor at the University of Chicago Press, for placing his confidence in the book and for his steadfast support. For their consummate professionalism, I also thank the team at the press, notably Nathan Petrie, Kristin Rawlings, and Stephen Twilley. Thanks to Joseph Brown for his diligent copyediting. I am grateful to the anonymous reviewers of the manuscript of the book for critical feedback and for making suggestions that prompted me to attend closely to its final organization and coverage.

For encouragement and advice, I thank Rick A. Pearson, Justine Baillie, Christine Battersby, Francesca Cauchi, Daniel W. Conway, Sarah Ellenzweig, Marta Faustino, Herwig Friedl, Rainer J. Hanshe, Nardina Kaur, Levan Kobakhidze, James I. Porter, Robert Spaven, Federico Testa, Yunus Tuncel, and Tina Watson. Paul Loeb has been a valuable interlocutor, both agonistic and generous, throughout the period of the writing of this book. I am grateful to both Daniel and Paul for the unstinting support they have offered me over many years. Rainer's Nietzsche-related creative offerings as a poet and storyteller provided regular stimulation. He was also instrumental in helping me decide on the final title for the book. I owe a special debt of gratitude to Lorenzo Serini for stimulating conversations about Nietzsche during our time together at Warwick University and since. The love I am fortunate to share with Nicky, Jazz, and Rick makes my life vital and real and has once again sustained me during the protracted period of the writing of a book.

Although the writing of this book has taken place in recent years, it is the summation of reading Nietzsche for almost fifty years and teaching him for over three decades. The experience of being educated and provoked by Nietzsche's writings and being able to share this with students and colleagues over many years has been the most fortunate intellectual experience of my life.

Chapter 1 draws on material that first appeared in Keith Ansell-Pearson and Lorenzo Serini, "Friedrich Nietzsche: Cheerful Thinker and Writer: A Contribution to the Debate on Nietzsche's Cheerfulness," *Nietzsche-Studien* 51, no. 1 (2022): 1–34. A version of chapter 4 appeared as Keith Ansell-Pearson, "Nietzsche on the Passions and Self-Cultivation: Contra the Stoics and Spinoza," *Continental Philosophy Review* 55 (2022): 245–65. Chapter 5 draws substantially on Keith Ansell-Pearson, "Nietzsche on the Task of the Poets in His Middle Writings," in *Nietzsche and Literary Studies*, ed. James I. Porter (Cambridge: Cambridge University Press, 2024), 91–120, © 2024 by Cambridge University Press. I thank the editors and publishers as well as my coauthor for granting permission to deploy material from these publications in this book and in modified and recontextualized form.

Notes

BOOK EPIGRAPH

Nietzsche, "The Dance Song," *Thus Spoke Zarathustra*, trans. Paul S. Loeb and David F. Tinsley.

INTRODUCTION

Epigraphs: Nietzsche, *The Gay Science*, trans. Walter Kaufmann; Nietzsche, note of 1885, trans. Adran Del Caro.

1. I readily acknowledge that aspects of the early Nietzsche—notably the *Unfashionable Observations* (1873–75)—have their strengths and continued relevance.

2. See the letter to Franz Overbeck dated August 5, 1886 (*KSB* 7, p. 223; Middleton 1996, 254). On Zarathustra and the song of solitude, see Hermann Hesse (1919/1974, esp. 88–91, 100). On Hesse's esteem of Nietzsche as a great solitary, see Hesse (1920/1975, 51).

3. See Nietzsche's 1888 letter to the American journalist Karl Knortz (*KSB* 8, p. 341; Middleton 1996, 299).

4. In aphorism 481 of *Dawn*, Nietzsche reveals that he prizes thinkers whose lives are punctuated by crises and catastrophes and offers a criticism of Schopenhauer as a philosopher who lacks development and has no history. In *Ecce Homo*, his text of 1878, *Human, All Too Human*, is said to stand as a monument to a crisis in his development. The crisis in question centers on his personal idealism and his realization that his "idealities" had not helped him at all. His lack of knowledge about "realities" pointed him in the direction of physiology, medicine, and natural science.

5. For insight, see chap. 7 below. In *Ecce Homo*, Nietzsche jokes that, when speaking of Stendhal as a profound psychologist to German professors, he has been asked to spell his name (*EH* "The Case of Wagner" 3). He also confesses to being envious of Stendhal for coming up with the atheist's best joke: God's only excuse is that he does not exist (*EH* "Why I Am So Clever" 3). He also offers his own witticism concerning the conditions for belief in God: "'God himself cannot exist without wise people,' said Luther with good reason. But 'God can exist even less without unwise people'—that our good Luther did not say" (*GS* 129).

6. Nietzsche discovered Dostoevsky in the winter of 1886–87 while resident in Nice and became familiar with, in French translations, *Memoirs from the House of the Dead*, *Notes from Underground*, *The Insulted and the Injured*, *The Idiot*, and *The Devils*. He writes about

his discovery to his friend Franz Overbeck on February 23, 1887, and a few weeks later, on March 7, to his amanuensis Peter Gast. To Overbeck he confides that an "instinct of affinity" spoke to him instantaneously and that his joy was beyond bounds: "[N]ot since my first encounter with Stendhal's *Red and Black* have I known such joy" (*KSB* 8, pp. 27–28; Middleton 1996, 261). The most perceptive study of Nietzsche and Dostoevsky remains Shestov (1900/1969). For valuable insight into Nietzsche's reception of Dostoevsky, see Miller (1973) and Stellino (2015). See also the final section of chap. 6 below. For an attempt to bring the two writers and thinkers into dialogue imaginatively, see Stepenberg (2019). André Gide was of the view that "[n]o one helped Nietzsche more than Dostoevsky" (1927, 178). George Steiner astutely notes that, like Nietzsche, Dostoevsky, whose nature was one of "enormous health," uses illness as an instrument of perception (1967, 23). For insight into the innovations Dostoevsky introduced into the psychological novel, see Belknap (2002). Regarding "psychology," we should consider the insight of Cynthia Ozick (2000, 23), who notes that Dostoevsky "is not psychological in the sense of understanding and portraying familiar human nature." On this see also Cowper Powys (1946a, 36–37).

7. Huxley gives two examples: Dostoevsky's *Notes from Underground* and Tolstoy's *Death of Ivan Ilyich.*

8. Nietzsche speaks of his "whole philosophical heterodoxy" in a letter to his friend Paul Deussen dated September 14, 1888 (*KSB* 8, p. 426; Middleton 1996, 310–11).

9. "[A]nyone who is related to me through the *loftiness* of their willing experiences true ecstasies of learning when they do: for I come from the heights to which no bird has yet flown, I know abysses into which no foot has yet strayed" (*EH* "Why I Write Such Good Books" 3).

10. For a translation of this draft, see Kaufmann (1967, 340).

11. See also the pertinent remarks Arthur Danto makes in the opening pages of *Nietzsche as Philosopher*: "He seems to belong to philosophy *faute de mieux*. But then Nietzsche felt that he had made a clean break with official philosophy; if it is true that he hardly fits with the subject he so often impugned, so much the worse, he would have said, for philosophy" (1965/2005, 3). Nietzsche was tremendously inspired by a rich intellectual and literary tradition of "European" books, including figures such as Montaigne, Pascal, and Stendhal, and he names four world thinkers whom he admires for having attained mastery in prose: Leopardi, Mérimée, Emerson, and Walter Savage Landor (*GS* 92). In addition, he draws inspiration for his philosophizing from the ancient schools of philosophy and their practice of philosophy as a way of life, including figures such as Epicurus and Epictetus. For further insight, see chaps. 2 and 3 below.

12. See also Nietzsche on Sterne as "the freest of writers" in *MOM* 113. On Sterne's importance for modern thought, see Price (1964, chap. 11).On Nietzsche and Sterne, see Large (1995).

13. See also the way Nietzsche writes in praise of the ancient Greek historian Thucydides: "[I]n him, the man as thinker and thinker as man, that *culture of the most impartial knowledge of the world*, attains a last magnificent flowering, that culture that had in Sophocles its writer, in Pericles its statesman, in Hippocrates its physician, in Democritus its natural philosopher" (*D* 168). He is not denying that imagination is not also at work in the craft of the historian: "[W]e **comprehend** only through a fantastic *anticipation* and experimenting, whether reality has *accidentally* been attained in the fantasy image, namely, in *history* etc. Thucydides and Tacitus *must* be *poets*. Even in the science of the simplest events imagination [*Phantasie*] is necessary" (*KSA*, vol. 9, fragment 11 [68]; *SUP*, 6:327).

14. For a comprehensive study of the aphorism in Nietzsche, see Westerdale (2013). See also Marsden (2006).

15. There are several pivotal appeals to the sublime in Nietzsche's texts and unpublished materials. Sometimes, however, and as we shall see, he privileges beauty over sublimity, and, when he does so, he is referring to the need to conquer one's playful or sportive monsters. When he deploys the concept positively, the sublime is being utilized to indicate the states of intellectual elevation that can be attained through new perceptions and the feelings that accompany them. A good example of this is when he signs off on his very first sketch of eternal recurrence in 1881 by referring to the "sublime states" he has reached in his thinking: "Early August 1881 in Sils-Maria, 6,000 feet above sea level and much higher above all human things!" (*KSA*, vol. 9, fragment 11 [141]; *SUP*, 6:351–52). For further insight into Nietzsche and the sublime, see Ansell-Pearson (2010, 2013).

16. In an interview with the *Paris Review*, Adam Phillips extols the virtues of the essay as a digressive form of writing since it gives the writer the opportunity to change the subject and meander. In a memorable phrase, he describes digression as "secular revelation" (2019, 236, 250). As Daniel Mendelsohn (2020, 24) points out in a consideration of Homer's *Odyssey*, digression is not a narrative or pithy style designed to promote distraction. This insight applies well to Nietzsche. Stendhal (1975, 61) says he aims to be truthful as a writer of his life but admits to also indulging in digressions.

17. Brian Leiter (2002) conceives Nietzsche as a methodological naturalist, Lawrence J. Hatab (2005) as an existential naturalist, and Christa Davis Acampora (2006) as an aesthetic naturalist. Marco Brusotti (2019) has articulated the reasons why one might choose to be skeptical about the wisdom of construing Nietzsche as a naturalist at all. On Nietzsche and naturalism, see also Emden (2019) and Schacht (2023, esp. 304–32). For an interpretation of Nietzsche that stresses the historical character of his approach to questions about human nature, see Lemm (2020). In Nietzsche's time, three forms of naturalism are identified: idealism, materialism, and monism. And these are seen to generate three systems of thought: theism, atheism, and pantheism. Emerson, for example, whose importance for Nietzsche is well-known, was taken to be a representative of idealist naturalism. Emerson's philosophy is described well by the now-forgotten French philosopher Jean-Marie Guyau (1887/1962, 482) as one of objective idealism in which the world is a precipitate of the soul. Guyau helpfully defines naturalism as follows: "We are content to admit, by a hypothesis at once scientific and metaphysical, the fundamental homogeneity of all things, the fundamental identity of nature. Monism, in our judgment, should be neither transcendent nor mystical, but immanent and naturalistic. The world is one continuous Becoming; there are not two kinds of existence nor two lines of development, the history of which is the history of the universe" (1887/1962, 494). Guyau was read attentively by Nietzsche in the 1880s. In his study of modern philosophers, Harald Höffding (1915) divided modern philosophers into different groupings, with Nietzsche appearing, along with Guyau and William James, in the group he labeled "The Philosophy of Value." This grouping recognizes that Nietzsche's concern is not only with philosophy as the guardian of truth but equally with philosophy as an advocate of value. For an interpretation of Nietzsche as a naturalist from this time, see Salter (1917).

18. Nietzsche writes about the need for us to cease anthropomorphizing nature in several notes of 1881 that eventually become aphorisms in *The Gay Science*. For example, he argues against the "modern-scientific counterpart to faith in God" where

the universe is construed as an organism (*KSA*, vol. 9, fragment 11 [201]; *SUP*, 6:374–75); he claims that the "assumption that the universe is an organism contradicts the *essence of the organic*" simply because in the universe we cannot identify an "infinitely growing force," and this means we cannot conceive of an "infinitely new becoming" (*KSA*, vol. 9, fragment 11 [213]; *SUP*, 6:377). Moreover, to naturalize the human being means being ready "for the absolutely sudden and annihilating" simply because "at any moment a comet could smash the sun, or an electrical force could appear in which the solar system is vaporized all at once" (*KSA*, vol. 9, fragment 11 [228]; *SUP*, 6:381). Even if Nietzsche's examples in this note are not especially well-chosen ones, his point about "the sudden and the annihilating" is valid and informs his call for the naturalization of humankind in *GS* 109.

19. The attempt to move knowledge beyond the level of human presumption and fancy as well as enthusiasm and vanity is what motivates Francis Bacon in *The New Organon*: "[M]an prefers to believe what he wants to be true" (1620/2000, aphorism 49). Bacon wants human beings to get used to "actual things," and he identifies four idols that stand in the way of knowledge: the tribe, the cave, the marketplace, and the theater (1620/2000, aphorism 39). As Stephen Gaukroger astutely notes, Bacon's reasons for starting afresh with philosophy and the pursuit of knowledge are not speculative in the sense that we encounter in Descartes and his hyperbolic doubt but real and compelling: "The doctrine of Idols sets out to show that we pursue natural philosophy with seriously deficient natural faculties, that we operate with a severely inadequate means of communication, and that we rely on a hopelessly corrupt philosophical culture: claims much more radical than anything we find in Descartes. The deficiencies of our faculties are not due to their inability to deal with a purely speculative form of doubt, but, quite the contrary, are wholly real and in constant evidence in our daily lives" (2001, 233). On Nietzsche and Bacon, see chap. 6, n. 4, below and the final section of chap. 7 below.

20. In his preface to the second edition of *Human, All Too Human* (1886), Nietzsche presents himself as a bird catcher, but one who seeks to catch as an "old immoralist" (*HH* preface 1). For Nietzsche on the immoral thinker as a moralist who is not to be confused with the preacher of morality, see *WS* 19.

21. Nietzsche subtitles *Beyond Good and Evil* "a prelude to a philosophy of the future." Paul Loeb (2018b, 257) notes correctly that this denotes both a philosophy about the future and a new kind of philosophy that may arrive in the future. However, as we shall see as this study unfolds, Nietzsche assigns futural aspects to philosophy from the time of the second volume of *Human, All Too Human*—made up of two texts (*Mixed Opinions and Maxims* and *The Wanderer and His Shadow*)—where it operates as an integral part of our working on ourselves and in the hope of something new emerging from the task. Nietzsche is not, of course, the first modern philosopher to declare a philosophy "of" the future. In his *Principles of the Philosophy of the Future*, Feuerbach writes of a "new" and "independent" philosophy that corresponds to the needs of humankind and the future. This new philosophy is a philosophy of joy, being "open-hearted and sensuous" (1843/1986, secs. 65, 36).

22. Janaway (forthcoming) brings his interpretation of *BGE* 230 to a conclusion by arguing that the question "Why pursue a naturalistic account of the human?" is to be answered solely in terms of some instrumental value. Moreover: "Nietzsche does not need to assign naturalistic inquiry any value in itself and can regard it as one means, perhaps not necessarily the most important, towards his evaluative goals."

23. Brian Leiter construes Nietzsche as a methodological naturalist, not a substantive one, because, he argues, he is not a reductive physicalist but takes seriously the reality of qualia, i.e., the qualitative experience of liking something and finding it beautiful. He interprets aphorism 373 of *The Gay Science* as lending support to this conception of Nietzsche. The aphorism in question is "Science as a Prejudice," and in it Nietzsche discusses the faith that materialistic natural scientists appear to rest content with, a faith centered on a world we have made familiar to ourselves, one that is "supposed to have its equivalent and measure in human thought and human valuations—a 'world of truth' that can be mastered completely and forever with the aid of our square little reason." He then asks if we really want the world to be degraded like this, reduced to little more than an indoor diversion for mathematicians, and divested of its rich ambiguity. Nietzsche contends that to interpret the world only in terms of "counting, calculating, weighing, seeing, and touching, and nothing more" is both crude and naive and quite possibly "a mental illness, an idiocy." Such an interpretation, he contends, is one of the most "stupid" interpretations since it is so poor in sense or meaning (*Sinn*). Indeed, he argues: "[A]n essentially mechanistic world would be an essentially *meaningless* [*sinnlose*] world." He then invites us to reflect on the example of music. If we think about the value of a piece of music, how much of it would we have *comprehended* if we subjected it to counting and calculation and then expressed this in simple formulas? Would we not lose sight of what is "music" in music? Interpreting existence only in terms of its most superficial and external aspect—"what is most apparent, its skin and sensualization"—is more than just an error and possibly fatal, revealing a will to death in the will to truth of a mechanistic-biased science. Nietzsche's focus in this aphorism, then, is on the *Sinn* (sense, meaning, direction, or movement) of music, not simply on the qualitative experience of listening to it and finding the experience beautiful. He does write about *quale*, but he does so in terms of thinking about the character of life: "A greater power implies a different consciousness, feeling, desiring, a different perspective; growth itself is a desire to be more; the desire for an increase in quantum grows from a *quale*; in a purely quantitative world everything would be dead, stiff, motionless" (*KSA*, vol. 12, fragment 2 [157]; *WP* 564). And, in a note that echoes his argument in *GS* 373, he writes "against the physical atom": "The calculability of the world, the expressibility of all events in formulas—is this really 'comprehension'? How much of a piece of music has been understood when that which in it is calculable and can be reduced to formulas has been reckoned up?" (*KSA*, vol. 12, fragment 7 [56]; *WP* 624).

24. On apathetic naturalism, see Santayana (1900/1989, 5). In contrast to ancient naturalists, Santayana finds modern materialists to have "vulgar and jejune minds" (1951/2017, 20). Santayana knew Nietzsche's writings quite well and describes him as a courageous thinker "who clings to what his soul *loves*" (2009, 579). See also his treatment of Nietzsche in his study of egotism in German philosophy (Santayana 1916/1939, chap. 11–13).

25. For further insight, see Ansell-Pearson (2006a).

26. The word *Geist* appears frequently in Nietzsche's writings and denotes "mind," "intellect," or "spirit." In his middle writings, it signifies several things, including the aesthetic sensibilities that inform a person's responses to other people and to the things of the world (see *MOM* 310). It can also be understood as a mode of self-cultivation that flourishes beyond the level of need or material necessity and personal advantage. Nietzsche also deploys the notion when he examines the tendencies of modern society

and the extent to which it squanders—e.g., in the pursuit of national security—"what is most precious, spirit" (*D* 179). It also characterizes the mode of life led by free spirits as a kind of driving force or power: "*Spirit* is what saves us from burning out entirely and turning to ashes; it lets us tear ourselves away from the sacrificial altar of justice or wraps us in asbestos" (*HH* 637). On "spirit" or "mind" as a stomach, see also *BGE* 230.

27. Nietzsche's reception of and relation to Augustine is examined in chap. 2 below.

28. Nietzsche's skepticism about the ancient practice of philosophy as a way of life that seeks to attain self-sufficiency, making us completely happy within ourselves, can also be found expressed in Hume when he writes that this is the voice of human pride speaking and not nature. See Hume (1985, 140 and esp. 150–51 [on the figure of the sage]). Watkins (2019, esp. 220–22) offers an instructive interpretation of Hume as a mitigated sage in addition to being a mitigated skeptic.

29. According to John Sellars: "The Stoic conception of the sage was nothing less than the ideal of a perfect individual, an individual described in terms that were usually reserved only for the gods. The sage is described in a variety of sources as one who does everything that he undertakes well, one who is never impeded in what he does, one who is infallible; he is more powerful than all others, richer, stronger, freer, happier" (2009, 60). See also Brouwer (2014) and Hadot (2020).

30. Hugo's novel *Les misérables* was criticized on its publication for its inane evangelism. Baudelaire, an erstwhile Hugo enthusiast, detested the ideas promoted in the book, such as the natural goodness of man. Nietzsche refers to Baudelaire's description of Hugo as an "ass of a genius" in a note of 1885 (*KSA*, vol. 11, fragment 38 [6], p. 601; *SUP*, 16:160). For further insight into the reception of Hugo and Baudelaire's relationship with him, see McAuliffe (2020, 170ff.).

31. As Michael Bell notes: "'His capacity to question the substantive *ego* is closely allied to his capacity . . . to experience his personal existence impersonally as a function of the historical culture. Nietzsche seems really to have lived a deconstructive *ego*'" (2007, 16).

CHAPTER ONE

Epigraph: Nietzsche, *Mixed Opinions and Maxims*, trans. Gary Handwerk.

1. Although Nietzsche is addressing in this aphorism a German moral culture, Santayana is surely correct when he notes: "[People] are not naturally sceptics, wondering if a single one of their intellectual habits can be reasonably preserved; they are dogmatists angrily confident of maintaining them all" (1923/1955, 11–12).

2. On the social mask and its dangers, see Jung (1983, 98–99, 124). On the conventional world as a world of masks, see the rich appreciation of Dickens in Santayana (1922/1967, chap. 18, esp. 65–67).

3. We will benefit from putting many human errors calmly on ice (*EH* "Human, All Too Human" 1). At the same time, however, in addition to refreshing us this coldness frees us for new, more mature ways of thinking and feeling. Iris Murdoch dramatizes the "cold" character of truth in her novel *The Philosopher's Pupil* (see Murdoch 1983, 194ff.).

4. Several philosophers have sought to show the importance of cheerfulness to individual health and flourishing. For example, Schopenhauer (1851/2014, 283) holds that the cheerful person can value its existence because cheerfulness is the genuine coin of happiness, as opposed to fake paper money: it makes us immediately happy in the present, which is, he claims, the only truly real dimension of time. (For further

insight, see Ansell-Pearson [2023b].) In Spinoza, cheerfulness (*hilaritas*) denotes a state of serenity that colors one's whole personality, a form of joy to which every part of the body contributes and that facilitates a feeling of presentness in the world. For insight into Spinoza and cheerfulness, see Naess (2008, 123–33).

5. Nietzsche admires Montaigne for his honesty, courage, cheerful skepticism, and naturalism. For insight, see Berry (2004), Donnellan (1986), Miner (2017), and Williams (1952). For insight into Montaigne and cheerfulness and his recommendation of "gay and sociable wisdom" (Montaigne 2003, 1044 [3.13]), see Hampton (2022, 83–99) and Lanier Anderson and Cristy (2017). See also Hazlitt on Montaigne: "He does not converse with us like a pedagogue with his pupil, whom he wishes to make as great a blockhead as himself, but like a philosopher and friend who has passed through life with thought and observation and is willing to enable others to pass through it with pleasure and profit" (1982, 271). Bertrand Russell (1996a, 61) refers to Montaigne and Voltaire as examples of cheerful skeptics.

6. See Emerson: "We live amid surfaces, and the true art of life is to skate well on them" (2000, 314 ["Experience"]).

7. According to the account Nietzsche gives of his development, while in the volumes of *Human, All Too Human* he presents himself as if cheerful even if he is not, in *Dawn* he believes he succeeds in achieving a perfect cheerfulness, which he then further cultivates in *The Gay Science*, *Thus Spoke Zarathustra*, *Twilight of the Idols*, and *Ecce Homo*. He does not mention late writings such as *On the Genealogy of Morality* and *The Anti-Christ* as cheerful works. His principal aim in these works appears to be not cheering the reader but rather communicating to us a sense of alarm motivated by the need to confront what he sees as an impending era of decadence and nihilism. Still, even here we may experience cheerfulness as a reward for carrying out diligent, subterranean inquiries. Cheerfulness, then, is not the opposite of seriousness but in this instance a reward for persevering as a serious critic of morality.

8. On "morality as a problem," see *GM* preface (esp. 6); and *GS* 345. In his middle writings, Nietzsche contests the idea that there is a single moral-making morality and seeks to develop a more audacious morality in defiance of the modern cult of the sympathetic affects, notably compassion (*Mitleid*, lit. "suffering with"). In his late writings, he seeks to make the case for a distinction to be made between lower and higher moralities and presents "morality" as the "danger of dangers" since it makes the present live at the expense of the future. We moderns also worryingly assume the nature and value of "morality" to be self-evident.

9. Nietzsche recognizes that the search after knowledge is fraught with the danger of lapsing into melancholy. See, e.g., *HH* 109, 628; *D* 317, 376, 492; *GS* 53, 68. On the melancholic mood that can be associated with philosophical activity, see Terry (2011, 81): "Melancholy could be seen as a precondition for philosophical inspiration, or as an occupational hazard uniquely incident to philosophers." Hume (1985, 159–81 ["The Sceptic"]) offers valuable insight into the temper of cheerfulness and disposition of melancholy. On melancholy and philosophy, and with reference to Hume and Spinoza, see Lemmens (2005). On Hume and philosophical melancholy, see Livingston (1998).

10. Nietzsche's claim that Schopenhauer, a notoriously embittered human being, is a cheerful thinker and writer might seem at first surprising. Lanier Anderson and Cristy illuminate the matter well: "However surprising the claim, Nietzsche does have a point, if one has ears for Schopenhauer's *tone* as a writer. Despite the gloomy content of his pessimistic message, Schopenhauer regularly manages to puncture the pieties

of optimistic claptrap with rhetoric sufficiently high-spirited to be a reliable source of mirth" (2017, 1541–42 [n. 20]).

11. While expressing a great interest in him as an important writer, Kierkegaard identifies in Schopenhauer, albeit concealed, "the most terrible and corrupting voluptuous melancholy: a profound misanthropy" (1958, 235). See also Hume's astute insights into how a gloomy, melancholic disposition leads to an embittered attitude toward life (1985, 179).

12. This might come as a surprise because in *The Birth of Tragedy* Nietzsche famously deems Socrates—or, more precisely, Socratism—to be responsible for the death of Greek tragedy and, with it, the profound, tragic cheerfulness of the Greeks (see esp. *BT* 19).

13. On Nietzsche's preference for the Old Testament, see *GM* 3.22. Nietzsche declares that in the Old Testament he finds great individuals, heroic landscape, a people, and something he thinks is especially rare on earth that he calls "the incomparable naiveté of the *strong heart*." In a note of 1887, he writes of the importance of intellectual cleanliness (*Sauberkeit*) and finds this lacking in the New Testament. It is characterized, he holds, by a shameless levity concerning the way the most intractable problems are dealt with—life, God, and the purpose of life—"as if they were not problems at all but simply things that these little bigots *knew*!" (*KSA*, vol. 12, fragment 10 [204]; *WP* 201).

14. *Cheerful seriousness* is precisely the term Carlyle (2015, 8) uses to describe the character of Goethe as a philosopher of wisdom. See also Emerson's essay "Goethe, the Writer" (1996, esp. 156–57).

15. On having a sense of humor as one of the Nietzschean virtues, and on the epistemic function of laughter in Nietzsche's writings, see Alfano (2021, 216–32).

16. Huizinga's *Homo Ludens* (1949) remains a highly instructive study of the importance of playfulness in human life and culture and that is central to the agonistic spirit. Specifically on Nietzsche, see ibid., 152. For a more recent and engaging study of play, see Bates (1999).

17. The German term *Munterkeit* (liveliness) is closely associated with *Heiterkeit* and intercepts some of its meanings. Indeed, the word can be also translated as *cheerfulness, brightness*, or *high spirits*. In addition to *HH2* preface 5, Nietzsche employs the term *Munterkeit* only one other time in his published writings, in aphorism 381 in bk. 5 of *The Gay Science*. Like *Heiterkeit, Munterkeit* is also used by Nietzsche to denote a style of thinking and writing: "The extraordinary vivaciousness [*Munterkeit*] of style, like [Machiavelli's] *il principe* (quite apart from the seriousness of its task), the brevity strength, a kind of joy in the thronging of difficult thoughts" (*KSA*, vol. 11, fragment 34 [102]).

18. Although Lanier Anderson and Cristy do not focus on Nietzsche's notion of "cricket-cheerfulness," their interpretation can help explain what is going on in the preface to the second volume of *Human, All Too Human*. According to them: "[Cheerfulness] is neither the natural response of immediate (pre-volitional, pre-deliberative) instinct, nor the reasoned conclusion of detached evaluative deliberation; rather, it can be achieved through practical learning, namely, habitual exercise of the spirit, resulting in the incorporation of a spiritual habit into a sort of second nature" (2017, 1529 [see also 1532]).

19. Nietzsche's personal experience and recommendation with respect to willfully enacting cheerfulness is not entirely unusual in philosophy and psychology. For instance, in thinking about the practical applications of his psychological doctrines to mental well-being, William James writes: "Action seems to follow feeling, but really action and feeling go together; and by regulating the action which is under the more

direct control of the will, we can indirectly regulate the feeling, which is not. Thus the sovereign voluntary path to cheerfulness, if our spontaneous cheerfulness be lost, is to sit up cheerfully, to look round cheerfully, and to act and speak as if cheerfulness were already there. If such conduct does not make you soon feel cheerful, nothing else on that occasion can" (1933, 45). While James here focuses on the experience of the feeling of cheerfulness on a specific occasion, Nietzsche by contrast is much more interested in the cultivation of a cheerful habitus of spirit.

20. In contrast, when Nietzsche thinks and writes about the future in *Human, All Too Human*, his mood and tone are not those of cheerfulness and hope (see, e.g., *HH* 37, 38, 109, 248).

21. Other aphorisms on hope in Nietzsche's corpus include *HH* 443; *D* 546; *GS* 268–72; *AC* 23; and *EH* "The Birth of Tragedy" 4. See also: "For *that man may be freed from the bonds of revenge*: that is the bridge to my highest hope and a rainbow after protracted storms" (*Z* 2 "Of the Tarantulas"). Like Nietzsche, Camus (1968, 92) opposes Christian hope for another life and sees it as an attitude of resignation when "to live is not to be resigned" (cf. de Beauvoir 1945/2004, 206; see also Mumford 1950, foreword; and Hadot 2023, 116–25). For a recent study of hope that includes a discussion of Nietzsche, see Potkay (2022). Bishop (2011, 33–36, 97–99, 229–30) incisively examines Nietzsche on hope. See also Eagleton's thought-provoking *Hope without Optimism* (2017).

22. Leopardi views the human mind as not only open to hope but also possessed by it, "even in the moment of its final desperation, even in the act of suicide" (2014, 100). There is, then, a deeply tragic side to human hope. As Cioran observes: "[I] t is when we no longer hope that we suffer the fascination of hope" (1949/2010, 167). Emerson writes astutely on the indefatigable character of hope: "There is a difference between one and another hour of life in their authority and subsequent effect. Our faith comes in moments; our vice is habitual. Yet there is a depth in those brief moments which constrains us to ascribe more reality to them than to all other experiences. For this reason the argument which is always forthcoming to silence those who conceive extraordinary hopes of man, namely the appeal to experience, is for ever invalid and vain. We give up the past to the objector, and yet we hope. He must explain this hope" (2000, 236).

23. On Nietzsche and Emerson taken together as skeptics, see Ansell-Pearson (2021). In addition to his essay "Montaigne; or, The Skeptic" (1850), there are significant treatments of skepticism in Emerson's essays "Spiritual Laws," "Experience," and "Character." In Emerson, skepticism is part of an affirmative philosophy, and it works in two ways. On the one hand, although philosophy endeavors to be affirmative, it "readily accepts the testimony of negative facts" (Emerson 2000, 184 ["Spiritual Laws"]). On the other hand, it maintains that a new picture of life is possible, one in which the "new statement will comprise the skepticisms as well as the faiths of society," acknowledging that such skepticisms are neither gratuitous nor lawless: "[T]he new philosophy must take them in and make affirmations outside of them" (Emerson 2000, 321 ["Experience"]). Much more than what he calls a "fine Pyrrhonism"—the equivalent and indifferent character of all actions—is at work, then, in Emerson. Nietzsche's copies of Emerson's *Essays* and *The Conduct of Life* were heavily annotated, but it cannot be established with certainty whether he was familiar with Emerson's essay on Montaigne. This is because the book in which the essay appears was never fully translated into German in Nietzsche's time, and this essay was one of those that were overlooked.

The essays on Goethe and Shakespeare were published in German as an independent text, and this is the book Nietzsche owned. Nevertheless, references to skepticism are to be found in a significant number of Emerson's *Essays*, and Nietzsche would most certainly have been exposed to these references given his great familiarity with them. Stanley Cavell did much in his work to defend Emerson's entitlement to being a philosopher and contra negative estimations of him. Cavell's work is also notable for the way it seeks to counter the threat posed to philosophy by skepticism. It is curious, then, that nowhere in his writings does he consider Emerson's essay on Montaigne with its advocacy of a *wise* skepticism. Cavell is a thinker perturbed by skepticism's role in philosophy: "I take skepticism not as the moral of a cautious science laboring to bring light into a superstitious, fanatical world, but as the recoil of a demonic reason, irrationally thinking to dominate the earth" (1988, 138).

24. Borges (2000, 417) shares Nietzsche's preference for Emerson over Carlyle: "Carlyle was a romantic writer, of plebeian virtues and vices; Emerson, a classical writer and a gentleman." He also finds him maniacal. Nietzsche is less severe, finding Carlyle simply "muddle-headed" (*BGE* 252). On Nietzsche's relation to Carlyle, with a focus on issues of perfectionism, see Meakins (2014). Thoreau (1846/2007) is incisive on Carlyle's relation to poetry and philosophy as well as instructive on his colloquial style and the role that humor plays in his writings.

25. Emerson's cheerful mode of thinking and writing, Nietzsche implies, offers the reader digested problems that have been confronted and overcome. Stanley Cavell recognizes that some readers might object that "Emersonian cheerfulness and hopefulness would simply express a childish ignorance of our real situation," and he notes that Emerson "is forever taken by his detractors, and not by them alone, to ignore the tragic facts of life." He ripostes as follows: "Emerson seems to take despair not as a recognition of life, not even a tragic recognition of it, but as a fear of life, an avoidance of it" (Cavell 1990, 130). Both Nietzsche and Emerson are perfectly aware of the tragic facts of life, and we should avoid patronizing Emerson on this issue. Emerson acknowledges: "[N]o theory of life can have any right, which leaves out of account the values of vice, pain, disease, poverty, insecurity, disunion, fear, and death" (2013, 334–35 ["The Tragic"]).

CHAPTER TWO

Epigraph: Nietzsche, note of 1881, translation mine.

1. Socrates refers to the Delphic inscription in the *Phaedrus* to acknowledge that he remains unable to know himself and so must keep looking into himself (Plato 1995, 229e, 244b). For an enlightening study of humanity's belief in signs and oracles, see Wood (2003).

2. Nietzsche's rendition of the doctrine of the eternal recurrence of the same is designed to add tremendous weight to this insight by posing to us, in the hour of our most solitary solitude, the question, How well-disposed would we have to become to ourselves and to life "*to crave nothing more fervently* than this ultimate eternal confirmation and seal?" (*GS* 341). On the significance of the "colossal moment" in Nietzsche's aphorism, see Loeb (2018a). On Nietzsche and eternal recurrence, see chap. 6 below.

3. Nietzsche's critique of Kant is not wholly reliable. For example, in *AC 11*, he construes Kant's ethics as espousing the "automaton of duty," but this is remote from what Kant puts forward. For Kant, virtue is not to be conceived as "a mere mechanism

of applying power." Instead, "virtue is *moral strength* in adherence to one's duty, which should never become habit but should always emerge entirely new and original from one's own way of thinking" (2006, 38). Still, Nietzsche is right to draw attention to the worrisome aspects of an ethics of duty where it entails an unquestioning morality of obedience. See esp. *D* 207.

4. There is one situation in his life where Nietzsche confesses to playacting. This is when he was acting as feeling cheerful when he was not. Reflecting on his middle period in 1885, he writes: "'Forward,' I said to myself, 'tomorrow you will be healthy, today it suffices for you to feign health.' Back then I gained mastery over everything 'pessimistic' in me: the will to health itself, the play-acting of health was my cure" (*KSA*, vol. 11, fragment 40 [65], p. 665; *SUP*, 16:217). For insight on this aspect of Nietzsche's cheerfulness, see chap. 1 above.

5. For Nietzsche on Pascal, see *DS* sec. 8; *HH* 282; *MOM* 5, 408; *D* 46, 64, 68, 79, 86, 91, 192, 549; *BGE* 45–46, 62; *GM* 3.17; *TI* "The Four Great Errors" 6; *TI* "Reconnaissance Raids of an Untimely Man" 9; *AC* 5; EH "Why I Am So Clever" 3. In *BGE* 45, Nietzsche describes Pascal's intellectual conscience as "profound," "wounded," and "monstrous." For insight into Nietzsche's reading of Pascal as critic of human illusion and human pride, see Williams (1952, 56–58, 79–85, 101–3). As Williams points out, Nietzsche reads Pascal in two ways: as a skeptic and as an agonized mystic. Aldous Huxley writes with great wit: "Pascal's metaphysic may be described as a kind of positivistic Pyrrhonism tempered, and indeed flatly denied, by dogmatic Christianity" (1929, 254). For insight into Nietzsche on Pascal, see also Parr (2023).

6. On honesty in Nietzsche, see also Page (2019), Reginster (2013), White (2001), Wurzer (1975, 1983), and Zaborowski (2010). In the translations on which I am relying, *Redlichkeit* is typically rendered as *honesty*, but it can also be translated as *integrity* or *probity*. Cognizance should be taken of Annette Baier's insight: "The Latin *honestas*, perhaps best translated as 'probity,' is a broad-ranging virtue, but then so is English honesty" (2009, 85). The final sketches of a notebook from the autumn of 1880 reveal that Nietzsche planned a work on honesty (*Redlichkeit*) in which he proposes to write of its history and its passion: "*Passio nova* oder Von der Leidenschaft der Redlichkeit" (*KSA*, vol. 9, fragment 6 [461]; see also *KSA*, vol. 9, fragment 6 [457–61]).

7. It is perhaps significant, then, that in *Zarathustra* Nietzsche presents the doctrine of the eternal recurrence in terms of a vision and a riddle.

8. On Epicurean naturalism, see Guyau (1878/2021) and Santayana (1910/2019). On the Christian rejection of Epicurus, see Augustine (2019, 6.16.26). In his late writings, Nietzsche is sometimes critical of Epicurean teaching, locating in it a denial of the strong will to life in favor of a life free of desire and with an aversion to pain (*AC* 30), even a "hypnotic feeling nothingness" (*GM* 3.17). In *The Ethics of Epicurus*, Guyau convincingly shows that Epicurus is a thinker of supreme affirmation whose work was motivated by a desire to attack the philosophies and religions of his time that sought to reduce life to nothingness and "to make nothingness more desirable than life" (1878/2021, 95). Nietzsche's notebooks and annotations show that he had an intimate knowledge of Guyau's *A Sketch of Morality without Obligation or Sanction* (1885/1896) and *The Non-Religion of the Future* (1887/1962), but evidence that would show he was familiar with *The Ethics of Epicurus* is not available. For further insight into Nietzsche's reception of Epicurus, see Ansell-Pearson (2018, esp. chaps. 1 and 6) and Acharya and Johnson (2020).

9. On why we might choose to be Epicureans today, see Ansell-Pearson (2018, esp. chap. 6) and Harrison (2008, chap. 7).

10. In *The Gay Science*, Nietzsche praises Stendhal as a writer "who may well have had more thoughtful eyes and ears than any other Frenchman of this century" (*GS* 95). And, in *Ecce Homo*, he praises Stendhal as a "profound psychologist" in the context of a biting critique of German philosophers—presented as "unconscious counterfeiters"—and the lack, as he sees it, in German culture of psychology in the form of "harsh self-examination" (*EH* "The Case of Wagner" 3). Stendhal's importance to Nietzsche is looked at in chap. 7 below.

11. For a recent instructive appreciation of Stendhal's autobiography, see Davis (2019).

12. For instructive insight into Stendhal's lifelong engagement with Rousseau, see Coe (1979) and Brombert (1988). For Nietzsche on Rousseau as a moral fanatic, see esp. the preface to sec. 3 of *Dawn*. On his "passionate follies and half-lies," see *HH* 463. Virginia Woolf touches on the importance of honesty when she lays down two strictures for a good essay. First, it must be fused by "the magic of writing" in which no fact "juts out" and no "dogma tears the surface of the texture." Second, although an exercise in the art of expressing one's personal peculiarities, it must be written in accordance with the dictates of intellectual honesty: "Confronted with the terrible spectre of themselves, the bravest are inclined to run away or shade their eye. And thus, instead of the honest truth which we should all respect, we are given timid side-glances in the shape of essays, which, for the most part, fail in the cardinal virtue of sincerity" (2008, 13, 5). On the difficulty of telling the truth about oneself and even of being oneself, see Woolf's essay on Montaigne (Woolf 2019, 127–43).

13. For insight into Hume's conception of a passion of knowledge, see Harris (2015, 102–3).

14. I examine Nietzsche's criticism of the limits of "objectivity" more fully in chap. 7 below.

15. Rousseau employs Juvenal's motto—*vitam impendere vero*—in his letter to D'Alembert on the theater and reaffirms it in *Emile* and his *Letters from the Mountain*. Schopenhauer employs the motto for the frontispiece of his two-volume *Parerga and Paralipomena* (1851). On Rousseau, see Kelly (2003). See also Baudelaire, who cites Joseph de Maistre: "If a writer adopts as his motto: *Vitam impendere vero*, the bets are on that he's a liar" (2022, 389).

16. On the importance of this, and on Augustine's love of wisdom, see Gilson (2020, chap. 1).

17. For insight into the relation of love to knowledge in Augustine, see Scheler (1992, 161–64).

18. Admittedly, Augustine pursued a kind of philosophical way of life by drawing on the tradition of Christian Platonism, which enabled him to attain a personal triumph over the skepticism of late antiquity after experiencing a skeptical period. His traditional conception of wisdom is one that takes seriously knowledge of both human and divine matters (Augustine 1995, 17). It is the interest in the divine that Nietzsche wishes us to lose in the new wisdom he calls for and pursues in his middle writings and that I highlight in the next chapter. For insight into the influence of the skeptical schools of philosophy on Augustine, see Augustine (2019, vi–xx [translator's introduction]), Gilson (1936, 209–28), Kenny (2005, 156–59), and Lane Fox (2015, 173–74, 227–28).

19. See also Unamuno: "We do not understand the existence of the world one whit the better by telling ourselves that God created it. It is a begging of the question,

or a merely verbal solution, intended to cover up our ignorance." And with respect to the so-called proofs of God's existence that refer to the God idea, a logical God of abstraction, they prove nothing more than the existence of this *idea* of God. Unamuno seeks to persuade us that "[t]he God whom we hunger after is the God to whom we pray, the God of the *Pater Noster*, of the Lord's Prayer" (1912/1962, 164, 181). On the remote character of the God of the philosophers, see also Bergson (1933/1977, chap. 3 ["Dynamic Religion"]). See also Cioran: "Theology is the negation of divinity. Looking for proofs of God's existence is a crazy idea. All the theological treatises put together are not worth a single sentence from Saint Teresa!" (1937/1995, 76).

20. A defense of the coherence of idea of the "hidden God" (*deus absconditus*) (Isa. 45:15; Job 23:9) against Nietzsche's attack is offered by Douglas Groothuis in his study of Pascal. Groothuis contends that Nietzsche's attack is an ad hominem one and begs the question. Moreover, he contends that Nietzsche's dismissal of theism is as much dispositional as it is philosophical (2024, 82). This riposte fails to recognize, however, that the dispositional character of Nietzsche's thinking is guided by his commitment to the *passion of knowledge*, which is a passion absent in theological thinking. On Pascal and the hidden God see the classic study by Lucien Goldmann (2016).

21. See also Diderot's view in sec. 31 of *Pensées philosophiques* that, if something has not been questioned, then it cannot be taken as proven: "Skepticism, then, is the first step toward truth. It should be made something general since it is its touchstone" (1746, 63–64). For Nietzsche on Diderot, see *MOM* 113 and *BGE* 28. On Diderot and skepticism, see Serini (2024). On Nietzsche and Diderot, see Porter (2023). Ernst Cassirer (1951, esp. 90–91) provides excellent insight into Diderot's philosophical nature, which he characterizes well as a flexible and perspectival manner of thinking that resists crystallization and expression in definitive formulas. For a glorious portrait of "Denis *le philosophe*," see Hazard: "To him, we owe that picture of Experiment in the guise of a giant, bringing down the pillars of the Temple of Error" (1965, 405 [and see 403–17 generally]).

22. In "Reading Montaigne," Merleau-Ponty persuasively argues against supposing the meaning of Montaigne's skepticism, along with the confession "what do I know?" is self-evident. His appreciation of Montaigne's skepticism brings him close to Nietzsche when he assumes the guise of a skeptic: "The fact of the matter is that true skepticism is movement toward the truth. . . . The critique of human understanding destroys it only if we cling to the idea of a complete or absolute understanding" (1964, 206–7). For insight into Montaigne and skepticism, see Hartle (2008) and Zalloua (2005). Jonathan Bate provides a defense of Montaigne's "what do I know?" by pointing out that Montaigne's "work is a perpetual critique of abstract wisdom in the name of experience" (2009, 388). In short, Montaigne knows what he knows only from experience and finds theory wanting in the face of action. See also Cowper Powys (1946b, 317–18).

23. The attachment to freedom of the will "in the superlative metaphysical sense," as Nietzsche has it, which would mean being the *causa sui* (self-caused), supposes that we can perform the impossible, namely, pulling ourselves up by the hair "out of the swamp of nothingness into existence." The *causa sui* "is the best self-contradiction conceived of to date, a kind of logical rape and violation of nature," and it is humanity's excessive pride that accounts for this error and how we have become so entangled in such nonsense for so long (*BGE* 21). In place of phantasmic notions of free will and unfree will, Nietzsche favors a notion of strong and weak wills. We see this at work in his commitment to a notion of "self-sovereignty" (*D* 191) and how he conceives freedom

of the will positively as the "power of self-determination" (*GS* 347) and in terms of the sovereign individual who has the prerogative to promise and is in possession of an enduring will that gives him or her consciousness of a rare freedom and power over himself or herself. This is "freedom of the will" as self-mastery (*GM* 2.2). On the "will" as the affect of command, see *BGE* 19.

24. For further insight into Nietzsche's reception of a priestly Kant, see Loeb (2019b).

25. For further insight into Nietzsche and skepticism, see Berry (2011) and Bett (2000). For a critical response to Berry, see Mitcheson (2016).

26. On the conservative character of "profound scepticism," see Santayana (1922/1967, 257). See also Horkheimer (1993). And see also Cioran (1972/2012, 137): "What then is the skeptic?—A ghost: a conformist skeptic."

27. Santayana echoes Nietzsche's description of Hamlet as a weak sceptic in *BGE* 208 when he writes: "This unreason is not madness, because his intellect remains clear, his discourse sound and comprehensive; but it is a sort of passionate weakness and indirection in his will, which mocks its own ends, strikes fantastic attitudes, and invents elaborate schemes of action useless for his declared purposes. . . . An apt pupil of philosophy, of politics, of art, of love, Hamlet is master in nothing. . . . Hamlet's sad reflections have in the end the merit of humor rather than of wisdom" (1968, 135, 137, 142).

28. On "sin's skepticism," see Kierkegaard (1844/2014, 22–25). Cioran notes: "A Greek would never have associated lamentation with doubt. He would recoil horror-struck before a Pascal" (2019, 95). See also Cioran (1956/1987, 196–97) and Cioran (1937/1995, 47, 50–51).

CHAPTER THREE

Epigraphs: Nietzsche, *Human, All Too Human*, trans. Gary Handwerk; Nietzsche, *The Gay Science*, trans. Walter Kaufmann; Nietzsche, *Dawn*, trans. Brittain Smith.

1. See the insights I offer in the section of chap. 4 below on the passions and self-cultivation and in chaps. 5 and 6 generally.

2. As the poet (and physician) William Carlos Williams noted, the approach to learning through the classics "can be lethal to the intelligence," and it is possible to imagine that a great and original naturalist like Shakespeare would have been thoroughly gelded by a classical training (1974, 140).

3. Today we associate the conception of philosophy as a way of life with the pioneering work of Pierre Hadot on the ancient schools of philosophy. However, an important, if now forgotten, attempt to remind us that philosophy is a way of life can be found in the work of Olaf Stapledon, who is better known today for writing novels in the genre we now call *science fiction*. He conceives philosophy in these terms: "Philosophy is a way of life. It is not simply an intellectual discipline. Of course, a rigorous intellectual discipline is included in philosophy; but no matter how rigorous, no matter how subtle and conscientious, intellectual activity alone is not by itself philosophy, in the fullest sense of that ambiguous but important word. Philosophy is an attitude taken up by the mind in relation to its whole world; a mental tone or temper which should affect the whole of a man's practical living, giving it sanity, a coherence, constancy of direction, which it could not otherwise have" (1939, 1:11–12). See also Jung: "Our philosophy is no longer a way of life, as it was in antiquity; it has turned into an exclusively intellectual and academic exercise" (1983, 383).

4. In this note, Nietzsche refers to Aristotle on the sage when speaking of philosophy's preoccupation with the divine. For relevant insight into Aristotle, see Cooper (2012, 154–55 [and chap. 3 generally]). Cooper helpfully clarifies Aristotle on the divine: "For Aristotle, as reasoners ourselves, we are indeed related to the thinking of the divine mind . . . but only through the divine mind's being the ultimate and highest object for us to grasp and understand through our own processes of reasoning. . . . The virtue of practical wisdom is knowledge of the human good, not of god—god's activity—as a good beyond us" (2012, 155).

5. In this instance I have translated *schwärmerisch* as *enthusiastic*. As Coleridge (1997, 19) points out in the *Biographia Literaria*, in its original import *schwärmerisch* is the German word for *fanaticism*, deriving from the swarming of bees (*Schwärmen*). In his translation of *MOM* 148 for the Cambridge University Press (Nietzsche 1991), R. J. Hollingdale omits the word completely and simply has "a *love* of philosophy and art"; in his translation for the Stanford University Press (Nietzsche 2013b), Gary Handwerk has "a visionary *love* for philosophy and art." The English word *enthusiasm* captures well what Nietzsche has in mind in the context of the aphorism as a whole, suggesting that, given our spiritual poverty as well as the extent to which we live in the grip of senseless delusions and passions, cultivating a love of philosophy in an enthusiastic manner may serve to drive us forward in our existence and enable us to attain a new level of self-understanding. Handwerk's translation of the German word as *visionary* is inventive and not without a degree of merit since it captures the idea implied in the aphorism that, by working through our poverty and delusions, we may arrive at a quite different place, enlightening ourselves in the process. It is the case, however, that Nietzsche will often deploy the word *schwärmerisch* (along with *Fanatismus*) to articulate his concerns about fanaticism. See, e.g., *D* preface 3; *D* 57–58, 66, 68, 204, 298; *BGE* 10; *GS* 347; and *AC* 11, 54. For further insight into Nietzsche on fanaticism, see Ansell-Pearson (2018, 47–63 [chap. 2]). See also *BGE* 230.

6. Nietzsche may have been influenced by Emerson's insight that history is biography: "We, as we read, must become Greeks, Romans, Turks, priest and king, martyr and executioner." And later: "The world exists for the education of each man. . . . He should see that he can live all history in his own person" (2000, 114, 115). Emerson begins his essay by positing a "universal mind" that is common to all human beings. The fact that there is this one mind means that all human beings have access to everything that has ever been thought and felt within history: "Who hath access to this universal mind is a party to all that is or can be done, for this is the only and sovereign agent" (2000, 113).

7. On Nietzsche and Heraclitus, see chap. 6 below.

8. For instructive insight into the two aphorisms taken together (*GS* 340 and 341), see Loeb (1998). On *GS* 340, see also Foucault (2012, 99ff.).

9. Pierre Hadot argues that for anyone who takes philosophy seriously the Platonic dictum of conceiving philosophy as training for death is "profoundly true" (1995, 95). If, in the words of La Rochefoucauld, what cannot be looked at directly are the sun and death, then it is philosophers who attempt the impossible: recognizing the need for lucidity in the face of death. For the Platonist, the Epicurean, and the Stoic, philosophy provides an apprenticeship in death. The meditation on death may be done, however, for different reasons and with different expectations: "From the perspective of pure thought, things which are 'human, all too human' seem awfully puny. This is one of the fundamental themes of Platonic spiritual exercises, and it is this which will allow us

to maintain serenity in misfortunes" (Hadot 1995, 96). As Plato puts it in *The Republic* (486a): "But that soul to which pertain grandeur of thought and the *contemplation of the totality* of time and of being, do you think that it can consider human life to be a matter of great importance? Hence such a man will not suppose death to be terrible" (cited in Hadot 1995, 97). Seneca argues, following Epicurus, that to learn how to die is to unlearn slavery: we are to free ourselves from the fear of death since it is death that puts the yoke about our necks, thus making us unfree and intimidated by an external sanction (Seneca 2005, letter 30). In Epicurean teaching, death is to be meditated on to liberate us for the joys and pleasures of life. See also Montaigne's essay, which takes its title from Cicero, "That to philosophize is to learn to die" (2003, 1.20). See also Cioran's witty and perceptive insight: "The thought of death enslaves those whom it haunts. It liberates only at the beginning; then it degenerates into an obsession, thereby ceasing to be a thought" (1992, 198). And, in his essay "Stoicism and Mental Health," Russell writes wisely about the harmfulness of brooding continually on death: "It is a mistake to think too exclusively about any one subject, more particularly when our own thinking cannot issue in action. . . . Fear of death makes a man feel himself the slave of external forces, and from a slave mentality no good result can follow" (1935/1996b, 149–50).

10. In the practical, ethical teaching of Socrates, Bergson identifies what he calls a *creative emotion*. Everything that raises humankind to a new level of perception and feeling—be it in art, philosophy, or science—requires the inspiration of such an emotion to beget new thoughts. In Socrates the gadfly, we also encounter a mystic of reason who seeks to inspire in others a love of philosophical questioning (1932/1977, 62–63). Cioran questions whether Socrates's daemon was a purely psychological phenomenon, a mere hallucination, or corresponded to some supposed metaphysical reality, noting that Hegel held it to be a subjective oracle with no external reality, while Nietzsche considered it to be the trick of an actor. Cioran then astutely notes: "[H]e was the first thinker to make himself into a *case*, and it is with him that the inextricable problem of sincerity begins" (1956/1987, 167–68).

11. On the significance for philosophy of Socrates and his death, see Foucault (2012, 113–14) and Hadot (2020, 43–55). For fresh insights into the image and meaning of Socrates for philosophy, see Long (2022, chap. 6).

12. For insight into Nietzsche's "Socrates," see Conway (2017), Dannhauser (1974), Porter (2006), and Nichols (2009, esp. 15–23, 207–12).

13. For further extensive insight into Nietzsche on morality as a problem, see Ansell-Pearson and Bamford (2021).

14. On this choice, see Hadot (2020, 59).

15. The other three pairs are: Goethe and Spinoza, Plato and Rousseau, and Pascal and Schopenhauer. In a note of 1881, Nietzsche writes of his felt affinity with the likes of Plato, Pascal, Spinoza, and Goethe, stating that their blood flows in his and that he is proud of this humaneness (*Menschlichkeit*) (*KSA*, vol. 9, fragment 12 [52]; *SUP*, 6:430).

16. In an essay on Lucretius's naturalism, Deleuze argues that in Epicurean teaching the products of nature are inseparable from an ontological diversity, including individuality and heterogeneity, in which species differ, members of the same species differ, and there is a diversity of parts that make up an individual. We encounter in nature, then, a diversity of matter and a heterogeneity of elements in which we can declare that there are no two shellfish or grains of sand that are indiscernible. While not a pregiven whole, nature can be conceived as a sum, and we can think of this in terms of

the image of the Harlequin's cloak, "made entirely of solid patches and empty spaces": "[Nature] is made of plenitude and void, beings and nonbeings." However: "[T]here is no combination capable of encompassing all the elements of Nature at once" (1961, 19–20). On Lucretius, see also Italo Calvino's remarkable essay "Lightness" (1996, 3–29).

17. As George Corbett (2013, 11–12) notes, the misinterpretation of the Epicurean teaching of *voluptas*—taken to denote the simple, mindless pursuit of positive sensual pleasure—appears to have assailed Epicurean ethics from its inception. It is captured in Horace's ironic reference to himself as a hog from the herd of Epicurus. See also Otto (1975). Nietzsche writes perceptively: "Epicurus has been alive at all times and is living now, unknown to those who have called and call themselves Epicureans and enjoying no reputation among philosophers. He has, moreover, himself forgotten his own name: it was the heaviest pack he ever threw off" (*WS* 227). On the rich character of Epicurean ethics, see Guyau (1878/2021).

18. While Nietzsche commits himself to hope, his attitude is never one of resignation or simple consolation. For further insight and references, see chap. 1 above.

19. As Santayana (1896/1955, 87) notes, a single philosophy could claim final victory only if it proved adequate to all experience. He wisely advises us to be skeptical of any philosophy that purported to have such a pretension.

20. Terse insight into Nietzsche as a philosopher-wanderer can be found in Coverley (2012, 30–31). For more substantial insight, see Sussman (2007, 21–42). See also the informed study of vol. 2 of *Human, All Too Human* in Brücker (2019).

21. Along with Hazlitt, Stendhal is the great analyst of idealized romantic love, and together the two writers contribute to the treasury of human knowledge by providing honest insight into it. Nietzsche did not know of Hazlitt's *Liber Amoris* (1823), but he knew well Stendhal's *On Love* (1822), as he did Benjamin Constant's novel *Adolphe* (1816), on the sufferings of the heart and the tragedy of sexual love (*KSA*, vol. 13, fragment 11 [305]). On numerous occasions, we find him referring to Stendhal's texts, including *On Love*, in his notebooks (e.g., *KSA*, vol. 9, fragment 7 [134], [140], [145], [148], and [297]; and *KSA*, vol. 10, fragment 7 [77], p. 269). Stendhal considers love to be the strongest of the passions, noting: "In the others, desires have to adapt to cold reality; with love, reality is eagerly reshaped according to your desires. Therefore, of all the passions, it is love that permits the greatest scope for pleasures in violent desires" (1957, 60 [chap. 12]). He observes how love can transport us to heights of a delirious sublime: "For romantic hearts, the more sublime the soul of your beloved, the more celestial and the further removed from the mire of all vulgar concerns will be the pleasures you find in her arms." Love, however, is also to be considered a species of madness: "Love is like a fever. It flares up and dies away, and the will has no sway over it" (1957, 60, 51 [chap. 5]). He astutely observes: "From the moment he begins to love, even the wisest man no longer sees any object *as it is*. . . . Now his fears and hopes enter the realm of the *romantic* (and *wayward*). Nothing can now be due to luck; he loses all sense of likeliness. Everything he imagines becomes real and present according to its effect on his happiness" (1957, 60 [chap. 12]). Ortega y Gasset notes that it is not so much that love is blind for Stendhal but rather that it is wholly imaginary: "Not only does it not see what is real, but it supplants the real" (1957/2012, 26). For rich insights into Stendhal on love, see also de Beauvoir (1949/1997) and Calvino (1997). On love's blindness, see also the nuanced insights offered by Rousseau in bk. 4 of *Emile* (2010, 363–65), and compare Ortega y Gasset (1957/2012, 203–4). Ortega y Gasset (1957/2012, 188–89) is excellent on romantic love as the summit of all eroticisms.

22. In some respects, we can see Rilke as building on Nietzsche's thinking about love. When young, we are bunglers of life and apprentices in love, absolute beginners. For example, in conceiving love as the strengthening of two neighboring solitudes, Rilke contests the prevailing conception of love as consisting in the merging of two people into a single entity. His reasoning on this point is incisive: "Love is at first not anything that means merging, giving over, and uniting with another: for what would be a union of something unclarified and unfinished?" When we fall in love, our feeling of isolation is shattered, but we go wrong in love when we neglect to attend to the fact that in love two separate existences need ripening and that only the work of love can bring this about. A good marriage, Rilke says, is not a matter of creating a "quick community of spirit by tearing down and destroying all boundaries, but rather one in which each appoints the other guardian of his solitude, and shows him this confidence, the greatest in his power to bestow" (2004, 38, 34).

23. For insight into the "deification of love" in the history of humanity, see the appendix "Moments in the History of Love" in Hacker (2018, esp. 426–37). See also May (2019). Chapter 34 of this excellent book is devoted to thoughts about romantic love (esp. May 2019, 221–28).

24. For Jung, the shadow is not simply something negative to be wholly transcended. There is a wisdom in our natural instincts that is often more profound than what we learn through culture and education: "A shadowless life tends to become shallow and spiritless" (Hall and Nordby 1973, 49).

25. On emotions and affects, see Jung (1983, 215–18). On the shadow, see Jung (1983, 242–43, 388–89, 399–403).

26. For insight into the shadow in *Zarathustra*, see Bishop (2017). Also well worth reading is Hough (1997) and Huskinson (2004).

27. In thinking about the "psychology" of the artist, Nietzsche claims that intoxication and the feeling of increased power and plenitude are required for "any kind of aesthetic doing and seeing," and this is because "idealization" is at work. This, however, has nothing to do with finding an alleged "true" self, let alone "the true world" (*TI* "Reconnaissance Raids of an Untimely" 8).

28. On Dionysus, see also Otto (1965), Harrison (1903/1991), Pater (2018, 277–98), and Fornari (2021). On Nietzsche and Dionysus, see Calasso (2002, 65–67), Fisher (1995, 515–36), and Murray (2018). Pater construes Dionysus as the liberator of human hearts (2018, 283) and relates him to the Orphic mysteries (2018, 297). On the presentation of Dionysus in *BGE* 295, Conway (2024, 201–9) is especially instructive.

29. On the "insanity" of the mob, see Emerson (2000, 167–68).

30. In his 1841 essay "Self-Reliance," Emerson echoes Schopenhauer in part when he writes: "Society everywhere is a conspiracy against the manhood of every one of its members. Society is a joint-stock company, in which the members agree, for the better security of his bread to each shareholder, to surrender the liberty and culture of the eater. The virtue in most request is conformity. Self-reliance is its aversion. It loves not realities and creators, but names and customs. . . . I am ashamed to think how easily we capitulate to badges and names, to large societies and dead institutions." Perhaps the key aspect of self-reliance, the one that explains it, is having trust in oneself: "Trust thyself: every heart vibrates to that iron string" (2000, 133). See also Emerson (2000, 324 ["Experience"]). For an instructive study of Emerson on self-reliance, which also includes some treatment of Nietzsche, see Kateb (2002).

31. Compare Emerson: "The soul is no traveller; the wise man stays at home.... Travelling is a fool's paradise" (2000, 149–50 ["Self-Reliance"]). See also Emerson (2003, 142): "The uses of travel are occasional and short." On the benefits of "wise travel," see Santayana (1964). Hazlitt's essay "On Going on a Journey" (1821) is also well worth reading (see Hazlitt 1982, 136–48).

32. These are the words uttered by the young widow Constance in Diderot's play *The Natural Son* (1757). Diderot sent the play to Rousseau, who was convinced the remark was aimed at him.

33. A similar claim is found in Montaigne, who writes of "the real solitude, which may be enjoyed in the midst of cities and the courts of kings": "[B]ut it is enjoyed more handily alone" (2003, 214 [1.39]).

34. Compare Montaigne: "[I]t is not enough to have gotten away from the crowd, it is not enough to move; we must get away from the gregarious instincts that are inside us, we must sequester ourselves and repossess ourselves." For Montaigne: "The greatest thing in the world is to know how to belong to oneself." However, he stresses that solitude is most appropriate for those who have given to the world their most active and flourishing years: "We have lived long enough for others; let us live at least this remaining bit of life for ourselves" (2003, 213, 216 [1.39]).

35. Nietzsche has adjusted here the four virtues he had listed as the good four in *Dawn*: honesty toward oneself and whatever else is a friend to us; displaying courage in the face of the enemy; showing magnanimity toward the defeated; and politeness (*D* 556).

36. Compare Diderot: "[T]here is a secret link between death and the night, which moves us without our realizing it. The resurrection is all the more wonderful and death all the more melancholy" (1994, 334). On the "untimely night" where the perception of time becomes anomalous, see Nietzsche, *KSA*, vol. 9, fragment 11 [260]; *SUP*, 6:390.

37. For the role the third eye plays in Indian philosophy, where it is conceived as an invisible eye that can provide perception beyond ordinary sight, see Napier (1986, 135ff. [chap. 5]).

38. For Nietzsche's teaching of the self, including the relation of the "self" to the "ego," see *Z* 1 "Of the Despisers of the Body." For insight into this discourse, see Gerhardt (2006).

39. Huxley provides a reliable conception of mystical experience: "It is a non-egoistic consciousness, a kind of formless and timeless consciousness, which seems to underlie the consciousness of the separate ego in time." His approach is to value it as a psychological experience in which the "fruits" of the knowledge (gnosis) gained from the experience are the fruits of the spirit, such as love, joy, and peace: "[O]ne is not committed by mysticism to any cut-and-dried statement about the structure of the universe" (1980, 208, 211). D. H. Lawrence is a writer much concerned with the need for us to view ourselves in terms of a cosmic consciousness, and in a more literal sense than Nietzsche intends: "There are millions of worlds, whole cosmic worlds, to us as yet unborn" (1999, 176).

40. See also Santayana's perceptive insight about mysticism: "It is not, however, in the least superhuman. It is hardly even abnormal, being only an exaggeration of a rational interest in the highest abstractions." Just as penetrating in exposing the conceits of mysticism is when Santayana argues that it "make us proud and happy to renounce the work of intelligence, both in thought and in life, and persuades us that we become divine by remaining imperfectly human." He gives the example of Whitman to illustrate

his critical point: “He feels his own cosmic justification and he would lend the sanction of his inspiration to all loafers and holiday-makers” (1900/1989, 16, 114).

CHAPTER FOUR

Epigraphs: Stendhal to his sister Pauline, January 29, 1803, trans. Andrew Brown; Nietzsche, note of 1881, trans. Adrian Del Caro; Nietzsche, *Dawn*, trans. Brittain Smith.

1. Rousseau is one writer and thinker who provides testimony to the vehement character of the passions in his *Confessions*: “My passions have made me live, and my passions have killed me” (Rousseau 1995, 183 [pt. 1, bk. 5]; see also Rousseau 1995, 373 [pt. 2, bk. 9]). Stendhal gives sound advice to his sister Pauline concerning Rousseau: “Read that great man; but remember that he was always in a bad mood” (2011, 41). On Rousseau’s vehemence, Carlyle writes: “A morbid, excitable, spasmodic man; at best, intense rather than strong. . . . A fundamental mistake to call vehemence and rigidity strength!” (1841/1983, 224–25).

2. Stoic teaching makes a distinction between “good affections” (*eupatheiai*) and “passions” (*pathe*), with the latter being construed as disordered affective states that do not participate in virtue. For further insight, see Russell (2012, 184–88). See also Graver (2007). With regard to the exceptions that I mention, one might refer to thinkers such as Malebranche, Hume, and Rousseau. Hume is famous for his claim that reason acting on its own can make nothing matter: “Tis not contrary to Reason to prefer the destruction of the entire world to the scratching of my finger” (2007, 2.3.3). For Hume, reason denotes the power to make discoveries about what is real and so is to be greatly valued. His critical point, however, is that reasoning alone can never give us a primary impulse to do anything or to make judgments of worth. Reason enables us to discover what is true or false about reality, but it cannot provide us with any motivating desire to act. Malebranche takes the Stoics to task on the emotions in his extensive treatment of the passions in bk. 5, chap. 2 of *The Search after Truth* (1997). Rousseau accords a crucial role to the passions in human education and holds that the “one who has lived most is not he who has counted the most years but he who has most felt life!” (2010, 7).

3. To be fair, Kant readily acknowledges that reason plays a role in the fostering of the passions, with passions presupposing “a maxim of the subject, namely, to act according to a purpose prescribed to him by his inclination” (2006, 173).

4. For a recent study of Nietzsche on the emotions, see Tuncel (2021).

5. See also: “Anyone who is about to fly into a rage or to fall intensely in love reaches a point where his soul is filled like a vessel; and yet one drop of water must still be added, a good will for passion (which we generally term a bad will). Only this droplet is necessary, then the vessel runs over” (*HH* 584).

6. Here one might give the example of early modern thinkers such as Montaigne and Spinoza. As Dominik Perler notes: “Montaigne gave practical advice on how to overcome feelings of sadness and loneliness, and Spinoza devoted the whole of the last part of the *Ethics* to the ‘power of reason’ over the affects” (2018, 15). For an instructive attempt to bring Nietzsche and Spinoza into rapport on the issue of the emotions and their mastery, see Armstrong (2013). The affinity that can be drawn between the two, she seeks to show, resides in their shared commitment to a principle of naturalistic immanence: the human being is fully immanent within the order of nature. As Spinoza makes clear in his *Ethics* (1992, bk. 3, preface), the human being has to be understood as fully implicated in the common order of nature, and this means that the human

being cannot be treated as if it was a kingdom within a kingdom that "disturbs" rather than "follows" nature's order; in short, and conceived as a finite mode, the human being is subject to the same causal laws and processes as everything else that exists in nature. For insight into the affects in Spinoza, including the active ones, see Nadler (2020, 24–28). Nadler helpfully defines Spinozist virtue as involving the cultivation of "the strength of one's rational ideas so that they are affectively more powerful than the passions on a consistent basis" (2020, 105). See also Jacquet (2019). I raise some doubts about the extent of Nietzsche's affinity with Spinoza later in this chapter.

7. On the "sins of passions" in general, see Augustine (2019, 3.8.15–16, 4.15.24). For Nietzsche on the origin of sin, see *GS* 135. Where it is conceived as a transgression against God-given law, the doctrine of sin relies on extreme mental states and encourages in those exposed to it extreme modes of behavior: "[E]verywhere, the sinner breaking himself on the cruel wheel of a restless and morbidly lustful conscience; everywhere, dumb torment, the most extreme fear, the agony of the tortured heart, the paroxysms of unknown happiness, the cry for 'redemption'" (*GM* 3.20). For Nietzsche's perspective on Christ and sin, see *AC* 33.

8. James Porter (2020) has argued that Roman Stoicism is a school of philosophy that ought to be conceived as challenging ideas of self-intactness and coherence, with the result that the model of human invulnerability can be shown to be too imprecise when applied to the Stoics. Nevertheless, it is this model of which Nietzsche is keen to expose the limits. My concern here is with assessing not whether he does justice to the Stoic teaching on the emotions but rather what his position on it reveals about his thinking on self-cultivation. Aspects of Schopenhauer's critical perspective on the figure of the Stoic sage—who is said to be "stiff and wooden, a mannequin that no one can engage with and who does not himself know what to do with his own wisdom"—may have exerted an influence on Nietzsche (Schopenhauer 1818/2010, 118). For further insight into Schopenhauer on Stoicism and the wisdom of life, see Ansell-Pearson (2023b).

9. Here I am drawing on the incisive reading of Nietzsche provided in Ure (2009).

10. For further helpful insight, see Ure (2009). For additional insight into Nietzsche's relation to Stoicism, focused on matters of suffering and the love of fate, see Mollison (2019). When considering Nietzsche's doctrine of *amor fati* (*GS* 276), we need to consider what he says in the following note: "Before fate [*Schicksal*] strikes us, we should lead it like a child and—show it the whip: but once it has struck us, then we should seek to love it" (*KSA*, vol. 10, fragment 5 [1] 194).

11. In a potent criticism of Stoic doctrine, Merleau-Ponty seeks to show that the Stoic separation of internal and external, of necessity and freedom, is abstract and destroys itself since "we are indivisibly within and without." Moreover, and echoing Nietzsche but without referring to him, he writes: "[W]e must enter the world's folly" (1964, 205). A. D. Nuttall claims: "Stoicism is at bottom a pusillanimous philosophy" (2007, 184). He advances this claim in the context of a reading of Shakespeare's *Julius Caesar* and what he regards as Shakespeare's criticism of Stoicism. For a thought-provoking perspective on Shakespeare's relation to philosophy, see Eliot (1951, 126–41 ["Shakespeare and the Stoicism of Seneca" (1927)]). Eliot suggests provocatively: "Stoicism is the refuge for the individual in an indifferent or hostile world too big for him; it is the permanent substratum of a number of versions of cheering oneself up. Nietzsche is the most conspicuous modern instance of cheering oneself up. The stoical attitude is the reverse of Christian humility" (Eliot 1951, 131–32). He is most

keen to argue that the task of the poet is not to think but to produce dramatic poetry. On "Shakespeare and the Stoicism of Seneca," see Santayana (1968, 209–21 ["Tragic Philosophy"]).

12. On Nietzsche's objection to Spinoza's intellectual form of love, see also chap. 6 below. Santayana's remark about Spinoza is also apposite here. While applauding him for bringing the human "back into nature . . . showing how he may recognise his environment and how he may master it," Spinoza, Santayana writes, seeks to make the human "a pious tame animal, with the stars shining above his head" (2011, 18).

13. Nietzsche points out that peace of soul can denote a number of different things depending on the person and his or her life situation, including "a rich animality radiating gently out into the moral (or religious) domain," "unwitting gratitude for successful digestion," "the state which follows the powerful satisfaction of our ruling passion," "the infirmity of our will, our desires, our vices" and hence "laziness persuaded by vanity to dress itself up in moral garb," or "the advent of certainty, even terrible certainty, after a long period of tension and torment at the hands of uncertainty." Finally, it may be an expression "of maturity and mastery in the midst of doing, creating, affecting, willing; breathing easily, 'freedom of the will' *achieved*" (*TI* "Morality as Anti-Nature" 3).

14. This concern also informs Nietzsche's criticism of Spinoza in his notebook of 1881: "How Spinoza fantasizes about *reason*! A *fundamental error* is the belief in harmony and the absence of struggle—this would simply be death!" (*KSA*, vol. 9, fragment 11 [132]; *SUP*, 6:347). On where Spinoza goes wrong in his conception of understanding and knowledge, see also *GS* 333.

15. For insight into Nietzsche's psychology of the drives, see Ansell-Pearson and Bamford (2021, chap. 6) and Katsafanas (2019).

16. For an instructive analysis of Nietzsche on the virtues, see Harcourt (2015).

17. Nidesh Lawtoo (2013) has constructed a thought-provoking reading of modernism, including Nietzsche's role in it, on the basis of insights into this aphorism from *Dawn*.

18. In his essay on Leonardo da Vinci, Freud seeks to show that "repression," "fixation," and "sublimation" all play "a part in determining the contribution of the sex drive" to Leonardo's mental life. He also gives due consideration to the passions in his analysis, noting that Leonardo did not lack passion, "the divine spark that is, directly or indirectly, the driving force—*il primo motore*—behind all human activity": "He had simply transformed his passion into a thirst for knowledge" (1910/2003, 101, 53). In his classic study *Life against Death*, Norman O. Brown (1959/1968, 130) pessimistically maintains that Freud had no solution to the general problem of sublimation, construed as a necessary but incomplete response to the levels of repression required by culture, and, therefore, could conceive of the psychoanalytically reconstructed ego continuing to function only in terms of instinctual repression in the form of stoic self-control and renunciation. On the notion of sublimation in Freud, see also Loewald (1988) and Phillips (1998, 25–32). Salomé offers an original view on sublimation, which she links to healthy self-development, and makes a strong case for not endowing sublimation "with the perilous role of standing in opposition to the natural" (Andreas-Salomé 1987, 146–47). For insight into Nietzsche as an original thinker of sublimation, see Gemes (2009), Kaufmann (1974, chaps. 7–8), and Swenson (2014). Gemes illuminates the role sublimation plays in Nietzsche's thinking by indicating how a modern self can achieve a healthy and fertile sense of unity and integrity free of negative emotions such as

ressentiment. For Swenson, the concept of sublimation is best seen as part of Nietzsche's attempt to develop a psychology "that aims to both naturalize our traditional conceptions of human spirituality and to spiritualize our modern conceptions of naturalism" (2014, 206). This is close to Salomé's view on sublimation. In a note of 1881, Nietzsche refers to Plato's view that the love of knowledge and philosophy is "a sublimated sex drive [*ein sublimirter Geschlechtstrieb*]" (*KSA*, vol. 9, fragment 11 [124]; *SUP*, 6:343).

19. In thinking through these points, we can also profit from taking stock of Emerson's insight that passion is to be conceived as both a bad regulator and a powerful spring: "[T]here is no man at some point indebted to his vices, as no plant that is not fed from manures. We only insist that man meliorate, and that the plant grow upward, and convert the base into the better nature" (Emerson 2003, 137–38).

CHAPTER FIVE

Epigraph: Nietzsche, *The Gay Science*, trans. Walter Kaufmann.

1. Grätz and Kaufmann (2017) is also worthy of note.

2. This conception of the poet is common in the history of thought and literature. See, e.g., the insights of Vico (1999, bk. 2, sec. 1). See also the discussion of the art of the poet, be it prose or verse, in Melville's essay "Hawthorne and His *Mosses*" (2018). According to Vico (1999, 145), great poetry has three main aims: (1) to invent "sublime myths" suitable to popular understanding; (2) to excite an audience to a state of ecstasy and in this way fulfill its sublime purpose; and (3) to teach the masses how to act virtuously just as the poets have taught themselves.

3. Woolf's "Poetry, Fiction, and the Future" (2008) is especially pertinent since, like Nietzsche, she focuses on the task of the poet in relation to the beautiful and the emotions. Mill's "What Is Poetry?" (1833/1999) remains instructive on the relation between poetry and the emotions and between poetry and truth.

4. One might argue that this is an exaggeration since surely Nietzsche's supreme teaching is the *Übermensch*. However, even humanity remains for Nietzsche something that needs cultivating. As he asks in the mouth of Zarathustra: "Yet tell me, my brothers: if a goal for humanity is still lacking, is there still not lacking—humanity itself?" (*Z* 1 "Of the Thousand and One Goals"). We should also pay attention to these words when Zarathustra utters: "The human being and the human earth are still unexhausted and undiscovered" (*Z* 1 "Of the Bestowing Virtue" 2). And in a note of 1881 Nietzsche writes that our time is the age of experiments: "Darwin's claims have to be proven—through experiments! . . . Experiments lasting 1000s of years have to be conducted! Educate apes into humans!" (*KSA*, vol. 9, fragment 11 [177]; *SUP*, 6:362).

5. For insight into the poet-seer as one with eyesight who opens a path between "sight" and "soul," see the appreciation of Whitman in Ziff (1981/1982, esp. 234–36 [and chap. 4 generally]). On the "seeing eye" of the poet, see also Carlyle (1841/1983, 128–30 [lecture 3]).

6. This conception of "(beautiful) possibilities of life" first appears in Nietzsche in his reflections on the pre-Platonic philosophers and the beginnings of philosophy. See *KSA*, vol. 8, fragment 6 [48]; *PT*, 144.

7. In his early period, Nietzsche holds to the view that philosophy is the selective knowledge drive in which the aim is to place knowledge in the service of the best life, even if this means that "[o]ne must even *desire illusion*" (*KSA*, vol. 7, fragment 19 [35]).

8. For Schopenhauer, the metaphysical need is a primordial need specific to the human animal, being bound up with the attitude of astonishment we adopt with respect to the world and from which "arises the *need for metaphysics* that is peculiar to man alone." Indeed, Schopenhauer calls man "an *animal metaphysicum*" (2014, 169 [chap. 17]). In the course of human history, the metaphysical need has been attended to by the religions of the world and by a special class of people, namely, priests and philosophers.

9. In his essay "Intellect" (2000, 269–70), Emerson notes that, while truth is our element of life, we distort our relation to it when we fasten our attention on a single aspect of it and then lose our balance through its exaggeration. Moreover, every thought can become a prison for us. These reflections—from an essay included in the first series of Emerson's *Essays*—may well have left an abiding impression on Nietzsche's own thinking about truth.

10. Nietzsche's worry over humanity's attachment to nothingness expresses itself dramatically in the third essay of *On the Genealogy of Morality*, including and especially its final lament: "And, to conclude by saying what I said at the beginning: one still prefers to *will nothingness*, than *not* will" (*GM* 3.28). As Santayana notes in the preface to his book *The Realm of Spirit*, the "desire to cease from willing is evidently a form of will" (1940, xii). See also Cioran: "[N]othingness is merely a *purer* version of God, which is why the mystics have plunged into it with such frenzy, as have, moreover, the unbelievers with a certain religious capital" (1992, 210). On the connection Nietzsche perceives between "the great Nothingness" and "world-weariness [*Weltmüde*]," see *Z* 3 "Of Old and New Law-Tables" 17. In *On the Genealogy of Morality*, Nietzsche defines *nihilism* as a condition in which "[t]he sight of the human now make us tired": "We are tired of *humans*" (*GM* 1.12). Today, this lament concerning nihilism resonates for us in ways Nietzsche perhaps could not have imagined. For a thought-provoking attempt to extend Nietzsche's insight into an analysis of a widespread cultural process of existential fatigue, see Sloterdijk (1989).

11. A translation of this sketch can be found in Nietzsche (1989, 243–44). In *The Case of Wagner*, Nietzsche refers to Wagner in terms similar to the "poetic people" addressed in this sketch. He is depicted as the old magician who sought to fool us all: "The first thing his art presents us with is a magnifying glass: you look through it and cannot believe your eyes—everything becomes big, *even Wagner becomes big*" (*CW* 3). See also *Z* 4 "The Magician." For insight into this discourse, see the section "The Mask" in chap. 6 below.

12. Harold Bloom holds to the view that Emerson's "lifelong obsession was with a poetry *yet to be written*, and which never could be written" (2011, 217). Jacques Rancière (2022, 40–46) has recognized the continuing importance of Emerson on the poet and instructively draws on his conception of a poetry to come to think afresh the time of modernity. See also Arendt (2007a).

13. There are copied excerpts from Emerson's *Essays* and utilization of ideas contained in them in Nietzsche's notebook 13 from the autumn of 1881 and notebook 17 from the beginning of 1882 (*KSA*, 9:618–23, 666–73; *SUP*, 6:460–64, 504–10). In "Emerson," a note from this period, Nietzsche writes: "I have never felt myself so at home and in my home in a book as—I must not praise it, it's too close to me" (*KSA*, vol. 9, fragment 12 [68]; *SUP*, 6:433). For insight into Nietzsche's "Emerson-Exemplar," see Golden (2013).

14. That the poet is a liar is acknowledged by Walter Ralegh, patron of poets, in his "History of the World" (1984, 58):

Readers, believe Historians, and not those
Which to the world Jove's thefts and vice expose.
Poets are liars, and for verse's sake
Will make the Gods of human crimes partake.

The opposition Ralegh draws between history and poetry may be in conversation with Aristotle on the distinction between the two, with poetry deemed to be more philosophical and serious than history since it provides universal truths and not, as history is said to do, particular statements (*Poetics* 9). In Aristotle, *poetry* refers not to the music of verses but to the construction of a fictional plot, and it shows how things can happen on account of their own possibility. See Rancière (2020, 129). On Aristotle on poetry, see also Wordsworth's 1802 preface to the *Lyrical Ballads* (Wordsworth and Coleridge 1991, 301). In Shakespeare's *As You Like It*, the young country woman Audrey asks Touchstone if the poetical is a true thing, to which the sententious fool replies: "No, truly, for the truest poetry is the most feigning, and lovers are given to poetry" (3.3.18–19). With the word *feigning*, we think of a person pretending to be affected by a feeling, but its archaic meaning is "to invent a story." For insight, see Nuttall (2007, 226–30). Hazlitt is perceptive on Touchstone as a fool: "He is a mixture of the ancient cynic philosopher with the modern buffoon, and turns folly into wit, and wit into folly, just as the fit takes him" (1817/1966, 242). At the beginning of act 5, Touchstone engages the country youth William with a saying about wisdom he remembers: "The fool doth think he is wise, but the wise man knows himself to be a fool" (5.1.30–32). As we shall see in the next chapter, this connection between the wise human being and foolishness is played out in the drama of Nietzsche's *Thus Spoke Zarathustra*.

15. As Iris Murdoch (1997, 463) astutely points out in *The Fire and the Sun*, Plato feared the consolations of art and did not provide a consoling theology. For a helpful appreciation of Plato on art and the poets, see Janaway (2009, 388–401). See also Gadamer (1986a, 1986b), Badiou (2005, 16–28 ["What Is a Poem?"]), and de Beauvoir (1946/2004, 274).

16. For Socrates's praise of these poets as well as of the dithyrambic poetry of Melanippides, see Xenophon (1990, 1.4).

17. Nietzsche is referring here to the derivation of poetry from the Greek verb ποιεῖν meaning "to fabricate and fashion."

18. As W. D. Williams perceptively notes, Nietzsche sees in Voltaire an ally not just against prejudice and superstition but "mainly against the inartistic wallowing in life, without any attempt to impose the stamp of form upon it" (1952, 42). In his late writings, Nietzsche expresses a concern about our modern "plebeian curiosity" and how it reveals that we lack a sense of proportion and measure (*BGE* 224). In a note of 1884, he writes of the "natural delight of aesthetic natures in measure, in the enjoyment of the beauty of measure" (*KSA*, vol. 11, fragment 25 [348]; *WP* 870).

19. For insight into Voltaire's attack on the cult of Shakespeare ("bardolatry"), see Mason (1995). Voltaire's view of Shakespeare is contested by Chesterton, who draws a distinction between what he describes as a "classical phrase," which means much more than it says, and a "violent modern phrase," which says much more than it means, with the former being a characteristic of Shakespeare's writing (1935/2012, 5–8). Chesterton provides an instructive example: "The cry of Othello goes far beyond the death of Desdemona; it goes far beyond death itself; it is a cry for life and the secret of life" (1935/2012, 6). Emerson lauds Shakespeare's power of expression for being able to

transfer "the inmost truth of things into music and verse," something that "throws him into natural history as a main production of the globe, and as announcing new areas and ameliorations," to the point where things are mirrored in his art without loss or blur, finishing "an eyelash or a dimple as firmly as he draws a mountain": "[Y]et these, like nature's, will bear the scrutiny of a solar microscope" (1996, 122). For instructive insight into Emerson on Shakespeare's "poetry" as an art of translation, see Hampton (2022, 175–79).

20. On the passions in Shakespeare, see Santayana (1900/1989, 91–103), an essay that focuses on what he sees as the absence of religion in the plays. For a different perspective, see "Shakespeare and Religion" in Huxley (2013, 286–302). See also the superb "Lear, Tolstoy and the Fool" in Orwell (1974, 101–21, esp. 114–17). Santayana also holds that Shakespeare kept his personal religion "passive" (1900/1989, 126). See also Wilson Knight (1967, 227–41).

21. For insight into Shakespeare as an engaged reader of Montaigne, see Bate (2009, 12, 142, and esp. 382ff. [chap. 22, "The Foolosopher"]). See also Hackett (2022, 335–37).

22. Harold Bloom maintains that *Julius Caesar* "was, and is, a deliberately ambiguous play" (1998, 114). James Shapiro (2005, 145–53, 156–64) provides valuable insight into the context in which Shakespeare wrote the play that helps explain why Shakespeare's handling of Caesar's assassination is both daring and cautious. A. D. Nuttall points out that Brutus "is that mildly paradoxical thing, an aristocratic republican" (2007, 172). Frank Kermode notes that in the thought of the time Brutus could be either a heroic tyrannicide or a republican hero and maintains judiciously: "No simple political position can be detected in the play" (2000, 87).

23. Nietzsche was familiar with Stendhal's *Racine and Shakespeare*. For references to the text that refer to notes Nietzsche made in 1880, see *KSA* 14:639–42. It is perhaps also worth noting that in his estimation of the virtues of French classicism Nietzsche stands apart from the German prejudice against it (e.g., August Wilhelm Schlegel and Schiller). On this prejudice, see Auerbach's essay on Racine and the passions (Auerbach 2014, 236–46). On Racine's amoralism, see the translator's introduction to Racine (1970). Gide is also insightful on French classicism, which he defines as "the art of expressing the more by saying the less" (1959, 199 [and 196–200 generally]). Hazlitt is especially good on Shakespeare's character as a dramatist. For example: "Other dramatic writers give us very fine versions and paraphrases of nature; but Shakespear, together with his own comments, gives us the original text, that we may judge for ourselves." Also: "Shakespear had more magnanimity than any other poet" (1817/1966, 82, 81). Stendhal was, in the words of Duncan Wu, "bowled over" by the essays and articles of Hazlitt that he read, including his writing on Shakespeare (Wu 2008, 291). For information on the two meetings that Stendhal and Hazlitt had, see Wu (2008, 359–60, 392–93). Compare Emerson (1996, 121–22).

24. See also Santayana's perceptive insight regarding Shakespeare's talent: "Doubtless Shakespeare, in the heat of dramatic vision, lived his characters, transported himself to their environment, and felt the passion of each, as we do in a dream, dictating their unpremeditated words. But all this is in imagination; it is true only in the framework of our dream. This transporting oneself into the heart of a subject is a loose metaphor: the best one can do is to transplant the subject into one's own heart and draw from oneself impulses as profound as possible with which to vivify tradition and make it over in one's own image" (1913/1940, 87).

25. Nietzsche contends, however, that neither a Goethe nor a Shakespeare would be able to "breathe for a moment" in the "immense passion and height" that is the "concept of 'Dionysian'" (*EH* "Zarathustra" 6).

26. Hazlitt interpreted Hamlet as "the prince of philosophical speculators," a figure full of weakness and melancholy, and "the most amiable of misanthropes" (1817/1966, 83, 88). On Hamlet as a figure of melancholy, see also Turgenev (1860/1965, 7). For an astute analysis of the psychology of Hamlet's character, see Coleridge (1969, esp. 174–82). Harold Bloom goes so far as to call Hamlet a "nihilist poet" (2000, 213). In his later work, Bloom (2003, esp. 94–103) reflects on his changed interpretation of Hamlet. He also writes about how he felt compelled no longer to accept Nietzsche's view of Hamlet as the "Dionysian man," an interpretation he had upheld for some time: "Nietzsche thought Hamlet to be the authentic Dionysiac hero" (Bloom 1998, 208). For a recent interpretation of Hamlet as a philosopher, see Lewis (2017, chap. 5).

27. Nietzsche admired and enjoyed reading Lesage's picaresque novel *The Adventures of Gil Blas of Santillane,* published in four volumes between 1715 and 1735. In a note from the end of 1880, he writes favorably about the novel and, in the process, reveals what he does not like about Shakespeare: "I do not tire of Gil Blas: I breathe freely, no sentimentality, no rhetoric as with Shakespeare" (*KSA*, vol. 9, fragment 7 [81]; *SUP*, 13:290). In *The Gay Science*, Nietzsche refers to the novel as "the Spanish novel of adventure" that is "most readily accessible for us in the French disguise of Gil Blas" (*GS* 77). His repeated enjoyment of reading *Gil Blas* (as well as the stories of Mérimée) is revealed in a note from autumn 1881 (*KSA*, vol. 9, fragment 15 [67]), and the two are linked again in a note from 1888–89 (*KSA*, vol. 13, fragment 25 [3]). For insight into Nietzsche on *Don Quixote*, see also chap. 7 below.

28. Nietzsche discovered Byron's *Manfred* at age thirteen, and at age seventeen he gave a lecture on his dramatic poetry in which he declared Byron to be the originator of modern weltschmerz. For insight into Nietzsche's long-standing fascination with Byron, see Thatcher (1974) and Pointner and Geisenhanslüke (2004). For insight into the early Nietzsche's attachment to Byron's melancholy and celebration of the dark aspects of life, see Blue (2016, 152–54). For Nietzsche on Byron's "immortal verses" that "sorrow is knowledge" and the tree of knowledge is never one with the tree of life, see *HH* 109. Nietzsche admires Byron for his belief in the privileges of higher human beings and identifies with the depiction of the self-reliant mind in Byron's *Manfred* that rejects the power of any supernatural being, demonic or divine. See *KSA* 11, fragment 34 [176]; *SUP*, 16: 51, and *EH* "Why I Am So Clever" 4. On Nietzsche and Byron's *Manfred* see Wilson Knight (1948, 145–47 and 203ff.); on Byron and Nietzschean virtue see Wilson Knight (1952, 33, 47, 160, 247, 269).

29. See also Gordon Pocock's (1973, 40–64) complementary analysis of *Cinna*.

30. Dostoevsky is another nineteenth-century figure who valued Racine and especially Corneille. See Steiner (1967, 129–30) and Steiner (1997, chap. 3).

31. When Nietzsche writes about vanity in the volumes of *Human, All Too Human*, he is largely, though not exclusively, influenced by La Rochefoucauld and his probing of the disguises of egoism, referring to him and other French masters who examine the human soul as "sharpshooting marksmen who hit the black bull's-eye again and again—but the black bull's-eye of human nature" (*HH* 36; see also *WS* 214). Throughout the 1870s he also enjoyed reading Swift, including a volume of his humoristic writings. In a note from the summer–autumn of 1873, he cites a saying by Swift: "Every man's vanity is directly proportional to his lack of intelligence" (*KSA*, vol. 7, fragment 29

[96], p. 239; *SUP*, 11:239). See also *HH* 44, 54. In his subsequent thinking, Nietzsche comes to develop a suspicion about La Rochefoucauld, as when, e.g., he declares him to have a noble way of thinking but to be ultimately "a disappointed idealist," someone who thought under the inspiration of Christianity and sought out "nasty names for the impulses of his time" (*KSA*, vol. 10, fragment 7 [40]; *SUP*, 14:228). He finds in La Rochefoucauld a Christian gloominess that extracts egoism from everything and leads him to the erroneous conclusion that he has "thereby *reduced* the value of things and of virtues!" Although it displays a melancholic astuteness, La Rochefoucauld's thinking ultimately "contains a pessimistic mistrustfulness of the basis of life" (*KSA*, vol. 12, fragment 7 [65], p. 319; *WP* 362). For insight into the influence of La Rochefoucauld on Nietzsche, see Abbey (2015) and Williams (1952). For an instructive examination of La Rochefoucauld and other thinkers on vanity, see Moriarty (2011).

32. Spinoza argues that pride can be as stubborn as vanity and just as much of a hindrance to self-development and the attainment of genuine self-understanding: "Pride [*superbia*] is thinking more highly of oneself than is just, out of love of oneself" (1992, pt. 3, proposition 26, scholium). By contrast, self-esteem has a more secure grounding since it does connect with a knowledge of our own powers of acting and it does not have to end in pride understood as an overweening estimation of oneself. For Spinoza, the truly free human person is neither proud nor humble. The self-esteem a free person feels comes from a confident conception he has of his own worth, not through social honors or reputation, and reflects his own power of understanding. Spinoza considers it a rational form of self-love that does not have its source in outside opinion and does not crave or seek it. It is a sense of self that provides one with serene pleasure and joy, and for Spinoza it is the best for which we can hope in our aspiration to be rational beings.

33. On the "madness" of contemporary envy, see Bertrand Russell (1991, 20–21).

34. On "ideal selfishness," conceived as a state of consecration, see also *D* 552.

35. On Phidias, cf. Emerson (2000, 162).

36. For instructive insight into Athena, see Deacy (2008). See also the powerful portrait of Athena offered in Cornford's (1937/1997, 363–64) study of Plato's cosmology. Cornford stresses that Athena's words to the Furies "Be persuaded by me" speak of the attempt to transform the desire for vengeance and justice into powers of fertility and blessing and foretell a reconciliation of Zeus and fate, reason and necessity.

37. Nietzsche provides an additional qualifying insight: "[I]t is self-evident that at certain times of life an art that is overwrought, agitated, averse to anything orderly, monotonous, simple or logical is an essential need that artists *must* acknowledge if the soul is not to discharge itself at such times in another way, by all sorts of mischief and bad behaviour" (*MOM* 173).

38. In his wide-ranging study of forests in Western thought and literature, Robert Harrison (1992, 41–46) considers the prologue to Nietzsche's *Zarathustra* in which Zarathustra has an encounter with a saint who, oblivious to the event of his death, has retreated into the forest to praise God. He does not reflect, however, on this aphorism from *The Gay Science* on the need for preparatory humans. While the forest can be a place of retreat for those who wish to withdraw from life, it is also depicted in Nietzsche as a place of purification for those whose task is to educate humanity and consecrate it to a new future.

39. See also: "Are you ugly? Very well, my brothers! Take the sublime about you, the mantle of the ugly!" (*Z* 1 "Of War and Warriors"). For insight into the sublime in *Z*, see Gooding-Williams (2001, esp. 176–82).

40. In his reflections on the nature and function of the poet, whom he calls "the man of Beauty," Emerson writes: "The sign and credentials of the poet are that he announces that which no man has foretold" (2000, 290). Nietzsche was also familiar with Schiller's 1793 essay "On Grace and Dignity," where *grace* is defined as "movable beauty." On grace and beauty in relation to the "sensible laws of art," see "Observations on the Laocoon" in Goethe (1980, 78–89). For further insight into Schiller and other thinkers on grace, including Nietzsche, see Spuybroek (2020). Commentators often note Nietzsche's predilection for Stendhal's conception of beauty as a "promise of happiness" (see Stendhal 1957, bk. 1, chap. 17). Nietzsche expresses his liking of Stendhal's conception in the third essay of *On the Genealogy of Morality* (*GM* 3.6), though he is already making use of it, contra the idea of disinterestedness, in a notebook of early 1884 (*KSA*, vol. 11, fragment 25 [154]). I find the conception of beauty he is developing in his middle writings and in *Zarathustra* to be more philosophically substantial. In *On the Genealogy of Morality*, he is writing polemically against Kant and Schopenhauer, and the claim that an aesthetic judgment of beauty involves disinterested contemplation (see also *TI* "Reconnaissance Raids of an Untimely Man" 22). He interprets Stendhal's "promise" as involving the excitement of the will. Baudelaire offers a judicious appreciation of Stendhal's conception of beauty, arguing that it has "the great merit of getting away from the mistake of the academicians" (2006, 393). He is keen, however, to stress that the conception oversteps the mark by subordinating beauty too much to an infinitely variable ideal (happiness) and by divesting it too lightly of its aristocratic character. For Nietzsche on Baudelaire on the beautiful, see *KSA*, vol. 13, fragment 11 [183].

41. Bertram was also the author of an earlier study of Stifter (see Bertram 1907). For the possible relevance of Stifter to an understanding of Nietzsche on decadence, see also chap. 7 below.

42. W. G. Sebald presents a challenging perspective on the issue of the relation of Stifter's novel to conceptions of utopia. He also writes trenchantly of "the difficult beauty" of Stifter's work contra the widespread reception of him as a Biedermeier poet of ladybugs and flowers (1994, 15). On interpretations of Stifter as a poet of *Biedermeier*, see Lukács (1976, 295–99). Stern (1971, 120) describes Stifter's literary method of composition as more reminiscent of Mallarmé or Joyce than of Biedermeier literature. For thought-provoking interpretations of Stifter, see also Benjamin (1989) and Kundera (2007a).

43. For instructive insight into the meaning the blessed isles have for Nietzsche, see Bishop (2017) and Kolb (2013, 105–26).

44. As Martin and Erika Swales note in their study of Stifter's writings, Nietzsche's interest in Stifter seems at first sight an unlikely meeting of minds. They venture the explanation that Nietzsche was well attuned to the *unzeitgemäss* impulses informing Stifter's art and that he admired him "because of what he perceived as the embattled integrity of his art, its uncompromising transcendence of the tangle and turmoil of human passion, its willed calm and repose beyond heartbreak and weariness." In addition, they note what Bertram also sees in Nietzsche's appreciation of Stifter: "Nietzsche esteemed Stifter's fierce resistance to his times, to their banality and meretriciousness" (Swales and Swales 1984, 21, 22).

45. In Stifter's novel, *King Lear* is given prominence. Although Nietzsche's corpus includes references to several of Shakespeare's plays, *King Lear* is not one of them. What appeals to the hero of Stifter's novel about the play is the strength of the emotions acted out in it; he is also interested in the fear of going mad staged in it. For valuable

insight into the references to *Lear* in Stifter, see Gump (1974, 104, 115) and Sjögren (1972, 93).

46. For echoes of this thought in Nietzsche, see *D* 45, 551. For an instructive interpretation of how nature and the cosmos are conceived in Stifter's novel, including "Indian summer" as a "school of seeing," see Wiedemann (2004, esp. chaps. 1, 5, and 6). See also Häge (2019, esp. chap. 6).

47. See also the instructive analysis of the hero's *Bildungsweg* in Sjögren (1972, 88–96).

48. Stifter's novel is often read as providing a little enclave of harmony, but it also expresses an openness to the future, a future that may well be very different from the present: "The distant future [*Entfernte Zeiten*] will build something out of all this material, something we can't even imagine. . . . Quite different notions will develop, people's vocabulary will be different. . . . How will it be when man can send news over the whole world with the speed of light? . . . Won't the goods of the Earth be shared more because of the ease of exchange? Won't everything be accessible to everyone? . . . [A] new era will dawn, the like of which the world has never seen" (Stifter 2005, 123, 521–22; Stifter 2009, 76, 300–301). Today, alas, Stifter's optimism strikes us as naive and misplaced.

49. Rousseau confesses to needing the rocks, the pines and the deep woods, and the mountains, with rough paths to climb and descend, and with precipices on both sides that make him feel truly afraid, so "that [his] eyes be struck by the ravishing spectacle of nature" (1995, 538 [pt. 2, bk. 12]). In *Winter in Majorca*, George Sand writes: "Rousseau is the true Christopher Columbus of Alpine poetry" (1842/1956, 11).

50. In *Twilight of the Idols*, Nietzsche esteems Goethe for his "reckless realism" that expresses itself in "a reverence for everything actual" (*TI* "Reconnaissance Raids of an Untimely Man" 50). See also *D* 540, where Goethe is depicted as a "great learner." This appreciation of Goethe is echoed in Pater's great insight, developed in the context of his claim that the speculative instinct of the modern mind cannot be satisfied with a vague scholastic abstraction, "that colourless, formless, intangible being" elevated by Plato: "[T]he true illustration of the speculative temper is not the Hindoo mystic lost to sense, understanding, individuality, but one such as Goethe, to whom every moment of life brought its contribution of experimental, individual knowledge; by whom no touch of the world of form, colour, and passion was disregarded" (2018, 149).

51. For insight into the importance of perspectives in Nietzsche, see Gemes (2013).

CHAPTER SIX

Epigraph: Nietzsche, note of 1881, trans. Adrian Del Caro.

1. On several occasions the translation of *Zarathustra* I have used in this chapter is the one by Loeb and Tinsley (see Nietzsche, forthcoming). I am immensely grateful to Paul Loeb and David Tinsley for affording me the opportunity to make use of their powerful new translation ahead of its publication.

2. See also the foreword to *The Anti-Christ* where Nietzsche states that to understand his seriousness and passion one "must be accustomed to living on mountains" and "to seeing the ephemeral chatter of politics and national egoism *beneath* one." Nietzsche commenced the writing of *Thus Spoke Zarathustra* in a time of winter and in poor health. He was living at the time "on the delightfully tranquil Bay of Rapallo, carved out between Chiavari and the foothills of Porto Fino" (*EH* "Zarathustra" 1). That the book

was written in such adverse circumstances, with his health not the best and inadequate sleep due to the high sea at night, provides him with proof that "everything crucial occurs 'nevertheless.'" On the mood of melancholy that he experienced during the time he composed the book, including his reference to *Z* 2 "Night-Song" as the "loneliest song," see *EH* "Zarathustra" 4.

3. On Nietzsche's relation to the Longinian sublime, see Ansell-Pearson (2013).

4. Francis Bacon concludes *The Wisdom of the Ancients* with an appeal to Orpheus, saying that he "kept himself from hearing the music of the Sirens" (1609/1935, 292). In a note of 1870–71, Nietzsche conceives of Orpheus as a Buddha-like figure (*KSA*, vol. 7, fragment 7 [56]). This conception is explained in his consideration of the cult of Orpheus: "The names of Orpheus, Musaeus and their cults, reveal what were the conclusions to which a continual exposure to a world of combat and cruelty led—to nausea at existence . . . to the belief that existence and indebtedness were identical" (Nietzsche 2017a, 178). Nietzsche considers the Orphic theogonies, including Plato's views on the Orphic verses, in his lecture course on the pre-Platonic philosophers (*PPP*, 10–14). He argues that in his relation to Pythagorean-Orphic mysticism Empedocles joins the religious instinct to scientific explanation and broadens it in scientific form with the result that the one who enlightens humankind is unloved by the faithful, which is an outcome many subsequent figures of enlightenment in the history of thought encounter (*PPP*, 113). In *The Birth of Tragedy*, Socrates is described at one point as a new Orpheus (sec. 12). In a note of 1884, Nietzsche refers to the musicians he favors—Mozart, Rossini, and Chopin—and looks ahead to a new German Orpheus who will steer the ship toward Grecian landscapes (*KSA*, vol. 11, fragment 28 [10], pp. 302–3). On the story of Orpheus (and Eurydice), see Ovid (1955, bk. 10). On the story of Orpheus and Orphic theogonies, see Guthrie (1952/1993). On Orpheus and the model of the storyteller, see Cavarero (2000, 94–102). See also the instructive studies by Henry (1992) and Segal (1989). It is worth noting that Nietzsche is stern in his criticism of Bacon: "Bacon signifies an *attack* on the philosophical spirit generally" (*BGE* 252). In him, he further contends in a notebook entry, we find "a kind of playacting as if one had an ideal" (*KSA*, vol. 9, fragment 11 [99]; *SUP*, 6:336). In part he is objecting to Bacon's view that imaginative speculation is an intellectual vice; Nietzsche maintains that "truth for its own sake" is an impossible ideal and a cliché. For an attempt to bring Nietzsche into rapport with Bacon (and Descartes), see Lampert (1993).

5. See also: "[C]onstantly, we have to give birth to our thoughts out of our pain and, like mothers, endow them with all we have of blood, heart, fire, pleasure, passion, agony, conscience, fate, and catastrophe" (*GS* preface 3). See also D. H. Lawrence: "That is why one cannot quite believe in Kant, or Spinoza. Kant thought with his head and his spirit, but he never thought with his blood" (Lawrence 1936, 732). On Kant's philosophy as the biography of a head, cf. *D* 481.

6. On poetry conceived as "musical Thought," see Carlyle (1841/1983, 101). On poetry as the language of the emotions "musicalized," see Valéry (1958, 59). On the "musicality" of *Zarathustra*, see Graham Parkes in Nietzsche (2005b, introduction).

7. On the story of Alcyone and Ceyx, see Ovid (1955, bk. 11).

8. In his final book, Harold Bloom (2020, 17) expressed his ultimate disappointment over Nietzsche that there is only what Vico called "poetic wisdom" to be found in him. Such an assessment does not do justice to the jesting subversion of wisdom to be encountered in *Zarathustra* or the varied conceptions of wisdom offered in it and throughout Nietzsche's corpus.

9. Gadamer is on firmer ground when he observes: "[H]is drama is not so much about the suffering of the one who knows and says Yes to everything as it is about the one who now wants to teach his wisdom and cannot find the human beings who are equal to his wisdom" (1998, 230).

10. Commentators on *Zarathustra* who have sought to illuminate Nietzsche on the poets in the text include Lampert (1986, 126–32) and Rosen (2004, 162–63). For incisive readings of the figuration of the poets and of the lie in *Zarathustra*, see also Hatab (2018) and Tuncel (2014). See also Grundlehner (1986, 184–212), Schulte (2017), and Kast (2017). In aphorism 551 of *Dawn*, Nietzsche declares that matters must be taken out of the hands of the poets because the "age of harmless counterfeiting" is coming to an end. Yunus Tuncel argues that Zarathustra aspires to be not just any poet but a poet of tomorrow and the day after tomorrow. Although this is correct, we should take cognizance of Zarathustra's acknowledgment of both his heritage and his promise. "'I am of today and of yesterdays,' he then said, 'but there is something within me which is of tomorrow and of the day after tomorrow and of a time still to come'" (*Z* 2 "Of Poets").

11. For a related reading of the book's subtitle, see Heidegger (1968, 50). On Nietzsche as a poet philosopher and Zarathustra as a poet, see Heidegger (2011, 5–8, 13–14). Heidegger is not, however, very enlightening, largely because he does not pay sufficient attention to Nietzsche's project as Nietzsche himself conceives it.

12. As Gary Saul Morson (2012, 158) points out, the sensibility that inspired Ecclesiastes has generated numerous works that accept the futility of human action and the absurdity of existence, including Tolstoy's *Confession* and a great deal of modern existentialist literature.

13. Nietzsche's claim about Goethe is not considered by Hadot (2023, 136–42) in the section he devotes to both figures in his book on Goethe and the tradition of spiritual exercises. For perceptive remarks on the limited character—as Nietzsche sees it—of Goethe's Hellenism, see Bertram (1918/2009, 165–70).

14. See also Jane Harrison's contention that for the ancients, such as the Cretans, the so-called mysteries denoted nothing mysterious since they were open to all and centered on purification rites and rituals: "'There was no revelation, no secret to be kept, only a mysterious *taboo* to be prepared for and finally overcome'" (1903/1991, 154).

15. For a thoughtful consideration of Unamuno on immortality, including his relation to Nietzsche, see Buben (2021). See also the interpretation of Nietzsche's idea of the "superman" as a "progressive" idea in Soloviev (2015). (Soloviev was a close friend of Dostoevsky's.) The essay was written in the year before Soloviev died in 1900. At one point in his interpretation, Soloviev writes: "'Man' and 'mortal' are synonyms. . . . A person is first and foremost 'mortal'—in the sense of *conquered, overcome* by death. And if so, then this means a 'superman' must be first of all, and particularly, a *conqueror of death*" (2015, 261). On Nietzsche, immortality, and transhumanism, see Buben (2022, chap. 3). See also Sorgner (2020) and Tuncel (2017). For some typically mature insights into human death, see Hume's essay "Of the Immortality of the Soul" (1985, 590–98). See also Coleridge's extraordinary poem "Human Life. On the Denial of Immortality" (1986, 321).

16. See Nietzsche: "Even though Christianity brought the doctrine of unselfishness and love to the fore, its real historical effect remains the *intensification of egoism*, of individual egoism, to the furthest extreme—that extreme is the belief in individual

immortality" (*KSA*, vol. 13, fragment 14 [5], p. 218; *WLN*, 24). In *Human, All Too Human*, Nietzsche conceives "real immortality" as bound up with movement: "[A]nything that has ever moved is included and eternalized in the total union of all that exists, like an insect in amber" (*HH* 208).

17. In identifying a counterfeit doctrine of immortality in eternal recurrence, Unamuno locates in it a "stupendous tragi-comedy or comi-tragedy" (1912/1962, 110 [see also 228, 234–35]). Compare Wilson Knight (1948, 191).

18. In an essay on Lucretius, Elizabeth Asmis provides a set of instructive insights into the wisdom of accepting the natural conditions of our existence as a prerequisite for the attainment of human well-being and flourishing: "It is futile to desire life beyond its natural boundary. . . . One must avail oneself of one's present opportunities so as to reach the goal of a complete life within a finite period" (2022, 127).

19. Consider Borges's insight in "A History of Eternity": "[E]eternity is the style of desire" (2000, 136). See also the beautifully composed "Immortality," which offers a wide-ranging response to the wish for personal immortality (Borges 2000, 483–91). On eternity, see also Huxley: "Eternity conceived as existing apart from life is life's enemy. . . . The only eternity known to life is that present eternity of ecstatic timelessness which is the consummation of intense living" (1929, 289). For further insight into Nietzsche and eternity, see Conche (2014, chap. 8), Michalski (2012), Loeb (2018a), Liessmann (2021), and Wilson Knight (1948, 176–77, 188–195).

20. On the poet as a fool, see fragment 43. Cioran notes: "Homer has been taken to task (Heraclitus himself claimed he deserved a whipping) because he made no bones about it: his gods, as much as his mortals, behaved like scoundrels. Philosophy had not yet appeared to weaken them, to sweeten them, to make them *suitable*" (1972/2012, 145).

21. As John Kerrigan (1996, 274–89) points out, the German word *Erlösung* that Nietzsche deploys for *redemption* partly means "unloosing." He also instructively examines Nietzsche on redemption and recurrence in relation to the figure of Job and the importance of Job for Kierkegaard, Dostoevsky, and Melville.

22. For insight into Nietzsche's teaching on redeeming time and gaining power over time, see Loeb (2001). For insight into the relation of Nietzsche's doctrine of eternal recurrence to Heraclitean flux, see Loeb (2021). See also Murray (2018, chap. 4). On the attempt to free humanity from the curse of vengeful and resentful thinking, see Sloterdijk (2013, 32–33) on Nietzsche's fifth gospel. See also Nietzsche: "Freedom from resentment, enlightenment about resentment—who knows what great debt of gratitude I ultimately owe my long illness in this respect too! The problem is not exactly simple: you need to have experienced it from a position of strength and from one of weakness" (*EH* "Why I Am So Wise" 6). On Nietzsche's fifth gospel, see also Steiner (2003, 115–18) and Corriero (2021).

23. See also: "A table of values hangs over every people. Behold, it is the table of its overcomings; behold, it is the voice of its will to power. . . . People were the creators at first; only later did individuals become creators. Indeed, the individual himself is still the latest creation" (*Z* 1 "Of the Thousand and One Goals").

24. Nietzsche holds that mechanism and matter are to be construed as expressions of lower stages of life, as "the most despiritualized form of affect (of 'will to power')" (*KSA*, vol. 12, fragment 9 [8]; *WP* 712). The human being is to be regarded as "a multiplicity of 'wills to power': each one with a multiplicity of means of expression and forms" (*KSA*, vol. 12, fragment 1 [58], and fragment 7 [1]; *WLN*, 128). On the will to

power, see Müller-Lauter (1999), Reginster (2006), and Richardson (1996, 2004). On the will to power and naturalism, see Meyer (2022).

25. Compare Guyau: "One does not always act with the view of seeking a *particular pleasure*—limited and exterior to the act itself. Sometimes we act for the pleasure of acting. . . . There is in us an accumulated force which demands to be used. If its expenditure is impeded, this force becomes desire or aversion; if the desire is satisfied, there is pleasure; if it is opposed, there is pain. But it does not follow from this that the stored-up activity unfolds itself solely *for the sake* of pleasure—with pleasure as motive. Life unfolds and expresses itself in activity because it is life. In all creatures pleasure accompanies, much more than it provokes, the search after life" (1885/1896, 77). For insight into the ideas about morality and life that Nietzsche and Guyau share, see Ansell-Pearson and Testa (2024, 137–50).

26. See Saint-Exupéry: "The earth teaches us more about ourselves than all the books in the world, because it is resistant to us. Self-discovery comes when man measures himself against an obstacle" (1995, foreword). See also the reference to Nietzsche and the notion of "self-surpassing adventure" in Saint-Exupéry (1995, introduction). On Saint-Exupéry's Nietzschean-inspired wisdom, see de Beauvoir (1944/2004, 133), de Beauvoir (1945/2004, 312), and Maurois (1970, 201–24). See also Schopenhauer: "Overcoming obstacles means the full enjoyment of our existence; they might be of a material nature, as in acting and doing, or of an intellectual nature, as in learning and investigating" (1851/2014, 386).

27. Max Scheler expresses Nietzsche's insight well when he writes: "Nietzsche came closest to the truth: the whole of the curve of life activity between profound pleasure and profound pain occurs 'prior' to pleasure and pain. These feelings are only the accidental terminal points reached by the pendulum of life in its full swing" (1992, 97).

28. When seen in the context of this criticism, Nietzsche's reference to the "damnable mania" for Anglo-Saxon ideas and his claim that Hobbes, Hume, and Locke represent a debasement and decline in value of the concept "philosopher" begin to make sense, even though we will surely find his remark an uncharitable one (*BGE* 252).

29. See also "To the Realists" where Nietzsche poses a challenge: "As if reality stood unveiled before you only, and you yourselves were perhaps the best part of it—O you beloved images of Sais!" (*GS* 57).

30. The invocation in *Zarathustra* of a new earth and new peoples to come is an echo of the words of Yahweh in Isaiah 65:17–18: "Behold, I create a new earth. Former things shall no longer be remembered. . . . [B]oundless realms I create." On the dedication to the earth in Nietzsche, see Creasy (2022), Del Caro (2004), Manschot (2021), Murray (2018, chap. 6), and Shapiro (2016).

31. The last humans are depicted by Huxley in *Brave New World* with reference to the famous utterance of Hamlet: "Getting rid of everything unpleasant. . . . Whether 'tis nobler in the mind to suffer the slings and arrows of outrageous fortune, or to take arms against a sea of troubles and by opposing end them. . . . But you don't do either. Neither suffer nor oppose. You just abolish the slings and arrows. It's too easy" (1932/1972, 186 [chap. 17]). For insight into the ongoing pertinence of Huxley's novel, see Atwood (2011, 184–94) and Le Guin (2019, 127–33). Our brave new digital world is wickedly satirized by Rainer Hanshe in his novel on the "digital Frankenstein" (2024).

32. One worry that Nietzsche has centers on the dangers presented by a burgeoning nationalism and militarism. An artificial nationalism that thrives on national animosities, he writes, is as dangerous as an artificial Catholicism. The "whole problem

of the Jews," he states, exists only within national states. This people's energy and higher intelligence, built up from generation to generation as an accumulated capital of spirit, reaches such a degree of preponderance that it awakens envy and hatred. We may witness, he speculates, Jews being led to the "slaughterhouse as scapegoats for every possible public and personal misfortune" (*HH* 475). On what "Europe owes to the Jews," see also *BGE* 250–51.

33. See also: "There are thousands of paths which remain untrodden; there are a thousand ways of being healthy, and there are a thousand islands of life which remain hidden. Human beings and the human earth have potential which has not yet been realized or discovered" (*Z* 1 "Of the Bestowing Virtue" 2).

34. We might also wish to consider Walter Otto on the "madness" of Dionysus and the claim that this is not to be regarded as a sickness or a debility of life, but rather as "a companion of life at its healthiest": "The deep emotion with which this emotion announces itself finds its expression in music and dance" (1965, 143). Here, Otto is, of course, echoing Nietzsche's account in *The Birth of Tragedy*. However, as Kerényi (1976, 134) points out, the concern is not with "mania" in any medical sense but rather with a kind of "visionary attempt" to explain states in which our vital powers are enhanced to the utmost and we may gain a glimpse of the superhuman.

35. On Dionysus and the symbol of the mask, see the excellent analysis in Otto (1965, 86–91).

36. In a note from 1884, Nietzsche sketches a new way of being in the world in the following terms: "No longer joy in certainty but in uncertainty; no longer 'cause and effect' but the continually creative; no longer will to preservation but power; no longer the humble expression, 'everything is merely subjective,' but 'it is also our work!—Let us be proud of it!'" (*KSA*, vol. 11, fragment 26 [284]; *WP* 1059).

37. In his observation in *The Case of Wagner*, cited above, Nietzsche is surely referring to Hamlet being certain that Claudius is the murderer of his royal brother, Hamlet's father, and his belief that his mother was an accomplice to the murder.

38. For Nietzsche's insights into the mask in his middle writings, see *MOM* 383 (on greatness as a mask) and *WS* 175 (on mediocrity as a mask). For further insight into the role played by masks in Nietzsche's thinking, see Fisher (1995), Kirkland (2004), and Parkes (1987).

39. In bk. 5 of *The Gay Science* (1887), Nietzsche reveals that the problem of the actor is the problem that has troubled him the longest (*GS* 361). For an instructive interpretation of this aphorism in connection with the character of the butler in Kazuo Ishiguro's novel *The Remains of the Day* (1989), see Patton (1991). In this essay, Patton also probes aspects of Nietzsche's *Zarathustra* to illuminate the problem of the actor.

40. On the paradox of the (dramatic) actor, see Diderot's classic essay on the topic (1994, 100–159). See also the excellent study of Diderot in Peretz (2013, chap. 4). Sander Gilman (1976, esp. 207–12) sensitively examines the issue of the mask and the figure of the poseur in Nietzsche by tracing his evolving reception of Heine.

41. On this conception of the superhuman, see also Feuerbach (1843/1986, sec. 8).

42. On locating the superhuman in *On the Genealogy of Morality*, see Loeb (2005).

43. Salter (1915) on Nietzsche's "superman" remains incisive. See also Conway (1989) and Marsden (2005). Also incisive in places is Ouspensky (1934/1984, 113–24 [and chap. 3 generally]). Several decades ago John Cowper Powys (1946b, 546) sought to make the case for translating Nietzsche's *Übermensch* as "Over-man." He conceives Nietzsche as the seeker of a new Being. The leonine symbol of the "superman" leads us astray if

it suggests a bunch of storybook characteristics, such as Herculean muscles, satanic wisdom, and godlike beauty. See also Wilson Knight (1948, 175–76).

44. In his study of the German tradition of self-cultivation, W. H. Bruford (1975, chap. 8) selects *Thus Spoke Zarathustra* as the principal text for his examination of Nietzsche. See also Bell (2007).

45. The discourse "On Child and Marriage" begins with a question: "I have a question for you alone, my brother: like a plummet, I cast this question into your soul, so that I might know how deep it is. You are young and wish for a child and marriage. But I ask you: Are you a human being entitled to wish [*wünschen darf*] for a child? Are you the victor, the self-conqueror, the commander of your senses, the master of your virtues? Or is it the animal and need that speak out of your wish? Or isolation? Or discord with yourself?"

46. It is in the body, Nietzsche says, that we will find an unknown sage (*Z* 1 "Of the Despisers of the Body").

47. "Do I exhort you to kill the senses? I exhort you to an innocence of the senses. Do I exhort you to chastity? With some, chastity is a virtue, but with many it is almost a vice. These people abstain, it is true: but the bitch Sensuality glares enviously out of all they do. This restless beast follows them even into the heights of their virtue and the depths of their cold spirit" (*Z* 1 "Of Chastity").

48. This insight is lost on many readers of Nietzsche. An instructive example is Nicolas Berdyaev, who can see in Nietzsche's idea of the "superman" only a "betrayal of man and of humanity" (1952, 163).

49. For insight into the character of Kirillov, see Allan (2014), Arendt (2007, 275–82), Camus (1942/2004, 577–81), and Frank (2010, 650–57). Paul Loeb (2008) provides highly instructive insight into the issue of suicide, as Camus dramatically presents it in *The Myth of Sisyphus*, from the perspective of an interpretation of Nietzsche, but he does not consider the character of Kirillov, either as depicted by Camus or as noted by Nietzsche. It is worth noting that at no point in his writings does Nietzsche provide intellectual succor to the fanciful thoughts and vengeful antics of revolutionary socialists and anarchists that so troubled Dostoevsky. On Kirillov and Nietzsche see Cowper Powys (1946b, 545).

50. In this final part of the book, Kirillov, expressing his ultimate conviction, declares that he is the only human being in history who has refused to invent God (Dostoevsky 1971, 613). This declaration is part of the material from the novel that Nietzsche copies into his notebook. On the difference between the man-god and god-man, see Dostoevsky (1971, 244 [pt. 2, chap. 1, sec. 5]). For another perspective on the doctrine of self-will, see Hesse (1919/1974, 71–77).

51. Lawrence is typically incisive and alive when he reflects on Dostoevsky as a writer and thinker in his 1930 essay on *The Grand Inquisitor*: "Dostoevsky is always perverse, always impure, always an evil thinker and a marvellous seer" (Lawrence 1936, 285).

52. Nietzsche copies dialogue from pt. 3, chap. 6, sec. 2 of the novel. See Dostoevsky (1872/1971, 611–14).

53. On the cosmology of recurrence, see Loeb (2006, 2010, 2013, 2022), Moles (1990, chap. 9), Small (2006, 2010), and Holub (2018). For insight into the ethical aspect of recurrence, see esp. Loeb (2018a) and Reginster (2006, esp. 222–27 [and chap. 5 generally]).

54. Nietzsche, in fact, says something subtly different to the view Kain attributes to him: "After the prospect of the superhumans the doctrine of recurrence now in

an awesome way endurable!" (*KSA*, vol. 10, fragment 15 [10] [my translation]; *SUP*, 14:434).

55. In the early 1950s, Maurice Nicoll developed an interpretation of eternal recurrence in terms of the evolving human being who remembers that he relates to the Orphic-Bacchic teaching that contained the idea of the repetition of our earthly existence. He refers to an Orphic fragment that speaks of the incalculable value of memory: where the impure and uninitiated soul passes into sleep and forgetfulness, into Lethe, in the Orphic ritual the soul drinks of the cold water of the Lake of Memory (Nicoll 1952, 181–82). Thus the moment of death becomes the moment of birth. Our whole impression of life is a confused one that needs to be overcome: "We do not think we are only *beginning* something, but merely coming to the end of something" (Nicoll 1952, 179). Only by remembering, then, can we make the *choice* in favor of this life and cease living according to the habits of a mere life. It is under the influence of the ideas of Ouspensky on eternal recurrence that Nicoll discusses in the book not only Nietzsche but also Plato, Proclus, the Stoics, Swedenborg, and others.

CHAPTER SEVEN

Epigraphs: Nietzsche, *Beyond Good and Evil*, trans. Adrian Del Caro

1. *Beyond Good and Evil* developed out of an attempt to rework *Human, All Too Human* and was originally conceived as a companion text to *Dawn*, and the final title settled on for the work was taken from a section of *Zarathustra* entitled "Retired." See Prange (2012, 232). On *Beyond Good and Evil*, see also Berkowitz (1995), Born (2015), Conway (2024), and Lampert (2001). For insight into the metaphilosophical dimension of Nietzsche's project in the late writings, including *Beyond Good and Evil*, see Brusotti (2019), Loeb (2019a), Meyer (2019), and Panaioti (2019).

2. On the outdated character of the traditional figure of the gentleman, see Hazard (1965, 177).

3. It is interesting to note that, in Dostoevsky's novel *The Devils*, the fearless character Kirillov signs himself in French as "*de Kiriloff, gentilhomme russe et citoyen du monde*" (Dostoevsky 1872/1971, 616–17). At the time of composing *Beyond Good and Evil*, Nietzsche had not yet made his discovery of Dostoevsky.

4. On the need for tests of feelings of self-overcoming with respect to solitude and silence, see also *BGE* 61.

5. Socrates is, of course, the classic instance of intellectual martyrdom. In this aphorism, however, Nietzsche has in mind forced hermits such as Spinoza and Giordano Bruno. He refers to Spinoza's philosophy as the "conceptual cobwebbery of a hermit" and claims that Spinoza both disguised and armored his philosophy in the "hocus-pocus of mathematical form." In Spinoza's case, then, the masquerade of the hermit betrays the timidity and vulnerability of the beatific kind of philosopher (*TI* "Reconnaissance Raids of an Untimely Man" 23; *BGE* 5). On the philosopher's "secret gardens," see also *GM* preface 3.

6. Proust takes Sainte-Beuve's method to task not from the perspective of the genuine philosopher, as we find in Nietzsche, but rather from the perspective of the creative writer and novelist. Taking issue with Taine's appreciation of him, which praises him for applying the methods of natural history to the history of moral philosophy, he finds in the work of Sainte-Beuve only the approach of reductive biography and its interest in the writer's "superficial self" and not his "innermost self"

that informs his creative writing. (He focuses on Sainte-Beuve writing on Stendhal to illustrate the limitations of this approach.) Thus, he contends, Sainte-Beuve displays only a "shallow conception of the creative mind" (Proust 1997, 107). For further insight into Sainte-Beuve's character as a critic concerned with literature and as an expression of individual personality as well as a skeptic, see the introduction to Sainte-Beuve (1924, ix–xl). The volume features essays in the original French on several writers also of great interest to Nietzsche, including Montaigne, Beaumarchais, La Fontaine, La Bruyère, and Taine. The essay on "method" provides a good introduction to Sainte-Beuve's appreciation of literary study as a form of moral study. Chapter 8, pp. 167–82. Brandes, who lectured on Nietzsche in Copenhagen in the late 1880s, devotes three chapters to Sainte-Beuve in his study of the Romantic school in France in his multivolume *Main Currents in Nineteenth Century Literature*, based on lectures first delivered in the early 1870s. He conceives him as an "epoch-making critic" who founded a new branch of art (Brandes 1904, 307). Nietzsche refers to Brandes's lectures in a March 27, 1888, letter to Brandes, and he expresses his admiration for Brandes's multivolume study in an August 26, 1888, letter to Carl Fuchs (*KSB* 8, pp. 278–80, 399–403). In a letter to Franz Overbeck from the early part of 1888, he refers to Brandes as an "intelligent and combative Dane," and, in a July 29, 1888, letter to Carl Fuchs, he expresses his satisfaction with the success of Brandes's lecture course on his writings and ideas (*KSB* 8, pp. 242–43, 374–76).

7. *Bouvard and Pécuchet* is discussed as a significant testament about the world by characters in Aldous Huxley's novel *Time Must Have a Stop*: "Incomparably the finest thing Flaubert ever did. It's one of the great philosophical poems of the world—and probably the last that will ever be written" (1944/1953, 130).

8. In a consideration of jokes and funny stories in the context of a discussion of Cervantes, Kundera (2007b) reflects on *Bouvard and Pécuchet* as an "extended joke." As de Madariaga (1961, 121) pointed out in a highly original study, superficial tradition has reduced the "marvellous psychological fabric" of Cervantes's story of Don Quixote and Sancho to a line of the simplest melody: the valiant knight and idealist and the matter-of-fact, cowardly rustic and skeptic.

9. Shestov maintains that under the cover of positivism Nietzsche pursued quite different goals and never was, in fact, a positivist. "For what has positivism in common with a new dawn?" (Shestov 1900/1969, 273), he asks rhetorically.

10. See also *KSA*, vol. 9, fragment 4 [19]; *SUP*, 13:89; *KSA*, vol. 9, fragment 4 [222], *SUP*, 13:133; and *KSA*, vol. 10, fragment 8 [7]; *SUP*, 14:293.

11. "What is the greatest thing you can experience? It is the hour of the great contempt. The hour in which even your happiness grows loathsome to you, and your reason and your virtue also" (*Z* prologue 3). On the harm done by moral contempt, see *KSA*, vol. 12, fragment 10 [50], p. 480; *WP* 740. Putting forth an equally critical and enlightening view of Cervantes's novel, Nabokov takes issue with critics who view it as "a kindly humane work" and wishes to draw attention to its "brutality" (1983, 15). Harold Bloom discusses Nabokov on *Don Quixote* in his introduction to the Vintage edition of the novel (Cervantes 2005, xxv–xxvi). On the figure of Don Quixote, see Turgenev's (1860/1965) thought-provoking essay contrasting Hamlet's "egotism" with Don Quixote's "altruism." More recently, James Wood (2019, 325–38) has provided a nuanced interpretation of the honesty and skepticism being played out in the novel, which he interprets as the founder of secular comedy.

12. Compare Aristotle's *Ethics*: "The wise men, then, must not only know all that follows from first principles, but must also have a true understanding of those principles" (1980, 6.7).

13. See also: "But all life is a dispute over taste and tasting! Taste: that is at the same time weight and scales and weigher; and woe to all living creatures that want to live without dispute over weight and scales and weigher!" (*Z* 2 "On the Sublime Ones"). The cultivation of taste is just as important as the exercise of reason in the development of one's character and the establishment of a mature way of life: "Now our taste is decisive in rejecting Christianity, no longer our reasons" (*GS* 132). Arendt (1961/2006, 194–223 ["The Crisis of Culture"]) seeks to provide enlightenment about taste—"that curious and ill-defined capacity," as she calls it.

14. Buckle's ideas are also attacked by the underground man in Dostoevsky's satirical novella *Notes from Underground* (1864), including the view that civilization results in a softening of human beings. See Dostoevsky (1864/1993, 22–23). Joseph Frank (2010, 422–23) shows that Dostoevsky was responding to the interest shown in Buckle's ideas by the Russian radicals of his time. Although Nietzsche is keen to attach his modes of thinking to the methods and procedures of science, as we saw in chapter 2 above, he also expresses a concern about modern science's preoccupation with the average: "It is the *mass* instinct that also reigns in knowledge." At bottom, he argues: "[T]he aim of science is to determine how *the human being*—**not** the individual—perceives in relation to all things and to himself, therefore, to *weed out* the idiosyncrasy of individuals and groups and determine the *enduring* relationship. Not truth, but *the human being* becomes known and moreover within all ages in which it exists. I.e., a phantom is *constructed*, everyone works constantly on finding that on which one *must agree*, because it belongs to the nature of human being. . . . Science therefore merely *continues* the process that has *constituted* the essence of the species" (*KSA*, vol. 9, fragment 11 [156]; *SUP*, 6:357, 356). *Notes from Underground* was the first book of Dostoevsky's that Nietzsche read. For details, see Miller (1973).

15. In his notebooks of 1888, Nietzsche also characterizes several "modern pessimists" as decadents, including Schopenhauer, Leopardi, and Dostoevsky (*KSA*, vol. 13, fragment 14 [222]; and *KSA*, vol. 13, fragment 15 [34]). On his reception of Baudelaire, see Pestalozzi (1978) and Baudelaire (2022, 60–66 [introduction]). Walter Benjamin finds it too simple to construe Baudelaire as a pessimist since spleen, he holds, serves as a bulwark against pessimism: "[W]ith Baudelaire, a taboo is placed on the future." Baudelaire is thus best seen as an incomparable brooder. Moreover, although "Baudelaire adheres to Catholicism, his experience of the universe is in exact accord with the experience comprehended by Nietzsche in the phrase 'God is dead'" (Benjamin 2006, 135, 154). Baudelaire's recognition of this death, Benjamin suggests, is what best accounts for his melancholy. Pearson (2021) seeks to show that Baudelaire understands *le Mal*—presented not as Christian evil but rather as secular ill-being—as a condition of melancholy synonymous with the human business of living. For profound reflections on melancholy in Nietzsche, see *GS* 291, 302, 368.

16. For Baudelaire on Wagner, see Baudelaire (2006, chap. 13). Baudelaire wrote Wagner on February 17, 1860, a few weeks after attending a concert at the Théâtre des Italiens on January 25, to let him know that he owes him "the greatest musical pleasure I've ever experienced." He explains that he experienced the music as his own: "[A]nd I recognized it, as any man recognizes those things he is destined to love." He also refers to the grandeur of the music and its sublime heights that drive "the listener on to the

heights" as well as to the solemnity of the music, which evokes both the solemnity of the great sounds of nature and the solemnity of the great human passions (1986, 145–46).

17. Compare Bourget (1883/2009, esp. 100–101) on Baudelaire. Also well worth consulting is the work of Arthur Symons on decadence and especially on Baudelaire as a decadent poet. Symons writes that Baudelaire "feeds himself on his nerves" (1920, 6). See also Symons (1899/1919/2014), a classic study of French symbolism. (The expanded 1919 edition includes a chapter on Baudelaire.) Symons had a strong interest in Nietzsche, whom he started to read in earnest (and in French) in 1902. Interestingly, he holds that Nietzsche's philosophy too "was made out of his nerves." He adds perspicaciously, referring to aphorism 481 of *Dawn*, that Nietzsche's "remarkable personality . . . stands to him in the place of a system. . . . His thoughts are the passionate history of his soul. It is for this reason that he is an artist among philosophers rather than a pure philosopher." Symons cited in Bridgwater (1972, 32).

18. Nietzsche could also have referred to the note "To the Reader" at the commencement of *Les Fleurs du Mal* (Baudelaire 1993, 5):

> Foolishness and error, stinginess and sin
> Possess our spirits and fatigue our flesh.
> And like a pet we feed our tame remorse
> As beggars take to nourishing their lice. . . .
> Truly the Devil pulls on all our strings!
> In most repugnant objects we find charms;
> Each day we're one step further into Hell,
> Content to move across the stinking pit.

19. On Goethe as Nietzsche's educator, see Prange (2013, chap. 7).

20. Compare Huxley: "For chastity, after all, is the proper, the natural complement of passion. After satisfaction, desire reposes in a cool and lucid sleep. Chastity enforced against desire is unquiet and life-destroying" (1929, 282).

21. Nietzsche refers to Bourget in *EH* "Why I Am So Clever" 3.

22. For a rich study of decadence in nineteenth-century French culture, see Swart (1964). On Nietzsche and decadence, see Bernheimer (2002), Conway (1997), Gogröf-Voorhees (2004), and Huddleston (2019).

23. See also *Twilight of the Idols* on "great style," in which power that no longer needs to prove itself or to please "reposes in *itself*, fatalistically, a law among laws" (*TI* "Reconnaissance Raids of an Untimely Man" 11).

24. *Perspectiva* is the Latin term for *optics*. For further insight, see Barasch (1985, 148–63). For Nietzsche on the "perspectival optics of life," see, e.g., *BGE* 11; and *GM* 3.12.

25. Henry James is a perceptive critic of Flaubert's hatred of bourgeois life, observing how it distorted his view of the world and impaired him as an artist. See James (1987, 96–103, 373–403). For further insight, see Seaton (2014, 95–101). See also Baudelaire (2006, 244–56) on *Madame Bovary*. In *The Family Idiot*, his highly challenging study of Flaubert, Sartre seeks to demonstrate that the misanthropy of the neurotic author needs to be understood in terms of an objective neurosis, namely, the neurosis of (French) bourgeois society. Sartre astutely points out that in a society "devoured by hatred one wants to satisfy hatred still more than contempt" (2023, 261). Sartre (2023, 242) is claiming not that the works of artists and poets will be neurotic under such conditions but rather that literary doctrines will be and that artists

themselves will have to act and be neurotic. In his introduction to *The Family Idiot*, Joseph S. Catalano notes that for Sartre *Madama Bovary* is a modern realist novel that aims to awaken in the reader despair, hatred of fellow human beings, and a sense of the futility of all human behavior: "And yet, most modern readers seem strangely unaware of the negative content of Flaubert's writings" (Sartre 2023, 4). In this respect, Sartre's study of Flaubert rigorously extends the concerns of Nietzsche and James. See also Nietzsche: "[T]he cultivated classes in European countries are thoroughly neurotic" (*HH* 244). For the way in which in *La nausée* a drama of misanthropy and hatred is played out, see Sartre (1938, 169–70) or Sartre (1965, 170–71).

26. On the issue of the "exception," we should bear in mind Nietzsche's reflection in an aphorism in *Dawn*: "'The rule is more interesting to me than the exception'—anyone who feels this way is far advanced in scholarship and belongs to the initiated" (*D* 442; see also *BGE* 26; and *KSA*, vol. 12, fragment 10 [175]; *WP* 893).

27. In *Afloat*, a logbook of a Mediterranean cruise, Maupassant expresses his deep pessimism about human beings: "[W]e'll just go on living, bearing the burden of the hateful customs, criminal prejudices, and savagery of our barbaric ancestors, for we're beasts and beasts we shall remain, dominated by our instincts in which nothing can change" (1888/2008, 31). Despite his pessimism, cynicism, and even misanthropy, Maupassant's writings contain elements that would have appealed to Nietzsche. They are perhaps best brought out by Joseph Conrad in the essay "The Austerity of Maupassant." Conrad writes of Maupassant's keenness for facts and observation and his wish to avoid empty phrases that demand of us only a vague susceptibility to emotion. Furthermore, his literary honesty is guided by the virtues of courage and justice, and he was "a true and dutiful lover of our earth" (1949, 31).

28. On Maupassant's skills as a psychologist and novelist, see the excellent reading developed in Henry James (1987, 230–57), where Maupassant's preface to *Pierre and Jean* is also discussed.

29. Valéry's views on the romantics and on Baudelaire's relation to Romanticism are also well worth considering. See Valéry (1972, 193–215, esp. 196–98 and 200–202). As Valéry points out, Romanticism needs to be treated as something of an arbitrary idea. For Baudelaire's attempt to answer the question "what is romanticism?" see "The Salon of 1846" (Baudelaire 2006, 52–54). For Baudelaire, the following inform the Romantic sensibility: "intimacy, spirituality, colour, yearning for the infinite" (2006, 53).

30. For insight into how urban experience affected Baudelaire as a poet and his efforts to create poetry that embodies "the immortal instinct of beauty," as he put it, see Prendergast (1995, esp. 126–64). On Baudelaire and the city, see also Pearson (2021, chaps. 18–19).

31. One facet of Turin that delighted Nietzsche when he took up residence there in 1888 was that he found it "[n]ot at all a metropolis, not at all modern" (*KSB* 8, p. 285 [letter to Peter Gast, April 7, 1888]; Middleton 1996, 291).

32. See also Benjamin (1978, 142). On De Quincey, see Beer (2012, chap. 5) and Hayter (1988, chaps. 5, 10). For further insight into Nietzsche on different kinds and states of consciousness, see Ansell-Pearson (2007). Nietzsche wishes us to be on guard against the tendency to substantialize entities and so-called faculties, such as "ego" and "will." When we take consciousness for a determinate magnitude, we deny its growth and intermittences, and posit it uncritically for the unity of the organism. Nietzsche proposes we make the body and physiology the starting point instead: "Essential to start from the body and use it as a guiding thread. It is the far richer phenomenon and

can be observed more distinctly" (*KSA*, vol. 11, fragment 40 [15]; *WLN*, 43; see also *GS* 11).

33. Cioran appears to be a writer resigned to the satanic: "Our suffering cannot be anything but futile and satanic. Any poem by Baudelaire says more to modern man than the saints' sublime excesses" (1937/1995, 49).

34. In this letter, Nietzsche also refers to Baudelaire's genius. See also Baudelaire: "There are in every man, at every hour, two simultaneous postulations, one toward God, the other toward Satan." Also: "Ever since childhood, a tendency toward mysticism. My conversations with God" (Baudelaire 2022, 188, 145).

35. In his study of Baudelaire, Roger Pearson (2021) does not refer to Eliot's "Baudelaire" (Eliot 1930/2015). He does, however, discuss the issue of Satan and other interpretations of Baudelaire as a Catholic writer. See, e.g., Pearson (2021, 115–18, 158, 159, 161, 173–75).

36. For insight into Baudelaire and the satanic, see also Huxley: "To this Christian, who accepted the doctrine of the Fall with all its consequences, Humanitarianism was simply criminal nonsense. Man was by nature malignant and stupid. The 'universal silliness of every class, individual, sex, and age' filled him, as it filled Flaubert, with a chronic indignation" (1929, 179 [and see generally 171–203]). See also Symons (1920, 29). Satanism was fashionable in Baudelaire's time. In a study of Symbolist art, Edward Lucie-Smith discusses the role that J.-K. Huysman's novels, such as *À rebours* (*Against nature*) and *Là bas*, played in this fashion, exemplifying the interest in decadence. He quotes a revealing remark made by Huysman after his conversion to orthodox Catholicism: "It was through a glimpse of the supernatural of evil that I first obtained insight into the supernatural of good. The one derived from the other" (cited in Lucie-Smith 1991, 51).

37. Charles Taylor (2024, 302–3) holds that, although a doctrine of original sin is central to Baudelaire, he wavers between telling a Christian story and a gnostic or even a Manichaean one that also involves Hermes Trismegistus, in whose teachings the interrelationship between the material and the divine is central.

38. Gide also admired Chopin: "[T]he *Barcarolle* is a kind of radiant, graceful and robust lyricism which explains Nietzsche's predilection . . . and mine" (1949, 119). Nietzsche found Wagner's music histrionic, overwhelming, and even destroying of thought. Aldous Huxley had a similar experience: "[T]he ceaseless torrent of Wagner's music is very poor in silence. . . . It 'says' less because it is always speaking" (1950, 19). Georges Liébert (2004) devotes a few pages to Nietzsche on Chopin in his study of Nietzsche and music. For a recent study of Nietzsche on Wagner, see Harvey and Ridley (2022). Although they provide many valuable insights, they do not explore the link Nietzsche makes between Wagner's art and the literary work of the "Parisian decadents."

39. Regarding the psychologists of France, Nietzsche says: "'[I]nstinct' is the most intelligent of all the different kinds of intelligence discovered so far" (*BGE* 218). In *Twilight of the Idols*, Nietzsche singles out for criticism the brothers Edmond and Jules de Goncourt: "[T]hey cannot string three sentences together without simply hurting the eye, the *psychologist's* eye" (*TI* "Reconnaissance Raids of an Untimely Man" 7; see also *KSA*, vol. 11, fragment 25 [184]; *SUP*, 15:53; and *KSA*, vol. 13, fragment 14 [47]; *WP* 821). Nietzsche also copies extracts from the journals of the brothers in his notebooks of 1887–88, including reflections on contemporary French melancholy. See, e.g., *KSA*, vol. 13, fragment 11 [296], pp. 117–21. Inspired by Nietzsche, Gide applies the insights advanced in *Twilight of the Idols* to an understanding of Dostoevsky, who, he says, never

observes for observation's sake. See Gide (1923/1967, 102–4). He also understands Dostoevsky to be nonpartisan. Partisanship for Nietzsche is a sign of intellectual slavery and reveals itself in the person who needs "to have a strict and necessary optic in all values" (*AC* 54). See Gide (1923/1967, 39). Gide's understanding of Dostoevsky as a novelist will strike many as far-fetched. Bloom is much nearer to the truth, I think, when he writes of him: "He is a partisan, whose fierce perspective is always explicit in what he writes. His design upon us is to raise us, like Lazarus, from our own nihilism and skepticism, and then convert us to Orthodoxy" (2000, 170). As he wittily adds, when one reads *Crime and Punishment*, it is as if one is reading *Macbeth* composed by Macbeth himself. On Dostoevsky as "a genius of spiritual morbidity," see Nabokov (1981, 130).

40. For a highly instructive interpretation of Pope on nature and art, see Price (1964, chap. 5).

41. Nietzsche also refers to Stendhal in *Beyond Good and Evil* as an "odd Epicurean and question mark of a man" (*BGE* 254). Stendhal can be conceived as an Epicurean since he shows an inquisitive Epicureanism in his pursuit of pleasure and happiness. Keeping in mind that the Epicurean school valued friendship over love, he is an "odd" (*wunderlich*) Epicurean since his great passion is for the pleasures of love, and he devotes his passion for knowledge to an honest study of it. For insight into this aspect of Epicurean teaching, see Guyau (2021, 113–18). In conceiving Stendhal as a curious Epicurean, Nietzsche may have been influenced by Paul Bourget's reading of him in the *Essais de psychologie contemporaine* (1883). Bourget's chapter on Stendhal has been translated into English by Nancy O' Connor (Bourget 1883/2017). Georg Brandes describes Stendhal as a "pronounced epicurean" when taken as a moral philosopher (1904, 218). For Nietzsche's acquaintance with Brandes's study of modern literature, see the discussion of Resa von Schirnhofer on some of the books Nietzsche esteemed in Gilman (1987, 154). Nietzsche shares Stendhal's admiration of Helvétius, who was an Epicurean-inspired thinker. For further insight into the appeal Stendhal has for Nietzsche as a psychologist, see Campioni (2015). For Nietzsche on Helvétius, see *WS* 216, *GS* 94, and *BGE* 228. In *BGE* 228, Nietzsche lampoons the English utilitarians for failing to see him as a dangerous thinker. For insight into Helvétius as an Epicurean political thinker, see also Force (2009). On Stendhal, see Zweig (1952), Wood (1971), and Wakefield (1984). See also the potent insights in de Beauvoir (1949/1997), de Beauvoir (1945/2004, 210), de Beauvoir (1946/2004, 269), and de Beauvoir (1947/2004, 311).

42. On the art of reading well with "delicate fingers and eyes," see *D* preface 5.

43. See also Cioran where he asks why we so rarely recall the Cynics: "It is better to forget the cynics. Their lack of timidity in front of knowledge betrays a dangerous lust for incurable diseases" (1937/1995, 67). See also Cioran (1949/2010, 51).

44. For further insight into Nietzsche's relationship to the Cynics, see Hutter (1989), Lemm (2020), Logan (2023), and Porter (2023). On cynicism as "the true life," see Faustino (2024).

45. In *CW* 5, Nietzsche refers to Wagner, the "modern artist par excellence," as "the Cagliostro of modernity." See also *EH* "The Case of Wagner" 1. For insight into Cagliostro see Elizabeth Butler's classic study of the figure of the magus (1948/1993, 207ff., 215ff.).

46. In the 1844 essay "The Poet," Emerson characterizes the poet as "the Namer, or Language-Maker" (2000, 296).

47. For further insight into the distinction Nietzsche draws between genuine free spirits and freethinkers, see Ansell-Pearson (2009). In *Dawn*, Nietzsche had already observed that today the attempt is being made to create a society of universal security. However, the price being paid for it, he argues, is much too high: "[T]he maddest thing is that what is being effected is the very opposite of universal security" (*D* 179). For further insight, see Ansell-Pearson and Bamford (2021, 168–71).

48. See also Emerson: "The poets are thus liberating gods" (2000, 301 ["The Poet"]). Roger Pearson holds that there is a difference between the poet as "legislator" and the poet as "lawgiver" (2021, ix–x). In the case of the lawgiver, Pearson argues that we can detect a tension between passive transmission and active creation, which leads him to pose the question: "Does the poet resemble Moses, receiving the Laws from God and handing them down to humankind? Or does the poet more closely resemble Orpheus, actively employing the power of poetry—of harmony—to bring order where there was originally chaos?" (2021, x). For Nietzsche on Orpheus, see *GS* 87, 286. See also chap. 6, n. 4, above.

49. On Shelley, see Howe (2021). For Nietzsche on Shelley, see *SE* 3; *BGE* 245; *KSA*, vol. 11, fragment 34 [95]; and *KSA*, vol. 13, fragment 11 [228].

50. In the preface to *De l'esprit* (1809, xix), Helvétius lays out his principles for studying the mind: "I imagined that morality ought to be treated like all other sciences, and founded on experiment, as well as natural philosophy." For insight into Nietzsche's reading of Helvétius, see Williams (1952, 119–21). For insight into Helvétius as a Pelagian figure, see Huxley (1980, 64–78 ["How Original Is Original Sin?"]).

51. In a note from 1885, Nietzsche refers to "brave Guyau" and describes him as a courageous thinker who has written, in his *A Sketch of Morality without Obligation or Sanction* (1885/1896), one of the few genuinely interesting books on ethics of modern times (*KSA*, vol. 11, fragment 35 [34], p. 525). Isaiah Berlin (2003, 11–27) provides instructive insight into the novel character of Helvétius's utilitarianism.

52. The importance of Emerson's conception of the thinker for Nietzsche cannot simply be restricted to his early period since it recurs in his both his middle and his late writings. For studies of Nietzsche and Emerson, see Mikics (2003), Stack (1992), and Zavatta (2019). See also Krell (2015) and La Rocca (2017).

53. Nietzsche provides several examples of figures he takes to be fanatics whom he also calls "sick spirits" and "conceptual epileptics": Savonarola, Luther, Rousseau, Robespierre, and Saint-Simon (*AC* 54). See also *AC* 32. While acknowledging "the fantastic, naive and ludicrous aspects" of Saint-Simon, Isaiah Berlin argues that his hypothesis about why the French Revolution failed is one of the most original put forward (2003, 120). For Nietzsche on the "pathetic and bloody quackery" of the Revolution, see *D* 534. See also *WS* 221.

54. Reflecting in the spring of 1880 on the experience of reading his earlier writings in a preface to the unpublished book of aphorisms that transmuted into *Dawn* entitled *In the Shadow of Venice*, Nietzsche says that he is shocked to find that they share the language of fanaticism (*Fanatismus*). Fanaticism, he notes, corrupts character as well as taste and ultimately one's health. He concludes by declaring that he wants his newest thoughts to be read with caution. *KSA*, vol. 9, fragment 3 [1]; *SUP*, 13:38.

55. On the uses of contempt in Nietzsche, see Jenkins (2022). It may be, as Iris Murdoch (1970, 50) has it, that contempt for the ordinary human condition can serve

to save a writer from real pessimism. See also Nietzsche's depiction of an exchange between a sage and a fool in *GS* 213.

56. The need for cleanliness runs throughout Nietzsche's writings as a refrain, starting with the unfashionable observations. Nietzsche argues that the sense for "cleanliness" (*Reinlichkeit*) should be kindled in a child to the point of passion, attending all its talents "like an aureole of purity" that bears happiness within it and spreading happiness around it (*MOM* 288). See also: "Every achievement, every step forwards in knowledge is the *consequence* of courage, of toughness towards oneself, of cleanliness [*Sauberkeit*] towards oneself" (*EH* foreword 3). See also: "I have an instinct for cleanliness that is utterly uncanny in its sensitivity. . . . The whole of my *Zarathustra* is a dithyramb to solitude, or, if I have been understood, to purity" (*EH* "Why I Am So Wise" 8).

57. Nietzsche's concern is echoed by Bergson in the conclusion of *The Two Sources of Morality and Religion* (1932/1977, 296ff.). Bergson's worry about the future is strikingly like Nietzsche's, namely, that humanity is trapped in an aphrodisiac culture it has created for itself. We find it pleasurable to love pleasure, and to this end we want more and more conveniences. We soon find ourselves, however, in the grip of a frenzy of consumption. Nietzsche's concern leads him to a depiction of "the last human" in *Zarathustra*. This is the human that thinks it has discovered happiness—perpetual bland contentment—and simply blinks (*Z* prologue 5).

58. In his final book, Berdyaev reflected on the two principal planes of being as he saw them, spirit and Caesar, and argued that today we are building a civilization that confines human life to one plane only, that of Caesar in the form of the "autonomous authority of technics" (1952, 54). He does not consider Nietzsche's conception of spiritual Caesarism and shows that he has a facile understanding of him. On Nietzsche and the machine, see my remarks in the coda.

59. For an informative study of Caesar, see Billows (2012). One of Billows's key arguments is that "the tradition of seeing Caesar as synonymous with autocratic power does the real Caesar a disservice" (2012, 262). For instructive insight into Nietzsche's reception of Roman figures and models, including Caesar, see Bett (2011).

60. For detailed insight into this whole issue, see Shapiro (2010, chap. 2). On Bacon and Shakespeare, see also Williams (1974, 68–70, 136–37). Nietzsche was aware of the speculations about Bacon in America, and he contrasts his own instinctive surety about Shakespeare's alleged real identity to "the pitiable prattle of American muddle-heads and blockheads" (*EH* "Why I Am So Clever" 4).

CODA

1. In addition to *Brave New World*, see Huxley's 1929 essay "The New Salvation" (Huxley 2001, 209–13). Like Nietzsche, Huxley considers the machine by itself to be not a teacher but a promoter of "boredom and discontent to such a pitch" that we are on the verge of mass imbecility and mass insanity (Huxley 2001, 212). See also the essay "Machinery, Psychology, and Politics" (Huxley 2001, 218–21). See also Mumford (1952, 1954, 1967). On the relevance of Mumford's writings today, see Sachs (2022).

2. Nietzsche, "The Desert Grows: Woe to Him Who Harbours Deserts . . . ," in *DD*, *27* (translation modified).

Bibliography

Abbey, Ruth. 2000. *Nietzsche's Middle Period*. Oxford: Oxford University Press.

———. 2015. "Skilled Marksman and Strict Self-Examination: Nietzsche on La Rochefoucauld." In *Nietzsche's Free Spirit Philosophy*, ed. Rebecca Bamford, 13–33. London: Rowman & Littlefield International.

———. 2020. *Nietzsche's Human, All Too Human: A Critical Introduction and Guide*. Edinburgh: Edinburgh University Press.

Acampora, Christa Davis. 2006. "Naturalism and Nietzsche's Moral Psychology." In *A Companion to Nietzsche*, ed. Keith Ansell-Pearson, 314–35. Malden, MA: Blackwell.

Acampora, Christa Davis, and Keith Ansell-Pearson. 2011. *Nietzsche's Beyond Good and Evil*. London: Continuum.

Acharya, Vinod, and Ryan J. Johnson, eds. 2020. *Nietzsche and Epicurus: Nature, Health, and Ethics*. London: Bloomsbury Academic.

Alfano, Mark. 2021. *Nietzsche's Moral Psychology*. Cambridge: Cambridge University Press.

Allan, Derek. 2014. "A Logical Redeemer: Kirillov in Dostoievskii's *Demons*." *Journal of European Studies* 44, no. 2: 97–111.

Andreas-Salomé, Lou. 1987. *The Freud Journal*. Translated by Stanley A. Leaby. London: Quartet Books.

Ansell-Pearson, Keith. 2006a. "A Dionysian Drama on the Fate of the Soul: An Introduction to Reading *On the Genealogy of Morality*." In *Nietzsche's On the Genealogy of Morals: Critical Essays*, ed. Christa Davis Acampora, 9–39. Lanham, MD: Rowman & Littlefield.

———. 2006b. "The Incorporation of Truth: Towards the Overhuman." In *A Companion to Nietzsche*, ed. Ansell-Pearson, 230–50. Malden, MA: Blackwell.

———. 2007. "Incorporation and Individuation: On Nietzsche's Use of Phenomenology for Life." *Journal of the British Society for Phenomenology* 38, no. 1:61–89.

———. 2009. "Free Spirits and Free Thinkers: Nietzsche and Guyau on the Future of Morality." In *Nietzsche, Nihilism, and the Philosophy of the Future*, ed. Jeffrey Metzger, 102–25. London: Bloomsbury.

———. 2010. "Nietzsche, the Sublime, and the Sublimities of Philosophy." *Nietzsche-Studien* 40:202–32.

———. 2013. "Holding on to the Sublime: On Nietzsche's Early 'Unfashionable' Project." *The Oxford Handbook of Nietzsche*, ed. Ken Gemes and John Richardson, 226–52. Oxford: Oxford University Press.

———. 2018. *Nietzsche's Search for Philosophy: On the Middle Writings*. London: Bloomsbury Academic.

———. 2019. "Nietzsche on Transforming the Passions into Joys: On the Middle Writings and *Thus Spoke Zarathustra*." *Nietzsche, penseur de l'affirmation: Relecture d'Ainsi parlait Zarathoustra*, ed. C. Bertot, J. Leclercq, N. Monseu, and P. Wotling, 73–91. Louvain: Presses universitaires de Louvain.

———. 2021. "How to Make Sense of Nietzsche as a Sceptic." In *Nietzsche on Making Sense of Nietzsche*, ed. M. Béland, C. Denat, C. Piazzesi, and P. Wotling, 71–91. Reims: Editions et presses de l'Université de Reims.

———. 2022. "Nietzsche on the Passions and Self-Cultivation: Contra the Stoics and Spinoza." *Continental Philosophy Review* 55:245–65.

———. 2023a. "Nietzsche on the Task of the Poets in His Middle Writings." In *Nietzsche and Literary Studies*, ed. James I. Porter, 91–120. Cambridge: Cambridge University Press.

———. 2023b. "Schopenhauer on Stoicism as a Way of Life and on the Wisdom of Life." In *The Schopenhaurian Mind*, ed. David Woods and Timothy Stoll, 376–90. London: Routledge.

Ansell-Pearson, Keith, and Rebecca Bamford. 2021. *Nietzsche's Dawn: Philosophy, Ethics, and the Passion of Knowledge*. Hoboken, NJ: Wiley Blackwell.

Ansell-Pearson, Keith, and Paul S. Loeb, eds. 2022. *Thus Spoke Zarathustra: A Critical Guide*. Cambridge: Cambridge University Press.

Ansell-Pearson, Keith, and Lorenzo Serini. 2022. "Friedrich Nietzsche: Cheerful Thinker and Writer: A Contribution to the Debate on Nietzsche's Cheerfulness." *Nietzsche-Studien* 51:1–34.

Ansell-Pearson, Keith, and Federico Testa. 2024. "Jean-Marie Guyau on Morality and Life." In *The Oxford Handbook of Modern French Philosophy*, ed. Mark Sinclair and Daniel Whistler, 137–50. Oxford: Oxford University Press.

Arendt, Hannah. 1961/2006. *Between Past and Future*. London: Penguin.

———. 2007a. "Emerson Address." In *Reflections on Literature and Culture*, ed. Susannah Young-Ah Gottlieb, 282–85. Stanford, CA: Stanford University Press.

———. 2007b. "Great Friend of Reality: Adalbert Stifter." In *Reflections on Literature and Culture*, ed. Susannah Young-Ah Gottlieb, 110–15. Stanford, CA: Stanford University Press.

Aristotle. 1980. *Ethics*. Translated by J. A. K. Thomson. Harmondsworth: Penguin.

———. 2013. *Poetics*. Translated by Anthony Kenny. Oxford: Oxford University Press.

———. 2018. *The Art of Rhetoric*. Translated by Robin Waterfield. Oxford: Oxford University Press.

Armstrong, Aurelia. 2013. "The Passions, Power, and Practical Philosophy: Spinoza and Nietzsche contra the Stoics." *Journal of Nietzsche Studies* 44, no. 1:6–24.

Asmis, Elizabeth. 2022. "'Love It or Leave It': Nature's Ultimatum in Lucretius' *On the Nature of Things*." In *Epicurus in Rome: Philosophical Perspectives in the Ciceronian Age*, ed. Sergio Yona and Gregson Davis, 111–29. Cambridge: Cambridge University Press.

Atwood, Margaret. 2011. "*Brave New World* by Aldous Huxley." *In Other Worlds: SF and the Human Imagination*, 184–93. London: Virago.

Auerbach, Eric. 2014. *Time, History, and Literature: Selected Essays of Eric Auerbach*. Edited by James I. Porter. Translated by Jane O. Newman. Princeton, NJ: Princeton University Press.

Augustine. 1995. *Against the Academicians and The Teacher*. Translated and with an introduction by Peter King. Indianapolis: Hackett.

———. 2019. *Confessions*. Translated and with an introduction by Thomas Williams. Indianapolis: Hackett.

Bacon, Francis. 1609/1935. *The Essays and The Wisdom of the Ancients*. London: Odhams.

———. 1620/2000. *The New Organon*. Edited by Lisa Jardine and Michael Silverthorne. Cambridge: Cambridge University Press.

———. 1626/2002. *The New Atlantis*. In *The Major Works*, ed. Brian Vickers, 457–91. Oxford: Oxford University Press.

Badiou, Alain. 2005. "What Is a Poem? or, Philosophy and Poetry at the Point of the Unnamable." In *Handbook of Inaesthetics*, trans. Alberto Toscano, 16–28. Stanford, CA: Stanford University Press. 16-28.

Baier, Annette C. 2009. "Why Honesty Is a Hard Virtue." In *Reflections on How We Live*, 85–111. Oxford: Oxford University Press.

Bamford, Rebecca, ed. 2015. *Nietzsche's Free Spirit Philosophy*. London: Rowman & Littlefield International.

Bate, Jonathan. 2009. *Soul of the Age: The Life, Mind and World of William Shakespeare*. London: Penguin.

Barasch, Moshe. 1985. *Theories of Art*. Vol. 1, *From Plato to Winckelmann*. New York: Routledge.

Bates, Catherine. 1999. *Play in a Godless World*. London: Open Gate.

Baudelaire, Charles. 1950. "The Poem of Hashish." In *My Heart Laid Bare and Other Prose Writings*, ed. Peter Quennell, trans. Norman Cameron, 73–125. London: Weidenfeld & Nicolson.

———. 1986. *Selected Letters of Charles Baudelaire: The Conquest of Solitude*. Translated and edited by Rosemary Lloyd. London: Weidenfeld & Nicolson.

———. 1993. *The Flowers of Evil*. Translated by James McGowan. Oxford: Oxford University Press.

———. 2006. *Selected Writings on Art and Literature*. Translated by P. E. Charvet. London: Penguin.

———. 2020. *My Heart Laid Bare and Other Texts*. Translated and with an introduction by Rainer J. Hanshe. New York: Contra Mundum.

———. 2022. *Late Fragments*. Translated by Richard Sieburth. New Haven, CT: Yale University Press.

Beebe, John. 2005. *Integrity in Depth*. College Station: Texas A&M University Press.

Beer, John. 2012. *Romantic Consciousness: Blake to Mary Shelley*. Basingstoke: Palgrave Macmillan.

Belknap, Robert L. 2002. "Dostoevskii and Psychology." In *The Cambridge Companion to Dostoevskii*, ed. W. J. Leatherbarrow, 131–48. Cambridge: Cambridge University Press.

Bell, Michael. 2007. *Open Secrets: Literature, Education, and Authority from J.-J. Rousseau to J. M. Coetzee*. Oxford: Oxford University Press.

Benjamin, Walter. 1978. "Hashish in Marseilles." In *Reflection: Essays, Aphorisms, Autobiographical Writings*, 137–46. New York: Harcourt Brace Jovanovich.

———. 1989. "Stifter." In *Selected Writings*, vol. 1, *1913–1926*, 111–13. Cambridge, MA: Harvard University Press.

———. 2006. *The Writer of Modern Life: Essays on Charles Baudelaire*. Edited by Michael W. Jennings. Cambridge, MA: Harvard University Press.

Berdyaev, Nicolas. 1952. *The Realm of Spirit and the Realm of Caesar*. Translated by Donald A. Lowrie. London: Victor Gollancz.

Bergson, Henri. 1919/2007. "Memory of the Present and False Recognition." In *Mind-Energy*, trans. H. Wildon Carr, 106–49. Basingstoke: Palgrave Macmillan.

———. 1932/1977. *The Two Sources of Morality and Religion*. Translated by R. Ashley Audra and Cloudesley Brereton. Notre Dame, IN: University of Notre Dame Press.

Berkowitz, Peter. 1995. *Nietzsche: The Ethics of an Immoralist*. Cambridge, MA: Harvard University Press.

Berlin, Isaiah. 2003. *Freedom and Its Betrayal*. Edited by Henry Hardy. London: Pimlico.

Bernheimer, Charles. 2002. *Decadent Subjects: The Idea of Decadence in Art, Literature, Philosophy, and Culture of the Fin de Siècle in Europe*. Edited by T. Jefferson Kline and Naomi Schor. Baltimore: Johns Hopkins University Press.

Berry, Jessica. 2004. "The Pyrrhonian Revival in Montaigne and Nietzsche." *Journal of the History of Ideas* 65, no. 3:497–514.

———. 2011. *Nietzsche and the Ancient Skeptical Tradition*. Oxford: Oxford University Press.

Bertram, Ernst. 1907. *Studien zu Adalbert Stifters Novellentechnik*. Dortmund: Wilh. Ruhfus.

———. 2009. *Nietzsche: Attempt at a Mythology*. Translated by Robert E. Norton. Urbana: University of Illinois Press. First published as Ernst Bertram, *Nietzsche: Versuch einer Mythologie* (Berlin: Georg Bondi, 1918).

Bett, Richard. 2000. "Nietzsche on the Skeptics and Nietzsche as Skeptic." *Archiv für Geschichte der Philosophie* 82, no. 1:62–86.

———. 2011. "Nietzsche and the Romans." *Journal of Nietzsche Studies* 42 (Autumn): 7–31.

———. 2019. *How to Be a Pyrrhonist*. Cambridge: Cambridge University Press.

Billows, Richard A. 2012. *Julius Caesar: The Colossus of Rome*. Abingdon: Routledge.

Bishop, Paul. 2011. *Reading Goethe at Midlife: Ancient Wisdom, German Classicism, and Jung*. New Orleans: Spring Journal Books.

———. 2017. *On the Blissful Islands with Nietzsche and Jung: In the Shadow of the Superman*. London: Routledge.

Blackhall, Eric A. 1948. *Adalbert Stifter*. Cambridge: Cambridge University Press.

Bloom, Harold. 1998. *Shakespeare and the Invention of the Human*. London: Fourth Estate.

———. 2000. *How to Read and Why*. London: Fourth Estate.

———. 2003. *Hamlet: Poem Unlimited*. Edinburgh: Canongate.

———. 2004. *Where Shall Wisdom Be Found?* New York: Riverhead.

———. 2011. *The Anatomy of Influence: Literature as a Way of Life*. New Haven, CT: Yale University Press.

———. 2020. *Take Arms against the Sea of Troubles*. New Haven, CT: Yale University Press.

Blue, Daniel. 2016. *The Making of Friedrich Nietzsche: The Quest for Identity, 1844–1869*. Cambridge: Cambridge University Press.

Blum, Léon. 1962. "A Theoretical Outline of 'Beylism.'" In *Stendhal: A Collection of Critical Essays*, ed. Victor Brombert, 101–14. Englewood Cliffs, NJ: Prentice-Hall.

Borges, Jorge Luis. 2000. *Selected Non-Fictions*. Edited by Eliot Weinberger. Translated by Esther Allen, Suzanne Jill Levine, and Eliot Weinberger. London: Penguin.

Born, Marcus Andreas. 2015. "Perspectives on a Philosophy of the Future in Nietzsche's *Beyond Good and Evil*." In *Nietzsche's Free Spirit Philosophy*, ed. Rebecca Bamford, 157–69. London: Rowman & Littlefield International.

Boswell, James. 1791/1980. *Life of Johnson*. Oxford: Oxford University Press.

Bourget, Paul. 1883/1993. *Essais de psychologie contemporaine*. Paris: Gallimard.

———. 1883/2009. "The Example of Baudelaire." Translated by Nancy O'Connor. *New England Review* 30, no. 2:90–104.

———. 1883/2017. "On Stendhal (Henri Beyle)." *New England Review* 38, no. 3:127–52.

Brandes, Georg. 1904. *Main Currents in Nineteenth Century Literature*. Vol. 5. New York: Macmillan.

Bridgwater, Patrick. 1972. *Nietzsche in Anglosaxony*. Leicester: Leicester University Press.

Brombert, Victor. 1988. *The Hidden Reader: Stendhal, Balzac, Hugo, Baudelaire, Flaubert*. Cambridge, MA: Harvard University Press.

Brouwer, René. 2014. *The Stoic Sage: The Early Stoics on Wisdom, Sagehood and Socrates*. Cambridge: Cambridge University Press.

Brown, Lee Rust. 1997. *Emerson's Museum: Practical Romanticism and the Pursuit of the Whole*. Cambridge, MA: Harvard University Press.

Brown, Norman O. 1959/1968. *Life against Death: The Psychoanalytical Meaning of History*. London: Sphere.

Brücker, Tobias. 2019. *Auf dem Weg zur Philosophie: Friedrich Nietzsche schreibt "Der Wanderer und sein Schatten"*. Paderborn: Wilhelm Fink.

Bruford, W. H. 1975. *The German Tradition of Self-Cultivation: "Bildung" from Humboldt to Thomas Mann*. Cambridge: Cambridge University Press.

Brusotti, Marco. 2019. "Metaphilosophy and 'Natural History': Nietzsche's *Beyond Good and Evil* on the Free Spirit." In *Nietzsche's Metaphilosophy: The Nature, Method, and Aims of Philosophy*, ed. Paul S. Loeb and Matthew Meyer, 9–22. Cambridge: Cambridge University Press.

Buben, Adam. 2021. "Unamuno on Making Oneself Indispensable and Having the Strength to Long for Immortality." *International Journal of Philosophy of Religion* 90:133–48.

———. 2022. *Existentialism and the Desirability of Immortality*. London: Routledge.

Buell, Lawrence. 2003. *Emerson*. Cambridge, MA: Harvard University Press.

Butler, E. M. 1948/1993. *The Myth of the Magus*. Cambridge: Cambridge University Press.

———. 1956. *Byron and Goethe: Analysis of a Passion*. London: Bowes & Bowes.

Calasso, Roberto. 2002. *Literature and the Gods*. Translated by Tim Parks. New York: Vintage.

———. 2012. *La folie Baudelaire*. Translated by Alistair McEwen. London: Penguin.

Calvino, Italo. 1996. *Six Memos for the Next Millennium*. Translated by Patrick Creagh. London: Vintage.

———. 1997. *The Literature Machine*. Translated by Patrick Creagh. London: Vintage.

Campioni, Giuliano. 2015. "Nietzsche and 'the French Psychologists': Stendhal, Taine, Ribot, Bourget." In *Nietzsche and the Problem of Subjectivity*, ed. João Constâncio, Maria-João Mayer Branco, Bartholomew Ryan, 219–34. Berlin: Walter de Gruyter.

Camus, Albert. 1942/2004. *The Myth of Sisyphus*. Translated by Justin O'Brien. New York: Everyman's Library.

———. 1951/1971. *The Rebel*. Translated by Anthony Bower. Harmondsworth: Penguin.

———. 1968. *Lyrical and Critical Essays*. Translated by Ellen Conroy Kennedy. New York: Vintage.

Čapek, Milič. 1983. "Eternal Recurrence—Once More." *Transactions of the Charles S. Peirce Society* 19, no. 2:141–53.

Carlyle, Thomas. 1841/1983. *On Heroes, Hero Worship, and the Heroic in History*. New York: Chelsea House.

———. 2015. *Selected Writings*. Edited and with an introduction by Alan Shelston. London: Penguin.

Cassirer, Ernst. 1951. *The Philosophy of the Enlightenment*. Translated by Fritz C. A. Koelln and James P. Pettegrove. Princeton, NJ: Princeton University Press.

Cavarero, Adriana. 2000. *Relating Narratives: Storytelling and Selfhood*. Translated by Paul A. Kottman. London: Routledge.

Cavell, Stanley. 1988. *In Quest of the Ordinary: Limits of Skepticism and Romanticism*. Chicago: University of Chicago Press.

———. 1990. *Conditions Handsome and Unhandsome: The Constitution of Emersonian Perfectionism*. Chicago: University of Chicago Press.

———. 2003. *Emerson's Transcendental Etudes*. Stanford, CA: Stanford University Press.

Caygill, Howard. 2006. "Under the Epicurean Skies." *Angelaki* 2, no. 3:107–15.

Cervantes. 1605/1615/2005. *Don Quixote*. Translated by Edith Grossman. With an introduction by Harold Bloom. London: Vintage.

Chesterton, G. K. 2012. *The Soul of Wit: Chesterton on Shakespeare*. New York: Dover.

Cicero. 1945. *Tusculan Disputations*. Translated by J. E. King. Loeb Classical Library. Cambridge, MA: Harvard University Press.

———. 1972. *The Nature of the Gods*. Translated by Horace C. P. McGregor. Harmondsworth: Penguin.

Cioran, E. M. 1937/1995. *Tears and Saints*. Translated and with an introduction by Ilinca Zarifopol-Johnston. Chicago: University of Chicago Press.

———. 1949/2010. *A Short History of Decay*. Translated by Richard Howard. London: Penguin.

———. 1952/2017. *All Gall Is Divided*. Translated and with an introduction by Richard Howard and with a new foreword by Eugene Thacker. New York: Arcade.

———. 1956/1987. *The Temptation to Exist*. Translated by Richard Howard. London: Quartet.

———. 1964/1970. *The Fall into Time*. Translated by Richard Howard. Chicago: Quadrangle.

———. 1972/2012. *Drawn and Quartered*. Translated by Richard Howard. New York: Arcade.

———. 1992. *Anathemas and Admirations*. Translated by Richard Howard. London: Quartet.

Clark, Maudemarie. 1990. *Nietzsche on Truth and Philosophy*. Cambridge: Cambridge University Press.

Coe, Richard N. 1979. "Stendhal, Rousseau and the Search for Self." *Australian Journal of French Studies* 16, no. 1 (January): 27–47.

Coleridge, Samuel Taylor. 1969. *Coleridge on Shakespeare*. Edited by Terence Hawkes. Harmondsworth: Penguin.

———. 1986. *Coleridge: Poems*. Edited by John Beer. London: J. M. Dent.

———. 1997. *Biographia Literaria*. Edited by Nigel Leask. London: J. M. Dent.

Conard, Mark T., ed. *Nietzsche and the Philosophers*. London: Routledge.

Conche, Marcel. 2014. *Philosophizing ad Infinitum: Infinite Nature, Infinite Philosophy*. Translated by Laurent Ledoux and Herman G. Bonne. Albany: State University of New York Press.

Conrad, Joseph. 1949. "The Austerity of Maupassant." In *Notes on Life and Letters*, 25–32. London: J. M. Dent.

Conway, Daniel W. 1989. "Overcoming the *Übermensch*: Nietzsche's Revaluation of All Values." *Journal of the British Society of Phenomenology* 20, no. 3:211–24.

———. 1997. *Nietzsche's Dangerous Game: Philosophy in the Twilight of the Idols*. Cambridge: Cambridge University Press.

———. 2017. "Twilight of an Idol: Nietzsche's Affirmation of Socrates." In *Nietzsche and the Philosophers*, ed. Mark T. Conard, 40–63. London: Routledge.

———. 2024. *Nietzsche's Beyond Good and Evil*. Edinburgh: Edinburgh University Press.

Cooper, John M. 2012. *Pursuits of Wisdom: Six Ways of Life in Ancient Philosophy from Socrates to Plotinus*. Princeton, NJ: Princeton University Press.

Corbett, George. 2013. *Dante and Epicurus*. London: Modern Humanities Research Association/Maney.

Cornford, Francis M. 1937/1997. *Plato's Cosmology: The Timaeus of Plato*. Indianapolis: Hackett.

Corriero, Emilio Carlo. 2021. *The "Gift" in Nietzsche's Zarathustra: Affirmative Love and Friendship*. Translated by Vanessa di Stefano. London: Bloomsbury Academic.

Coverley, Merlin. 2012. *The Art of Wandering: The Writer as Walker*. Harpenden: Oldcastle.

Cowper Powys, John. 1946a. *Dostoievsky*. London: Bodley Head.

———. 1946b. *The Pleasures of Literature*. London: Cassell.

Creasy, Kaitlyn. 2022. "Nietzsche on the Re-Naturalization of Humanity in *Thus Spoke Zarathustra*." In *Thus Spoke Zarathustra: A Critical Guide*, ed. Keith Ansell-Pearson and Paul S. Loeb, 225–47. Cambridge: Cambridge University Press.

Crotty, Kevin. 2009. *The Philosopher's Song: The Poet's Influence on Plato*. Lanham, MD: Lexington.

Curran, Andrew S. 2019. *Diderot and the Art of Thinking Freely*. New York: Other Press.

Dannhauser, Werner J. 1974. *Nietzsche's View of Socrates*. Ithaca, NY: Cornell University Press.

Danto, Arthur C. 2005. *Nietzsche as Philosopher*. Expanded ed. New York: Columbia University Press.

Davis, Lydia. 2019. "Stendhal's Alter Ego: *The Life of Henry Brulard*." In *Essays*, 371–80. London: Penguin.

Deacy, Susan. 2008. *Athena*. London: Routledge.

de Beauvoir, Simone. 1944/2004. "Pyrrhus and Cineas." In *Philosophical Writings*, ed. Margaret A. Simons with Marybeth Timmermann and Mary Beth Mader, 77–151. Urbana: University of Illinois Press.

———. 1945/2004. "Existentialism and Popular Wisdom." In *Philosophical Writings*, ed. Margaret A. Simons with Marybeth Timmermann and Mary Beth Mader, 195–221. Urbana: University of Illinois Press.

———. 1946/2004. "Literature and Metaphysics." In *Philosophical Writings*, ed. Margaret A. Simons with Marybeth Timmermann and Mary Beth Mader, 261–79. Urbana: University of Illinois Press.

———. 1947/2004. “An Existentialist Looks at Americans.” In *Philosophical Writings*, ed. Margaret A. Simons with Marybeth Timmermann and Mary Beth Mader, 299–317. Urbana: University of Illinois Press.

———. 1949/1997. “Stendhal; or, The Romantic of Reality.” In *The Second Sex*, ed. and trans. H. M. Parshley, 268–78. London: Vintage.

Del Caro, Adrian. 2004. *Grounding the Nietzsche Rhetoric of Earth*. Berlin: Walter de Gruyter.

———. 2023. Afterword to *The Joyful Science / Idylls from Messina / Unpublished Fragments*, trans. Adrian Del Caro, 647–729. Stanford, CA: Stanford University Press.

Deleuze, Gilles. 1961. “Lucrèce et le naturalisme.” *Les études philosophiques* 16:19–29.

———. 1983. *Nietzsche and Philosophy*. Translated by Hugh Tomlinson. London. Athlone.

de Madariaga, Salvador. 1961. *Don Quixote: An Introductory Essay in Psychology*. Rev. ed. London: Oxford University Press.

De Quincey, Thomas. 1821/1971. *Confessions of an English Opium Eater*. London: Penguin.

Diderot, Denis. 1746. *Pensées philosophiques*. The Hague: Aux dépens de la Compagnie.

———. 1994. *Selected Writings on Art and Literature*. Translated by Geoffrey Bremner. London: Penguin.

Donnellan, Brendan. 1982. *Nietzsche and the French Moralists*. Bonn: Bouvier.

———. 1986. “Nietzsche and Montaigne.” *Colloquia Germanica* 19, no. 1:1–20.

Dostoevsky, Fyodor. 1848/1999. “White Nights.” In *A Gentle Creature and Other Stories*. Translated by Alan Myers, 1–57. Oxford: Oxford University Press.

———. 1864/1993. *Notes from Underground*. Translated by Richard Pevear and Larissa Volokhonsky. New York: Everyman’s Library.

———. 1872/1971. *The Devils*. Translated by David Magarshack. Harmondsworth: Penguin.

Dunne, J. W. 1927/2023. *An Experiment with Time*. San Antonio, TX: Bibliotech.

Eagleton, Terry. 2017. *Hope without Optimism*. New Haven, CT: Yale University Press.

Eliot, T. S. 1930/2015. “Baudelaire.” In *The Complete Prose of T. S. Eliot: The Critical Edition*, ed. Jason Harding and Ronald Schuchard, 4:155–68. London: John Hopkins University Press/Faber & Faber.

———. 1951. *Selected Essays*. London: Faber & Faber.

Emden, Christian. 2019. *Nietzsche’s Naturalism: Philosophy and the Life Sciences in the Nineteenth Century*. Cambridge: Cambridge University Press.

Emerson, Ralph Waldo. 1996. *Representative Men: Seven Lectures*. Cambridge, MA: Harvard University Press.

———. 2000. *The Essential Writings of Ralph Waldo Emerson*. Edited by Brooks Atkinson. New York: Modern Library.

———. 2003. *The Conduct of Life*. Cambridge, MA: Harvard University Press.

———. 2007. *Society and Solitude*. Cambridge, MA: Harvard University Press.

———. 2010a. “Poetry and Imagination.” In *Letters and Social Aims*, 1–42. Cambridge, MA: Harvard University Press.

———. 2010b. *Selected Journals, 1820–1842*. Edited by Lawrence Rosenwald. New York: Library of America.

———. 2012. "Literary Ethics." In *The Annotated Emerson*, ed. David Mikics, 120–38. Cambridge, MA: Harvard University Press.
———. 2013. *Uncollected Prose Writings*. Edited by Ronald A. Bosco and Joel Myerson. Cambridge, MA: Harvard University Press.
Erasmus. 1511/1994. *Praise of Folly*. London: Penguin.
Faustino, Marta. 2017. "Nietzsche's Therapy of Therapy." *Nietzsche-Studien* 46:82–104.
———. 2024. "'A Broken Mirror': Cynicism and the Scandal of the True Life." In *Practices of Truth in Philosophy: Historical and Comparative Perspectives*, ed. Pietro Gori and Lorenzo Serini, 42–61. New York: Routledge.
Feuerbach, Ludwig. 1843/1986. *Principles of the Philosophy of the Future*. Translated by Manfred Vogel. Indianapolis: Hackett.
Fisher, David H. 1995. "Nietzsche's Dionysian Masks." *Historical Reflections / Réflexions historiques* 21, no. 3 (Fall): 515–36.
Flaubert, Gustave. 1881/1976. *Bouvard and Pécuchet*. Translated by A. J. Krailsheimer. Harmondsworth: Penguin.
Force, Pierre. 2009. "Helvétius as an Epicurean Political Theorist." *Studies on Voltaire and the Eighteenth Century*, 105–18.
Fornari, Giuseppe. 2021. *Dionysus, Christ, and the Death of God*. East Lansing: Michigan State University Press.
Foucault, Michel. 1988. *Politics, Philosophy, Culture: Interviews and Other Writings, 1977–1984*. Edited by Lawrence D. Kritzman. Translated by Alan Sheridan. London: Routledge.
———. 2012. *The Courage of Truth: Lectures at the College de France, 1983–1984*. Translated by Graham Burchell. Basingstoke: Palgrave Macmillan.
Frank, Joseph. 2010. *Dostoevsky: A Writer in His Time*. Edited by Mary Petrusewicz. Princeton, NJ: Princeton University Press.
Frederick, Samuel. 2012. *Narratives Unsettled: Digression in Robert Walser, Thomas Bernhard, and Adalbert Stifter*. Evanston, IL: Northwestern University Press.
Frederick the Great. 2021. *Philosophical Writings*. Edited by Avi Lifschitz. Translated by Angela Scholar. Princeton, NJ: Princeton University Press.
Freud, Sigmund. 1910/2003. "Leonardo da Vinci and a Memory of His Childhood." In *The Uncanny*, trans. David McLintock, 43–121. London: Penguin.
Friedl, Herwig. 2019. "Emerson; or, The Neopyrrhonist Skeptic." In *Thinking in Search of a Language: Essays on American Intellect and Intuition*, 41–61. London: Bloomsbury Academic.
Gadamer, Hans-Georg. 1986a. "Philosophy and Poetry." In *The Relevance of the Beautiful and Other Essays*, 131–40. Cambridge: Cambridge University Press.
———. 1986b. "Poetry and Mimesis." In *The Relevance of the Beautiful and Other Essays*, 116–23. Cambridge: Cambridge University Press.
———. 1998. "The Drama of Zarathustra." Translated by Thomas Heilke. In *Nietzsche's New Seas: Explorations in Philosophy, Aesthetics, and Politics*, ed. Michael Allen Gillespie and Tracy B. Strong, 220–33. Chicago: University of Chicago Press.
Gaukroger, Stephen. 2001. *Francis Bacon and the Transformation of Early-Modern Philosophy*. Cambridge: Cambridge University Press.
Gemes, Ken. 2009. "Freud and Nietzsche on Sublimation." *Journal of Nietzsche Studies* 38:38–59.
———. 2013. "Life's Perspectives." In *The Oxford Handbook of Nietzsche*, ed. Ken Gemes and John Richardson, 553–76. Oxford: Oxford University Press.

Gerhardt, Volker. 2006. "The Body, the Self, and the Ego." In *A Companion to Nietzsche*, ed. Keith Ansell-Pearson, 273–97. Malden, MA: Blackwell.

Gide, André. 1923/1967. *Dostoevsky*. With an introduction by Arnold Bennett. Harmondsworth: Penguin/Secker & Warburg.

———. 1927. "Nietzsche." In *Prétextes: Réflexions sur quelques points de littérature et de morale*, 166–85. Paris: Mercvre de France. The original French edition of *Prétextes* contains a set of reflections on Nietzsche composed in the form of a letter to Angèle dated December 10, 1898, and not included in the 1959 English translation.

———. 1949. *Notes on Chopin*. Translated by Bernard Frechtman. New York: Philosophical Library.

———. 1959. *Pretexts: Reflections on Literature and Morality*. Edited and with an introduction by Justin O'Brien. London: Secker & Warburg.

Gilman, Sander L. 1976. "Parody and Parallel: Heine, Nietzsche, and the Classical World." In *Studies in Nietzsche and the Classical Tradition*, ed. James C. O' Flaherty, Timothy F. Sellner, and Robert M. Helm, 199–213. Chapel Hill: University of North Carolina Press.

———, ed. 1987. *Conversations with Nietzsche: A Life in the Words of His Contemporaries*. Translated by David J. Parent. Oxford: Oxford University Press.

Gilson, Etienne. 1936. *The Spirit of Mediaeval Philosophy* (Gifford Lectures, 1931–32). Translated by A. H. C. Downes. New York: Charles Scribner's Sons.

———. 2020. *The Christian Philosophy of Saint Augustine*. Translated by L. E. M. Lynch. Providence, RI: Cluny.

Girard, René. 2001. *I See Satan Fall Like Lightning*. Translated by James G. Williams. Maryknoll, NY: Orbis.

Goethe, Johann Wolfgang von. 1796/1995. *Wilhelm Meister's Apprenticeship*. Ed. and trans. Eric A. Blackhall in cooperation with Victor Lange. Princeton, NJ: Princeton University Press.

———. 1980. *Goethe on Art*. Edited and translated by John Gage. London: Scolar.

Gogröf-Voorhees, Andrea. 2004. *Defining Modernism: Baudelaire and Nietzsche on Romanticism, Modernity, Decadence, and Wagner*. New York: Peter Lang.

Golden, Mason. 2013. "Emerson-Exemplar: Friedrich Nietzsche's Emerson Marginalia: Introduction." *Journal of Nietzsche Studies* 44, no. 3:398–409.

Goldmann, Lucien. 1981. *Racine*. Translated by Alastair Hamilton. London: Writers and Readers Publishing Cooperative/Rivers Press.

———. 2016. *The Hidden God: A Study of Tragic Vision in the "Pensées" of Pascal and the Tragedies of Racine*. Translated by Philip Thody. London: Verso.

Gooding-Williams, Robert. 2001. *Zarathustra's Dionysian Modernism*. Stanford, CA: Stanford University Press.

Grätz, Katharina, and Sebastian Kaufmann. 2017. *Nietzsche als Dichter: Lyrik-Poetologie-Rezeption*. Berlin: Walter de Gruyter.

Graver, Margaret R. 2007. *Stoicism and Emotion*. Chicago: University of Chicago Press.

Groothuis, Douglas. 2024. *Beyond the Wager: The Christian Brilliance of Blaise Pascal*. Downers Grove, IL: InterVarsity.

Grossman, Évelyn. 2023. *The Creativity of the Crisis*. Translated by Rainer J. Hanshe. New York: Contra Mundum.

Grundlehner, Philip. 1986. *The Poetry of Friedrich Nietzsche*. Oxford: Oxford University Press.

Gump, Margaret. 1974. *Adalbert Stifter*. New York: Twayne.

Guthrie, W. K. C. 1952/1993. *Orpheus and Greek Religion.* Princeton, NJ: Princeton University Press.

Guyau, J. M. 1878/2021. *The Ethics of Epicurus.* Edited by Keith Ansell-Pearson and Federico Testa. Translated by Federico Testa. London: Bloomsbury Academic.

———. 1885/1896. *A Sketch of Morality without Obligation or Sanction.* Translated by Gertrude Kapteyn. London: Watts.

———. 1887/1962. *The Non-Religion of the Future.* With an introduction by Nahum N. Glatzer. New York: Schocken.

———. 1895. "The Philosophy of Hope." Translated by Mitchell Abidor. https://www.marxists.org/archive/guyau/1895/hope.htm.

Hacker, P. M. S. 2018. *The Passions: A Study of Human Nature.* Hoboken, NJ: Wiley Blackwell.

Hackett, Helen. 2022. *The Elizabethan Mind.* New Haven, CT: Yale University Press.

Hadot, Pierre. 1995. *Philosophy as a Way of Life.* Translated by Michael Chase. Oxford: Blackwell.

———. 2002. *What Is Ancient Philosophy?* Translated by Michael Chase. Cambridge, MA: Harvard University Press.

———. 2020. *The Selected Writings of Pierre Hadot.* Translated by Matthew Sharpe and Federico Testa. London: Bloomsbury Academic.

———. 2023. *Don't Forget to Live: Goethe and the Tradition of Spiritual Exercises.* Translated by Michael Chase. Chicago: University of Chicago Press.

Häge, Elisabeth. 2019. *Dimensionen des Erhabenen bei Adalbert Stifter.* Berlin: Walter de Gruyter.

Hall, Calvin S., and Vernon J. Nordby. 1973. *A Primer of Jungian Psychology.* London: Meridian/Penguin.

Hampton, Timothy. 2022. *Cheerfulness.* New York: Zone.

Hanshe, Rainer. 2024. *Dionysus Speed.* London: Contra Mundum Press.

Harcourt, Edward. 2015. "Nietzsche and the Virtues." In *The Routledge Companion to Virtue Ethics*, ed. Lorraine Besser-Jones and Michael Slote, 165–81. London: Routledge.

Harris, James A. 2015. *Hume: An Intellectual Biography.* Cambridge: Cambridge University Press.

Harris, Kenneth Marc. 2013. *Carlyle and Emerson: Their Long Debate.* Cambridge, MA: Harvard University Press.

Harrison, Jane Ellen. 1903/1991. *Prolegomena to the Study of Greek Religion.* Princeton, NJ: Princeton University Press.

Harrison, Robert Pogue. 1992. *Forests: The Shadow of Civilization.* London: University of Chicago Press.

———. 2008. *Gardens: An Essay on the Human Condition.* Chicago: University of Chicago Press.

Hartle, Ann. 2008. *Michel de Montaigne: Accidental Philosopher.* Cambridge: Cambridge University Press.

Harvey, Ryan, and Aaron Ridley. 2022. *Nietzsche's The Case of Wagner and Nietzsche contra Wagner.* Edinburgh: Edinburgh University Press.

Hatab, Lawrence J. 2005. *Nietzsche's Life Sentence.* London: Routledge.

———. 2018. "What Kind of Text Is Zarathustra?" *The Agonist*, vol. 11, no. 2 (Spring). https://agonist.nietzschecircle.com/wp/what-kind-of-text-is-zarathustra-by-lawrence-j-hatab.

Hayter, Alethea. 1988. *Opium and the Romantic Imagination*. Wellingborough: Crucible/Thorsons.

Hazard, Paul. 1965. *European Thought in the Eighteenth Century*. Translated by J. Lewis May. Harmondsworth: Penguin.

Hazlitt, William. 1817/1966. *Characters of Shakespeare's Plays*. London: Oxford University Press.

———. 1982. *Selected Writings*. Edited by Ronald Blythe. Harmondsworth: Penguin.

Heidegger, Martin. 1968. *What Is Called Thinking?* Translated by Fred D. Wieck and J. Glenn Gray. San Francisco: Harper & Row.

———. 1984. "Who Is Nietzsche's Zarathustra?" In *Nietzsche: Volumes I and II*, trans. David Farrell Krell, 209–37. San Francisco: Harper & Row.

———. 1987. "The Overman." In *Nietzsche: Volumes III and IV*, trans. David Farrell Krell, 216–35. San Francisco: Harper & Row.

———. 2011. *Introduction to Philosophy—Thinking and Poetizing*. Translated by Phillip Jacques Braunstein. Bloomington: Indiana University Press.

Heller, Erich. 1988. "Rilke and Nietzsche with a Discourse on Thought, Belief and Poetry." In *The Importance of Nietzsche: Ten Essays*, 87–127. Chicago: University of Chicago Press.

Helvétius, Charles A. 1809/2005. *De l'esprit; or, Essays on the Mind and Its Several Faculties*. London: Elibron Classics.

Henry, Elisabeth. 1992. *Orpheus with His Lute: Poetry and the Renewal of Life*. London: Bristol Classical.

Heraclitus. 2001. *Fragments*. Translated by Brooks Haxton. London: Penguin.

Hesse, Hermann. 1919/1974. *If the War Goes On*. Translated by Ralph Manheim. London: Pan.

———. 1920/1975. *Wandering*. Translated by James Wright. London: Picador.

Höfele, Andreas. 2016. "Nietzsche's Shakespeare." In *No Hamlets: German Shakespeare from Nietzsche to Carl Schmitt*, 26–54. Oxford: Oxford University Press.

Höffding, Harald. 1915. *Lectures on Modern Philosophers and Bergson*. London: Macmillan.

Holub, Robert C. 2018. *Nietzsche in the Nineteenth Century: Social Questions and Philosophical Interventions*. Philadelphia: University of Pennsylvania Press.

Holzer, Angela. 2009. "'Nietzsche Caesar': The Turn against Dynastic Succession and Caesarism in Nietzsche's Late Works." In *Nietzsche, Power, and Politics: Rethinking Nietzsche's Legacy for Political Thought*, ed. Herman Siemens and Vasti Roodt, 371–91. Berlin: Walter de Gruyter.

Horkheimer, Max. 1993. "Montaigne and the Function of Skepticism." In *Between Philosophy and Social Science*, trans. G. Frederick Hunter, Matthew S. Kramer, and John Torpey, 265–313. Cambridge, MA: MIT Press.

Hough, Sheridan. 1997. *Nietzsche's Noontide Friend: The Self as Metaphoric Double*. University Park: Penn State University Press.

Howe, Anthony. 2021. "Poetic Defences and Manifestos." In *The Oxford Handbook of British Romanticism*, ed. David Duff, 264–79. Oxford: Oxford University Press.

Huddleston, Andrew. 2019. *Nietzsche on the Decadence and Flourishing of Culture*. Oxford: Oxford University Press.

Hui, Andrew. 2019. *A Theory of the Aphorism*. Princeton, NJ: Princeton University Press.

Huizinga, Johan. 1949. *Homo Ludens: A Study of the Play-Element in Culture*. London: Routledge & Kegan Paul.

Humboldt, Alexander von. 2018. *Selected Writings.* Edited by Andrea Wulf. New York: Everyman's Library.

Hume, David. 1985. *Essays Moral, Political, and Literary.* Edited by Eugene F. Miller. Indianapolis: Liberty Fund.

———. 1993. *Dialogues and Natural History of Religion.* Edited by J. C. A. Gaskin. Oxford: Oxford University Press.

———. 1998. *Selected Essays.* Edited by Stephen Copley and Andrew Edgar. Oxford: Oxford University Press, 1998.

———. 1999. *An Enquiry concerning Human Understanding.* Edited by Tom L. Beauchamp. Oxford: Oxford University Press.

———. 2007. *A Treatise of Human Nature: Volume One.* Edited by David Fate Norton and Mary J. Norton. Oxford: Oxford University Press.

Huskinson, Lucy. 2004. *Nietzsche and Jung: The Whole Self in the Union of Opposites.* Hove: Brunner-Routledge.

Hutter, Horst. 1989. "With the 'Nightwatchman of Greek Philosophy': Nietzsche's Way to Cynicism." In *Nietzsche and the Rhetoric of Nihilism,* ed. Tom Darby, Béla Egyed, and Ben Jones, 117–33. Ottawa: Carleton University Press.

Huxley, Aldous. 1929. *Do What You Will: Essays.* London: Chatto & Windus.

———. 1932/1972. *Brave New World.* Harmondsworth: Penguin.

———. 1950. *Music at Night.* London: Penguin.

———. 1953. *Time Must Have a Stop.* London: Vintage.

———. 1980. *The Human Situation: Lectures at Santa Barbara, 1959.* Edited by Piero Ferruci. London: Triad Granada.

———. 2000. *Complete Essays: Volume Two.* Edited by Robert S. Baker and James Sexton. Chicago: Ivan R. Dee.

———. 2001. *Complete Essays: Volume Three.* Edited by Robert S. Baker and James Sexton. Chicago: Ivan R. Dee.

———. 2013. *The Divine Within: Selected Writings on Enlightenment.* Edited by Jacqueline Hazard Bridgeman. New York: Harper Perennial.

Isherwood, Christopher. 1969. *Exhumations.* Harmondsworth: Penguin.

James, Henry. 1987. *The Critical Muse: Selected Literary Criticism.* Edited and with an introduction by Roger Gard. London: Penguin.

James, William. 1933. "The Gospel of Relaxation." In *On Vital Reserves,* 43–78. New York: Henry Holt.

Janaway, Christopher. 2006. "Naturalism and Genealogy." In *A Companion to Nietzsche,* ed. Keith Ansell-Pearson, 337–53. Malden, MA: Blackwell.

———. 2009. "Plato and the Arts." In *A Companion to Plato,* ed. Hugh H. Benson, 388–401. Malden, MA: Wiley Blackwell.

———. Forthcoming. "Why Naturalism? Translating *Homo natura* Back into Nietzsche's Text." *The Monist.*

Jaquet, Chantal. 2019. *Affects, Actions and Passions in Spinoza: The Unity of Body and Mind.* Translated by Tatiana Reznichenko. Edinburgh: Edinburgh University Press.

Jenkins, Scott. 2022. "Zarathustra's Contempt." In *Nietzsche's Thus Spoke Zarathustra: A Critical Guide,* ed. Keith Ansell-Pearson and Paul S. Loeb, 168–87. Cambridge: Cambridge University Press.

Johnson, Samuel. 1759/2009. *The History of Rasselas Prince of Abissinia.* Edited and with an introduction by Thomas Keymer. Oxford: Oxford World Classics.

Jung, C. G. 1983. *Selected Writings.* With an introduction by Anthony Storr. London: Fontana.

Kahn, H. Charles. 1979. *The Art and Thought of Heraclitus*. Cambridge: Cambridge University Press.

Kain, Philip J. 1983. "Nietzsche, Skepticism, and Eternal Recurrence." *Canadian Journal of Philosophy* 13, no. 3:365–87.

Kant, Immanuel. 1964. *Groundwork of the Metaphysics of Morals*. Translated by H. J. Paton. New York: Harper Torchbooks.

———. 1989. *Critique of Judgment*. Translated by Werner S. Pluhar. Indianapolis: Hackett.

———. 2006. *Anthropology from a Pragmatic Point of View*. Translated and edited by Robert B. Louden. Cambridge: Cambridge University Press.

Kast, Christina. 2017. "'Nur Narr! Nur Dichter!' Nietzsches Versuch einer Neubegründung der Philosophie in der Dichtung." In *Nietzsche als Dichter: Lyrik-Poetologie-Rezeption*, ed. Katharina Grätz and Sebastian Kaufmann, 377–401. Berlin: Walter de Gruyter.

Kateb, George. 2002. *Emerson and Self-Reliance*. Lanham, MD: Rowman & Littlefield.

Katsafanas, Paul. 2019. *The Nietzschean Self: Moral Psychology, Agency, and the Unconscious*. Oxford: Oxford University Press.

Kaufmann, Walter, ed. 1967. *On the Genealogy of Morals / Ecce Homo*, by Friedrich Nietzsche. New York: Random House.

———, ed. and trans. 1968. *The Portable Nietzsche*. London: Viking Penguin.

———. 1974. *Nietzsche: Philosopher, Psychologist, and Antichrist*. 4th ed. Princeton, NJ: Princeton University Press.

———. 1980a. "Nietzsche and Rilke." In *From Shakespeare to Existentialism*, 219–41. Princeton, NJ: Princeton University Press.

———. 1980b. "Philosophy versus Poetry." In *From Shakespeare to Existentialism*, 263–83. Princeton, NJ: Princeton University Press.

Kelly, Christopher. 2003. *Rousseau as Author*. Chicago: University of Chicago Press.

Kenny, Anthony. 2005. *Medieval Philosophy*. Oxford: Oxford University Press.

Kerényi, Carl. 1976. *Dionysos: Archetypal Image of Indestructible Life*. Translated by Ralph Mannheim. Princeton, NJ: Princeton University Press.

Kermode, Frank. 2000. *Shakespeare's Language*. London: Penguin.

Kerrigan, John. 1996. *Revenge Tragedy: Aeschylus to Armageddon*. Oxford: Oxford University Press.

Kierkegaard, Søren. 1844/2014. *The Concept of Anxiety*. Edited and translated by Alastair Hannay. London: Norton.

———. 1958. *The Journals of Kierkegaard, 1834–1854*. Edited and translated by Alexander Dru. London: Fontana.

Kirkland, Paul E. 2004. "Nietzsche's Honest Masks: From Truth to Nobility beyond Good and Evil." *Review of Politics* 66, no. 4 (Fall): 575–604.

Kolb, Martina. 2013. *Nietzsche, Freud, Benn, and the Azure Spell of Liguria*. Toronto: University of Toronto Press.

Krell, David Farrell. 2015. "Emerson—Nietzsche's Voluptuary?" *Comparative and Continental Philosophy* 7, no. 1:8–17.

Kundera, Milan. 2007a. "Bureaucracy According to Stifter." In *The Curtain: An Essay in Seven Parts*, 130–33. London: Faber & Faber.

———. 2007b. "In Praise of Jokes." In *The Curtain: An Essay in Seven Parts*, 75–77. London: Faber & Faber.

Lampert, Laurence. 1986. *Nietzsche's Teaching*. New Haven, CT: Yale University Press.

———. 1993. *Nietzsche and Modern Times: A Study of Bacon, Descartes, and Nietzsche.* New Haven, CT: Yale University Press.

———. 2001. *Nietzsche's Task: An Interpretation of Beyond Good and Evil.* New Haven, CT: Yale University Press.

Lane, Melissa. 2007. "Honesty as the Best Policy: Nietzsche on *Redlichkeit* and the Contrast between Stoic and Epicurean Strategies of the Self." In *Histories of Postmodernism*, ed. Mark Bevir, Jill Hargis, and Sara Rushing, 25–53. London: Routledge.

Lane Fox, Robin. 2015. *Augustine: Conversions and Confessions.* London: Penguin.

Lanier Anderson, R., and Rachel Cristy. 2017. "'What Is the Meaning of Our Cheerfulness?' Philosophy as a Way of Life in Nietzsche and Montaigne." *European Journal of Philosophy* 25:1514–49.

Large, Duncan. "'The Freest Writer': Nietzsche on Sterne." *The Shandean: An Annual Volume Devoted to Laurence Sterne and His Works* 7:9–29.

La Rocca, David. 2017. "Emerson Recomposed: Nietzsche's Use of His American Soul-Brother." In *Nietzsche and the Philosophers*, ed. Mark T. Conard, 211–31. London: Routledge.

La Rochefoucauld. 2007. *Collected Maxims and Other Reflections.* Translated and with an introduction by E. H. Blackmore, A. M. Blackmore, and Francine Gigère. Oxford: Oxford University Press.

Lawrence, D. H. 1931/1974. *Apocalypse.* London: Penguin.

———. 1936. *Phoenix: The Posthumous Papers of D. H. Lawrence.* Edited by Edward D. McDonald. London: William Heinemann.

———. 1986. *Selected Essays.* With an introduction by Richard Aldington. London: Penguin.

———. 1999. *Sketches of Etruscan Places and Other Italian Essays.* London: Penguin.

———. 2019. "Poetry of the Present." In *Life with a Capital L*, ed. Geoff Dyer, 77–83. London: Penguin.

Lawtoo, Nidesh. 2013. *The Phantom of the Ego: Modernism and the Mimetic Unconscious.* Ann Arbor: University of Michigan Press.

Le Guin, Ursula K. 2019. "Huxley's Bad Trip." In *Words Are My Matter: Writings on Life and Books*, 127–33. New York: Mariner Books.

Leiter, Brian. 2002. *Nietzsche on Morality.* London: Routledge.

Lemm, Vanessa. 2020. *Homo Natura: Nietzsche, Philosophical Anthropology and Biopolitics.* Edinburgh: Edinburgh University Press.

Lemmens, Willem. 2005. "The Melancholy of the Philosopher: Hume and Spinoza on Emotions and Wisdom." *Journal of Scottish Philosophy* 3, no. 1:47–65.

Leopardi, Giacomo. 2014. *Passions.* Translated by Tim Parks. New Haven, CT: Yale University Press.

Lesage, Alain René. 1715–35/1887. *Adventures of Gil Blas of Santillane.* London: Frederick Warne.

Lewis, Rhodri. 2017. *Hamlet and the Vision of Darkness.* Princeton, NJ: Princeton University Press.

Liébert, Georges. 2004. *Nietzsche and Music.* Translated by David Pellauer and Graham Parkes. Chicago: University of Chicago Press.

Liessmann, Konrad Paul. 2021. *Alle Lust will Ewigkeit: Mitternächtliche Versuchungen.* Vienna: Zsolnay.

Livingston, Donald W. 1998. *Philosophical Melancholy and Delirium: Hume's Pathology of Philosophy*. Chicago: University of Chicago Press.

Loeb, Paul S. 1998. "The Moment of Tragic Death in Nietzsche's Dionysian Doctrine of Eternal Recurrence: An Exegesis of Aphorism 341 of *The Gay Science*." *International Studies in Philosophy* 30, no. 3:131–44.

———. 2001. "Time, Power, and Superhumanity." *Journal of Nietzsche Studies* 21:27–47.

———. 2005. "Finding the *Übermensch* in Nietzsche's Genealogy of Morality." *Journal of Nietzsche Studies* 30:70–101.

———. 2006. "Identity and Eternal Recurrence." In *A Companion to Nietzsche*, ed. Keith Ansell-Pearson, 171–89. Malden, MA: Blackwell.

———. 2008. "Suicide, Meaning, and Redemption." In *Nietzsche on Time and History*, ed. Manuel Dries, 163–91. Berlin: Walter de Gruyter.

———. 2010. *The Death of Nietzsche's Zarathustra*. Cambridge: Cambridge University Press.

———. 2013. "Eternal Recurrence." In *The Oxford Handbook of Nietzsche*, ed. Ken Gemes and John Richardson, 645–75. Oxford: Oxford University Press.

———. 2018a. "The Colossal Moment in Nietzsche's *The Gay Science* §341." In *The Nietzschean Mind*, ed. Paul Katsafanas, 428–48. London: Routledge.

———. 2018b. "Nietzsche's Futurism." *Journal of Nietzsche Studies* 49, no. 2:253–59.

———. 2019a. "Genuine Philosophers, Value-Creation, and Will to Power: An Exegesis of Nietzsche's *Beyond Good and Evil* §211." In *Nietzsche's Metaphilosophy: The Nature, Method, and Aims of Philosophy*, ed. Paul S. Loeb and Matthew Meyer, 83–106. Cambridge: Cambridge University Press.

———. 2019b. "Nietzsche's Critique of Kant's Priestly Philosophy." In *Nietzsche and The Antichrist: Religion, Politics, and Culture in Late Modernity*, ed. Daniel Conway, 89–117. London: Bloomsbury Academic.

———. 2021. "Nietzsche's Heraclitean Doctrine of the Eternal Recurrence of the Same." *Nietzsche-Studien* 50:70–101.

———. 2022. "Nietzsche's Solution to the Philosophical Problem of Change." In *Thus Spoke Zarathustra: A Critical Guide*, ed. Keith Ansell-Pearson and Paul S. Loeb, 125–48. Cambridge: Cambridge University Press.

Loewald, Hans. 1988. *Sublimation: Inquiries into Theoretical Psychoanalysis*. New Haven, CT: Yale University Press.

Logan, Fraser. 2023. "*Ehrlichkeit* and *Parrhesia*: The Development of Nietzsche's Cynicism from *Schopenhauer as Educator* to *Ecce Homo*." *Journal of Nietzsche Studies* 54, no. 1:51–76.

Long, A. A. 2022. *Selfhood and Rationality in Ancient Greek Philosophy: From Heraclitus to Plotinus*. Oxford: Oxford University Press.

Longinus. 1965. *On the Sublime*. Translated by T. S. Dorsch. Harmondsworth: Penguin.

Lowell Young, Charles. 1941. *Emerson's Montaigne*. New York: Macmillan.

Löwith, Karl. 1997. *Nietzsche's Philosophy of the Eternal Recurrence of the Same*. Translated by J. Harvey Lomax. Berkeley and Los Angeles: University of California Press.

Lucie-Smith, Edward. 1991. *Symbolist Art*. London: Thames & Hudson.

Lukács, Georg. 1976. *The Historical Novel*. Translated by Hannah Mitchell and Stanley Mitchell. London: Peregrine.

Malebranche, Nicolas. 1997. *The Search after Truth*. Translated by Thomas M. Lennon. Cambridge: Cambridge University Press.

Manschot, Henk. 2021. *Nietzsche and the Earth: Biography, Ecology, Politics*. Translated by Liz Walters. London: Bloomsbury Academic.

Marsden, Jill. 2005. "Sensing the Overhuman." *Journal of Nietzsche Studies* 30:102–14.

———. 2006. "Nietzsche and the Art of the Aphorism." In *A Companion to Nietzsche*, ed. Keith Ansell-Pearson, 22–39. Malden, MA: Blackwell.

Mason, Hadyn. 1995. "Voltaire versus Shakespeare: The *Lettre à L'Académie française* (1776)." *Journal for Eighteenth-Century Studies* 18, no. 2 (September): 173–84.

Maupassant, Guy de. 1888/2008. *Afloat*. Translated by Douglas Parmée. New York: New York Review of Books.

Maurois, André. 1940. *The Art of Living*. London: English Universities Press.

———. 1970. *From Proust to Camus: Profiles of Modern French Writers*. Translated by Carl Morse and Renaud Bruce. London: Weidenfel and Nicolson.

May, Simon. 2019. *Love: A New Understanding of an Ancient Emotion*. Oxford: Oxford University Press.

McAuliffe, Mary. 2020. *Paris, City of Dreams*. Lanham, MD: Rowman & Littlefield.

Meakins, William. 2014. "Nietzsche, Carlyle, and Perfectionism." *Journal of Nietzsche Studies* 45, no. 3:258–78.

Melville, Herman. 2018. "Hawthorne and His *Mosses*." In *Moby-Dick*, ed. Hershel Parker, 544–59. New York: Norton.

Mendelsohn, Daniel. 2020. *Three Rings: A Tale of Exile, Narrative and Fate*. London: William Collins.

Mérimée, Prosper. 1989. "The Etruscan Vase." In *Carmen and Other Stories*, trans. Nicholas Jotcham, 93–116. Oxford: Oxford University Press.

Merleau-Ponty, Maurice. 1964. *Signs*. Translated by Richard C. McCleary. Evanston, IL: Northwestern University Press.

Meyer, Matthew. 2019. "The Dialectics of Nietzsche's Metaphilosophies." In *Nietzsche's Metaphilosophy: The Nature, Method, and Aims of Philosophy*, ed. Paul S. Loeb and Matthew Meyer, 22–42. Cambridge: Cambridge University Press.

———. 2022. "Nietzsche's Naturalism and *Thus Spoke Zarathustra*." In *Thus Spoke Zarathustra: A Critical Guide*, ed. Keith Ansell-Pearson and Paul S. Loeb, 104–25. Cambridge: Cambridge University Press.

Meyer, Michel. 2000. *Philosophy and the Passions: Toward a History of Human Nature*. Translated by Robert F. Barsky. University Park: Penn State University Press.

Michael, John. 1988. *Emerson and Skepticism: The Cipher of the World*. Baltimore: Johns Hopkins University Press.

Michalski, Krzysztof. 2012. *The Flame of Eternity: An Interpretation of Nietzsche's Thought*. Princeton, NJ: Princeton University Press.

Middleton, Christopher, ed. and trans. 1996. *Selected Letters of Friedrich Nietzsche*. Indianapolis: Hackett.

Mikics, David. 2003. *The Romance of Individualism in Emerson and Nietzsche*. Athens: Ohio University Press.

Mill, J. S. 1833/1999. "What Is Poetry?" In *The Broadway Anthology of Victorian Poetry and Poetic Theory*, ed. Thomas J. Collins and Vivienne J. Rundle, 1212–20. Peterborough, ON: Broadway.

Miller, Charles A. 1973. "Nietzsche's Discovery of Dostoevsky." *Nietzsche-Studien* 2:202–57.

———. 1975. "The Nihilist as Tempter-Redeemer: Dostoevsky's 'Man-God' in Nietzsche's Notebooks." *Nietzsche-Studien* 4:165–226.

Miller, Jon. 2015. *Spinoza and the Stoics*. Cambridge: Cambridge University Press.

Miner, C. Robert. 2017. *Nietzsche and Montaigne*. Basingstoke: Palgrave Macmillan.

———. 2021. *Nietzsche's Gay Science*. Edinburgh: Edinburgh University Press.

Mitcheson, Katrina. 2015. "The Experiment of Incorporating Unbounded Truth." In *Nietzsche's Free Spirit Philosophy*, ed. Rebecca Bamford, 139–57. London: Rowman & Littlefield International.

———. 2016. "Scepticism and Self-Transformation in Nietzsche—on the Uses and Disadvantages of a Comparison to Pyrrhonian Scepticism." *British Journal of the History of Philosophy* 25, no. 1:63–83. https://doi.org/10.1080/09608788.2016.1225564.

Moles, Alistair. 1990. *Nietzsche's Philosophy of Nature and Cosmology*. New York: Peter Lang.

Mollison, James A. 2019. "Nietzsche contra Stoicism: Naturalism and Value, Suffering and *Amor fati*." *Inquiry* 62, no. 1:93–115.

Montaigne, Michel de. 2003. *The Complete Works*. Translated by Donald M. Frame. New York: Everyman's Library.

Montinari, Mazzino. 2003. *Reading Nietzsche*. Translated by Greg Whitlock. Urbana: University of Illinois Press.

Moriarty, Michael. 2011. *Disguised Vices: Theories of Virtue in Early Modern French Thought*. Oxford: Oxford University Press.

Morson, Gary Saul. 2012. *The Long and Short of It: From Aphorism to Novel*. Stanford, CA: Stanford University Press.

Müller-Lauter, Wolfgang. 1999. *Nietzsche: His Philosophy of Contradictions and the Contradictions of His Philosophy*. Translated by David J. Parent. Urbana: University of Illinois Press.

Mumford, Lewis. 1926/1953. *Golden Day: A Study in American Literature and Culture*. New York. Dover.

———. 1950. *Man as Interpreter*. New York: Harcourt, Brace.

———. 1952. *The Conduct of Life*. London: Secker & Warburg.

———. 1954. *In the Name of Sanity*. New York: Harcourt, Brace.

———. 1967. *The Myth of the Machine*. New York: Harcourt, Brace.

Murdoch, Iris. 1970. *The Sovereignty of Good*. London: Routledge & Kegan Paul.

———. 1983. *The Philosopher's Pupil*. London: Penguin.

———. 1997. *Existentialists and Mystics: Writings on Philosophy and Literature*. Edited by Peter Conradi. London: Penguin.

Murray, Peter Durno. 2018. *Nietzsche and the Dionysian: A Compulsion to Ethics*. Leiden: Brill Rodopi.

Nabokov, Vladimir. 1981. *Lectures on Russian Literature*. Edited by Fredson Bowers. New York: Harcourt.

———. 1983. *Lectures on Dox Quixote*. Edited by Fredson Bowers. San Diego: Harcourt Brace Jovanovich.

Nadler, Steven. 2020. *Think Least of Death: Spinoza on How to Live and How to Die*. Princeton, NJ: Princeton University Press.

Naess, Arne. 2008. *Ecology of Wisdom*. Edited by Alan Drengson and Bill Devall. London: Penguin.

Napier, A David. 1986. *Masks, Transformation, and Paradox*. Berkeley and Los Angeles: University of California Press.

Nichols, Mary P. 2009. *Socrates on Friendship and Community: Reflections on Plato's Symposium, Phaedrus, and Lysis*. Cambridge: Cambridge University Press.

Nicoll, Maurice. 1952. *Living Time and the Integration of the Life*. London: Vincent Stuart.

Nietzsche, Friedrich. 1911. "The Relation of Schopenhauer's Philosophy to German Culture." In *The Complete Works of Friedrich Nietzsche*, ed. Oscar Levy, 2:65–69. London: T. N. Foulis.

———. 1962. *Philosophy in the Tragic Age of the Greeks*. Translated by Marianne Cowan. Washington, DC: Regnery.

———. 1967–. *Werke: Kritische Gesamtausgabe*. Edited by Giorgio Colli and Mazzino Montinari. 40 vols. Berlin: Walter de Gruyter.

———. 1968. *The Will to Power*. Translated by Walter Kaufmann and R. J. Hollingdale. New York: Random House.

———. 1969. *Thus Spoke Zarathustra*. Translated by R. J. Hollingdale. London: Penguin.

———. 1974. *The Gay Science*. Translated by Walter Kaufmann. New York: Random House.

———. 1975–84. *Sämtliche Briefe: Kritische Studienausgabe*. Edited by Giorgio Colli and Mazzino Montinari. 8 vols. Berlin: Walter de Gruyter.

———. 1979. *Philosophy and Truth: Selections from Nietzsche's Notebooks of the Early 1870s*. Translated by Daniel Breazeale. Atlantic Highlands, NJ: Humanities Press International.

———. 1981. *Nietzsche Briefwechsel: Kritische Gesamtausgabe*. Edited by Giorgio Colli and Mazzino Montinari. Berlin: Walter de Gruyter.

———. 1984. *Dithyrambs of Dionysus*. Translated by R. J. Hollingdale. London: Anvil.

———. 1967–88. *Sämtliche Werke: Kritische Studienausgabe*. Edited by Giorgio Colli and Mazzino Montinari. 14 vols. Berlin: Walter de Gruyter; Munich: Deutscher Taschenbuch.

———. 1989. "On the Poet." In *Friedrich Nietzsche on Rhetoric and Language*, ed. Sander L. Gilman, Carole Blair, and David J. Parent, 243–44. Oxford: Oxford University Press.

———. 1991. *Human, All Too Human*. Translated by R. J. Hollingdale. 2 vols. Cambridge: Cambridge University Press.

———. 1995a. *Human, All Too Human*. Translated by Gary Handwerk. Stanford, CA: Stanford University Press.

———. 1995b. *Unfashionable Observations*. Translated by Richard T. Gray. Stanford, CA: Stanford University Press.

———. 1995c. *Unpublished Fragments from the Period of "Unfashionable Observations"*. Translated by Richard T. Gray. Stanford, CA: Stanford University Press.

———. 1999. *The Birth of Tragedy*. Translated by Ronald Speirs. Cambridge: Cambridge University Press.

———. 2001. *The Pre-Platonic Philosophers*. Translated and edited by Greg Whitlock. Urbana: University of Illinois Press.

———. 2003. *Writings from the Late Notebooks*. Translated by Kate Sturge. Cambridge: Cambridge University Press.

———. 2004. *On the Future of Our Educational Institutions*. Translated by Michael W. Grenke. South Bend, IN: St. Augustine's.

———. 2005a. *"The Anti-Christ", "Ecce Homo", "Twilight of the Idols" and Other Writings*. Translated by Judith Norman. Cambridge: Cambridge University Press.

———. 2005b. *Thus Spoke Zarathustra*. Translated by Graham Parkes. Oxford: Oxford University Press.

———. 2006. "European Nihilism (Notebook of 1887)." In *The Nietzsche Reader*, ed. Keith Ansell-Pearson and Duncan Large, 385–90. Malden, MA: Blackwell.

———. 2007. *Ecce Homo*. Translated by Duncan Large. Oxford: Oxford University Press.

———. 2011. *Dawn: Thoughts on the Presumptions of Morality*. Translated by Brittain Smith. Stanford, CA: Stanford University Press.

———. 2013a. *Human, All Too Human II and Unpublished Fragments from the Period of "Human, All Too Human II" (Spring 1878–Fall 1879)*. Translated by Richard T. Gray. Stanford, CA: Stanford University Press.

———. 2013b. *"Mixed Opinions and Maxims" and "The Wanderer and His Shadow"*. Translated by Gary Handwerk. Stanford, CA: Stanford University Press.

———. 2014. *Beyond Good and Evil*. Translated by Adrian Del Caro. Stanford, CA: Stanford University Press.

———. 2017a. "Homer's Contest." In *On the Genealogy of Morality*, trans. Carole Diethe, 177–85. Cambridge: Cambridge University Press.

———. 2017b. *On the Genealogy of Morality*. Translated by Carole Diethe. Cambridge: Cambridge University Press.

———. 2019. *Unpublished Fragments from the Period of "Thus Spoke Zarathustra" (Summer 1882–Winter 1883/84)*. Translated by Paul S. Loeb and David F. Tinsley. Stanford University Press.

———. 2020. *Unpublished Fragments (Spring 1885–Spring 1886)*. Translated by Adrian Del Caro. Stanford, CA: Stanford University Press.

———. 2021a. *The Case of Wagner, Twilight of the Idols, The Antichrist, Ecce Homo, Dionysus Dithyrambs, Nietzsche contra Wagner*. Translated by Carol Diethe et al. Stanford, CA: Stanford University Press.

———. 2021b. *Unpublished Fragments from the Period of "Human, All Too Human I" (Winter 1874/75–Winter 1877/78)*. Translated by Gary Handwerk. Stanford, CA: Stanford University Press.

———. 2022. *Unpublished Fragments from the Period of "Thus Spoke Zarathustra" (Spring 1884–Winter 1884/85)*. Translated by Paul S. Loeb and David F. Tinsley. Stanford, CA: Stanford University Press.

———. 2023a. *The Joyful Science / Idylls from Messina / Unpublished Fragments*. Translated by Adrian Del Caro. Stanford, CA: Stanford University Press.

———. 2023b. *Unpublished Fragments from the Period of "Dawn" (Winter 1879/80–Spring 1881)*. Translated by J. M. Baker Jr. and Christiane Hertel. Stanford, CA: Stanford University Press.

———. Forthcoming. *Thus Spoke Zarathustra*. Translated by Paul S. Loeb and David F. Tinsley. Stanford, CA: Stanford University Press.

Nozick, Robert. 1989. *The Examined Life: Philosophical Meditations*. New York: Simon & Schuster.

Nussbaum, Martha. 1994. "Pity and Mercy: Nietzsche's Stoicism." In *Nietzsche, Genealogy, Morality*, ed. Richard Schacht, 139–67. Berkeley and Los Angeles: University of California Press.

Nuttall, A. D. 2007. *Shakespeare the Thinker*. New Haven, CT: Yale University Press.

O'Keefe, Tim. 2010. *Epicureanism*. Durham: Acumen.

Ortega y Gasset, José. 1914/1961. *Meditations on Quixote*. Translated by Evelyn Rugg and Diego Marín with an introduction by Julián Marías. New York: Norton.

———. 1957/2012. *On Love: Aspects of a Single Theme*. Translated by Toby Talbot. Mansfield Centre, CT: Martino.

Orwell, George. 1974. *Inside the Whale and Other Essays*. Harmondsworth: Penguin.

Ouspensky, P. D. 1934/1984. *A New Model of the Universe*. London: Arkana.

Otto, Walter F. 1965. *Dionysus: Myth and Cult*. Translated by Robert B. Palmer. Bloomington: Indiana University Press.

———. 1975. *Epikur*. Stuttgart: Ernst Klett.

Ovid. 1955. *Metamorphoses*. Translated by Rolf Humphries. Bloomington: Indiana University Press.

Ozick, Cynthia. 2000. *Quarrel and Quandary*. New York: Vintage International.

Page, Jeremy. 2019. "Nietzsche on Honesty." *The Monist* 102:349–68.

Panaioti, Antoine. 2019. "Nietzsche as Metaphilosopher." In *Nietzsche's Metaphilosophy: The Nature, Method, and Aims of Philosophy*, ed. Paul S. Loeb and Matthew Meyer, 42–63. Cambridge: Cambridge University Press.

Parkes, Graham. 1987. "Facing the Masks: Persona and Self in Nietzsche, Rilke and Mishima." *Mosaic* 20, no. 3:65–79.

———. 1994. *Composing the Soul: Reaches of Nietzsche's Psychology*. Chicago: University of Chicago Press.

Parr, Jamie. 2023. "'What Do I Matter!': Nietzsche on Pascal, Self-Obsession, and Good Cheer." In *Joy and Laughter in Nietzsche's Philosophy*, ed. Paul E. Kirkland and Michael J. McNeal, 105–23. London: Bloomsbury Academic.

Pater, Walter. 2018. *Selected Essays*. Edited by Alex Wong. Manchester: Carcarnet.

Patton, Paul. 1991. "Postmodern Subjectivity: The Problem of the Actor (Zarathustra and the Butler)." *Social Analysis: The International Journal of Anthropology* 30:32–41.

Paz, Octavio. 1973. *The Bow and the Lyre*. Translated by Ruth L. C. Simms. Austin: University of Texas Press.

———. 1986. *On Poets and Others*. Translated by Michael Schmidt. New York: Seaver.

Pearson, Roger. 1988. *Stendhal's Violin: A Novelist and His Reader*. Oxford: Clarendon.

———. 2016. *Unacknowledged Legislators: The Poet as Lawgiver in Post-Revolutionary France*. Oxford: Oxford University Press.

———. 2021. *The Beauty of Baudelaire: The Poet as Alternative Lawgiver*. Oxford: Oxford University Press.

Peretz, Eyal. 2013. *Dramatic Experiments: Life according to Diderot*. Albany: State University of New York Press.

Perler, Dominik. 2018. *Feelings Transformed: Philosophical Theories of the Emotions, 1270–1670*. Translated by Tony Crawford. Oxford: Oxford University Press.

Pestalozzi, Karl. 1978. "Nietzsches Baudelaire-Rezeption." *Nietzsche-Studien* 7:158–78.

Phillips, Adam. 1998. *The Beast in the Nursery*. London: Faber & Faber.

———. 2019. *In Writing: Essays on Literature*. London: Penguin.

Pippin, Robert B. 2010. *Nietzsche, Psychology, and First Philosophy*. Chicago: University of Chicago Press.

Plato. 1968. *The Republic*. Translated by Allan Bloom. New York: Basic.

———. 1993. *The Last Days of Socrates*. Translated by Hugh Tredennick and Harold Tarrant. London: Penguin.

———. 1995. *Phaedrus*. Translated and with an introduction by Alexander Nehamas and Paul Woodruff. Indianapolis: Hackett.

Pocock, Gordon. 1973. *Corneille and Racine: Problems of Tragic Form*. London: Cambridge University Press.

Poe, Edgar Allan. 1986. "Philosophy of Composition." In *The Fall of the House of Usher and Other Writings*, ed. David Galloway, 430–43. London: Penguin.

Pointner, Frank Erik, and Achim Geisenhanslüke. 2004. "The Reception of Byron in German-Speaking Lands." In *The Reception of Byron in Europe*, ed. Richard Cardwell, 3:236–69. London: Thoemmes Continuum.

Pope, Alexander. 1969. *Poetry and Prose of Alexander Pope*. Edited by Aubrey Williams. Boston: Houghton Mifflin.

Porter, James I. 2006. "Nietzsche and the 'Problem of Socrates.'" In *A Companion to Socrates*, ed. Sara Ahbel-Rappe and Rachana Kamtekar, 406–25. Oxford: Blackwell.

———. 2020. "Living on the Edge: Self and World *in Extremis* in Roman Philosophy." *Classical Antiquity* 39, no. 2:225–83.

———. 2023. "Nietzsche *Ludens*: Subversions of Literature and Philosophy in the Later Writings." In *Nietzsche and Literary Studies*, ed. James I. Porter, 142–65. Cambridge: Cambridge University Press.

Potkay, Adam. 2022. *Hope: A Literary History*. Cambridge: Cambridge University Press.

Prange, Martine. 2012. "Beyond Good and Evil." In *A Companion to Friedrich Nietzsche*, ed. Paul Bishop, 232–51. Rochester, NY: Camden House.

———. 2013. *Nietzsche, Wagner, Europe*. Berlin: Walter de Gruyter.

Prendergast, Christopher. 1995. *Paris and the Nineteenth Century*. Oxford: Blackwell.

Price, Martin. 1964. *To the Palace of Wisdom: Studies in Energy and Order from Dryden to Blake*. Carbondale: Southern Illinois University Press.

Proust, Marcel. 1997. *Proust on Art and Literature*. Translated by Sylvia Townsend Warner. New York: Carroll & Graf.

———. 2011. *On Reading*. Edited and translated by Damion Seals. London: Hesperus.

Racine, Jean. 1970. *Iphigenia/Phaedra/Athaliah*. Translated by John Cairncross. London: Penguin.

Ragg-Kirkby, Helena. 2002. "'Warum nun dieses?' *Verblendung* and *Verschulden* in the Stories of Adalbert Stifter." *German Life and Letters* 55, no. 1:24–41.

Ralegh, Walter, Sir. 1984. *Selected Writings*. With an introduction by Gerald Hammond. Harmondsworth: Penguin.

Rancière, Jacques. 2020. *The Edges of Fiction*. Translated by Steve Corcoran. Cambridge: Polity.

———. 2022. *Modern Times: Temporality in Art and Politics*. Translated by Gregory Elliott. London: Verso.

Ransome, Arthur. 1913. "Friedrich Nietzsche: An Essay in Comprehension." In *Portraits and Speculations*. London: Macmillan.

Read, Herbert. 1953. *The True Voice of Feeling: Studies in English Romantic Poetry*. London: Faber & Faber.

Reginster, Bernard. 2006. *The Affirmation of Life: Nietzsche on Overcoming Nihilism*. Cambridge, MA: Harvard University Press.

———. 2013. "Honesty and Curiosity in Nietzsche's Free Spirits." *Journal of the History of Philosophy* 51, no. 3:441–63.

Richardson, John. 1996. *Nietzsche's New System*. Oxford: Oxford University Press.

———. 2004. *Nietzsche's New Darwinism*. Oxford: Oxford University Press.

Rilke, Rainer Maria. 2004. *On Love and Other Difficulties.* Translated by John L. Mood. New York: Norton.
———. 2011. *Letters to a Young Poet.* Translated by Charlie Louth. London: Penguin.
Robertson, Michael. 2012. "Nietzsche's Poet-Philosopher: Towards a Poetics of Response-ability, Possibility, and the Future." *Mosaic* 45, no. 1:187–202.
Rosen, Stanley. 2004. *The Mask of Enlightenment: Nietzsche's Zarathustra.* New Haven, CT: Yale University Press.
Rousseau, Jean-Jacques. 1995. *Confessions.* Translated by Christopher Kelly. Hanover, NH: University Press of New England.
———. 1782/2000. *Reveries of a Solitary Walker.* Edited by Christopher Kelly. Translated by Charles E. Butterworth, Alexandra Cook, and Terence E. Marshall. Hanover, NH: University of Press of New England.
———. 2010. *Emile; or, On Education.* Translated and edited by Christopher Kelly and Allan Bloom. Hanover, NH: Dartmouth College Press.
Russell, Bertrand. 1991. *Sceptical Essays.* London: Routledge.
———. 1996a. *In Praise of Idleness and Other Essays.* London: Routledge.
———. 1996b. *Why I Am Not a Christian.* London: Routledge.
Russell, Daniel C. 2012. *Happiness for Humans.* Oxford: Oxford University Press.
Sachs, Aaron. 2022. *Up from the Depths: Herman Melville, Lewis Mumford, and Rediscovery in Dark Times.* Princeton, NJ: Princeton University Press.
Saint-Exupéry, Antoine de. 1995. *Wind, Sand and Stars.* Translated by William Rees. London: Penguin.
Sainte-Beuve, Charles Augustin. 1924. *Selections from Sainte-Beuve.* Edited by Arthur Tilley. London: Cambridge University Press.
Salomé, Lou. 2001. *Nietzsche.* Edited and translated by Siegfried Mandel. Urbana: University of Illinois Press.
Salter, William Mackintire. 1915. "Nietzsche's Superman." *Journal of Philosophy, Psychology and Scientific Methods* 12, no. 16:421–38.
———. 1917. *Nietzsche the Thinker: A Study.* New York: Henry Holt.
Sand, George. 1956. *Winter in Majorca.* Translated by Robert Graves. Mallorca: Valldemosa Edition.
Santaniello, Weaver. 2005. *Zarathustra's Last Supper: Nietzsche's Eight Higher Men.* Aldershot: Ashgate.
Santayana, George. 1896/1955. *The Sense of Beauty: Being the Outline of Aesthetic Theory.* New York: Dover.
———. 1900/1989. *Interpretations of Poetry and Religion.* Cambridge, MA: MIT Press.
———. 1910/2019. *Three Philosophical Poets: Lucretius, Dante, and Goethe.* Edited by Kellie Dawson and David E. Spiech. Cambridge, MA: MIT Press.
———. 1913/1940. *Winds of Doctrine: Studies in Contemporary Opinion.* London: J. M. Dent.
———. 1916/1939. *Egotism in German Philosophy.* London: J. M. Dent.
———. 1922/1967. *Soliloquies in England and Later Soliloquies.* Ann Arbor: University of Michigan Press.
———. 1923/1955. *Scepticism and Animal Faith.* New York: Dover.
———. 1936. *Obiter Scripta: Lectures, Essays and Reviews.* Edited by Justus Buchler and Benjamin Schwartz. London: Constable.
———. 1940. *The Realm of Spirit.* London: Constable.
———. 1942. *Realms of Being.* 1-vol. ed. New York: Charles Scribner's Sons.

———. 1951/2017. *Dominations and Powers*. London: Routledge.

———. 1964. "The Philosophy of Travel." *Virginia Quarterly Review* 40, no. 1:1–10.

———. 1968. *Selected Critical Writings of George Santayana: Volume One*. Edited by Norman Henfrey. Cambridge: Cambridge University Press.

———. 1998. *The Genteel Tradition: Nine Essays*. Edited by Douglas L. Wilson. Lincoln: University of Nebraska Press.

———. 2009. *The Essential Santayana: Selected Writings*. Edited by the Santayana Edition. Bloomington: Indiana University Press.

———. 2011. *The Life of Reason: Introduction and Reason in Common Sense*. Edited by Marianne S. Wokeck and Martin A. Coleman. Cambridge, MA: MIT Press.

———. 2016. *Reason in Science*. Edited by Marianne S. Wokeck and Martin A. Coleman. Cambridge, MA: MIT Press.

Sartre, Jean-Paul. 1938. *La nausée*. Paris: Gallimard.

———. 1965. *Nausea*. Translated by Robert Baldick. Harmondsworth: Penguin.

———. 2023. *The Family Idiot: Gustave Flaubert, 1821–1857*. Translated by Carol Cosman. Edited and abridged by Joseph S. Catalano. Chicago: University of Chicago Press.

Schaberg, William H. 1995. *The Nietzsche Canon: A Publication History and Bibliography*. Chicago: University of Chicago Press.

Schacht, Richard. 2023. *Nietzsche's Kind of Philosophy*. Chicago: University of Chicago Press.

Scheler, Max. 1992. *On Feeling, Knowing, and Valuing*. Edited by Harold J. Bershady. Chicago: University of Chicago Press.

Schiller, Friedrich. 2001. "On the Sublime." In *Essays*, ed. Walter Hinderer and Daniel O. Dahlstrom, 22–45. New York: Continuum.

Schopenhauer, Arthur. 1818/2010. *The World as Will and Representation: Volume 1*. Translated by Judith Norman, Alistair Welchman, and Christopher Janaway. Cambridge: Cambridge University Press.

———. 1844/2018. *The World as Will and Representation: Volume 2*. Translated by Judith Norman, Alistair Welchman, and Christopher Janaway. Cambridge: Cambridge University Press.

———. 1851/2014. *Parerga and Paralipomena: Volume 1*. Translated and edited by Sabine Roehr and Christopher Janaway. Cambridge: Cambridge University Press.

———. 1851/2015. *Parerga and Paralipomena: Volume 2*. Translated and edited by Adrian Del Caro and Christopher Janaway. Cambridge: Cambridge University Press.

Schulte, Natalie. 2017. "Nur Narr, Nur Dichter? Das *Lied der Schwermuth* in Nietzsches *Zarathustra*." In *Nietzsche als Dichter: Lyrik-Poetologie-Rezeption*, ed. Katharina Grätz and Sebastian Kaufmann, 273–97. Berlin: Walter de Gruyter.

Seaton, James. 2014. *Literary Criticism from Plato to Postmodernism: The Humanistic Alternative*. Cambridge: Cambridge University Press.

Sebald, W. G. 1994. "Bis an den Rand der Natur: Versuch über Stifter." In *Die Beschreibung des Unglücks: Zur österreichischen Literatur von Stifter bis Handke*, 15–38. Frankfurt a.M.: Fischer.

Segal, Charles. 1989. *Orpheus: The Myth of the Poet*. Baltimore: Johns Hopkins University Press.

Sellars, John. 2009. *The Art of Living: The Stoics on the Nature and Function of Philosophy*. London: Bloomsbury Academic.

Seneca. 2015. *Letters on Ethics*. Translated by Margaret Garver and A. A. Long. Chicago: University of Chicago Press.

Serini, Lorenzo. 2024. "Skepticism as a Truth-Seeking Practice: The Pyrrhonists, Diderot, and Regulative Epistemology." In *Practices of Truth in Philosophy: Historical and Comparative Perspectives*, ed. Pietro Gori and Lorenzo Serini, 103–28. New York: Routledge.

Serres, Michel. 1997. *The Troubadour of Knowledge*. Translated by Sheila Faria Glaser with William Paulson. Ann Arbor: University of Michigan Press.

Shakespeare, William. 2005. *The Complete Works*. Edited by John Jowett, William Montgomery, Gary Taylor, and Stanley Wells. 2nd ed. Oxford: Oxford University Press.

Shapiro, Gary. 2016. *Nietzsche's Earth: Great Events, Great Politics*. Chicago: University of Chicago Press.

Shapiro, James. 2005. *1599: A Year in the Life of William Shakespeare*. London: Faber & Faber.

———. 2010. *Contested Will: Who Wrote Shakespeare?* London: Faber & Faber.

Sharpe, Matthew, and Michael Ure. 2021. *Philosophy as a Way of Life: History, Dimensions, Directions*. London: Bloomsbury Academic.

Shelley, Percy Bysshe. 2003. "In Defence of Poetry." In *The Major Works*, ed. Zachery Leader and Michael O'Neill, 674–702. Oxford: Oxford University Press.

Shestov, Lev. 1900/1969. *Dostoevsky, Tolstoy, and Nietzsche*. Translated by Bernard Martin and Spencer Roberts. Athens: Ohio University Press.

Simmel, Georg. 1986. *Schopenhauer and Nietzsche*. Translated by Helmut Loiskandl, Deena Weinstein, and Michael Weinstein. Amherst: University of Massachusetts Press.

Sjögren, Christine Oertel. 1972. *The Marble Statue as Idea: Collected Essays on Adalbert Stifter's Der Nachsommer*. Chapel Hill: University of North Carolina Press.

Slater, Joseph, ed. 1964. *The Correspondence of Emerson and Carlyle*. New York: Columbia University Press.

Sloterdijk, Peter. 1989. "Eurotaoism." In *Nietzsche and the Rhetoric of Nihilism*, ed. Tom Darby, Béla Egyed, Ben Jones, 99–117. Ottawa: Carleton University Press.

———. 2013. *Nietzsche Apostle*. Translated by Steven Corcoran. Los Angeles: Semiotext(e).

Small, Robin. 2006. "Nietzsche and Cosmology." In *A Companion to Nietzsche*, ed. Keith Ansell-Pearson, 189–208. Malden, MA: Blackwell.

———. 2010. *Time and Becoming in Nietzsche's Thought*. London: Continuum.

Smith, Adam. 2009. *The Theory of Moral Sentiments*. Edited by Ryan Patrick Hanley. London: Penguin.

Solomon, Robert C. 2003. *Living with Nietzsche: What the Great "Immoralist" Has to Teach Us*. Oxford: Oxford University Press.

Soloviev, V. S. 2015. "The Idea of a Superman." In *Politics, Law, Morality*, ed. and trans. Vladimir Woznuik, 255–63. New Haven, CT: Yale University Press.

Sorgner, Stefan. 2020. *On Transhumanism*. Translated by Spencer Hawkins. University Park: Penn State University Press.

Spinoza, B. 1985. *The Collected Works of Spinoza: Volume 1*. Edited and translated by Edwin Curley. Princeton, NJ: Princeton University Press.

———. 1992. *Ethics*. Translated by Samuel Shirley. Indianapolis: Hackett.

Sprigge, T. L. S. 1984. *Theories of Existence*. Harmondsworth: Penguin.

Spuybroek, Lars. 2020. *Grace and Gravity*. London: Bloomsbury Academic.

Stack, George. 1992. *Nietzsche and Emerson*. Athens: Ohio University Press.

Stapledon, Olaf. 1939. *Philosophy and Living*. 2 vols. London: Pelican.

Steiner, George. 1967. *Tolstoy or Dostoevsky: An Essay in Contrast*. Harmondsworth: Penguin.

———. 1997. *Errata: An Examined Life*. London: Weidenfeld & Nicolson.

———. 2003. *Lessons of the Masters*. Cambridge, MA: Harvard University Press.

Stellino, Paolo. 2015. *Nietzsche and Dostoevsky: On the Verge of Nihilism*. Bern: Peter Lang.

Stendhal. 1957. *On Love*. Translated by Gilbert Sale and Suzanne Sale. London: Penguin.

———. 1962. *Racine and Shakespeare*. Translated by Guy Daniels. Richmond: Crowell-Collier.

———. 1973. *The Life of Henry Brulard*. Translated by Jean Stewart and C. J. G. Knight. London: Penguin.

———. 1975. *Memoirs of an Egotist*. Translated by David Ellis. New York: Horizon.

———. 2011. *Letters to Pauline*. Translated by Andrew Brown. London: Hesperus Classics.

Stepenberg, Maïa. 2019. *Against Nihilism: Nietzsche Meets Dostoevsky*. Montreal: Black Rose.

Stern, J. P. 1971. *Idylls and Realities: Studies in Nineteenth-Century Literature*. London: Methuen.

Stevens, Wallace. 1997. "A Collect of Philosophy." In *Wallace Stevens: Collected Poetry and Prose*, 850–67. New York: Library of America.

Stifter, Adalbert. 1994. *Bunte Steine*. Stuttgart: Reclam.

———. 2005. *Nachsommer*. Stuttgart: Reclam.

———. 2009. *Indian Summer*. Translated by Wendell Frye. Bern: Peter Lang.

———. 2021. *Motley Stones*. Translated by Isabel Fargo Cole. New York: New York Review Books.

Strauss, Leo. 2017. *On Nietzsche's "Thus Spoke Zarathustra"*. Chicago: University of Chicago Press.

Sussman, Henry. 2007. *Idylls of the Wanderer*. New York: Fordham University Press.

Swales, Martin, and Erika Swales. 1984. *Adalbert Stifter: A Critical Study*. Cambridge: Cambridge University Press.

Swart, Koenraad W. 1964. *The Sense of Decadence in Nineteenth Century France*. The Hague: Martinus Nijhoff.

Swenson, Joseph. 2014. "Sublimation and Affirmation in Nietzsche's Psychology." *Journal of Nietzsche Studies* 45, no. 2:196–209.

Symons, Arthur. 1899/1919/2014. *The Symbolist Movement in Literature*. Manchester: Carcanet. First published in 1899, and then expanded in 1919.

———. 1920. *Charles Baudelaire: A Study*. London: Elkin Mathews.

Taub, Liba. 2009. "Cosmology and Meteorology." In *The Cambridge Companion to Epicureanism*, ed. James Warren, 105–24. Cambridge: Cambridge University Press.

Taylor, Charles. 2024. *Cosmic Connections: Poetry in the Age of Disenchantment*. Cambridge, MA: Harvard University Press.

Terry, Richard. 2011. "Philosophical Melancholy." In *Melancholy Experience in Literature of the Long Eighteenth Century*, ed. Allan Ingram, Stuart Sim, Clark Lawlor, Richard Terry, John Baker, and Leigh Wetherall Dickson, 54–82. Basingstoke: Palgrave Macmillan.

Thatcher, David S. 1974. "Nietzsche and Byron." *Nietzsche-Studien* 3:130–52.

Thoreau, Henry David. 1998. *A Week on the Concord and Merrimack Rivers*. London: Penguin.

———. 2007. "Thomas Carlyle and His Works." In *Henry David Thoreau: Walden, The Maine Woods, Collected Essays and Poems*, 691–729. New York: Library of America.

Tillich, Paul. 1962. *The Courage to Be*. London: Collins.

Tuncel, Yunus. 2014. "Why Do Poets Lie Too Much? Nietzsche, Poetry and the Different Voices of Zarathustra." *The Agonist*, vol. 8, nos. 1–2 (Fall). https://agonist.nietzschecircle.com/wp/poets_tuncel.

———, ed. 2017. *Nietzsche and Transhumanism: Precursor or Enemy?* Cambridge: Cambridge Scholars.

———. 2021. *Nietzsche on Human Emotions*. Basel: Schwabe.

Turgenev, Ivan. 1860/1965. "Hamlet and Don Quixote." Translated by Moshe Spiegel. *Chicago Review* 17, no. 4:92–109.

Unamuno, Miguel de. 1912/1962. *The Tragic Sense of Life*. London: Collins.

Ure, Michael. 2008. *Nietzsche's Therapy: Self-Cultivation in the Middle Works*. Lanham, MD: Lexington/Rowman & Littlefield.

———. 2009. "Nietzsche's Free Spirit Trilogy and Stoic Therapy." *Journal of Nietzsche Studies* 38:60–84.

———. 2019. *Nietzsche's The Gay Science: An Introduction*. Cambridge: Cambridge University Press.

Valéry, Paul. 1958. *The Art of Poetry*. Translated by Denise Folliot. With an introduction by T. S. Eliot. London: Routledge & Kegan Paul.

———. 1964. *Selected Writings of Paul Valéry*. New York: New Directions.

———. 1968. *Masters and Friends*. Translated by Martin Turnell. Princeton, NJ: Princeton University Press.

———. 1972. *Leonardo, Poe, Mallarmé*. Translated by Malcolm Cowley and James R. Lawler. London: Routledge & Kegan Paul.

Vico, Giambattista. 1999. *New Science*. Translated by David Marsh. London: Penguin.

Wakefield, David. 1984. *Stendhal: The Promise of Happiness*. Bedford: Newstead.

Warner, William Beatty. 1986. *Chance and the Text of Experience: Freud, Nietzsche, and Shakespeare's Hamlet*. Ithaca, NY: Cornell University Press.

Watkins, Margaret. 2019. *The Philosophical Progress of Hume's Essays*. Cambridge: Cambridge University Press.

Westerdale, Joel. 2013. *Nietzsche's Aphoristic Challenge*. Berlin: Walter de Gruyter.

White, Alan. 2001. "The Youngest Virtue." In *Nietzsche's Postmoralism: Essays on Nietzsche's Prelude to Philosophy's Future*, ed. Richard Schacht, 63–79. Cambridge: Cambridge University Press.

Whitman, Walt. 1996. *Poetry and Prose*. New York: Library of America.

Wiedemann, Eva Sophie. 2004. *Adalbert Stifters Kosmos*. Frankfurt a.M.: Peter Lang.

Wilkerson, Dale. 2006. *Nietzsche and the Greeks*. London: Continuum.

Williams, Bernard. 1985. *Ethics and the Limits of Philosophy*. London: Fontana & William Collins.

———. 2002. *Truth and Truthfulness: An Essay in Genealogy*. Princeton, NJ: Princeton University Press.

Williams, William Carlos. 1974. *The Embodiment of Knowledge*. Edited by Ron Loewinsohn. New York: New Directions.

Williams, W. D. 1952. *Nietzsche and the French*. Oxford: Basil Blackwell.

Wilson Knight, G. 1948. *Christ and Nietzsche: An Essay in Poetic Wisdom*. London: Staples.

———. 1952. *Lord Byron: Christian Virtues*. London: Routledge & Kegan Paul.

———. 1967. *Shakespeare and Religion: Essays of Forty Years*. London: Routledge & Kegan Paul.

Wood, James. 2019. *Serious Noticing: Selected Essays*. London: Vintage.

Wood, Michael. 1971. *Stendhal*. Ithaca, NY. Cornell University Press.

———. 2003. *The Road to Delphi: The Life and Afterlife of Oracles*. London: Chatto & Windus.

Woolf, Virginia. 1977. *Books and Portraits*. Edited by Mary Lyon. London: Hogarth.

———. 2008. "Poetry, Fiction, and the Future." In *Selected Essays*, 74–85. Oxford: Oxford University Press.

———. 2019. *Genius and Ink: Virginia Woolf on How to Read*. London: TLS/HarperCollins.

Wordsworth, William. 2013. "The Sublime and the Beautiful." In *Fragments*, ed. Rainer J. Hanshe, 26–48. New York: Contra Mundum.

Wordsworth, William, and Samuel Taylor Coleridge. 1991. *Lyrical Ballads*. Edited by R. L. Brett and A. R. Jones. London: Routledge.

Wotling, Patrick. 2020. "Enjoying Riddles: Epicurus as a Forerunner of the Idea of Gay Science?" In *Nietzsche and Epicurus: Nature, Health, and Ethics*, ed. Vinod Acharya and Ryan R. Johnson, 159–72. London: Bloomsbury Academic.

Wu, Duncan. 2008. *William Hazlitt: The First Modern Man*. Oxford: Oxford University Press.

Wurzer, Wilhelm. 1975. "Nietzsche's Dialectic of Intellectual Integrity: A Propaedeutic Study." *Southern Journal of Philosophy* 13, no. 2:235–45.

———. 1983. "Nietzsche's Hermeneutic of *Redlichkeit*." *Journal of the British Society for Phenomenology* 14, no. 3:258–70.

Xenophon. 1990. *Conversations of Socrates*. Translated by Hugh Tredennick and Robin Waterfield. London: Penguin.

Yeats, W. B. 1925/2008. *A Vision*. Edited by Catherine E. Paul and Margaret Mills Harper. New York: Scribner.

Youpa, Andrew. 2020. *The Ethics of Joy: Spinoza on the Empowered Life*. Oxford: Oxford University Press.

Zaborowski, Holger. 2010. "From Modesty to Dynamite, from Socrates to Dionysus: Friedrich Nietzsche on Intellectual Honesty." *American Catholic Philosophical Quarterly* 84, no. 2:337–57.

Zalloua, Zahi. 2005. *Montaigne and the Ethics of Skepticism*. Charlottesville, VA: Rockwood.

Zavatta, Benedetta. 2019. *Individuality and Beyond: Nietzsche Reads Emerson*. Oxford: Oxford University Press.

Ziff, Larzer. 1981/1982. *Literary Democracy: The Declaration of Cultural Independence in America*. Harmondsworth: Penguin.

Zweig, Stefan. 1952. *Adepts in Self-Portraiture: Casanova, Stendhal, Tolstoy*. London: Cassell.

Index